大学专业英语系列教程

Selected Readings in History
历史学专业英语教程

沙露茵
[美] 马紫梅(Mary G. Mazur) 编著

北京大学出版社
·北 京·

图书在版编目(CIP)数据

历史学专业英语教程/沙露茵,(美)马紫梅(Mary G. Mazur)编著. —北京:北京大学出版社,2005.8
(大学专业英语系列教程)
ISBN 978-7-301-07527-2

Ⅰ.历… Ⅱ.①沙…②马… Ⅲ.史学-英语-高等学校-教材 Ⅳ.H31

中国版本图书馆 CIP 数据核字(2004)第 057340 号

书　　　名：	Selected Readings in History
	历史学专业英语教程

著作责任者：沙露茵　[美]马紫梅（Mary G. Mazur）　编著
责任编辑：李　颖
标准书号：ISBN 7-301-07527-2/H · 1028
出　版　者：北京大学出版社
地　　　址：北京市海淀区成府路 205 号　100871
网　　　址：http://www.pup.cn　新浪官方微博:@北京大学出版社。
电　　　话：邮购部 62752015　发行部 62750672　编辑部 62754382　出版部 62754962
电子信箱：zpup@pup.pku.edu.cn
印　刷　者：北京宏伟双华印刷有限公司
发　行　者：北京大学出版社
经　销　者：新华书店
　　　　　787×1092　16 开本　18.75 印张　450 千字
　　　　　2005 年 8 月第 1 版　2024 年 8 月第 7 次印刷
定　　　价：58.00 元

未经许可，不得以任何方式复制或抄袭本书之部分或全部内容。
版权所有，侵权必究
举报电话：010-62752024　电子信箱：fd@pup.pku.edu.cn

大学专业英语系列教程

北京大学英语系大学英语教研室
北京大学文学文化与翻译研究会

顾　问：李赋宁
主　编：辜正坤　　黄必康
编委会：安美华　　石春祯　　沙露茵　　索玉柱　　范　红
　　　　赵白生　　林庆新　　刘红中　　王　伶　　傅国英
　　　　张　华　　张　政　　高艳丽　　余苏凌　　孟凡君

专家委员会：
胡壮麟（北京大学）
刘意青（北京大学）
申　丹（北京大学）
沈　虹（北京大学）
袁可嘉（社科院）
李文俊（社科院）
何其莘（北京外国语大学）
裘克安（外交部）
方　平（上海译文出版社）
程慕胜（清华大学）
彭镜禧（台湾大学）
刘士聪（南开大学）
黄新渠（四川师范大学）
David Bevington, University of Chicago
Tsao Michelle, State University of New York
Tanya Viger, Graduate School of City University of New York

总　序

辜正坤

　　西学东渐给东方的外语出版界造成一种奇特的景观：在相当短的时间内，外语出版物的数量扶摇直上，使他种民族语出版物相对汗颜，这是可以理解的。日本明治维新之后，出现过类似的情形，外语（尤其是英语）原著注释读物动辄一套就是数百本，洋洋大观。毫无疑问，这对推进日本的外语教学起到了非常重要的作用。时至今日，其效应已经明显昭示出来：当今的中国各大学发表的论文为 SCI 所收录者，最多者一年达 500 篇，而东京大学一年就达 4 万篇，两者相距 80 倍！如果以为日本的论文数量必与其科学水平成正比，因而中国大学的科学研究水平就落后了东大 80 倍的话，恐怕是一种很大的误解。其中的奥妙之一，就在于日本学者的英语水平普遍较高，许多论文是直接用英文写成，因此容易被世界各地的媒体注意到，其入选 SCI 的机会也就相对增多。反观中国学者的论文，绝大多数用汉语写成，少量靠懂英语的学者翻译，只有极少量的学者能够自己用英文直接写作。因此，大多数的中国论文是难以进入西方学者的视野的。当然入选 SCI 的机会也就相对少得多了。当然，这并非是说，中国的科研水平就反过来比日本高，而是说，由于中国学者英语写作水平普遍偏低的原因，其实际的科研水平未能在英语世界的文献中充分显示出来。由此可以明白，提高中国学者的英语能力（尤其是阅读文献与用英语写作的能力）是一件非常迫切的事。

　　然而，改革开放 20 多年来的英语学习大潮虽然使许多中国人在英语学习方面获得了较高的造诣，上了一个较为理想的台阶，但是有更多的人却老在一个水平上徘徊不前：要学的教材已经学了，该考的科目已经通过了，但是，面对英语的殿堂，人们并没有登堂入室的感觉。听说能力未能应付裕如或许情有可原，因为学习者可以抱怨没有相应的可以一试身手的客观条件，但是在阅读方面，例如阅读文史哲数理化的专业文献方面，却仍是磕磕绊绊、跋前踬后，字典不离手，冷汗不离身。这种处于瓶颈地带、欲罢不可、欲进不能的促迫感，源于一个关键的原因：缺乏专业外语文献阅读训练。学校里使用的基础英语教材编得再好，也只能解决基础问题，不能解决超过基础的专业阅读问题。正如要做游泳健儿的人只在游泳池里按照游泳要领奋力拨拉了一阵池水，自觉亦有劈波斩浪之感，但与真正的河涛海潮相比，终究属于两重洞天。

　　于是，就产生了这一整套专业英语阅读教程。

　　它的目标非常明确，无非是要把英语知识与技能的培训和高层次系统知识的灌输二者有机结合起来，达到既学语言又学知识的目的；即温故，又知新。照我看来，这是最有效率的学习与巩固方略。

　　如前所述可以明白，这套教程不只是对一般想要提高英语实际水平的人有用，对于专家学者或研究人员，也有很大的好处。一个人无论多么博学多才，也不太可能对各个专业的英语经典文献和地道表达都了然于胸，因此，当需要在尽可能短的时间内对某专业的英语经典文献或概念有所把握时,这一整套书无疑不会使人们失望。

  这套书的编选思路最初萌发于1991年,当时称作《注释本英文世界文化简明百科文库》。编者当时曾会同北京大学英语系大学英语教研室教师和北京大学出版社若干编辑共商过具体编选事宜,并由北京大学出版社出版。尔后还进行过多次类似的讨论。文库分上、中、下三编,每编含精选名著100种左右。在编选思路上,力求达到雅俗共赏,深入浅出,系统全面。在系统性方面,注意参照《大英百科全书》和《中国大百科全书》的知识框架,用英文把更为完备的知识系统介绍给读者。在实用性方面,亦注意选材的内容与词汇量同现行的英语教材、实际英语教学水平相呼应。

  本编为上编,除可供大学英语分科专业阅读选用教材之用外,亦可供社会上一般读者提高英语水平、直接经由阅读原著而掌握某一专业知识之用。基本的编辑方针是:第一,选目必须系统、广泛,尽可能把大学的重要专业都包容进去(包括人文社会科学和理工科专业)。第二,选目可大致分三类:A. 简史类;B. 名篇名著类;C. 比较规范的或经典的西方专业教材类。第三,每册书的字数最好在20万字上下(个别可以例外)。至于其他具体事项,则随书说明。

  教育部在1999年亦强调大学英语教学不能停留在基础英语教学上,而要逐步过渡到教授专业分科英语,使学生尽可能进入阅读专业英语文献的水平。因此这套教材的产生是适得其时的。

  当然,它的具体效果如何,还有待检验。好在这套教材的编注与出版都是一个较长的过程,这期间可望获得有关方面的建议与批评,以期使它精益求精,日臻完善。

  是为序。

2001年于北京大学英语系

前　言

　　《历史学专业英语教程》由美国历史学家、《时代之子吴晗》的作者、芝加哥大学马紫梅博士(Dr. Mary G. Mazur)和本人共同精选。所选篇幅内容丰富，题材广泛，体裁多样。文章都是由历史学各个不同领域的权威人士和知名历史学家所撰写。这本教程恰似一座桥梁，使得有一定英语基础、对历史学以及相关学科有兴趣的学生和自学者通过这一桥梁，到达能正确阅读、理解英文历史原著、历史文献的彼岸。

　　为了帮助读者更好地理解原著，马紫梅博士对英文原著的作者及其著作做了注释，并编写了启发性强、令人深思的阅读理解练习和讨论题。为方便读者学习，编者除了对重要的历史人物和事件做了简单的注释外，对语言也进行了注释。为了让读者更好地理解文章中所出现的常用词和短语在上下文中的意义，所注释的词和短语都没有脱离语境。对超出2000年出版的《大学英语教学大纲》四级词汇表的词汇做了注释，并附有例句，还编写了相关的练习。对长难句的句子结构做了分析，并对语言点进行了解释。这样，读者自己就能把这些句子译成汉语，对经注释后还不容易理解的句子，附有汉语译文，或者编入了英译汉练习。书后附有练习答案和词汇表，供读者参考。本书没有按照语言的难易程度编排，教师使用时，可以按照自己的实际需要打乱原来编排的次序。

　　此书是在原北京大学历史系主任王天有教授倡导下而编写的。在编写过程中，又得到了北京大学出版社的支持，同时还得到了美国罗伯特·梅兹尔博士的大力帮助，在此表示深切的感谢。最后，欢迎专家、学者和读者对此书给予批评指正。

沙露茵
2003 年 11 月

Preface

This collection of history readings in English is for all who want to improve their English skills and enjoy history. The need of history students for such a collection was originally recommended to the editors by Professor Wang Tianyou, Chairman of History Department, Peking University. With this encouragement Professor Sha Luyin of Peking University and I planned a collection of history readings in English intended for both students and general reades who have a strong interest in history and are at an advanced level of English usage. Study and discussion of these selections in class or by self will improve the reading and spoken English of specialists in history as well as general readers with interest in social sciences, literature and the global situation. Readers who want to increase fluency in reading and ease in discussing historical subjects will find this collection of short readings interesting and worthwhile.

In order to provide acquaintance with a variety of historical topics and periods and methodologies, the editors have chosen short selections from histories and articles in English by well known historians who are authorities in various specialty fields. There are also some selections which are primary sources from the past, such as Martin Luther King's speech.

The plan the book follows is to assist the reader in increasing English language skills and to encourage the broadening of the reader's view of the historical literature in English. The book is arranged in two sections. In the first, following each of the readings, there are extensive notes of explanation on vocabulary and information. The second section includes additional supplementary readings with short vocabulary notes. Although all of the selections are short they introduce ideas and concepts about the past and the study of the past that will lead students into further reading, research, and historical analysis. In the first section in notes 1 and 2 following each of the selections there is information about the author and the significance of the work the excerpt was taken from. Extensive notes for each selection and a glossary provide extra help but all advanced readers should become accustomed to using a dictionary, either an English dictionary or an English-Chinese dictionary. If one wants to explore and study independently, the personal use of a dictionary is absolutely necessary. Language exercises are included for each selection to help the student check comprehension and English usage. Language teachers will use these exercises directly or utilize them as models for classroom use.

In the main section, the first unit on concepts and meanings introduces some ideas about what history is and what historians do. Of course, to some extent we are all historians in our thinking. The second unit of this main section offers several readings on World History, a new and very lively field of historical study. Next the reader will find a unit on the ancient world of Greece, then two selections on China. Next comes a unit on Japan, followed by units on South Asia, the Islamic World, Sub-Saharan Africa, Europe, Russia, and the United States. Then there is a separate unit on Environmental History and finally in the main section, a unit on some basic aspects of the practice of historical writing. The specialties of the historians who wrote the selections include geography, economic history, comparative history, history of science, political history, social history, popular cultural history, environmental history, intellectual history as well as the basic tools of writing and publishing. Following the main section is the supplementary section of very interesting readings for further study.

None of the selections are simple, nor were they originally prepared or rewritten for students. This is the real thing, real historical writing. There are many challenges and many rewards in this volume for the student, whether a general self-study reader or a university student. The world of history is ahead!

Mary G. Mazur

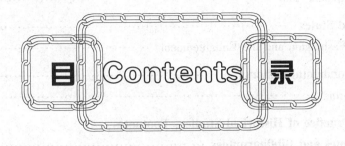

Unit 1　Introduction to Concepts of History and Historical Writing ……… (1)
　1. The Meanings of the Term History ……… (1)
　2. An Overview of the Debates about Historical Writing ……… (6)
　3. History's Nature ……… (16)
　4. Culture and Society ……… (23)
　5. The Historian and His Day ……… (31)

Unit 2　World History ……… (41)
　6. Introduction to World History ……… (41)
　7. A Definition of Civilization ……… (53)
　8. A Comparative Analysis of France, Russia, and China ……… (60)

Unit 3　Ancient Greece ……… (69)
　9. How the Greek World Grew ……… (69)

Unit 4　China ……… (81)
　10. Chinese Economic History in Comparative Perspective ……… (81)
　11. Chinese Science Explorations of an Ancient Tradition ……… (91)

Unit 5　Japan ……… (100)
　12. Ideology and Imperial Japan ……… (100)

Unit 6　South Asia ……… (114)
　13. On Some Aspects of the Historiography of Colonial India ……… (114)

Unit 7　Islamic World ……… (126)
　14. Muhammad and the Appearance of Islam ……… (126)

Unit 8　Sub-Saharan Africa ……… (139)
　15. Africa after Independence ……… (139)

Unit 9　Europe ……… (150)
　16. From Balance of Power to World Politics ……… (150)

Unit 10　Russia and the Soviet Union ……………………………………… (161)
　　17. A Geographical Note ……………………………………………………… (161)

Unit 11　United States ………………………………………………………… (172)
　　18. George Washington and the Enlightenment ……………………………… (172)

Unit 12　Environmental History ……………………………………………… (187)
　　19. Silent Spring …………………………………………………………………… (187)

Unit 13　The Practice of Historical Studies: Footnotes,
　　　　　Endnotes and Bibliographies ………………………………………… (198)
　　20. Chicago Manual of Style …………………………………………………… (198)

Supplementary Reading Materials

Section 1　Europe ……………………………………………………………… (207)
　　21. The Fundamental Characteristics of European Feudalism ……………… (207)
　　22. The Coming of the French Revolution ……………………………………… (211)

Section 2　Latin America ……………………………………………………… (214)
　　23. Latin America since 1800 …………………………………………………… (214)

Section 3　United States ……………………………………………………… (218)
　　24. The Cuban Missile Crisis …………………………………………………… (218)
　　25. I Have a Dream ……………………………………………………………… (224)

Section 4　History of Popular Culture ……………………………………… (229)
　　26. The River of Rock …………………………………………………………… (229)
　　27. Rock and Roll ………………………………………………………………… (235)

Section 5　Women's History ………………………………………………… (242)
　　28. The Creation of Patriarchy ………………………………………………… (242)

Key to Exercises ………………………………………………………………… (249)
Glossary …………………………………………………………………………… (261)

Unit 1

Introduction to Concepts of History and Historical Writing

> 最近几十年,一直在广泛讨论什么是历史,历史学家应该如何写历史。在这一部分,首先选择了两篇短文,第一篇对历史的一般概念进行了讨论,第二篇短文概述了历史和历史学近来的辩论情况。随后所选的三篇文章都由重要的历史学家所撰写,他们发展了撰写历史著作的思想并对此做出了贡献。

1. The Meanings of the Term History[1]

from Encyclopedia Britannica

HISTORY[2]

The word "history" is used in two senses. It may mean either the record of events or events themselves. Originally limited to inquiry and statement, it was only in comparatively modern times that the meaning of the word was extended to include the phenomena which form or might form their subject. ... Now indeed it is the commoner meaning[3]. The "history of England" is used without reference to any literary narrative. Kings and statesmen are termed the "makers of history"[4] and sometimes it is said that the historian only records the history which they make. History in this connection is obviously not the record, but the thing to be recorded.[5]

1

History in the wider sense is all that has happened, not merely all the phenomena of human life, but those of the natural world as well. It includes everything that undergoes change; and as modern science has shown that there is nothing absolutely static, therefore the whole universe and every part of it has its history.

HISTORY AND HISTORIOGRAPHY

History, in its broadest sense, is the totality of all past events, although a more realistic definition would limit it to the known past. Historiography is the written record of what is known of human lives and societies in the past and how historians have attempted to understand them.[6] Of all the fields of serious study and literary effort, history may be the hardest to define precisely, because the attempt to uncover past events and formulate an intelligible account of them necessarily involves the use and influence of many auxiliary disciplines and literary forms.[7] The concern of all serious historians has been to collect and record facts about the human past and often to discover new facts. They have known that the information they have is incomplete, partly incorrect, or biased and requires careful attention. All have tried to discover in the facts patterns of meaning addressed to the enduring questions of human life.[8]

. . . .

Except for the special circumstance in which historians record events they themselves have witnessed, historical facts can only be known through intermediary sources. These include testimony from living witnesses; narrative records, such as previous histories, memoirs, letters, and imaginative literature; the legal and financial records of courts, legislatures, religious institutions, or businesses; and the unwritten information derived from the physical remains of past civilizations, such as architecture, arts and crafts, burial grounds, and cultivated land.[9] All these, and many more sources of information provide the evidence from which the historian deciphers historical facts.[10] The relation between evidence and fact, however, is rarely simple and direct. The evidence may be biased or mistaken, fragmentary, or nearly unintelligible after long periods of cultural or linguistic change. Historians, therefore, have to assess their evidence with a critical eye.

. . . Moreover, the purpose of history as a serious endeavor to understand human life is never fulfilled by the mere sifting of evidence for facts.[11] Fact-finding is only the foundation for the selection, arrangement, and explanation that constitute historical interpretation. The process of interpretation informs all aspects of historical inquiry, beginning with the selection of a subject for investigation, because the very choice of a particular event or society or institution is itself an act of judgment that asserts the importance of the subject. Once chosen, the subject itself suggests a provisional model or hypothesis that guides research and helps the historian to assess and classify the available evidence and to present a detailed and coherent account of the subject. The historian must respect the facts, avoid ignorance and error as far as possible, and create a convincing, intellectually satisfying interpretation. Until modern times, history was regarded primarily as a special kind of literature that shared many techniques and effects with fictional narrative.[12] Historians were committed to factual materials and personal truthfulness,[13] but like writers of fiction they wrote detailed narratives of events and vivid character sketches with great attention to language and style. The complex relations between literary art and historiography have been and continue to be a subject of serious debate.

【Notes】

①These definitions of history are taken from two encyclopedias *Encyclopedia Britannica* and *Encarta Encyclopedia*. The first is from the *1957 Encyclopedia Britannica*, the most well known English language encyclopedia. The second definition is from the *1993 Encarta*, the computer software encyclopedia published by Microsoft.

②The definition of history is a debated subject. What is history? Some think of it as the origin and unfolding of the historical process of events in the past through the passage of time. Others see it, not as the process itself, but the knowledge, and the inquiry after that knowledge, which we, in later times, have of the past.

③the commoner meaning: 平民的历史。
commoner /'kɔmənə/ n. 平民(指个人);(牛津大学等的)自费生;普通学生;fellow commoner 可与研究员同桌吃饭的大学生。

④The "history of England" is used without reference to any literary narrative. Kings and statesmen are termed the "makers of history"...:
reference n. 参考;查询;reference book 参考书;reference to... 提到,提及,如:Her speeches have special reference to the African situation. 她的演讲对非洲形势有特定的意义。
reference to one's plan 提到某人的计划。
in reference to 关于;with reference to 关于;without reference to 不管,不顾;和……无关。
term vt. 称为,把……叫做,如:His life may be termed happy. 他的生活可称之为幸福。

⑤History in this connection is obviously not the record, but the thing to be recorded.
connection 联系,关系,如:There appeared to be no connection between the two crimes. 显然这

两件犯罪案没有联系。

in this connection 关于这一点,就此而论,如: In this connection, the agreement can be seen as a step toward peace. 在此环境下,该协议可视为是迈向和平的一步。

⑥Historiography is the written record of what is known of human lives and societies in the past and how historians have attempted to understand them: 这个句子是由主句与 what 和 how 引导的两个介词宾语从句而构成的复合句。在 what 引导的从句中,谓语部分 is known 把主语 what 与它的修饰语 of human lives and societies in the past 分隔开了。

historiography /ˌhɪstɔːrɪˈɒɡrəfɪ/ n. 历史编纂学,编史工作;史评,历史学。

⑦...because the attempt to uncover past events and formulate an intelligible account of them necessarily involves the use and influence of many auxiliary disciplines and literary forms: 在这个原因状语从句中,主语部分为 the attempt to uncover past events and formulate an intelligible account of them necessarily, 谓语部分为 involves the use and influence of many auxiliary disciplines and literary forms。

intelligible /ɪnˈtelɪdʒəbl/ adj. 可以理解的,易领悟的,如: intelligible speech 清晰的演说 intelligible explanation 明白的解释; make oneself intelligible 使人了解自己的思想(言语等); an intelligible account of past events 清晰地描述过去的事件。

many auxiliary disciplines and literary forms 许多辅助学科和文字记载。

⑧...patterns of meaning addressed to the enduring questions of human life:
address 提出,提交……以引起……的注意,如:address a protest to the faculty senate 向校评议会提交抗议书;忙于,专注于 address oneself to a task 投入一项工作。enduring /ɪnˈdjʊərɪŋ/ adj. 持久的,耐久的

⑨These include testimony from living witnesses; narrative records, such as previous histories, memoirs, letters, and imaginative literature; the legal and financial records of courts, legislatures, religious institutions, or businesses; and the unwritten information derived from the physical remains of past civilizations, such as architecture, arts and crafts, burial grounds, and cultivated land. 这个长句子是一个简单句。谓语 include 后面有由三个分号连接的四个宾语短语。

testimony from living witnesses 仍然还健在的证人的证词。memoir /ˈmemwɑː/ n. 实录,传略,论文;[pl.]自传,回忆录;学术论文集。unwritten information derived from the physical remains of past civilizations 来自过去文明遗留物的非文献的资料。

⑩...provide the evidence from which the historian deciphers historical facts:
decipher /dɪˈsaɪfə/ vt. 译解(密码等);解释(古代文学);辨认,辨读(潦草字迹)。

⑪Moreover, the purpose of history as a serious endeavor to understand human life is never fulfilled by the mere sifting of evidence for facts.

endeavor /ɪnˈdevə/ n. 努力,尽力;v. (与 to 连用)努力,尽力,如: We must always endeavour to improve our work. 我们总要努力改进自己的工作。sift v. 筛出;滤除;选拔;详审,细审,如:sift the candidates for the job 筛选该职务的候选人;sift the evidence 细审证据;by the mere sifting of evidence for facts 只通过仔细考证找出事实真相。

⑫Until modern times, history was regarded primarily as a special kind of literature that shared many techniques and effects with fictional narrative.

share *vt.*, *vi.* 共用;分摊;共有。如: Bill and Bob shared the work equally between them. 比尔和鲍勃两人把工作平分了。as a special kind of literature that shared many techniques and effects with fictional narrative 作为一种特殊的文学形式,使用同样的文学技巧并取得了与文学相同的效果

⑬Historians were committed to factual materials and personal truthfulness...: 历史学家致力于真实的资料和个人的诚实……

commit sb. to do/doing sth. 使某人承诺做某事;致力于约束或强制,如通过誓言等:They were committed to follow orders. 他们对命令全力以赴。

【 Exercises 】

I. Comprehension Questions

(1) The *Encarta Encyclopedia* tells us a realistic definition of "history" would limit it to the known past. How is it the past becomes "known" to us?

(2) What are the sources listed that the historian can use to know the historical facts? Can you think of more?

(3) After the fact-finding what process must the historian follow with the evidence he/she has found? List the steps that the *Encarta* writer thinks the historian must follow to create an interpretation.

II. Points for Discussion

In the *Encyclopedia Britannica* the word "history" is said to have two meanings: one the written record or narrative and two, the events themselves called by the author "the thing to be recorded." The passage continues: how much does history include? Give your own examples to explain the author's ideas.

III. Complete the following sentences, using the words or expressions from the passage according to the given meaning in brackets. Change the form where necessary.

(1) The same pride in being part of a well-coordinated, successful unit _____ (come from) being part of larger collectivity.

(2) We have _____ (associations) with various international corporations in Europe.

(3) At the end of his career in politics, he retired and wrote his _____ (biography).

(4) There is a widespread _____ (evidence) that this ominous fact is due to inherent biological defects in the crowded life of cities.

(5) The municipal government _____ (attempt) to improve the quality of life in the inner city.

IV. Complete the following sentences with the words or expressions from the passage given below. Change the form where necessary.

| commit | as far as possible | reference |
| undergo | address | assess |

(1) She made frequent _____ to her promotion when we were in the office.

(2) The statement says that they are _____ to a life-and-death struggle against terrorism.

(3) If your friend did something wrong, you should always _____ a warning to him.

(4) Since there were plenty of surprises on that journey our opinions _____ a change.

(5) The data available will help students _____ the present state of the economy.

V. Translate the following from English into Chinese.

(1) The "history of England" is used without reference to any literary narrative. Kings and statesmen are termed the "makers of history" and sometimes it is said that the historian only records the history which they make.

(2) History in the wider sense is all that has happened, not merely all the phenomena of human life, but those of the natural world as well.

(3) The evidence may be biased or mistaken, fragmentary, or nearly unintelligible after long periods of cultural or linguistic change.

2. An Overview of the Debates about Historical Writing

Peter Burke[1]

> 这篇文章介绍了一些国际知名历史学家的论文集。这些文章论述了20世纪后期所撰写的新史学的发展过程和实践。这本书所探讨的题目不仅包括了诸如妇女史、大众史等多种历史,而且还讨论了诸如政治史这样传统领域的发展新方向。

In the last generation or so[2] the universe of historians has been expanding at a dizzying rate. National history, which was dominant in the nineteenth century, now has to compete for attention with world history and with local history.[3] There are many new fields, often supported by specialized journals. Social history, for example, became independent of economic history only to fragment, like some new nation, into historical demography, labor history, urban history, rural history, and so on.[4]

There has been a shift among economic historians from a concern with production to a concern with consumption, a shift which makes it increasingly difficult to separate economic from social and cultural history. The history of management is a new interest, but one which blurs[5]... the boundaries between economic and administrative history. Another specialization, the history of advertising, straddles[6] economic history and the history of communication. Today, the very identity of economic history is threatened by a takeover bid[7] from a youthful but ambitious enterprise, the history of the environment, sometimes known as eco-history.

Political history too is divided between historians concerned with centres of government and those interested in politics at the grassroots. The territory of the political has expanded, in the sense that historians (following theorists such as Michel Foucault)[8] are increasingly inclined to discuss the struggle for power at the level of the factory, the school, or even the family. The price of such expansion, however, is a kind of identity crisis. If politics is everywhere, is there any need for political history? A similar problem faces cultural historians, as they turn away from a narrow but precise definition of culture in terms of art, literature, music etc, towards a more anthropological definition of the field.

In this expanding and fragmenting universe, there is an increasing need for orientation. What is the so-called new history? How new is it? Is it a temporary fashion or a long-term trend? Will it—or should it—replace traditional history, or can the rivals coexist in peace?... It may be useful to confront these problems at the start, and to place them in the context of long-term changes in the writing of history.

What is the New History?

The phrase "the new history" is best known in France... it is the history associated with the so-called *école des Annales*, grouped around the journal *Annales*: *économies, sociétés, civilizations.*[9]

What is this *nouvelle histoire*[10]? A positive definition is not easy; the movement is united only in what it opposes, and the pages which follow will demonstrate the variety of the new approaches. It is therefore difficult to offer more than a vague description, characterizing the new history as total history (*histoire totale*) or as structural history. Hence there may be a case for imitating medieval theologians faced with the problem of defining God, and opting for a *via negativa*,[11] in other words for defining the new history in terms of what it is not, of what its practitioners oppose.

The new history is history written in deliberate reaction against the traditional "paradigm," that useful if imprecise term put into circulation by the American historian of science Thomas Kuhn.[12] It will be convenient to describe this traditional paradigm as "Rankean history," after the great German historian Leopold von Ranke

(1795—1886)[13]... We might also call this paradigm the common-sense view of history, not to praise it but to make the point that it has often—too often—been assumed to be the way of doing history, rather than being perceived as one among various possible approaches to the past. For the sake of simplicity and clarity, the contrast between old and new history might be summed up in [six] points.

(1) According to the traditional paradigm, history is essentially concerned with politics... Politics was assumed to be essentially concerned with the state; in other words it was national and international rather than local. However, it did include the history of the Church as an institution and also what the military theorist Karl von Clausewitz[14] defined as' the continuation of policies by other means, that is, war. Although other kinds of history—the history of art, for example, or the history of science—were not altogether excluded by the traditional paradigm, they were marginalized in the sense of being considered peripheral to the interests of "real" historians.[15]

The new history, on the other hand, has come to be concerned with virtually every human activity. "Everything has a history,"... that is, everything has a past which can in principle be reconstructed and related to the rest of the past. Hence the slogan "total history," so dear to the *Annales* historians. The first half of the century witnessed the rise of the history of ideas. In the last thirty years we have seen a number of remarkable histories of topics which had not previously been thought to possess a history, for example, childhood, death, madness, the climate, smells, dirt and cleanliness, gestures, the body..., femininity..., reading, speaking, and even silence. What had previously been considered as unchanging is now viewed as a "cultural construction," subject to variation over time as well as in space.

The cultural relativism implicit here deserves to be emphasized. The philosophical foundation of the new history is the idea that reality is socially or culturally constituted. The sharing of this idea, or assumption, by many social historians and social anthropologists helps explain the recent convergence[16] between these two disciplines... This relativism also undermines the traditional distinction between what is central in history and what is peripheral.

(2) In the second place, traditional historians think of history as essentially a narrative of events, while the new history is more concerned with the analysis of structures. One of the most famous works of history of our time, Fernand Braudel's *Mediterranean*, dismisses the history of events... as no more than the foam on the

waves of the sea of history.[17] According to Braudel, economic and social changes over the long term la longue durée) and geo-historical changes over the very long term are what really matter. Although there has recently been something of a reaction against this view... and events are no longer dismissed as easily as they used to be, the history of structures of various kinds continues to be taken very seriously.

(3) In the third place, traditional history offers a view from above, in the sense that it has always concentrated on the great deeds of great men, statesmen, generals, or occasionally churchmen. The rest of humanity was allocated a minor role in the drama of history. The existence of this rule is revealed by reactions to its transgression.[18] When the great Russian writer Alexander Pushkin was working on an account of a peasant revolt and its leader Pugachev, Tsar Nicholas's comment was that "such a man has no history."[19] In the 1950s, when a British historian wrote a thesis about a popular movement in the French Revolution, one of his examiners asked him, " Why do you bother with these bandits?"

On the other hand..., a number of the new historians are concerned with "history from below," in other words with the views of ordinary people and with their experience of social change. The history of popular culture has received a great deal of attention. Historians of the Church are beginning to examine its history from below as well as from above. Intellectual historians too have shifted their attention away from great books, or great ideas—their equivalent of great men—to the history of collective mentalities or to the history of discourses or "languages," the language of scholasticism, for example, or the language of the common law...

(4) In the fourth place, according to the traditional paradigm, history should be based on the documents. One of Ranke's greatest achievements was his exposure of the limitations of narrative sources—let us call them chronicles—and his stress on the need to base written history on official records, emanating from governments and preserved in archives.[20] The price of this achievement was the neglect of other kinds of evidence... However, the "history from below" movement in its turn exposed the limitations of this kind of document. Official records generally express the official point of view. To reconstruct the attitudes of heretics and rebels,[21] such records need to be supplemented by other kinds of source.

In any case, if historians are concerned with a greater variety of human activities than their predecessors, they must examine a greater variety of evidence. Some of this evidence is visual, some of it oral... There is also statistical evidence: trade figures, population figures, voting figures, and so on... In Britain, for example, an Association for History and Computing was founded in 1987.

(5) According to the traditional paradigm, memorably articulated by the philosopher-historian R. G. Collingwood, "When an historian asks 'Why did Brutus stab Caesar?' he means 'What did Brutus think, which made him decide to stab Caesar?'" This model of historical explanation has been criticized by more recent historians on a number of grounds, principally because it fails to take account of the variety of historians' questions, often concerned with collective movements as well as individual actions, with trends as well as events.

Why, for example, did prices rise in sixteenth-century Spain? Economic historians do not agree in their answer to this question, but their various responses (in terms of silver imports, population growth and so on) are very far from Collingwood's model. In Fernand Braudel's famous study of the sixteenth-century Mediterranean... only the third and last part, devoted to the history of events, asks questions remotely like Collingwood's, and even here the author offers a very different kind of answer, emphasizing the constraints on his protagonist, King Philip II,[22] and the king's lack of influence on the history of his time.

(6) According to the traditional paradigm, History is objective. The historian's task is to give readers the facts, or as Ranke put it... to tell "how it actually happened." His modest disclaimer of philosophical intentions was interpreted by posterity as a proud manifesto for history without bias.[23] In a famous letter to his international team of contributors to the *Cambridge Modern History*, published from 1902 onwards, its editor, Lord Acton,[24] urged them that "our Waterloo must be one that satisfies French and English, Germans and Dutch alike" and that readers should be unable to tell where one contributor laid down his pen and another took it up.

Today, this ideal is generally considered to be unrealistic. However hard we struggle to avoid the prejudices associated with colour, creed, class or gender,[25] we cannot avoid looking at the past from a particular point of view. Cultural relativism obviously applies as much to historical writing itself as to its so-called objects. Our minds do not reflect reality directly. We perceive the world only through a network of conventions, schemata and stereotypes,[26] a network which varies from one culture to another. In this situation, our understanding of conflicts is surely enhanced by a presentation of opposite viewpoints, rather than by an attempt, like Acton's, to articulate a consensus.[27] We have moved from the ideal of the Voice of History to that of heteroglossia, defined as "varied and opposing voices"...

Rankean history was the territory of the professionals. The nineteenth century was the time when history became professionalized, with its departments in universities and its trade journals like the *Historische Zeitschrift* and the *English Historical Review*. Most of the leading new historians are also professionals... One way to describe the achievements of the *Annales* group is to say that they have shown that economic, social and cultural history can meet the exacting professional standards set by Rank for political history.

All the same, their concern with the whole range of human activity encourages them to be inter-disciplinary in the sense of learning from and collaborating with social anthropologists, economists, literary critics, psychologists, sociologists, and so on. Historians of art, literature and science, who used to pursue their interests more or less in isolation from the main body of historians, are now making more regular contact with them. The history-from-below movement also reflects a new determination to take ordinary people's views of their own past more seriously than professional historians used to do...

【 Notes 】

①Peter Burke is a member of the faculty at the University of Cambridge, England where he teaches Cultural History. This article is taken from "Overture: The New History, Its Past and Its Future" in *New Perspectives on Historical Writing* edited by Peter Burke, Pennsylvania State University Press, 1991, pp. 1—6.
This article is the introduction to a collection of articles by a group of internationally known historians on the development and practice of "new history" writing in the late 20th century. The subjects discussed in the book include women's history, history "from below," the history of reading, oral history, the history of the body, and microhistory, as well as new directions in traditional fields such as political history. A discussion of the "revival of narrative" considers the role of events in history.

②or so:左右,……上下,如: a week or so's sunshine 一个星期左右的日照

③... now has to compete for attention with world history and with local history:
compete (against/with sb,in sth,for sth)竞争；对抗；比赛。如: Several companies are competing (against/with each other) for the contract/to gain the contract. 几家公司正为争取一项合同而互相竞争。

④Social history, for example, became independent of economic history only to fragment, like some new nation, into historical demography, labor history, urban history, rural history, and so on.

这是一个简单句。主语是 social history,谓语部分是 became independent of... into , independent of 意思是"与……分开", into"而成为……", for example 和 like some new nation 是插入语。demography /di'mɔgrəfi/ *n.* 人口统计学;人口学。

⑤blur /blə:/ *v.* (使某事物)变得模糊不清,如:Her eyes blurred with tears. 她泪眼迷离。blurred writing 模糊不清的字迹;Mist blurred the view. 雾模糊了视线。His memory is blurred by his illness. 他因患病记忆力减退。

⑥straddle /'strʃædl/ *v.* 跨坐或跨立在(某物)上,如:straddle a fence (ditch, horse) 跨在栅栏(沟、马)上

⑦bid /bid/ *v.* (过去时 bade 或 bid,过去分词 bidden 或 bid)❶企图:The party is bidding to seize power. 这个党企图夺取政权。❷宣布,公开表示:bid defiance to sb. 表示对某人蔑视。❸喊价:What am I bid (for this painting)? (这幅画)给我个价,诸位愿意出多少钱?She bid 500 (for the painting). 她喊价 500 英镑(买这幅画)。

⑧ Michel Foucault:傅科(1926—1984),法国结构主义哲学家,以研究社会运作所凭依的观念与法则而闻名,特别是以研究一个社会自我界定所依据的"排除原则"而著称于世。

⑨école des Annales:年鉴学派

Annales:*économies*,*sociétiés*,*civilizations*:《年鉴:经济史,社会史,文明史》

⑩nouvelle histoire:[法]新历史

⑪opt for a via negativa:选择反证的方式。

opt /ɔpt/ *v.* 决定做某事;选择:He opted to go to Paris rather than London. 他决定去巴黎,不去伦敦。opt for(between) 决定某事物;选择某事物:opt for persuasion over force 选择用说服方式而不用武力。

⑫The new history is history written in deliberate reaction against the traditional "paradigm," that useful if imprecise term put into circulation by the American historian of science Thomas Kuhn. paradigm /'pærədaim/ 范例,样式:history written in deliberate reaction against the traditional "paradigm" 通过对比这种传统的范例,经过仔细思考而写成的历史。

Thomas Samuel Kuhn:库恩(1922—),是美国科学史学家,以《科学革命的结构》(1962)而闻名,该书是 20 世纪历史和哲学方面最具有影响力的著作之一。它彻底改革了科学的史学和哲学。他的范例转换概念扩展到政治学、经济学、社会学甚至商业管理等学科。

⑬"Rankean history":兰克学派。Leopold von Ranke (1795—1886):德国历史学家,兰克学派的创始人。他主张撰史要"如实叙述",强调原始资料和辨析考订的重要性,被西方学者奉为以"科学态度"和"科学方法"治学的第一人。

⑭Karl von Clausewitz:克劳塞维茨(1780—1831),德国军事理论家,普鲁士将军。编写了《军事训练概论》、《信念三标志》等著作。写了三卷著名的军事理论著作《战争论》。

⑮... they were marginalized in the sense of being considered peripheral to the interests of "real" historians.

marginalize /'mɑːdʒinəlaiz/ 使处于社会边缘,使脱离社会发展进程;忽视;排斥。in the sense of 从这个意义上来说。peripheral /pə'rifərəl/ *adj.* 外围的,边缘的:a peripheral member of a group 一个团体的外围人员，China's peripheral provinces 中国的边缘省份。

⑯convergence /kən'vɜːdʒəns/ n. 趋于相同，相似

⑰One of the most famous works of history of our time, Fernand Braudel's *Mediterranean*, dismisses the history of events... as no more than the foam on the waves of the sea of history.

Fernand Braudel's *Mediterranean*：费尔南·布罗代尔（1902—1985）的《地中海史》。布罗代尔是当代法国最著名的史学家，在世界史坛也享有盛誉。《地中海史》是他的成名作，被公认为一部经典著作。

dismiss... as... 对……某人（某事物）不予理会或不屑一提：He is dismissed as a dreamer. 人们认为他是一个空想家而不予理会。

⑱The rest of humanity was allocated a minor vole in the drama of history. The existence of this rule is revealed by reactions to its transgression.

allocate /'æləkeit/ vt. 分配；配给，拨出：allocate funds for new projects 为新的工程项目拨出资金。transgression /træns'greʃən/ n. 违反，违法，罪过，过失，错误：Apologize at once for your transgression. 对你所犯的错误立即表示道歉。

⑲When the great Russian writer Alexander Pushkin was working on an account of a peasant revolt and its leader Pugachev, Tsar Nicholas's comment was that "such a man has no history".

Alexander Pushkin：亚历山大·普希金（1799—1837），俄罗斯伟大的作家，他在作品《上尉的女儿》一书中描写农民起义领袖普加乔夫（Pugachev）。Tsar Nicholas：沙皇尼古拉。

⑳..., emanating from governments and preserved in archives：

emanate /'eməneit/ v. (~ from) 来自某物（某人）；从某物（某处）流出，飘出：The idea originally emanated from his brother. 这个主意最初是他哥哥出的。archives /'ɑːkaivz/ n. [pl.] 公文，档案；档案处。

㉑heretic /'herətik/ n. 异教徒，持异端者

㉒... emphasizing the constrains on protagonist, King Philip II：强调了主人公国王菲利普二世的局限性。

protagonist /prəu'tægənist/ n. （故事的）主人公；现实事件（尤指冲突或争端的）主要参与者，主要人物；领导者；拥护者：She is a leading protagonist of the women's movement. 她是妇女运动的领导者。

㉓His modest disclaimer of philosophical intentions was interpreted by posterity as a proud manifesto for history without bias.

disclaimer /dis'kleimə/ n. 否认某事物的声明；放弃某事物的声明：issue/send a disclaimer 发表声明加以否认。posterity /pɔ'sterəti/ n. 后裔，后代，子孙：for the sake of posterity 为了子孙后代的利益。

㉔Lord Acton：阿克顿（John Emerich Edward Dalberg Acton, 1834—1902），英国历史学家。主编《剑桥近代史》。遗稿出版的有《自由的历史》、《近代史讲稿》、《阿克顿论文与著作》等。

㉕creed /kriːd; krid/ n. [C] 信条，教义（尤指宗教信仰）；各种肤色和各种宗教信仰的人，如：What is your political creed? 你的政治信仰如何？

㉖... through a network of conventions, schemata and stereotypes：

schema /'skiːmə/ ([复]-mata) n. 图表;纲要;计划,方案:I condensed this into the following schema. 我将此缩略成下列概要。stereotype /'steriəutaip/ n. 陈规,老套,刻板模式: break through the stereotypes 打破陈规。

㉗to articulate a consensus:

articulate /ɑːˈtikjuleit/ v. 清楚明白地说:I'm a little deaf, please articulate (your words) carefully. 我有点耳背,请把话仔细说清楚。consensus /kənˈsensəs/ n. [C, U] (~on)意见一致,共同看法:The two countries have reached a consensus. 这两个国家取得了共识。

【 Exercises 】

I. Comprehension Questions

(1) According to the first paragraph, _____?
   A. when was national history dominant
   B. what kinds of history does it compete with now
   C. what kinds of history have developed from social history

(2) In the seventh paragraph what does the author say the traditional historical paradigm was called? Where does this name come from?

(3) Applying Burke's six points of comparison answer these questions.
   1) Does the "new history" cover politics and the state only?
   2) According to Burke which one of the following approaches would be least likely to follow the "analysis of structures" (structuralist) approach to doing history?
      A. A comparative historical study of population changes in Guangzhou and Gansu during the Qing period.
      B. The story of Sun Yatsen's life.
      C. An analysis of Shang dynasty's economic and social conditions made from archeological and textual evidence.

(4) According to the "new history" paradigm, history is _____.
   A. objective—tells how it actually happened
   B. not true—impossible to know
   C. relative—written from a particular view point

II. Points for Discussion

(1) Discuss the meaning of "cultural relativism" and its implications for studying and writing history.

(2) From your careful reading of this passage discuss your ideas of the meaning of "history-from-above" and "history-from-below." Cite 2 or 3 illustrative examples.

(3) Applying what you have learned from this passage discuss the difference between Social History and Socialist History.

III. **Complete the following sentences, using the words or expressions from the passage according to the given meaning in brackets. Change the form where necessary.**

(1) More and more students _____ (choose) science courses nowadays.

(2) He was excommunicated from the church on a morals _____ (mistake) 20 years ago.

(3) It is obvious that our previously opposed views are beginning to _____ (become to be similar).

(4) Since delicious smells _____ (come/flow from) the kitchen we felt hungry.

(5) As is well known, there is broad _____ (agreement in opinion) in the country on this issue.

(6) One fifth of the total expenditure has been _____ (assigned to) the public services.

IV. **Fill in the gaps with the words or expressions given below. Change the form where necessary.**

bid	turn away	on the grounds	associate with
in terms of	rather than	view	as related
concentrate	subject	take account of	independent
more or less	competing		

(1) We had hoped to get the house but another couple was _____ against us, ie repeatedly offering a higher price than us.

(2) Some doctors may slip into deceptive practices _____ that it would do more harm than good to tell the truth to the incurably ill.

(3) Mr. White resigned _____ get himself involved in the dirty dealings.

(4) There are two neighboring countries as closely _____ as lips and teeth.

(5) Mr. Thorp is in the habit of knitting his brows whenever he _____ on a difficult problem.

(6) _____ money, she is quite rich. However, this does not mean that she is happy.

(7) The author brings the first chapter of his book to a close by _____ a brief _____ the advances science has made since liberation.

(8) We demand an _____ inquiry into the government's handling of the affair.

(9) Several companies are _____ with each other to gain the contract.

V. **Translate the following from English into Chinese.**

(1) Social history, for example, became independent of economic history only to fragment, like some new nation, into historical demography, labor history, urban history, rural history, and so on.

(2) One of the most famous works of history of our time, Fernand Braudel's *Mediterranean*, dismisses the history of events... as no more than the foam on the waves of the sea of

history.

(3) It is therefore difficult to offer more than a vague description, characterizing the new history as total history (histoire totale) or as structural history.

(4) What had previously been considered as unchanging is now viewed as a "cultural construction," subject to variation over time as well as in space.

3. History's Nature[1]

R. G. Collingwood[2]

> 这篇文章选自《历史观念》一书。这本书被认为是发展现代史学的一本奠基之作。作者认为,历史是研究人类的往事而不是研究整个过程。历史是通过解释历史事件而发展的。历史学家必须注意过去的思想。但是,作者没有考虑到,在描叙和解释历史的过程中,历史条件及其环境是值得考虑的。他忽略了研究千差万别的必要性,而强调历史因素的统一性。尽管如此,他指出,对过去作历史的研究,它的重要性在于理解文化和文明,这一贡献对繁荣现代历史学学派起了重要的作用。

What history is, what it is about, how it proceeds, and what it is for, are questions which to some extent different people would answer in different ways. But in spite of differences there is a large measure of agreement between the answers.[3] And this agreement becomes closer if the answers are subjected to scrutiny with a view to discarding those which proceed from unqualified witnesses.[4] History, like theology or natural science, is a special form of thought. If that is so, questions about the nature, object, method, and value of this form of thought must be answered by persons having two qualifications.

First, they must have experience of that form of thought. They must be historians. In a sense we are all historians nowadays. All educated persons have gone through a process of education which has included a certain amount of historical thinking. But this does not qualify them to give an opinion about the nature, object, method, and value of historical thinking. For in the first place, the experience of historical thinking which they have thus acquired is probably very superficial; and the opinions based on it are therefore no better grounded than a man's opinion of the French people based on a single weekend visit to Paris. In the second place, experience of anything whatever gained through the ordinary educational channels, as well as being superficial, is invariably out of date. Experience of historical thinking, so gained, is modeled on text-books, and text-books always describe not what is now being thought by real live historians, but what was thought by real live historians at some time in the past when the raw material was being created out of which the text-book has been put together.[5] And it is not only the results of historical thought which are out of date by the time they get into the text-book. It is also the principles of historical thought: that is, the ideas as to the nature, object, method, and value of historical thinking. In the third place, and connected with this, there is a peculiar illusion incidental to all knowledge[6] acquired in the way of education: the illusion of finality. When a student is in *statu pupillari* with respect to any subject whatever,[7] he has to believe that things are settled because the text-books and his teachers regard them as settled. When he emerges from that state and goes on studying the subject for himself he finds that nothing is settled. The dogmatism[8] which is an invariable mark of immaturity drops away from him. He looks at so-called facts with a new eye. He says to himself: ' My teacher and text-books told me that such and such was true; but is it true? What reasons had they for thinking it true, and were these reasons adequate?' On the other hand, if he emerges from the status of pupil without continuing to pursue the subject he never rids himself of this dogmatic attitude. And this makes him a person peculiarly unfitted to answer the questions I have mentioned. No one, for example, is likely to answer them worse than an Oxford philosopher who, having read Greats in his youth,[9] was once a student of history and thinks that this youthful experience of historical thinking entitles him to say what history is, what it is about, how it proceeds, and what it is for.

The second qualification for answering these questions is that a man should not only have experience of historical thinking but should also have reflected upon that experience. He must be not only an historian but a philosopher; and in particular his philosophical thought must have included special attention to the problems of historical thought. Now it is possible to be a quite good historian (though not an historian of the highest order) without thus reflecting upon one's own historical thinking. It is even easier to be a quite good teacher of history (though not the very best kind of teacher) without such reflection. At the same time, it is important to remember that experience comes first, and reflection on that experience second. Even the least reflective historian has the first qualification. He possesses the experience on which to reflect; and when he is asked to reflect on it his reflections have a good chance of being to the point. An historian who has never worked much at philosophy will probably answer our four questions in a more intelligent and valuable way than a philosopher who has never worked much at history.

I shall therefore propound answers to my four questions[10] such as I think any present-day historian would accept. Here they will be rough and ready answers, but they will serve for a provisional definition of our subject-matter[11] and they will be defended and elaborated as the argument proceeds.

(a) *The definition of history.* Every historian would agree, I think, that history is a kind of research or inquiry. What kind of inquiry it is I do not yet ask. The point is that generically it belongs to what we call the sciences: that is, the forms of thought whereby we ask questions and try to answer them. Science in general, it is important to realize, does not consist in collecting what we already know and arranging it in this or that kind of pattern. It consists in fastening upon something we do not know, and trying to discover it. Playing patience with things we already know may be a useful means towards this end, but it is not the end itself. It is at best only the means. It is scientifically valuable only in so far as the new arrangement gives us the answer to a question[12] we have already decided to ask. That is why all science begins from the knowledge of our own ignorance: not our ignorance of everything, but our ignorance of some definite thing-the origin of parliament, the cause of cancer, the chemical composition of the sun, the way to make a pump work without muscular exertion on the part of a man or a horse or some other docile animal.[13] Science is finding things out: and in that sense history is a science.

(b) *The object of history.* One science differs from another in that it finds out things of a different kind. What kind of things does history find out? I answer, res gestae: actions of human beings that have been done in the past. Although this answer raises all kinds of further questions many of which are controversial, still, however they may be answered, the answers do not discredit the proposition that history is the science of res gestae,[14] the attempt to answer questions about human actions done in the past.

(c) *How does history proceed?* History proceeds by the interpretation of evidence: where evidence is a collective name for things which singly are called documents, and a document is a thing existing here and now, of such a kind that the historian, by thinking about it, can get answers to the questions he asks about past events. Here again there are plenty of difficult questions to ask as to what the characteristics of evidence are and how it is interpreted. But there is no need for us to raise them at this stage. However they are answered, historians will agree that historical procedure, or method, consists essentially of interpreting evidence.

(d) *Lastly, what is history for*? This is perhaps a harder question than the others; a man who answers it will have to reflect rather more widely than a man who answers the three we have answered already. He must reflect not only on historical thinking but on other things as well, because to say that something is "for" something implies a distinction between A and B, where A is good for something and B is that for which something is good[15]. But I will suggest an answer, and express the opinion that no historian would reject it, although the further questions to which it gives rise are numerous and difficult.

My answer is that history is "for" human self-knowledge. It is generally thought to be of importance to man that he should know himself: where knowing himself means knowing not his merely personal peculiarities, the things that distinguish him from other men, but his nature as man. Knowing yourself means knowing, first, what it is to be a man; secondly, knowing what it is to be the kind of man you are; and thirdly, knowing what it is to be the man you are and nobody else is. Knowing yourself means knowing what you can do; and since nobody knows what he can do until he tries, the only clue to what man can do is what man has done. The value of history, then, is that it teaches us what man has done and thus what man is.

【 Notes 】

①This selection is taken from *The Idea of History*, 1956 edition, pp. 7—10 (London: Oxford University Press, 1946). his lectures published after his death. This book is considered to be a basic text in the development of modern historiography. The selection briefly summarizes some of the central points Collingwood makes on the nature of history. In his view history is the study of human affairs, not of all processes, and it proceeds by the interpretation of evidence. The historian must pay attention to past thought but he does not consider the environment of the historical situation worth considering in the historical account and its interpretation. He ignores the difference between subjective evidence and objective analysis in historical writing and omits any necessity of studying differences and distinctions, emphasizing unity in the historical elements. Nonetheless, Collingwood's contribution pointing out the central importance of historical study of the past to the understanding of cultures and civilizations was fundamental to the flourishing of modern historiographic schools.

② R. G. Collingwood (1889—1943) is an English historian and philosopher of history whose work was a major 20th century contribution to uniting history and philosophy. A teacher at Oxford, as a practicing historian he was a leading authority on the Roman Empire in Britain. He developed the idea that philosophical inquiry is dependent on the study of history, that the presuppositions of all civilizations should be viewed as historically developed conceptions, not as eternal truths. He thought that the patterns of cultures and civilizations can only be discovered by rethinking the past events to understand the reasons people acted as they did. Although he made major contributions he has been criticized for being too idealistic, for not admitting the importance of material factors in events, and for assuming the actors in history were always rational beings, not motivated by passion or influenced by context.

③ ...a large measure of agreement between the answers:这些答案大部分都是一致的。
a measure of sth:一定量(程度)的。

④ ...if the answers are subjected to scrutiny with a view to discarding those which proceed from unqualified witnesses:
"subject sth to scrutiny" 认真仔细地审阅。
scrutiny /ˈskrutini/ n. 认真,仔细审阅
with a view to (后面跟动名词) 为了,为的是……,如:He is studying with a view to going to university. 他一直在学习为的是上大学。
discard /diˈskɑrd/ vt. 扔掉,丢弃,不再使用:discard one's winter clothes in spring 春天里把冬天的衣服处理掉。

⑤ Experience of historical thinking, so gained, is modeled on text-books, and text-books always describe not what is now being thought by real live historians, but what was thought by real live historians at some time in the past when the raw material was being created out of which the text-book has been put together:由此所获得的历史思维方式是教科书所塑造成的。教科书所描写的东西常常不是现在活着的、真实的历史学家的想法,而是生活在过去某个时期历史学家的真实想法。在整理这些原材料的过程中,教科书也就编写好了。
这个句子是一个并列复合句。"and"连接了两个分句。在第一个分句中,"model on or after"意思是"take...as an example","使模仿,使仿效";在第二个分句中,"not...but..."连接了两个由"what"引导的宾语从句。"when"引导了一个状语从句。"which"引导了一个定语从句,修饰"raw material"。

⑥ incidental /ˌinsiˈdentl/ adj. ❶伴随的,细小的,次要的:My new CD has incidental music along with the main songs. 我的新光盘主要是歌曲,伴随着音乐。❷偶然发生的:an incidental meeting of an old friend on the street 在街上与老朋友的邂逅。

⑦ When a student is in *statu pupillari* with respect to any subject whatever:
statu pupillari:[Latin] the status of a student 学生身份。
with respect to 涉及,至于,关于:With respect to your inquiry, I enclose an explanatory leaflet. 有关你的问题,我附上说明资料。

⑧dogmatism /ˈdɔgmətizm/ n. [U] 教条主义,武断。dogmatic adj. 教条主义的,武断的
⑨great: n. ❶大人物,伟人;伟大的事物:the greats 伟人们; the literary great 文豪 ❷Greats (英口)(牛津大学的)古典人文学科课程
⑩propound /prəˈpaund/ vt. 提请考虑,提出(某事物)以求解决: propound an idea /a theory 提出一个想法／一种理论。
⑪provisional /prəˈviʒənl/ adj. 临时的,暂时的: a provisional driving license 实习驾驶执照。
⑫in so far as 由于,鉴于,至……程度:You will learn your lessons only in so far as you are willing to keep studying them. 你要学会这门课程取决于你坚持学习的程度。
⑬docile /ˈdəusail/ adj. 容易控制的,驯服的
⑭…,however they may be answered, the answers do not discredit the proposition that history is the science of *res gestae*:

discredit /disˈkredit/ vt. 损害,败坏名声;不可信,受怀疑: The government was discredited by the scandal. 政府由于这件丑闻而身败名裂。His theories were discredited by scientists. 他的理论科学家很怀疑。

proposition /prɔpəˈziʃən/ n. (to do/that) 观点,见解,定理,命题: proposition to merge the two firms 合并两家商行的建议。

res gestae：[Latin] things done 人们过去的所作所为。

⑮He must reflect not only on historical thinking but on other things as well, because to say that something is "for" something implies a distinction between A and B, where A is good for something and B is that for which something is good: 他必须不仅对历史思维方式,而且对其他东西都进行反思。因为说某事物是"为了"某事物暗示了甲和乙之间有区别。区别在于甲有利于某事,乙就是某事的受益者。
这个句子是一个主从复合句。"because"引导了一个原因状语从句。"where"引导一个非限定性定语从句。

【 Exercises 】

I. **Comprehension Questions**
(1) List the four questions about history Collingwood gives in paragraph one.
(2) The author says unqualified people will be unable to answer his four questions. Decide whether the following statements are true or false.
  1) To be qualified one must have experience with the historical form of thought.
  2) Historical thinking based only on textbooks is not out of date.
  3) Collingwood believes that all students learn that what is in textbooks is the final unchanging truth.
(3) According to Collingwood, history is a science. (See his definition of history paragraph.) The reason he gives for this is _____.
  A. science tests a hypothesis against facts that have been gathered

B. he thinks both are trying to inquire into something unknown, trying to discover something
C. history always wants to understand all of the conditions of the environment in which an event happened or a person acted

II. Points for Discussion

(1) Collingwood asks four questions; what are they and how does he answer them?
(2) What are the two most important qualities a man must have to be an historian? Why?
(3) If someone wants to discover what it means to be human how should he do this according to Collingwood? What do you think about his answer to this question?
(4) How does Collingwood's idea of history differ from yours? How does it differ from the Twenty Four Dynastic Histories? From Sima Qian's?

III. Complete the following sentences with words or expressions from the passage similar in meaning to the words in brackets.

(1) The budget did not include _____ (minor, relatively unimportant) costs, such as paper and pens.
(2) The student _____ his attentie _____ (direct one's attention to) the teacher.
(3) She _____ (release, free) of bad habits like smoking cigarettes.
(4) _____ (the most one can expect) you will get only a small increase in salary.
(5) An old man _____ (think deeply about) what he had done in his lifetime.
(6) That pass _____ (allow, authorize) you to enter the concert for free.
(7) Coming from the chairman himself, the company's announcement about closing the factory had an air of _____ (a condition of definiteness) about it.
(8) Although the _____ (topic being discussed) of her talk was rather dull her witty delivery kept the audience interested.

IV. Complete the following sentences with the words or expressions from the passage given below. Change the form where necessary.

give rise to	find out	consist in	the point
in particular	unfit	emerge from	regard as
as to	with respect to	get into	put together
with an eye	go through	superficial	

(1) _____ your job application, please come for an interview tomorrow.
(2) He's buying land _____ to building a house on it someday.
(3) I thought the whole meal was good, but the soup _____ was delicious.
(4) Will you please try to _____ what time the airplane arrives?
(5) I can't believe what she _____ to get that job. She had four interviews with the hiring committee in one week.

(6) After the teenage took the broken video game apart and fixed it. He was unable to _____ it back _____ again.

(7) Hal _____ tennis while his wife goes for painting and sculpture.

(8) Let's stop discussing trivial details and come to _____.

4. Culture and Society

Raymond Williams[1]

> 作者是文化研究的一位奠基人。他的著作《1780 至 1950 的文化和社会》使他赢得了很高的威望。他的著作与其说是注重实际和思考历史的著作,还不如说是一本理论著作。在这篇文章中,他介绍了他对工业、民主、阶级、艺术和文化这些基本概念的看法以及这些概念在现代生活和思想中所显示出来的广泛变化。

In the last decades of the eighteenth century, and in the first half of the nineteenth century, a number of words, which are now of capital importance, came for the first time into common English use, or, where they had already been generally used in the language, acquired new and important meanings.[2] There is in fact a general pattern of change in these words, and this can be used as a special kind of map by which it is possible to look again at those wider changes in life and thought to which the changes in language evidently refer.

Five words are the key points from which this map can be drawn. They are *industry*, *democracy*, *class*, *art and culture*. The importance of these words, in our modern structure of meanings, is obvious. The changes in their use, at this critical period, bear witness[3] to a general change in our characteristic ways of thinking about our common life: about our social, political and economic institutions; about the purposes which these institutions are designed to embody; and about the relations to these institutions and purposes of our activities in learning, education and the arts.

The first important word is *industry*, and the period in which its use changes is the period which we now call the Industrial Revolution. *Industry*, before this period, was a name for a particular human attribute, which could be paraphrased as skill, assiduity, perseverance, diligence.[4] This use of *industry* of course survives. But, in the last decades of the eighteenth century, *industry* came also to mean something else; it became a collective word for our manufacturing and productive institutions, and for their general activities. Adam Smith[5], in *The Wealth of Nations* (1776), is one of the first writers to use the word in this way, and from his time the development of this use is assured. *Industry*, with a capital letter, is thought of as a thing in itself—an institution, a body of activities—rather than simply a human attribute. *Industrious*, which described persons, is joined, in the nineteenth century, by *industrial*, which describes the institutions. The rapid growth in importance of these institutions is seen as creating a new system, which in the 1830s is first called *Industrialism*. In part, this is the acknowledgement[6] of a series of very important technical changes, and of their transforming effect on methods of production. It is also, however, an acknowledgement of the effect of these changes on society as a whole, which is similarly transformed. The phrase *Industrial Revolution* amply[7] confirms this, for the phrase, first used by French writers in the 1820s, and gradually adopted, in the course of the century, by English writers, is modeled explicitly on an analogy with the French Revolution of 1789. As that had transformed France, so this has transformed England; the means of change are different, but the change is comparable in kind: it has produced, by a pattern of change, a new society.

The second important word is *democracy*, which had been known, from the Greek, as a term for "government by the people," but which only came into common English use at the time of the American and French Revolutions. Weekley, in *Words Ancient and Modern*[8], writes:

It was not until the French Revolution that democracy ceased
to be a mere literary word, and became part of the political vocabulary.

In this he is substantially[9] right. Certainly, it is in reference to[10] America and France that the examples begin to multiply, at the end of the eighteenth century, and it is worth noting that the great majority of these examples show the word being used unfavourably: in close relation with the hated *Jacobinism*[11], or with the familiar *mob-rule*. England may have been (the word has so many modern definitions) a democracy since Magna Carta[12], or since the Commonwealth, or since 1688, but it certainly did not call itself one. Democrats, at the end of the eighteenth and the beginning of the nineteenth centuries, were seen, commonly, as dangerous and subversive[13] mob agitators. Just as *industry* and its derived words record what we now call the Industrial Revolution, so *democracy* and *democrat*, in their entry into ordinary speech, record the effects, in England, of the American and French Revolutions, and a crucial phase of the struggle, at home, for what we would now call democratic representation.

Industry, to indicate an institution, begins in about 1776; *democracy*, as a practical word, can be dated from about the same time. The third word, *class*, can be dated, in its most important modern sense, from about 1772. Before this, the ordinary use of *class*, in English, was to refer to a division or group in schools and colleges: "the usual Classes in Logick and Philosophy." It is only at the end of the eighteenth century that the modern structure of class, in its social sense, begins to be built up. First comes *lower classes*, to join *lower orders*, which appears earlier in the eighteenth century. Then, in the 1790s, we get *higher classes*; *middle classes* and *middling classes* follow at once; *working classes* in about 1815; *upper classes* in the 1820s. *Class prejudice*, *class legislation*, *class consciousness*, *class conflict* and *class war* follow in the course of the nineteenth century. The *upper middle classes* are first heard of in the 1890s; the *lower middle class* in our own century.

It is obvious, of course, that this spectacular history of the new use of *class* does not indicate the beginning of social divisions in England. But it indicates, quite clearly, a change in the character of these divisions, and it records, equally clearly, a change in attitudes towards them. Class is a more indefinite word than *rank*, and this was probably one of the reasons for its introduction. The structure then built on it is in nineteenth-century terms: in terms, that is to say, of the changed social structure, and the changed social feelings, of an England which was passing through the Industrial Revolution, and which was at a crucial phase in the development of political democracy.[14]

The fourth word, *art*, is remarkably similar, in its pattern of change, to *industry*. From its original sense of a human attribute, a "skill", it had come, by the period with which we are concerned, to be a kind of institution, a set body of[15] activities of a certain kind. An *art* had formerly been any human skill; but *Art*, now, signified a particular group of skills, the "Imaginative" or "creative" arts. *Artist* had meant a skilled person, as had *artisan*[16]; but it now referred to these selected skills alone. Further, and most significantly, Art came to stand for a special kind of truth, "Imaginative truth", and *artist* for a special kind of person, as the words *artistic* and *artistical*, to describe human beings, new in the 1840s, show. A new name, *aesthetics*, was found to describe the judgement of art, and this, in its turn, produced a name for a special kind of person—*aesthete*. The *arts*—literature, music, painting, sculpture, theatre—were grouped together, in this new phrase, as having something essentially in common which distinguished them from other human skills. The same separation as had grown up-between *artist* and *artisan* grew up between *artist* and *craftsman*. *Genius*, from meaning "a characteristic disposition," came to mean "exalted ability,"[17] and a distinction was made between it and talent. As *art* had produced *artist* in the new sense, and *aesthetics aesthete*, so this produced a *genius*, to indicate a special kind of person. These changes, which belong in time to the period of the other changes discussed, form a record of a remarkable change in ideas of the nature and purpose of art, and of its relations to other human activities and to society as a whole.

The fifth word, *culture*, similarly changes, in the same critical period. Before this period, it had meant, primarily the "tending of natural growth," and then, by analogy, a process of human training. But this latter use, which had usually been a culture of something, was changed, in the nineteenth century, to *culture* as such, a thing, in itself. It came to mean, first, "a general state or habit of the mind," having close relations with the idea of human perfection. Second, it came to mean "the general state of intellectual development, in a society as a whole." Third, it came to mean "the general body of the arts." Fourth, later in the century it came to mean "whole way of life, material, intellectual and spiritual." It came also, as we know, to be a word which often provoked either hostility or embarrassment.

The development of *culture* is perhaps the most striking among all the words named. It might be said, indeed, that the questions now concentrated in the meanings of the word *culture* are questions directly raised by the great historical changes which the changes in *industry*, *democracy* and *class*, in their own way, represent, and to which the changes in *art* are a closely related response. The development of the word *culture* is a record of a number of important and continuing reactions to these changes in our social, economic and political life, and may be seen, in itself, as a special kind of map by means of which the nature of the changes can be explored...

The word which more than any other comprises[18] these relations is *culture*, with all its complexity of idea and reference—for the recognition of a separate body of moral and intellectual activities, and the offering of a court of human appeal, which comprise the early meanings of the word, are joined, and in themselves changed, by the growing assertion of a whole way of life, not only as a scale of integrity[19], but as a mode of interpreting all our common experience, and, in this new interpretation, changing it. Where *culture* meant a state or habit of the mind, or the body of intellectual and moral activities, it means now, also, a whole way of life. This development, like each of the original meanings and the relations between them, is not accidental, but general and deeply significant.

【 Notes 】

①Raymond Williams (1921—1988) is an English historian became Professor in the Faculty of English at Cambridge University in 1961. The son of a Welsh miner, he attended Cambridge University and in his youth, was a member of the Communist Party. He became one of the founders of cultural studies. His work was historical and meditative, pragmatic rather than theoretical. William's reputation grew from his major work, *Culture and Society*, *1780—1950*, New York: Columbia University Press, 1983.
It has been said that Williams "forced the first important shift into a new way of thinking about the symbolic dimensions of our lives." He took the idea of "culture" from the privileged space of artistic production and specialist knowledge, or "high culture," and introduced it into the lived experience of everyday life. In this passage he introduces his thinking about the expression in language of the central ideas of industry, democracy, class, art and culture and the changes in the meanings of those ideas that reveal broad change in modern life and thought.

②In the last decades of the eighteenth century, and in the first half of the nineteenth century, a number of words, which are now of capital importance, came for the first time into common English use, or where they had already been generally used in the language, acquired new and important meanings：很多词在18世纪末和19世纪上半叶开始用作英语普通词汇，而现在却有着重要的意义，或者说，过去这些词在语言中用作一般词汇，而现在有了新颖和重要的意义。
这个句子是一个主从复合句。主句的主语是 a number of words，谓语部分是 came into common English use, 和 acquired new and important meanings; which 引导的非限定性定语从句以及 where 引导的状语从句把主语和谓语分隔开了。
capital *adj.* 重要的，主要的；come into 开始进入某种行为或状态。

③bear witness(to sth.)：证明，作证，如：His evidence bore witness to my testimony. 他的证据可以证实我的证词。

④... was a name for a particular human attribute, which could be paraphrased as ,skill, assiduity, perseverance, diligence.
attribute ❶ *n.* 属性，特点，它可以表示某一典型事物，表示肯定意义时，比 characteristic 所表示的中性含义强一些：Eagerness to learn is an often overlooked attribute in small children. 渴望学习是小孩的特性，但是常被忽略。❷ *vt.* 认为某事物属于某人（某事），认为某事物由某人（某事）引起或产生：She attributes her success to hard work and a bit of luck. 她认

为,她的成功是由于勤奋加上一点儿运气而得来的。
assiduity /ˌæsiˈdjuːiti/ n. [U]专心致志,勤勉

⑤Adam Smith:亚当·斯密(1723—1790),英国著名经济学家。所著《国富论》(*The Wealth of Nations*)是一部伟大的、完整的政治经济学著作。

⑥acknowledgement n. ❶[U] 承认,确认:The fact is the acknowledgement of his own fault. 事实是他承认了自己的过失。❷[C] 确认通知,回音:I didn't receive an acknowledgement of my application. 我尚未收到确认已经接到我申请的回音。❸[C,U] 答谢的表示,(作者的)鸣谢:We are sending you some money in acknowledgement of your valuable help. 我们谨奉薄酬,对你的大力帮助表示感谢。

⑦amply /ˈæmpli/ adv. 充裕地,足够地:Facts amply prove that the policy is right. 事实充分证明了,这个政策是对的。

⑧*Words Ancient and Modern*:《古代与现代词汇》。其作者是 E. Weekly,该书于 1926 年出版,以下两句话摘自第 34 页。

⑨substantially /səbˈstænʃəli/ adv. 大量地,实质上,大体上

⑩in/with reference to:关于,就……而论,如:He is working on a collection of documents in reference to World War I. 他正在搞一本关于第一次世界大战的文献汇编。

⑪Jacobinism /ˈdʒækəubinizəm/ n. ❶(法国)雅各宾派的政治主张,雅各宾主义;❷(尤指政治上的)极端激进主义

⑫Magna Carta:大宪章

⑬subversive /səbˈvəsiv/ adj. 颠覆性的:subversive propaganda 颠覆性的宣传;subversive mob agitator 反叛暴民的鼓动者

⑭The structure then built on it is in nineteenth-century terms:in terms, that is to say, of the changed social structure, and the changed social feelings, of an England which was passing through the Industrial Revolution, and which was at a crucial phase in the development of political democracy. 这是一个主从复合句,主句中的主语是 structure,谓语由 is of... 结构表示,which 引导定语从句修饰 England。

in nineteenth-century terms:在 19 世纪时期;in terms:明确地,用确切的词语;at a crucial phase:在关键时期,紧要关头。

⑮a body of:大量,大片等,如:a body of evidence 大量证据;bodies of water 大片水域

⑯artisan /ˈɑːtizn/ n. 技工,工匠;aesthetics /isˈθetiks/ n. 美学;aesthete /ˈesθiːt/ n. 审美家

⑰...,from meaning "a characteristic disposition," came to mean "exalted ability":characteristic 是形容词,意思是"典型的、特有的",如:He spoke with characteristic enthusiasm. 他以特有的热情说话。characteristic 作名词时,表示某一事物的特点或特征。character 则指心理特征与情绪特征的集合,常与品格有关,如:This is a town that has all the characteristics of a typical seaside resort. 这是一座具有典型海滨休养地一切特色的城镇。They were only drinking companions of questionable character. 他们只不过是品格成问题的酒肉朋友。

disposition *n.* 性情,性格,意向,倾向,如:There was a general disposition to ignore the problem. 这里曾经存在忽视这个问题的倾向。

exalted *adj.* 提拔的,高的:a person of exalted rank 地位高的人。

⑱comprise /kəm'praɪz/ *v.* 包含,包括,由……组成。如:House of commons and the House of lords comprise the British Parliament. 下议院和上议院组成了英国议会。The British Parliament comprises House of commons and the House of lords. 英国议会由下议院和上议院组成。

⑲integrity *n.* ❶正直:a man of integrity 一个正直的人 ❷完整,完全,完善:mutual respect for territorial integrity 互相尊重领土完整

【 Exercises 】

I. Comprehension Questions

(1) Following is a list of eight key words which can be applied to the nineteenth and twentieth centuries. Which three are not William's key words?

Art, science, democracy, class, industry, politics, culture, and technology.

(2) Which of the following is true and which is false?

1) Thomas Jefferson introduced the use of the word "industry" as a collective word in the Wealth of Nations in the 18th century.

2) Democracy became a part of the commonly used political vocabulary after the French and American Revolutions.

3) The use of "class" in it's social and political sense is related to the rise of modern "industry" and "democracy" according to Williams. (Hint: paragraphs 5 and 6)

4) Williams says that before the changes in meaning occurred the word "culture" meant simply tending or caring for natural growth and the process of human training-that is becoming a well behaved and educated person. (Hint: paragraph 8)

(3) On what event in what other country was the use of the phrase "Industrial Revolution" in England was modeled? (Hint: paragraph 3)

(4) Which of the following two does the new use of the word "Art" mean?

A. Any human skill.

B. A kind of institution of "creative" or "imaginative" arts.

(5) Which is not one of Williams' explanations of how the meaning of "culture" developed in the following statement?

The new idea of "culture" that emerged included the following: a general state of mind having to do with the idea of human perfection, the general state of intellectual development in society as a whole, the general body of the arts, the body of political and economic philosophy, and a whole way of material, intellectual, and spiritual life.

II. Points for Discussion

(1) Williams tells us "culture" is the most central of the five key ideas he has identified. Discuss his idea about the concept of culture briefly, including an illustration of how this idea adds to the understanding of some particular historical case you chose.

(2) Relate Williams' ideas about culture to the contemporary expression "political culture."

III. Complete the following sentences with appropriate forms of words or expressions from the passage according to the given meaning in brackets.

(1) She shows great _____ (constant and careful attention to a task) in all her work.

(2) He says his brother is a man of _____ (of medium size) height.

(3) I wonder why he broke off all _____ (links between people, groups) with his family.

(4) On the American flag, each star _____ (represent) one of the fifty states and each stripe _____ (represent) one of the original thirteen colonies of the 1800s.

(5) There is a large _____ (amount) of support for nuclear disarmament.

(6) I am writing _____ (concerning, about) your job application.

(7) The time you spend in high school is an important _____ (a period of time, a stage of development) of your education.

(8) The new housing _____ (provide evidence) to the energy of the Council.

IV. Fill in blanks with the appropriate forms of the words and expressions listed below.

character	characteristic	attribute	acknowledgement
substantially	impetus	body	mitigate
in part	build up	build on	by means of
at least	in the least	rally	

(1) We planted the garden _____ with flowers, but in large part we planted vegetables.

(2) It has been proved that the insurance business is _____ trust.

(3) The professional athlete exercises regularly to _____ her strength.

(4) Mike claims that he drinks _____ a quart of water every day.

(5) _____ monthly payments, people can buy more than in the past.

(6) These flowers are a small _____ of your great kindness.

(7) Your assessment is _____ correct.

(8) Cool breezes _____ the heat of the day.

(9) The boy _____ on hearing the good news.

(10) What _____ distinguish the Americans from Canadians?

(11) Patience is one of the most important _____ in a teacher.

(12) He has _____ but no personality.

5. The Historian and His Day[1]

J. H. Hexter[2]

> 海克斯特(J. H. Hexter)在他的著作中把历史学家分成两类:理想主义历史学家和现实主义历史学家。在这篇文章的标题"历史学家和他的时代"中,时代具有双重意义。它既包含历史学家撰写著作时所生活的时代,也包含了历史学家所研究的事件所发生的时代。因此,这个具有特定意义的时代不但体现了历史学家本人的经历,而且还表达了他对所研究专题的理解和看法。

For a good while now a fairly strenuous contest has been in progress between two opposed schools of historical thought... The division lies roughly between the "present-minded" and the "history-minded" historians. In the course of time many historians have joined one side or the other in the controversy... In general,... the kind of scholar who, distrustful of ideas and theories, believes that history is all facts has tended to take the side of the history-minded historians.[3] For more obvious reasons the chronic do-gooder, who believes that knowledge justifies itself only by a capacity to solve current problems, lines up with the present-minded position[4].

This peculiar alignment has frequently obscured[5] the issues at stake.[6] It is easy to expose the feebleness and absurdity of those who want only facts and of those who want only current problem-solving; and it is fun, too. Consequently the attacks on both sides have often been directed mainly against these vulnerable positions... There is nothing intrinsic to the history-minded position that precludes ideas or theories or, if you prefer, generalization. Nor is there anything in present-mindedness that demands an optimism as to the efficacy[7] of history as a panacea[8] for current social ills... In a sense the present-minded are realists with respect to the study of history, the history-minded are idealists.

The approach of the latter to the problem is that we ought not to intrude our contemporary value systems and preconceptions[9] and notions into our reconstruction of the past. They insist that it is our duty as historians to understand the past in its terms, not in our own; and they document their thesis with some undeniably horrible examples of what has happened in the last century to historians who looked at the past with the dubious[10] prepossessions, current in their own day... We do not like to see the nineteenth-century present-minded [historian] transforming the roughneck barons

of Runnymede into harbingers[11] of nineteenth-century democracy and nationalism...
We are unhappy when we watch a historian adding Victorian liberalism to the cargo
that the 5th and 6th century Anglo-Saxons brought with them to England from their
North German forests...

Convinced by the dreadful examples... we resolve to eschew[12] the wickedness of
modernism and thenceforth hew to our obligation to be history-minded.[13] And then a
clear and chilly voice says: "But my dear fellows, you can't be history-minded. It
might be nice if you could, or it might not, but in any case it is impossible. So all
this... about the obligation to be history-minded is rather silly."... The harsh fact
of life is that, willy-nilly[14] the present-day historian lives not in the past but in the
present, and this fact cannot be altered by any pious[15] resolve to be history-minded.

What we say about any historical epoch in some ways reflects our experience;
and that experience was accumulated not in the fifteenth, in the sixteenth, or in any
other century than the twentieth. When we look back on the past, we do so from the
present. We are present-minded just as all earlier historians were present-minded in
their day because for better or worse we happen to live in our own day. So the best
thing for us to do is to recognize that every generation reinterprets the past in terms of
the exigencies of its own day[16]...

We must admit that in some respects all historians are present-minded, even the
most determined proponents of history-mindedness. All historians are indeed engaged
in rewriting past history in the light of at least one aspect of present experience, that
aspect which has to do with the increments to our positive knowledge[17] that are the
fruit of scientific investigation. Consider a single example. Up to a few decades ago
the Dark Ages before the twelfth century were considered an era of total regression,
technological as well as political, social and culture. Then Lefebvre de Noëttes[18] described results of certain experiments he had made with animal power. He had reproduced antique harnesses for draft horses. In such harness the pulling power of the
horse proved to be less than a quarter of what it is in modern harness. But "modem"
harness, involving the use of a rigid horse collar, makes its appearance in Europe in
the tenth century. So in the Dark Ages a horse could deliver about four times the
tractive force[19] that it could in antiquity... When we do apply the results of
Lefebvre's experiments to medieval agriculture we are being present-minded in at
least two ways. In the first and more simple way we are rewriting the history of the
Middle Ages in the light of the present because until the present the particular bit of

light that was the work of Lefebvre did not exist... Furthermore historians in earlier ages would not have thought of going about the investigation of medieval agriculture as Lefebvre did... Lefebvre was distinctly reflecting the preoccupations of his own age with science... In this particular area of study at any rate, scientific-mindedness is present-mindedness.

It seems to me that the proponents of history-mindedness must, and in most cases probably do, concede the validity of this kind of present-mindedness in the writing of history; and if this is all that present-mindedness means, then every historian worth his salt[20] is present-minded. No sane[21] contemporary scientist in his investigations of the physical world would disregard nineteenth-century advances in field theory, and no sane historian in his work would rule out of consideration insights achieved in the past century concerning the connection of class conflict with historical occurrences. But this is only to say that... in the nature of things no one can... use any device before it exists... The historian's situation is no different from that of the scientist. Adequate investigation of optical isomers in organic chemistry,[22] for example, had to wait on the development of the techniques of spectroscopy.[23] If this is what present-mindedness means, then present-mindedness is not just the condition of historical knowledge. For all knowledge at any time is obviously limited by the limits of the means of gaining knowledge at that time; and historians are simply in the same boat as all others whose business it is to know.

... But, the present-minded see a greater problem. They contend that in writing history no historian can free himself of his total experience and that that experience is inextricably involved[24] not only in the limits of knowledge but also... in the events, crises and tensions of his own day. Therefore those passions, prejudices, assumptions, prepossessions, events, crises and tensions of the historian's own day inevitably permeate what he writes about the past.[25] This is the crucial allegation of the present-minded,[26] and if it is wholly correct, the issue must be settled in their favor and the history-minded pack up their ... categorical-imperative baggage and depart in silence. Frequently discussions of this crucial issue have got bogged down[27] because the history-minded keep trying to prove that the historian can counteract the influence of his own day, while the present-minded keep saying that this is utterly impossible.

... For a small part of my day I live under a comfortable rule of bland intellectual irresponsibility vis-à-vis[28] the Great Issues of the Contemporary World,... But during most of my day—that portion of it that I spend in dealing with the Great and Not-So-Great Issues of the World between 1450 and 1650—I live under an altogether different rule. The commandments of that rule are:

1. Do not go off half-cocked.[29] ... [be irresponsible].
2. Get the story straight.
3. Keep prejudices about present-day issues out of this area.

The commandments are counsels of perfection, but they are not merely that; they are enforced by sanctions, both external and internal. The serried array of historical trade journals[30] equipped with extensive book-review columns provides the most powerful external sanction....

The reviewing host seems largely to have lined up with the history-minded. This seems to be a consequence of their training.... Consequently most of us have been conditioned to feel that it is not quite proper to characterize John Pym as a liberal, or Thomas More as a socialist, or Niccolo Machiavelli as a proto-Fascist, and we tend to regard this sort of characterization as at best a risky pedagogic device.[31] Not only the characterization but the thought process that leads to it lie under a psychological ban...

The austere rule[32] we live under as historians has some curious consequences. In my case one of the consequences is that my knowledge of the period around the sixteenth century in Europe is of a rather different order than my knowledge about current happenings. Those large segments of my own day spent in the discussion, investigation and contemplation of that remote era[33] ... are spent in an orderly, systematic, purposeful way.

......

In the controversy that provided the starting point of this... essay, the essential question is sometimes posed with respect to the relation of the historian to his own day, in other instances it is posed with respect to his relation to his own time.[34] Recognizing how idiosyncratic[35] is the day of one historian we may inquire whether his time is also peculiar. The answer is, "Yes, his time is a bit odd." And here it is possible to take a welcome leave of the first person singular. For, although my day is peculiar to me, my time, as a historian, is like the time of other historians.

For our purposes the crucial fact about the ordinary time of all men, even of historians in their personal as against their professional capacity, is that in no man's time is he really sure what is going to happen next. This is true, obviously, not only of men of the present time but also of all men of all past times.

......

But it is precisely characteristic of the historian that he does know. He is really sure what is going to happen next, not in his time as a pilgrim[36] here below, but in his own time as a historian. The public servant Conyers Read, for example, when he worked high in the councils of the Office of Strategic Services did not know what the outcome of the maneuvers he helped plan would be. But for all the years... during which he painstakingly investigated the public career of Francis Walsingham, the eminent Tudor historian Conyers Read knew that the Spanish Armada would come against England and that the diplomatic maneuvers of Mr. Secretary Walsingham would assist in its defeat...

...The historian alone lives systematically in the historian's own time. And from what we have been saying it is clear that this time has a unique dimension. Each man in his own time tries to discover the motives and the causes of the actions of those people he has to deal with; and the historian does the like with varying degrees of success. But, as other men do not and cannot, the historian knows something of the results of the acts of those he deals with: this is the unique dimension of the historian's time...

This knowledge makes it impossible for the historian to do merely what the history-minded say he should do—consider the past in its own terms, and envisage events as the men who lived through them did. Surely he should try to do that; also he must do more than that simply because he knows about those events what none of the men contemporary with them knew; he knows what their consequences were. To see the events surrounding the obscure monk Luther as Leo X saw them—as another "monks' quarrel" and a possible danger to the perquisites of the Curia—may help us understand the peculiar inefficacy of Papal policy at the time; but that does not preclude the historian from seeing the same events as the decisive step towards the final breach of the religious unity of Western Civilization. We may be quite sure however that nobody at the time, not even Luther himself, saw those events that way. The historian who resolutely refused to use the insight that his own peculiar time gave him would not be superior to his fellows; he would be merely foolish, betraying a singular failure to grasp what history is. For history is a becoming, an ongoing, and it is to be understood not only in terms of what comes before but also of what comes after.

......

He would be bold indeed who would insist that all historians should follow one and the same line of experience in their quest, or who would venture to say what this single line is that all should follow... History thrives in measure as the experience of each historian differs from that of his fellows[37]. It is indeed the wide and varied range of experience covered by all the days of all historians that makes the rewriting of history—not in each generation but for each historian—at once necessary and inevitable.

【 Notes 】

①J. H. Hexter, *Reappraisals in History*: *New Views on History and Society in Early Modern Europe*, New York: Harper Torchbooks, 1961, pp. 1—13. In this excerpt from his book, *Reappraisals of History* he divides historians into two categories: the idealists or history-minded and the realists, or present-minded.

The title he has chosen for his essay, "The Historian and His Day," is a double play on the meaning of time. He writes about the individual relationship of the historian to the period in which he lives (for example, mid-20th century) and also to the period he studies and writes about (for example, medieval England). The "historian's day" means the actual day of historical work in the historians' life but he extends it beyond to include the historian's understanding and ideas abut the period of the events studied. So the historians day includes his experience today and also his understanding and insight into the subject he studies. He uses the word "time" in a broader sense of the whole social contest of the general period in which the historian lives and also of the period he studies.

②J. H. Hexter, known as "Jack" Hexter, (1910—1996), professor of history at Yale University and Washington University in the US, was an American historian of early modern Europe and England who also wrote on the practice of historiography in his time. He was the author of a highly regarded series of books on the writing of history in the 1960s and 70s in which he advocated the idea that history can be written objectively. He promoted narrative historical writing.

③In general,... the kind of scholar who, distrustful of ideas and theories, believes that history is all facts has tended to take the side of the history-minded historians. 在这个主从复合句中，主句中的主语 the kind of scholar 与谓语 has tended 被以 who 引导的定语从句所分割。定语从句中的主语 who 与谓语 believes 被形容词短语 distrustful of ideas and theories 所分割。

④lines up with the present-minded position:

line up alongside/with: 与……站在一起，与……联合，如: He is lining up with the minority in his class. 他与班上的少数派站在一起。

⑤obscure /əbˈskjuə/ *vt.* 使不分明；遮掩，如: The moon was obscured by clouds. 月亮被云彩遮住了。Mist obscured the view. 薄雾笼罩着周围的景色。

⑥at stake:胜败关头,在冒险,如:This decision puts our lives at stake. 这项决定使我们的生命吉凶难卜。Our children's education is at stake. 我们孩子的教育难以预料。

⑦efficacy /'efikəsi/ 功效,效验:The efficacy of the latest medicine in relieving headache is well known. 这种新药医治头疼的功效是众所周知的。
efficiency 效率:raise efficacy 提高效率。

⑧panacea /ˌpænə'siə/ n. 治百病的药,万灵药

⑨preconception /ˌpri:kən'sepʃən/ n. 事先形成的观点或思想,先入之见:This small, determined woman upset all his preconceptions about the opposite sex. 这位个子矮小而坚强的女子改变了他对异性的一切成见。

⑩dubious /'dju:biəs/ adj. [尤作表语]❶半信半疑;可疑的:I remain dubious about her motives. 我对她的动机仍存疑念。❷结果未定的;不能确定的,有争议的:The results of this policy will remain dubious for some time. 这项政策的效果短期内难以确定。

⑪transforming roughneck barons of Runnymede into harbingers....:把兰尼米德这位粗鲁的男爵变成……的先驱。
baron /'bærən/ n. 男爵;Runnymede 兰尼米德,英格兰萨里郡西北部一个区和市。
harbinger /'hɑ:bindʒə(r)/ n. (~ of sb/sth) (修辞)预告者;先驱;前兆:The crowing of the cock is a harbinger of dawn. 鸡啼报晓。The cuckoo is a harbinger of spring. 布谷鸟预告春天的来临。

⑫eschew /is'tʃu:/ v. [文]避开(某事物);戒除;回避:eschew political discussion 回避政治讨论。

⑬hew /hju:; hju/ v. ❶用斧、刀剑等砍,劈(某物/某人):hewing wood 劈木。❷开辟:They hewed a path through the jungle. 他们在丛林中开辟出一条路。❸砍掉某物:hew off dead branches 砍去枯枝;hew sth out 努力做成某事物,奋力开创一番事业。hew to 坚持,遵守:hew to principle 坚持原则;hew to rules 遵守规则

⑭willy-nilly /'wili'nili/ adv. 无论想要不想要;不管愿意不愿意:They all had to take part, willy-nilly. 他们都得参加,不论他们愿意不愿意。

⑮pious /'paiəs/ adj. 虔诚的:pious utterance 虔诚的话;pious attempt 可贵的尝试。

⑯exigency /'eksidʒənsi/ n. [作可数名词时常作复数,亦作不可数名词][文]紧急的需要或要求;紧急情况;危急关头:The people had to accept the harsh exigencies of war. 人们要承受战乱的严酷现实。

⑰increment /'inkrimənt/ n. 增加,增长,增值:the increment of knowledge 知识的增长;an annual increment of $300 in salary 年薪300美元的增额。

⑱Lefebvre de Noëttes:法国历史学家

⑲the tractive force: 牵引力

⑳worth one's salt:称职的,胜任的,有能力的,应受尊敬的:Any worker worth his salt should know how that machine works. 任何一位称职的工人都应知道那台机器怎样运作。

㉑sane /sein/ adj. ❶心智健全的;神志正常的:It's hard to stay sane under such awful pressure. 处于这种可怕的压力之下,不疯才怪呢。❷(比喻)明智的;稳健的;理智的:a sane person, decision, policy 明智的人、决定、政策。her sane, democratic views 她的理智、民主的见解。sanely adv.

㉒insomer /ˈaisəumə(r)/ n. （同分）异构体,（同分）异构物

㉓spectroscopy /spekˈtrɔskəpi/ n. 光谱学；波谱学

㉔inextricably /inˈekstrikəbli/ adv. 无法摆脱地,解决不了地,不可避免地

㉕permeate /ˈpəːmieit/ v. ❶漫遍,遍布；充满：History permeated this ancient conference room. 这间古老的会议室洋溢着历史气息。❷影响,感染：be permeated with a good deal of Chinese culture 深受中国文化的熏陶；The sense of urgency permeated their thought. 他们的心中充满着紧迫感。permeate sb. with an ethic 向某人灌输一种伦理思想。

㉖allegation /ˌæliˈgeiʃən/ n. 断言,宣称；陈述,说法：The police man made serious allegations that he was a thief. 警察郑重其事地断言他是小偷。

㉗bog /bɔg/ v. (-gg-) bog (sth) down (usu passive 通常用于被动语态) ❶（使某物）陷入泥沼：The tank (got) bogged down in the mud. 坦克陷入泥沼之中。❷（比喻）(cause sth to)（使某物）陷入困境不能前进。n. [C, U]（地面为腐朽植物的）沼泽（地区）：a peat bog 泥炭沼；Keep to the path—most parts of the moor are bog. 沿着这条小路走——荒野上多处是沼泽地。

㉘vis-à-vis /ˈviːzɑːˈviː/ prep. (法) ❶关于（某事物）：discuss plans for the company vis-a-vis a possible merger 洽谈公司可能合并的事宜。❷和（某事物）相比：Women's salaries are low vis-a-vis what men earn for the same work. 女子的薪水比同工种的男子低。

㉙go off half-cocked /go off at half cock v. 草率、鲁莽行事：Tom often goes off half cocked. 汤姆常常草率行事。

㉚serried /ˈserid/ adj. [通常作定语]（旧或文）(指人或物的行列)排紧的,密集的：serried rows/ranks/lines 密集的排(列/行)。

㉛pedagogic /pedəˈgɔdʒik/ adj. 教师的,教学法的；教育学的：contemporary pedagogic thinking 当代教育思想。

㉜austere /ɔˈstiə/ adj. ❶(指人或行为)束身自修的,苦行的：monks leading simple, austere lives 过着清苦生活的僧侣。❷(指建筑物或地方)简朴的,无装饰的,简陋的：The room was furnished in austere style. 这间屋子的陈设都很简单朴素。

㉝contemplation /ˌkɔntemˈpleiʃən/ n. ❶凝视；沉思,出神：be sunk (lost) in religious contemplation 沉陷于宗教冥想。❷意图,预期：a new school now under contemplation 正在计划修建的新学校。

㉞In the controversy that provided the starting point of this... essay, the essential question is sometimes posed with respect to the relation of the historian to his own day; in other instances it is posed with respect to his relation to his own time. 作者在这一句中用"day"表示历史学家所生活的时代,而用"time"表示他生活的特定时期。例如,作者生活在20世纪这个时期,而研究更早的时期,例如,西周或晚唐,这就形成一种独特的时代范围,也就是作者所说的历史学家的时代(the historian's time)。

㉟idiosyncratic /ˌidiiəsiŋˈkrætik/ adj. 具有个人气质、癖性、风格的

㊱pilgrim /ˈpilgrim/ n. 朝圣者；香客：pilgrims on their way to Mecca 赴麦加的朝圣者；pilgrims visiting the shrine 到圣徒墓地朝圣的人。

㊲History thrives in measure as the experience of each historian differs from that of his fellows. 在这个句子中，in measure 这个介词短语的意思是相当地；as 引导一个原因状语从句。in considerable measure 相当大地，in some measure 部分地。

【 Exercises 】

I. Comprehension Questions

(1) According to Hexter, the idealist (history-minded) historian says historians ought to push their contemporary value systems into their reconstructions of the past. True _____ or False _____? (Hint：look at first 3 paragraphs.)

(2) Hexter states that present-mindedness (realism) is inevitable for historians. True _____ or False _____? (Hint：look at paragraph 5.)

(3) In the sixth paragraph the author seems to be saying that historians inevitably are both history-minded and present-minded. True _____ or False _____?

(4) Present-minded historian claims that the passions, prejudices, assumptions, events, crises, and tensions of the historian's own time influence what he writes about the past. True _____ or False _____?

II. Points for Discussion

(1) Choose one of the following questions to discuss in the light of Hexter's point that historians are inevitably both history-minded idealists and present-minded realists. For example, in environmental history you might choose to discuss the Li Bing Dujiang yan irrigation system as a water conservation project (near Chengdu in Szechwan, constructed in the Warring States period). Or an issue in women's history or one in Chinese population (demographic) history.

(2) Applying Hexter's ideas of idealism and realism in the writing of history, chose and analyze your own example of history-mindedness and/or present-mindedness in the reconstruction of history.

(3) How does the historian who is history-minded differ from the men of the time he studies? (See second to last paragraph.)

III. Complete the following sentences with words or expressions from the passage similar in meaning to the words in brackets.

(1) The president of our university _____ (postponed) the meeting _____ because she had to leave town.

(2) The main theme of the book is _____ (hidden from view) by frequent digressions.

(3) The farmers were more anxious for rain than the people in the city because they had more _____ (being risked).

(4) The effects of technology _____ (pass through) the lives of every human being alive.

(5) Mr. Jones was thinking about quitting his job, but his wife told him not to _____ (go off at half-cocked).

IV. **Complete the following sentences with the words or expressions from the passage given below. Change the form where necessary.**

> *go about   in terms of   in the light of   for better or worse*
> *rule out   pack up   in controversy   for a good while*

(1) We tended to risk change in our own values and perceptions _____ so as to comprehend why someone thinks and acts differently from us.

(2) The money was "enough" to enable them to "avoid indignity" _____.

(3) I can say nothing _____ his competence as a workman, as I have no knowledge of it.

(4) The point _____ is not whether we should do it, but whether we can do it.

(5) Lucy _____ applying to college in Texas because she would rather go to school in Canada.

V. **Translate the following sentences into English, using the words and phrases given below.**

> *preconception   worth its salt   vis-à-vis   panacea   bog*

(1) 国家经济弊病百出,又无万灵药可以医治。
(2) 早先对这一地区的生活所形成的看法越来越站不住脚了。
(3) 没有一次名副其实的工会运动会允许那种事情发生。
(4) 我们的讨论纠缠在无关紧要的细节上。
(5) 他的薪水比起全国平均水平高出很多。

Unit 2

World History

6. Introduction to World History[1]

Kevin Reilly, Lynda Shaffer[2]

> 这篇文章选自美国历史学会 1995 年出版的参考书的世界史部分。本文描述了第二次世界大战以后,世界史作为历史学科的一种新形式以一种新风格创立的过程,并阐述了八个不同作者的八种不同的世界史模式。每一种模式都运用了不同的历史分析法。上面提到的这本参考书是各种世界史的参考书目录,对世界史的学生来说,是难得的珍贵资料。

The antecedents of world history in the West can be found in some of the cultural traditions of the ancient world. A small "culture-in-between" like the ancient Greek, in the shadow of Egypt and threatened by Persia, developed historical writing as early as Herodotus in the fifth Century BCE[3] in order to know the other as well as the self. Then, along the trade and pilgrimage routes of the Eurasian ecumene, Christian and Buddhist travelers and thinkers evolved comparative and even presumed universal views of humankind.[4] Medieval Christianity contributed a theological framework that demanded a single narrative, a providential vision that applied to all people, and a useful tool in universal chronology.[5]

The vast house of Islam combined theological universalism and hemispheric coordination, but it was Islam under siege[6] (by the Mongols and the Spanish in the thirteenth to fourteenth century) that produced a world history. Ibn Khaldun, from a displaced Spanish family in North Africa, contributed a secular anthropology,[7] a comparative method, and a scientific ideal that was directed toward revealing the causes of Islamic defeat. And in Iran, the victorious Mongol rulers, especially after their conversion to Islam, called on local scholars such as Rashid al-din Fadl Allah.[8] This Jewish convert to Islam, while vizier to the Il-khans in Persia, wrote *The Collection of Histories* which covered almost all of Eurasia from the Franks to the Chinese, thus combining the universalism of Islam and Mongol dominion into a work that might lay claim to be the first global history.[9]

While the expansion of Europe created a single world, well-stocked northern museums, and a comparative method suitable for political and cultural critique (in such figures as Thomas More or Voltaire), the advent of an historical anthropology or global history[10] was remarkably late. Despite early prototypes for historical cultural comparisons in preindustrial Europe (e. g., works of Montesquieu or Vico), it was not until the end of the nineteenth century that Europeans used their hegemony and knowledge of the world[11] to develop the elements of a world history. These elements were the historical anthropology and historical sociology of primarily British and German system builders (foremost among them, Max Weber).[12]

In the twentieth century the historical sociological tradition continued in the work of Oswald Spengler... and Pitirim Sorokin... and the Christian providential vision in the work of Arnold J. Toynbee....[13] But it was not until after World War II that world history emerged as a scholarly subdiscipline of history, one that still included the work of generalists,[14] but was not limited to them. This new world history owed much to the phenomenal growth[15] after the war of area studies programs and institutes, any of which defined their areas (East Asia, Middle East, Latin America, South and Southeast Asia, Africa, etc.), more or less as world historians such as Spengler and Toynbee had defined civilizations. Governments, foundations, and universities funded language study and research at these institutes, vastly increasing our knowledge of the world's various regions, but also aiding the emergence of a world history that was more than the sum of its parts.[16]

Two Canadian American historians working in recent Greek history as World War changed to Cold War created important models of world history in the United States. Both William H. McNeill and L. S. Stavrianos wrote world history textbooks for the newly globally conscious (post-Sputnik) American schools.[17] In many ways their books created paradigms for world history that continue today. Stavrianos offered a stage theory for human development, drawn from European historical sociology (Marx and Weber) and mid-twentieth century archaeology (V. Gordon Childe) to delineate the technological stages of history:[18] hunting-gathering, agricultural, urban, and industrial. McNeill, in his influential *Rise of the West* which combined scholarly erudition and wide-ranging hypotheses for a general audience[19] and in his textbooks, offered a model for world history based on increasing human interaction, the "expanding ecumene" of technological diffusion, migration, and cultural (later even microbiological) contact.[20]

It was not until the 1980s that other models began to emerge, two from scholars working on Africa, an area that had received little attention from Stavrianos and McNeill. Philip Curtin[21] (perhaps as much by his teaching at Wisconsin-Madison, and Johns Hopkins as by his important monographs)[22] influenced a generation of Africanists to see Africa's role in world history, to study the Atlantic as a global region, and to develop manageable monographs on topics of trade, migration, and cross-cultural contact across regional "intercommunicating zones."

Another Africanist, the sociologist Immanuel Wallerstein, developed a very different model of world history, one less concerned with centering attention on areas like Africa, the South Atlantic, and the Indian Ocean, and more concerned with delineating the Marxist dialectic of capitalist development in the core northern European countries at the expense of increasingly remote "peripheries" that were exploited for their labor, resources, and markets.[23] Wallerstein's world-systems theory has proved an extremely influential approach to the study of both the development of capitalism and the history of the Third World. In recent years, however, his model has been criticized for displaying the same Eurocentrism as its Marxist forerunners. Some scholars such as economist Andre Gunder Frank and sociologist Janet Abu-Lughod have rejected the uniqueness of Europe's world system[24] and offer instead an earlier date for capitalism or core-periphery tension: Abu-Lughod argues for a thirteenth-century Islamic world trading system; Gunder Frank poses an ancient world system.

Wallerstein named the Fernand Braudel[25] Center—after the leader of the French Annales school, who founded a world history in France in mid-century that we must account a fifth model (if it were not actually first). Braudel initiated a route to world history as early as 1949 with the publication of his *The Mediterranean and the Mediterranean World of Philip II*. This two-volume masterpiece made two important contributions to world history. First, it chose as its area of study not France, or even Europe but a vast region, from North Africa to the Alps, from the Atlantic to the Levant, that encompassed the Mediterranean as its lake.[26] In this way, Braudel taught other historians to move from national history to regional and transregional histories and to explore the way seas and deserts integrated different cultures over vast areas. The work of his student K. N. Chaudhuri on the Indian Ocean from Persia to China as a trading and cultural area is instructive in this regard. Second *The Mediterranean* and Braudel's more explicit world history, his three-volume *Civilization and Capitalism...* contributed to world history the focus on the longue durée.[27] By beginning each of these major works with an examination of the longest historical processes—geology, geography, climate-and then moving gradually to lengthy social processes-food, clothing, housing—Braudel called attention to the vast territorial regions in which these continuities took place. Further, the definition of cultures by the use of butter or oil, camel or wheel, viticulture or transhumance betrayed history's obsession with such transitory phenomena as nations and states.[28] In Braudel's history, politics (some critics argued, even people) flicker fleetingly far from the stage.[29]

In much the way Braudel moved from a new kind of regional history in *The Mediterranean* to a genuine world history, the American Islamic historian Marshall G. S. Hodgson in the 1950s and 1960s developed a history of Islam that assumed hemispheric boundaries and a context of global history for his subject, and, had he lived, would have written an explicit world history, but one in which the Afro-Eurasian landmass rather than Europe would be central.[30] Even his magnum opus, *The Venture of Islam...*, which includes much of his work on a future world history, was published posthumously.[31] In *The Venture*, he not only situated Islam in a global context, he redrew that global history, centering it geographically in the middle of Eurasia in the "Nile to Oxus" region and chronologically in the "agrarianate cities" age[32] that lasted until the modern "technical" age beginning around 1800. With this periodization, Hodgson emphasized the vitality of Islam into the period of "gunpowder empires" in the sixteenth to eighteenth centuries, underscoring the limits of European hegemony before 1800.[33]

Such periodizations by Hodgson, his followers, and many other historians of Africa and Asia have often been used to counter a Europe-centered world history that charts a straight line from the Renaissance to the modern world, or posits an ever dynamic West surrounded by a static "traditional" world.[34] This view is most unapologetically expressed by proponents of modernization theory, initiated by C. E. Black's *The Dynamics of Modernization*. In its extreme form modernization theory has been equivalent to a belief in a single-line historical process, that experienced by the West, and the conviction that westernization was an inevitable and advantageous model for the rest of the world. Recently there have been more subtle works in the tradition of modernization theory (often by political scientists).

Seven models would seem more than sufficient, but the rapid proliferation of works and approaches to world history has continued unabated in recent decades.[35] The newness of the field (the World History Association dates from 1982, its Journal of World History from 1990), and growing global interaction, account for its vitality.[36] Like a newly opened country, world history draws its numbers from immigrants.[37] Historians and other social scientists come from various specialties that gain coherence and perspective from comparison, regionalization, or globalization.[38] Only within the last few years have graduate departments initiated programs to train world historians.

So perhaps an eighth model should be added to our list—one that draws on the specialties of the "immigrants" to the field. We might call this the composite[39] world history. This is the encyclopedic survey[40] that is based not so much on a single vision, but on an accumulation of insights from area specialists who attempt to elicit the globally relevant from their areas of expertise.[41] Most college textbooks are produced according to this method, gaining in current expertise what might be lost in coherence. It is also the method of one of the earliest modern world histories, the UNESCO[42] *History of Mankind*, the multivolume international project of the 1950s and 1960s.

【 Notes 】

①This selection, taken from the World History section of the 1995 reference book published by the American Historical Association as a guide to historical literature, describes the recent post World War II establishment of World History as a new type or genre of academic historical discipline. Eight models of world history by eight different authors are described, each one utilizing a different analytical structure of history. In the reference book, but not included here, is a bibliography of world histories, arranged chronologically and topically. This reference book is an invaluable resource for the student of world history.

②Kevin Reilly, Professor of History at Raritan Community College has published a number of studies on world history. Lynda Shaffer is Associate Professor of History at Tufts University and is a student of American Indian history.

③as early as Herodotus in the fifth Century BCE: Herodotus 希罗多德（约公元前484—前

452),古希腊历史学家;古罗马作家西塞罗称之为"历史之父"。BCE (Before the Christian Era),公元前,与 BC 同义。

④Then, along the trade and pilgrimage routes of the Eurasian ecumene, Christian and Buddhist travelers and thinkers evolved comparative and even presumed universal views of humankind.
pilgrimage /ˈpilgrimidʒ/ n. 朝圣,朝山进香,参拜圣地;人生的旅程,一生;远游: go on pilgrimage to 去……朝圣; make one's pilgrimage to 参拜。ecumene /ekjuˈmiːn/ n. 世界上有人居住的地区;定居区,核心区;发达区。presume /priˈzjuːm/ vt., vi(常与that 连用)假定;假设;认为: You must presume no such thing. 你不该这样设想。(与on, upon 连用)指望;寄希望于……: We must not presume too mush on the reliability of such sources. 我们不应过分指望/相信这类消息来源的可靠性。

⑤... a providential vision that applied to all people, and a useful tool in universal chronology:
providential /prɔviˈdenʃəl/ 神助的;天意的,幸运的。chronology /krəˈnɔlədʒi/ 年代学,年表。

⑥The vast house of Islam combined theological universalism and hemispheric coordination, but it was Islam under siege...:
theological /θiəˈlɔdʒikəl/ adj. 神学的。universalism /juːniˈvəːsəlizəm/ n. 宇宙神教,普遍性,普遍主义,普救说。hemispheric /hemiˈsferik/ adj. 半球的,半球状的。siege /siːdʒ/ n. 包围,围城,长期努力,不断袭击,围攻。be in/ under the state of siege 处于被围状态。

⑦Ibn Khaldun, from a displaced Spanish family in North Africa, contributed a secular anthropology...:
Ibn Khaldun:伊本赫勒敦(1332—1406),阿拉伯历史学家,哲学家。著有《阿拉伯人、波斯人、柏柏尔人历史的殷鉴和原委》。他的史学著作代表了阿拉伯历史的最高峰,有的学者认为他是文化史的奠基者,堪称阿拉伯的"历史哲学家"。secular /ˈsekjulə/ adj. 不受宗教约束的,非宗教的;现世的,世俗的: secular education 世俗教育(与宗教教育相对而言);普通教育; secular affairs 俗事,世事。

⑧... especially after their conversion to Islam, called on local scholars such as Rashid al-din Fadl Allah:
conversion /kənˈvəːʃən/ 改变,转变;改变信仰。address conversion 地址转换; channel conversion 频道变换; code conversion 代(码)变换。call on 拜访: I'll call on him tomorrow. 明天我去拜访他。号召;呼吁: The president called on the citizens to work hard for national unity. 总统号召公民们为了国家的统一而努力工作。
Rashid al-din Fadl Allah:拉施特(1247—1318),伊尔汗国历史学家,政治家。祖先为犹太人。著作甚多,主编的《史集》,主要叙述蒙古及伊朗的史事,亦涉及法兰克人、犹太人和中国人的历史,具有重要的史料价值。

⑨This Jewish convert to Islam, while vizier to the Il-khans in Persia, wrote *The Collection of Histories* which covered almost all of Eurasia from the Franks to the Chinese, thus combining the universalism of Islam and Mongol dominion into a work that might lay claim to be the first global history.

vizier /vɪˈzɪə/ n. (伊斯兰教国家元老,高官)维齐尔,(伊斯兰国家的)高官;大臣。khan n. 可汗(古代土耳其、鞑靼、蒙古、突厥各族最高统治者的尊称),汗(古代中亚、阿富汗等国统治者和官吏的尊称)。dominion /ˈdɔminjən/ n. 统治权;主权,领土;领地;(英联邦的)自治领。exercise(have, hold) dominion over 对……行使统治(管辖,支配)权。lay claim to v. 要求,主张,自以为。lay claim to an inheritance, an estate, a property, etc. 声称对遗传、房产、财产有权利。

⑩ ... the advent of an historical anthropology or global history:

advent /ˈædvənt/ 出现,到来。

⑪ Despite early prototypes for historical cultural comparisons in preindustrial Europe (e. g., works of Montesquieu or Vico),... that Europeans used their hegemony and knowledge of the world...:

prototype /ˈprəutətaip/ n. 原型(体),样机(品),典型;样板;模范,标准。the prototype for future school buildings 学校建筑物未来的模型;biological prototype 生物原型。Montesquieu: 孟德斯鸠,法国法学家,启蒙思想家,著作对早期世界史做出了贡献。hegemony /hiˈgemən i/ n. 霸权,霸权主义;(尤指数国联盟中的)盟主权:maritime hegemony 海上霸权。

⑫ Max Weber:欧洲历史社会学家。

⑬ ... in the work of Oswald Spengler... and the Christian providential vision in the work of Arnold J. Toynbee...:

Oswald Spengler:施本格勒(1880—1936),德国哲学家、历史学家,著有《西方的没落》、《抉择的时刻》等。Arnold J. Toynbee:阿诺德·约瑟夫·汤因比(1889—1975),英国历史学家,历史形态学派主要代表,代表作有《历史研究》,共十二卷。

⑭ ... one that still included the work of generalists, ...:

generalist /ˈdʒenərəlist/ n. 知识渊博者,有多方面才能的人,多面手。

⑮ ... owed much to the phenomenal growth...:

owe... to... 应该把……归功于……:She owes her success to her hard work. 她把成功归因于勤奋工作。phenomenal /fiˈnɔminl/ adj. 异常的;非凡的;现象的;关于现象的:a phenomenal feat of memory 非凡的记忆力。

⑯ ... but also aiding the emergence of a world history that was more than the sum of its parts:但是,同样也促进了世界史的出现,使它有更强大的整体力量。

(be) greater (或 more) than the sum of 比……的总和更强。

⑰ Both William H. McNeill and L. S. Stavrianos wrote world history textbooks for the newly globally conscious (post-Sputnik) American schools:

Willicm H. Mc Neill 麦克尼尔(1917—)杰出的历史学家,所著《西方的兴起》涵盖人类有文字记载的全部历史,对史学理论产生了重大的影响。L. S. Stavrianos:见 Unit 2 第7篇文章的注释。post-Sputnik:苏联发射人造卫星以后。

⑱ ... and mid-twentieth century archaeology (V. Gordon Childe) to delineate the technological stages of history....:

V. Gordon Childe 柴尔德(1892—1957),英国考古学家,著作甚多,主要有《人创造了自己本身》、《苏格兰的史前史》、《欧洲的曙光》、《欧洲社会的史前史》、《进步与考古》等。delineate /diˈlinieit/ vt. 描画,画出;描述详情,详细记述:delineate the technological stages of history 按技术的发展情况来描述历史的阶段。

⑲...which combined scholarly erudition and wide-ranging hypotheses for a general audience...:
erudition /eruːˈdiʃən/ n. 博学;学识;学问。hypothesis n. (复数-ses)假设;前提:absolute-income hypothesis(与消费相关的)绝对收入假设。

⑳..., the "expanding ecumene" of technological diffusion, migration, and cultural (later even microbiological) contact:
diffusion /diˈfjuːʒən/ n. 传播,流传;扩散,弥漫。migration /məiɡˈreiʃn/ n. 移动;移居;迁徙的人;成群的候鸟:data migration 数据移动。这个短语的意思是扩大了技术传播、转移以及文化(后来,甚至微生物学的)交往的区域。

㉑Philip Curtin:研究非洲的历史学家。见 Unit 8 注释。

㉒monograph /ˈmɔnəɡrɑːf/ n. 专题文章;专著;专论:advanced research monograph 高级研究专论集。

㉓...the Marxist dialectic of capitalist development in the core northern European countries at the expense of increasingly remote "peripheries" that were exploited for their labor, resources, and markets.
dialectic /daiəˈlektik/ n. (与单数动词连用)辩证;辩证法;逻辑论证:materialistic dialectic 唯物辩证法。adj. 辩证的。at the expense of sth 在损失或损害某事的情况下:achieved speed at the expense of accuracy 获得了速度但丧失了精确性。periphery /pəˈrifəri/ n. 外围;界限;周边;外围设备,辅助设备:fibre periphery 纤维周边,纤维外缘。

㉔...the uniqueness of Europe's world system...:
uniqueness /juːˈniːknis/ n. 惟一性;单值性;独特性:uniqueness of solution 解的惟一性。

㉕Fernand Braudel:布劳德尔(1902-08-24—1985-11-28)法国历史学家和教育家,20 世纪最重要的史科编纂者之一。

㉖...from North Africa to the Alps, from the Atlantic to the Levant, that encompassed the Mediterranean as its lake.
the Alps /ˈælps/ n. 阿尔卑斯山。the Levant /liˈvænt/ n. 地中海东部沿岸诸国家和岛屿(包括叙利亚、黎巴嫩等在内的自希腊至埃及地区)。encompass /inˈkʌmpəs/ vt. 包括,包含;包围;围绕;完工,促使:a reservoir encompassed by mountains 群山环绕的水库;a survey that encompassed a wide range of participants 一份包括了广泛参与者的评论。Mediterranean /meditəˈreinjən/ n. 地中海(= Mediterranean sea,位于欧、亚、非三大洲之间);地中海沿岸的居民。adj. 地中海的,地中海民族的。

㉗...Braudel's more explicit world history...the focus on the longue durée.
explicit /iksˈplisit/ adj. 详述的,明晰的;明确的;清楚的,直率的;不含糊的:explicit statement 明确的陈述(指示); be explicit about 对某事态度鲜明。They were explicit in

their criticism. 他们直截了当地表达了他们的批评。longue durée 法语，表示 very long era。

㉘Further, the definition of cultures by the use of butter or oil, camel or wheel, viticulture or transhumance betrayed history's obsession with such transitory phenomena as nations and states.

viticulture /ˈvitikʌltʃə/ n. 葡萄栽培。transhumance /trænsˈhjuːməns/ n. 季节性牲畜移动（指迁移至合适的放牧地）。betray 显示出，暴露出：His accent betrayed the fact that he was foreign. 他的口音显露出他是外国人。obsession /əbˈseʃən/ n. 困扰；固定的想法；分心，分神；迷念；（精神）强迫观念：be under an obsession of 在思想[情感]上被……缠住；suffer from an obsession 耿耿于怀。transitory /ˈtrænsitəri/ adj. 刹那间的，短暂的，暂时的：the disorder of his life: the succession of cities, of transitory loves 他混乱的生活：不断地变换他生活的城市和转瞬即逝的爱情。

㉙In Braudel's history, politics (some critics argued, even people) flicker fleetingly far from the stage. 在布劳德尔的历史书中，政治只是一闪而过，并没有占重要的地位。

flicker /ˈflikə/ vi. 闪现；忽隐忽现；摇晃：The candle flickered out. 蜡烛闪烁不定。leaves flickering in the wind 在风中摇晃的树叶。fleetingly adv. 飞快地，疾驰地。

㉚... had he lived, would have written an explicit world history, but one in which the Afro-Eurasian landmass rather than Europe would be central. 这个分句中，用于虚拟语气条件状语从句中的连接词 if 省略，用主语和谓语部分倒装（had he lived）来表示。

landmass n. 大片陆地。

㉛Even his magnum opus, *the Venture of Islam*..., which includes much of his work on a future world history, was published posthumously.

magnum /ˈmægnəm/ adj. 大的，发射能量大的；n. 大酒瓶（容量约为 2/5 加仑）。opus /ˈəupəs/ 作品：magnum opus（文学、艺术上的）杰作，巨著；个人的重大事业。posthumously /ˈpɔstʃuməsli/ adv. 身后地；posthumous adj. 身后的，作者死后出版的：posthumous works 遗著。

㉜... centering it geographically in the middle of Eurasia in the "Nile to Oxus" region and chronologically in the "agrarianate cities" age...：

"Nile to Oxus" 从尼罗河（埃及）到阿姆河（古代称奥克苏斯河，塔吉克斯坦与阿富汗之间边界的一部分）。

chronologically /krɔnəˈlɔdʒikəli/ adv. 按年代顺序排列地；chronological adj. 按年代顺序排列的。agrarian /əˈgreəriən/ adj. 土地的，农民的，农业的：a new agrarian reform program 一项新的土地改革计划；an agrarian movement 农民运动。

㉝With this periodization, Hodgson emphasized the vitality of Islam into the period of "gunpowder empires" in the sixteenth to eighteenth centuries, underscoring the limits of European hegemony before 1800：

periodization /piəriədaiˈzeiʃən/ n. （历史等的）时期（或时代）划分，周期化。vitality /vaiˈtæliti/ n. 生命力，活力；体力；生气；生动性（文艺作品等的）持久性；（物体的）使用寿命：economic vitality 经济活跃；inferior vitality 低生活力；the vitality of an old tradition

旧传统的生存力。underscore /ˌʌndərˈskɔː/ vt. 在……下划线；强调。hegemony /hɪˈɡeməni/ n. 霸权，霸权主义；（尤指数国联盟中的）盟主权：maritime hegemony 海上霸权。

㉞…that charts a straight line from the Renaissance to the modern world, or posits an ever dynamic West surrounded by a static "traditional" world.

Renaissance /rəˈneɪsəns/ n.（前面与 the 连用）文艺复兴时期；文艺复兴式艺术；复兴，新生：Early Renaissance，文艺复兴初期（1378—1500）的艺术风格，早期文艺复兴式；High Renaissance 文艺复兴时期盛期（1500—1530）；Late Renaissance 文艺复兴后期（1530—1600）。posit /ˈpɒzɪt/ v. 假设，假定；提出以供考虑或研究；论断；安(布)置，安排：If a book is hard going, it ought to be good. If it posits a complex moral situation, it ought to be even better. 如果一本书很难读，那么它应该是一本好书；如果它提出了一个复杂的道德状况，那么它就更应该是本好书了。static /ˈstætɪk/ adj. 静止的，静态的；呆板的；乏味的；[电]静止的，静态的：static electricity 静电；a play full of static characters 一出全是呆板人物的戏。

㉟…but the rapid proliferation of works and approaches to world history has continued unabated in recent decades.

proliferation /prəʊlɪfəˈreɪʃn/ n. 再育，增生（现象）；增殖，扩散：cell proliferation 细胞增殖；nuclear proliferation 核扩散。unabated /ˌʌnəˈbeɪtɪd/ adj. 不减弱的，不减轻的，猛烈如初的：The storm continued unabated. 暴风雨持续着，没有减弱。

㊱…account for its vitality：account for sth. 对某事物作解释：Please account for your disgraceful conduct. 请对你的可耻行为作解释。

㊲…world history draws its numbers from immigrants. 世界史从不同的移民中获得五彩缤纷的形式。draw sth from sth 获取，吸取（经验、教训等）：What conclusions did you draw from your study? 你从研究中得出什么结论？

㊳…that gain coherence and perspective from comparison, regionalization, or globalization.

coherence /kəʊˈhɪərəns/ n. 黏合性；连贯性；一致性。regionalization /riːdʒənəlaɪˈzeɪʃn/ n. 地区化，区域化：natural-historical regionalization 按自然历史区划。globalization /ɡləʊbəlaɪˈzeɪʃn/ n. 全球化，普及到世界范围。

㊴composite /ˈkɒmpəzɪt/ adj. 合成的；混成的；拼凑成的（事物）：composite photograph 合成照片；n. 合成物：English is a composite of many languages. 英语是多种语言混合而成的。

㊵encyclopedic survey：百科全书式的研究。encyclopedic /ɛnsaɪkləʊˈpiːdɪk/ adj. 如百科辞典的，百科全书式的。

㊶…who attempt to elicit the globally relevant from their areas of expertise.

elicit /ɪˈlɪsɪt/ vt. 引出，得出，探出：elicit a fact 得出事实。expertise /ˌekspɜːˈtiːz/ n. 专门技能，知识；专家评价，鉴定：technical expertise 技术专长。

㊷the UNESCO：United Nations Educational, Scientific and Cultural Organization 联合国教育、科学及文化组织，总部设在巴黎。

【 Exercises 】

I. Comprehension Questions

(1) From the first four paragraphs in this selection list as many forerunners who contributed to the recent emergence of world history as you can find.

(2) The first 2 authors of world history models this article selects are William McNeill and L. S. Stavrianos. Give the characteristic theme of each model.

(3) Which of the following was Philip Curtin's contribution to World History scholarship? There may be more than one correct answer.

    A. Influenced historians to study the Atlantic as a region in the globe.

    B. Influenced scholars to see that Africa had no important role in world history.

    C. Encouraged study of regional cross-cultural contact.

    D. Discouraged monographs on trade and migration.

(4) True or False? Immanuel Wallerstein's world-systems theory emphasized the development of capitalism and the history of the Third World but has been criticized for emphasizing the uniqueness of Europe's world system.

(5) Which of the following focuses was emphasized by Fernand Braudel's concept of world history?

    A. Cross-cultural context.

    B. Stage theory of development.

    C. Longue durée (continuity).

    D. Emphasis on centrality of Afro-Eurasian landmass.

    E. Modernization theory.

(6) True or False?

Those who advocate modernization theory have claimed that the historical process through which the West has gone was an inevitable model for the rest of the world.

II. Points for Discussion

Assume you are planning a project to write a world history. Choose one of these eight models. Obviously China will be in your world history. Explain in several paragraphs what your plan is for structuring the history to accomplish the objectives of the model you choose. Explain why you think this model is better than the others for your objectives.

III. Complete the following sentences with appropriate forms of words or expressions from the passage according to the given meaning in brackets.

(1) Social institutions are now being _____ (appeal to) to provide assistance to the homeless.

(2) The course is worth selecting because it will _____ (include) physics, chemistry and biology.

(3) She said she was sorry, but her eyes _____ (show unintentionally) her secret delight.

(4) Historical linguists _____ (presume) a common ancestor from which both Romance and Germanic languages descend.

(5) After much questioning among the people concerned, the headmaster at last _____ (bring out) the truth about the incident.

(6) It was odd that he didn't come to class, but his illness _____ (explain the cause) his absence.

IV. Fill in blanks with the appropriate forms of the words and expressions listed below.

chronological	center attention on	venture
owns ... to	focus on	hypothesis
at the expense of	apply to	migration
more than the sum of	make contributions to	draw on

(1) All these customs and cultures have _____ a very significant _____ the way the Americans live.

(2) This is only a sort of scientific _____ which has not been proved by experiments.

(3) When they are playing together, they add up to _____ their own instruments.

(4) Scientists have studied the _____ of fish over long distances in the river.

(5) American education _____ a great debt _____ Thomas Jefferson, who believed that only a nation of educated people could remain free.

(6) He built up a successful business but it was all done _____ his health.

(7) I would _____ to guess that Anon., who wrote so many poems without signing them, was often a woman?

(8) We've found it less difficult to learn the _____ table of the Chinese dynasties in chronological order.

(9) Mr. Smith _____ his childhood memories for the material of most of his stories.

V. Translate the following sentences from English to Chinese.

(1) Then, along the trade and pilgrimage routes of the Eurasian ecumene, Christian and Buddhist travelers and thinkers evolved comparative and even presumed universal views of humankind.

(2) The vast house of Islam combined theological universalism and hemispheric coordination, but it was Islam under siege (by the Mongols and the Spanish in the thirteenth to fourteenth century) that produced a world history.

(3) Such periodizations by Hodgson, his followers, and many other historians of Africa and Asia have often been used to counter a Europe-centered world history that charts a straight line from the Renaissance to the modern world, or posits an ever dynamic West surrounded by a static "traditional" world.

7. A Definition of Civilization[1]

Leften S. Stavrianos, et al[2]

> 本文的作者是首批用新的世界史科学原则来撰写世界史的一位作家。他认为人类的进步是按阶段来发展的。历史发展的技术阶段是狩猎和采集；农业；城市和工业。

What do we mean when we say that "People became civilized"? We mean that they have achieved all or most of the following: writing; cities; arts and sciences; formal political organization; social classes; and taxation.[3] People could not have achieved these characteristics of civilization as long as they had been food gatherers and always on the move.[4] They could not have built cities, for example, when they had to move their camp frequently to new grounds for hunting, fishing, picking berries, and digging roots. Agriculture therefore made civilization possible.

......

STYLES OF ANCIENT CIVILIZATIONS

All these civilization had the same general characteristics writing, cities, arts and sciences, rich and poor classes, and so forth. Despite these similarities, there were also basic differences among these civilizations. Each had its own distinctive style.

Geography explains some of these differences. The Mesopotamians,[5] for example, lived in a land threatened by sudden floods, by difficult irrigation problems, and by constant invasions of barbarians (nomadic people) The Egyptians, by contrast, enjoyed a land protected by almost impassable deserts. They benefited from a river that flooded regularly and predictably. It is not surprising, then, that the usual attitude of the Mesopotamians was one of pessimism and uncertainty, while the Egyptians tended to be optimistic and confident.

This difference can be seen clearly in architecture. The uncertain Babylonians built for the moment,[6] the confident Egyptians for eternity. The Mesopotamians normally use sun-dried bricks, even in areas where stone was easily available. They did not care that temples built of bricks would not last long; the gods probably would soon want them changed anyway. But the Egyptians, who began by imitating the Mesopotamians, soon changed from brick to stone. They built gigantic temples for their gods, and vast pyramids to house the mummified bodies of their kings, or pharaohs.[7] The Karnak Temple at Thebes[8] includes a hall 122 meters (400 feet) long, 53 meters (175 feet) wide, and 24 meters (80 feet) high. The roof is supported by rows of columns, some so large that 100 people could stand on top of one of them,

Likewise the Great Pyramid of Khufu, or Cheops[9]... is one of the Seven Wonders of the World. It is a solid mass of limestone blocks covering 5 hectares (13 acres), and originally it was 234 meters (768 feet) square and 147 meters (482 feet) high. So enormous is this pyramid that its limestone blocks would build a wall 3 meters (10 feet) high and 23 centimeters (9 inches) thick around the boundaries of France.[10] To the present day these huge monuments dominate the Egyptian landscape, whereas the many large structures built by the Mesopotamians have mostly crumbled away.[11]

The differences in style can be seen also in the case of the island of Crete. The Minoan civilization of Crete[12] was derived, as we have seen, from the older civilizations of Mesopotamia and Egypt. Yet the Minoans stamped everything they borrowed with their own style. Their civilization was a thalassocracy,[13] or sea civilization. They did not till the soil of a single river valley. Instead they sailed freely from one end of the Mediterranean to the other. With their single-masted ships they served as the middle-men of this great inland sea. They carried back and forth the food-stuffs, ivory, and glass of Egypt; the horses and wood of Syria; the silver, pottery, and marble of the Cyclades; and copper of Cyprus.[14]

Their manner of life reflected this freedom and breadth of horizons. Minoan artists never tried to impress by mere size. They did not build colossal pyramids[15] or carve huge shapes of gods or humans. Instead they reproduced the life about them on their household utensils, on the walls of their houses, and in their works of art. They found models everywhere—in natural objects such as birds, flowers, sea shells, and sea life of all types; and in scenes from life, such as peasants returning from fields, athletes wrestling with bulls, and women dancing in honor of the Great Goddess. In architecture, the Minoans were more interested in personal comfort than outward appearance. Their palaces lacked the size of the Egyptian buildings, but they were well ventilated and shaded, and had plumbing systems. Water for drinking and excellent bathing was piped into the palaces, and a drainage system carried off the waste water and the rain.

SIGNIFICANCE OF ANCIENT CIVILIZATIONS

The civilizations of the ancient world differed from each other in their styles, or in their ways of looking at life and carrying on everyday life. But they were similar in one basic respect, they were all much more complicated societies than those in the earliest villages.

We have seen that during the centuries between the beginning of agriculture and the development of civilization, people lived in socially homogeneous villages.[16] They did the same thing as their neighbors. They lived in the same way that their neighbors did. They grew their own food to feed themselves. But when people became civilized, two important changes took place. One was a great increase in productivity and the other wa s division of labor, so that everybody no longer did the same thing.

The increase in productivity occurred because they now used irrigation in farming. They also used various metals in place of stone. They also improved old crafts and created new ones. These advances made it possible for them to build up food surpluses instead of living from hand to mouth[17] as they had in the past. In other words, farmers for the first time were growing more than they needed for themselves. This extra is known as surplus. and it was this surplus that made possible specialization, or division of labor. The surplus was taken away by taxes, and taxes were used to support the new governmental, religious, and military leaders. In return for their services, the leaders were supported by the tax moneys, so that they did not have to grow their own food.

This meant that there no longer was only "one class" that the Odawa Indian remembered. Society no longer was homogeneous. Whereas in the early villages there could not be poor people at one end and rich at the other, now there were rich and poor in the villages and in the new cities. In the villages there were poor peasants with no land and rich peasants with much land. In the cities there were the palaces and temples and mansions of the governmental, religious, and military leaders. And there were the shacks of the artisans[18] who labored in the workshops. Civilized societies from now on were no longer homogeneous. They were divided into rich and poor, into rulers and ruled.

This division is clear even in the graveyards of these civilizations. Archaeologists have found that the graves of the early villagers were all very much the same, but in later times the graves became as different from each other as the housing of the living. Diggings have shown[19] that the graves of the poor contain only a little cheap pottery for use in afterlife. The graves of the rich have copper vessels and expensive jewelry. As for royal tombs, they are found to have not only fine clothing, precious ornaments, and beautifully carved weapons, but also the skeletons of dozens of attendants—soldiers, harem ladies, charioteers, and servants[20]— who were killed and placed in the grave in order to take care of their wealthy and powerful master—in afterlife as they had done in earthly life.

Although the coming of civilization ended the early equality between individuals, civilization did bring great achievements and gains. The military leaders provided protection against invaders. The religious leaders preserved and advanced culture at the same time that they offered religious guidance. And the governmental leaders furnished the organization needed by the complex new civilizations with their vast irrigation works, their tax systems, and their bureaucracies.[21]

The end result was that civilized people had more control over the forces of nature and therefore were more independent of nature. For example, they no longer had to suffer from repeated floods; instead they used the floods to increase their food supply. Civilized people also knew how to gather and organize knowledge, and how to pass it on in written form to future generations. This meant a constantly growing fund of knowledge rather than the same skills that formerly had been passed on orally from parent to child for generation after generation. Finally, civilized people developed various arts that made possible new forms of human expression in addition to the traditional ones of the village.

It is true that all these advances were based to a large extent on the exploitation of the many and benefited them very little. But the important point, so far as the whole history of people is concerned, is that advances were made and continue to be made with growing speed. And it was these advances that finally enabled people in modern times to gain such mastery over nature, such fantastic productivity through science and industry, that the many are now benefiting along with the few.

【 Notes 】

①This selection is taken from *A Global History* published by Allyn and Bacon in 1979, pp. 19, 24—27. The Stage theory of World History which Stavrianos applies includes ideas from anthropology and historical sociology that developed in 19th century Europe.

②Leften S. Stavrianos is one of the first historians to write a world history in the new academic discipline of World History. He sees human development as happening through stages: the technological stages of history are hunting and gathering, agriculture, urban and industrial.

③taxation /tæk'seiʃən/ n. 征税；税制；税，税款；估价征税；测树，材积测定：be subject to taxation 应纳税；be exempt from taxation 免税；taxation bureau 税务局。

④... as long as they had been food gatherers and always on the move.
on the move 在行进；在奔波；在迁移；在发展；活跃：a wandering people continually on the move 不断迁移的游牧民族。Science is always on the move. 科学一直在发展。

⑤Mesopotamian /mesəpə'teimiən/ adj. & n. 美索不达米亚 [西南亚一地区] (亦称"两河流域"，即底格里斯和幼发拉底两河流域平原，在叙利亚东部和伊拉克境内)。the Mesopotamians 美索不达米亚人。

⑥... Babylonians built for the moment:
Babylonian /bæbi'ləvnjən/ adj. 巴比伦城的；巴比伦人的；巴比伦王国的；n. 巴比伦人；巴比伦语。for the moment 暂时，目前：What can we do for the moment? 目前我们能做些什么呢? for a moment 片刻，一会儿。

⑦They built gigantic temples for their gods, and vast pyramids to house the mummified bodies of their kings, or pharaohs.
gigantic /ʤai'gæntik/ adj. 巨大的，庞大的。mummify /'mʌmifai/ vt. -fied, -fying 使成为木乃伊；使干枯。pharaoh /'fɛrəu/ n. 法老（古埃及王的尊称）；暴君。

⑧The Karnak Temple at Thebes...:
Thebes 底比斯：古代著名城市之一，古埃及帝国全盛时期的都城，坐落在尼罗河东岸。The Karnak Temple：凯尔奈克阿蒙大神庙。凯尔奈克在尼罗河东岸古埃及中王国、新王国时期首都 底比斯遗址的北半部，阿蒙大神庙废墟所在地，位于今上埃及基纳省凯尔奈克村。

⑨... the Great Pyramid of Khufu, or Cheops...:
Khufu 胡夫，希腊语作 Cheops，埃及第 4 王朝（公元前约 2575～前约 2465）第 2 代国王，吉萨大金字塔的建造者，这是当时惟一的大建筑物。

⑩So enormous is this pyramid that its limestone blocks would build a wall 3 meters (10 feet) high and 23 centimeters (9 inches) thick around the boundaries of France. 这是一个主从复合句。在主句中，表语 (so enormous) 提到句首，主语 (this pyramid) 和谓语 (is) 倒装。that 引导一个程度状语从句。

⑪... whereas the many large structures built by the Mesopotamians have mostly crumbled away.
crumble /'krʌmbl/ vt., vi. 弄碎；把……弄成碎屑；崩毁；倒塌；瓦解；灭亡：Her hopes crumbled to nothing. 她的希望落空了。His influence was crumbling away. 他的影响在逐渐消失。

⑫The Minoan civilization of Crete：克里特岛的米诺斯文化。克里特岛是爱琴海青铜时代文化的发祥地。米诺斯是希腊传说中克里特岛的某一朝代的名称或某一统治者的名字。米诺斯文化兴盛期约为公元前 3000—前约 1100 年。

⑬thalassocracy /θæləˈsɔkrəsi/ n. 制海权，海权

⑭... the horses and wood of Syria; the silver, pottery, and marble of Cyclades; and copper of Cyprus.

Syria /ˈsiəriə/ 叙利亚。历史上,叙利亚是地中海东岸一古国,在今叙利亚、黎巴嫩、约旦和巴勒斯坦一带。Cyclades /ˈsiklədiz/ [希腊]基克拉迪群岛(在爱琴海南部)。Cyprus /ˈsaiprəs/ [西亚岛国]塞浦路斯(岛)(在地中海东部)。

⑮colossal pyramids:

colossal /kəˈlɔsl/ adj. 巨像(似)的,巨大的;[口]异常的;非常的:a colossal monument 巨大的纪念碑。

⑯... in socially homogeneous villages:

homogeneous /hɔməuˈgiːniəs/ adj. 同类的,相似的,均一的,均匀的: a tight-knit, homogeneous society 一个紧密相连的同种社会。

⑰... instead of living from hand to mouth...:

live from hand to mouth 勉强度日,朝不保夕。These Indians live from hand to mouth on berries, nuts, and roots. 这些印第安人靠草莓、坚果和植物根部勉强度日。

⑱the shacks of the artisans:

shack /ʃæk/ n. 简陋木屋,棚屋。工匠的棚屋。

⑲Diggings have shown...:

digging /ˈdigiŋ/ n. 采掘,开凿;(pl.) 开采物。

⑳... soldiers, harem ladies, charioteers, and servants...:

harem /ˈhɛərem/ n. (伊斯兰教国家中的)闺房,后宫;(伊斯兰教家庭中的)女眷们。

charioteer /tʃæriəˈtiə/ n. 战车的御者,驾车者。

㉑bureaucracy /bjuəˈrɔkrəsi/ n. 官员;(公司的)管理人员;官僚政治;官僚机构

【 Exercises 】

I. Comprehension Questions

(1) What does Stavrianos say determines the existence of civilization? What key stage makes it possible for people to be civilized?

(2) Among the civilizations there are great differences. For Stavrianos geography was one reason for the differences.

   1) What was the reason for the Minoan civilization being so different from the Mesopotamian and Egyptian civilizations?

   2) hat was the nature of the Minoan civilization?

(3) Once there were civilizations people usually lived in homogeneous villages. True or False?

(4) The key to the increase in agricultural productivity was _____.

   A. development of classes

   B. rrigation

   C. heeled vehicles

D. ivision of labor

(5) According to Stavrianos what ended in the historic societies with the arrival of civilization?

II. Points for Discussion

In these pages from Stavrianos Global History there is a good deal about the relationship between nature and the rise of civilization. Locate what he says (in more than one place) and formulate what conclusions you might make as an historian if this were your book.

III. Fill in the gaps with the words or expressions given below. Change the form where necessary.

derive from	on the move	by contrast	serve as
for the moment	build up	in return	in the case of
live from hand to mouth	carry off	in place of	

(1) It was vacation time, and the highways were full of families _____.

(2) I want to leave this _____ and talk about something else.

(3) Mr. Johnson got very little pay, and the family _____ when he had no job.

(4) The Vice-President talked at the meeting _____ the President, because the President was sick.

(5) How much did John give you _____ for your bicycle?

(6) The overwhelming majority of patients want to be told the truth, even _____ grave illness.

(7) Each of us wants to feel he or she has the ability to do something that is meaningful and that _____ a tribute to our inherent abilities.

(8) The same pride in being part of a well-coordinated, successful unit is _____ being part of a larger collectivity.

IV. Translate the following from English into Chinese.

(1) So enormous is this pyramid that its limestone blocks would build a wall 3 meters (10 feet) high and 23 centimeters (9 inches) thick around the boundaries of France.

(2) This extra is known as surplus and it was this surplus that made possible specialization, or division of labor.

(3) And it was these advances that finally enabled people in modern times to gain such mastery over nature, such fantastic productivity through science and industry, that the many are now benefiting along with the few.

8. A Comparative Analysis of France, Russia, and China[1]

Theda Skocpol[2]

> 作者是哈佛大学教授,美国社会学家。在研究历史和历史事件时,她用历史对比法从宏观历史或世界史层次上来解释社会革命的性质。在这本书中,她不仅考虑到阶级冲突的问题,并以此来分析、对比法国、俄罗斯和中国的社会革命现象,而且在涉及大规模的社会进程时,尽力用宏观社会学家的眼光来考虑问题。

A COMPARATIVE HISTORICAL METHOD

"Social revolutions" as defined at the beginning of this work—rapid, basic transformations of a society's state and class structures, accompanied and in part carried through by class-based revolts from below—have been relatively rare occurrences in modern world history. Each such revolution, furthermore, has occurred in a particular way in a unique set of social-structural and international circumstances. How, then can a sociologist hope to develop historically valid explanations of social revolution as such?

......

WHY FRANCE, RUSSIA, AND CHINA?

...In the following chapters, the French, Russian, and Chinese Revolutions are to be treated together as basically similar examples of successful social-revolutionary transformations. At this point, therefore, some words are in order to justify this selection of cases.

There are some important practical reasons why these social revolutions rather than others were chosen for analysis. All of them, for one thing, happened in countries whose state and class structures had not been recently created or basically altered under colonial domination. This consideration eliminates many complexities that would need to be systematically included in any analysis of revolutions in postcolonial or neocolonial settings. Furthermore, the French, Russian, and Chinese Revolutions all broke out and—after more or less protracted processes of class and political struggle—culminated in the consolidation of revolutionary state power, long-ago enough in the past to allow a study and comparison to be made of all three as entire revolutionary transformations.[3] It is possible, in other words, to trace each Revolution from the demise of the old regime[4] through to the emergence of a distinctively structured new regime. For comparative history, Hegel's maxim indubitably holds: The owl of Minerva flies at dusk.[5]

Stronger reasons than these, however, are needed to explain not only why France, Russia, and China have each been selected for intense study, but also why all three have been grouped together as fundamentally similar cases of social revolution. For, according to most existing ways of defining and grouping revolutions for comparative study, France, Russia, and China simply do not belong together—certainly not all of them in one set. France was a pre-twentieth-century European revolution, typically understood as bourgeois-capitalist or liberal-democratic in nature. Depending upon one's category scheme, Russia was either an antiabsolutist revolution, or a statist-developmental revolution,[6] or a proletarian-communist revolution. Some analysts might be willing to group it with France, others with China, but none would agree that it belongs together with both. For China, especially, is not considered legitimately classifiable with France, either because the French Revolution was "bourgeois" or "liberal" and the Chinese obviously neither, or else because China should be grouped with Third World national-liberation revolutions and not with European revolutions of any sort.

But it is the premise of this work[7] that France, Russia, and China exhibited important similarities in their Old Regimes and revolutionary processes and outcomes—similarities more than sufficient to warrant their treatment together as one pattern calling for a coherent causal explanation.[8] All three Revolutions occurred in wealthy and politically ambitious agrarian states, none of which was ever colonially subjugated.[9] These Old Regimes were proto-bureaucratic autocracies[10] that suddenly had to confront more economically developed military competitors. In all three Revolutions, the externally mediated crises combined with internal structural conditions and trends to produce a conjuncture of:[11] (1) the incapacitation of the central state machineries of the Old Regimes; (2) widespread rebellions by the lower classes, most crucially peasants; and (3) attempts by mass-mobilizing political leaderships to consolidate revolutionary state power. The revolutionary outcome in each instance was a centralized, bureaucratic, and mass-incorporating nation-state with enhanced great-power potential in the international arena.[12] Obstacles to national social change associated with the prerevolutionary positions of the landed upper class were removed (or greatly curtailed[13]), and new potentials for development were created by the greater state centralization and mass political incorporation of the New Regimes.

Whatever other category systems may assume, the French and Chinese Revolutions—the two "polar" cases of my trio[14]—were not so different from one another, nor so similar (respectively) to early European, liberal revolutions and to Third World, nation-building revolutions, as their contrasting spatio-temporal and cultural settings might suggest.[15] The French Revolution actually was in important respects strikingly different from the English Revolution of the seventeenth century, and rather similar to the Chinese and Russian Revolutions. Peasant revolts played a key role in the process of the French Revolution, and the political result was a more centralized and bureaucratic state, not a liberal-parliamentary regime. As for the Chinese Revolution, it seems remarkably shortsighted in historical terms to regard it as a new-nation-building revolution of the mid-twentieth century. China had an imperial Old Regime with a cultural and political history stretching back many hundreds of years. And the Chinese Revolution as an entire process was launched in 1911 by an upper-class revolt against an absolute monarchical state, not unlike the aristocratic revolt that started the French Revolution. Furthermore, the Chinese Revolution eventually gave rise to a developmentally oriented Communist regime that is certainly as much or more similar to the post-revolutionary Soviet regime as to contemporary, noncommunist Third World governments.

Given that there are, indeed, sufficient similarities to allow these three Revolutions to be grouped together for comparative historical analysis, much is to be gained by actually doing so. The similar sociopolitical features of the French, Russian, and Chinese Revolutions can be high-lighted and explained in ways that would necessarily be missed by analysts determined to keep them segregated in separate type categories.[16] Above all, there is much to be learned from the juxtaposition of these Revolutions[17] about the causes and results of peasant participation in social revolutions. There is also much to be learned about the dynamics of the breakdown and reconstruction of state administrative and coercive organizations[18] from old to new regimes. It is not incidental that these aspects of revolutions tend either to be played down or assumed away by many other comparative analyses.[19] This happens because most of the alternative category schemes serve to highlight instead either bourgeois/proletarian class configurations or patterns of legitimate political authority and the ideological self-conceptions[20] of old and new regimes.

But we shall not only emphasize the common patterns shared by the French, Russian, and Chinese Revolutions. Given the flexibility and the historical sensitivity of the comparative method, attention can also be paid to the particular features of each of the three Revolutions. There will be no need to deny that the French Revolution had bourgeois and liberal features, that the Russian Revolution was extremely statist in its outcome, or that the Chinese Revolution had in its process elements of a national-liberation struggle. For even as we primarily look for and attempt to explain patterns common to France, Russia, and China, we can also attend to the variations[21] that characterize pairs of cases or single cases. These can then be explained as due in part to variations on the shared causal patterns, in part to contrasts among the social structures of France, Russia, and China, and in part to differences in the world-historical timing and succession of the three great Revolutions. As a result, exactly those distinctive characteristics of the Revolutions and their world-historical setting that have prompted other scholars to segregate them into separate type categories will be cast in a new explanatory light as they are studied against the background of the patterns shared by all three Revolutions.

LOOKING AHEAD

The chapters to come present a comparative historical analysis of the French, Russian, and Chinese Revolutions—an analysis conceived and executed within the frame of reference developed in this first chapter. Part I discusses the structural and historical conditions for the emergence of objective revolutionary situations in old-regime France, Russia, and China: Chapter 2 focuses upon the political crises of the absolutist states, and Chapter 3 analyzes the situation of the peasantry. In order to help validate the main lines of the argument,[22] particular subsections of Chapters 2 and 3 briefly show that the conditions hypothesized to be crucial for producing social-revolutionary situations in France, Russia, and China[23] were absent, or not present all together, at relevant periods in Japan, Prussia/Germany, and England. Thus the logic of comparison in Part I primarily stresses ways in which France, Russia, and China were similar. And this is underlined through contrasts to negative cases.

In Part II, on the other hand, the logic of comparison focuses entirely upon the similarities and differences among the positive cases of social revolution. For in Part

II it is taken for granted that France, Russia, and China shared similarly caused revolutionary situations. The objective is to explain the revolutionary outcomes against that background. Hence this part demonstrates how the conflicts unleashed in the revolutionary crises[24] led to social-revolutionary outcomes, with certain patterns common to all three Revolutions and others distinctive to one or two of them...

【 Notes 】

① This selection is taken from *States and Social Revolution*: *A Comparative Analysis of France, Russia, and China*, Cambridge University Press, 1979, pp. 33, 40—43. The comparative historical method in general focuses on common patterns in historical events in different contexts and different times. Although somewhat influenced by Karl Marx and Max Weber, Skocpol takes a macrosociological perspective that is more flexible and historically sensitive than those generally found in studies firmly committed to Marx. In this book she not only analyzes and compares the phenomenon of social revolution in France, Russia, and China with questions of class conflict in mind, but also is part of a larger effort of macrosociologists to consider the state when dealing with large-scale social processes.

② Theda Skocpol, Professor at Harvard University, is an American sociologist who uses the comparative method in the study of history and historical events to explain the nature of social revolution on a macro or world history level.

③ Furthermore, the French, Russian, and Chinese Revolutions all broke out and—after more or less protracted processes of class and political struggle—culminated in the consolidation of revolutionary state power, long-ago enough in the past to allow a study and comparison to be made of all three as entire revolutionary transformations. 这个长句是一个简单句,主语是 revolutions,谓语是 broke out and culminated, 破折号引出的插入语把谓语部分分隔开了,long-ago enough 至 transformations 是一个形容词短语,修饰 revolutionary state power。
protract /prəuˈtræctid/ adj. 延长的,引长的,拖延的:a protracted war 一场拖长的战争
culminate /ˈkʌlmineit/ vi. (与 in 连用) 达到……的顶点,达到……的顶峰;告终,完结
(in): The tower culminates in a 40-foot spire. 这塔的顶端是一个40英尺高的塔尖。vt. 使达到顶点;使告终: A reading from Shakespeare culminates the performance. 朗诵莎士比亚的一篇作品结束了这场演出。

④ ...from the demise of the old regime:
demise /diˈmaiz/ n. (不动产的)转让;遗赠;让位;逝世,死: the demise of the French monarchy 法国帝制的告终。v. 转让,遗赠;传(位),让(位) demise the Crown 让位。

⑤ ...Hegel's maxim indubitably holds: The owl of Minerva flies at dusk.
Hegel 黑格尔(1770—1831),德国哲学家。maxim /ˈmæksim/ n. 格言,箴言;谚语;主义;原理;座右铭;普遍真理,行为准则:"A stitch in time saves nine" is a popular maxim.

"小洞不补，大洞吃苦"是人们熟悉的谚语。Aesop's fables illustrate moral maxim. 伊索寓言阐明了道德准则。indubitably /in'dju:bitəbli/ adv. 无疑地，确实地。Minerva /mi'nə:və/ n. （罗神）密涅瓦（掌管智慧、工艺和战争的女神，即希腊神话中的雅典娜女神——Athene）。后半句的意思是雅典娜的猫头鹰也在夜幕降临时飞出（意思是有共性）。

⑥...Russia was either an antiabsolutist revolution, or a statist-developmental revolution:
antiabsolutist /'ænti'æbsəlu:tist/ n. 专制主义者，专制政治论者，绝对论者。statist n. 国家主义者，主张国家（中央集权下）统制经济者；统计学家，统计人员。

⑦the premise of this work:
premise /'premis/ n. 前提: If your premise is established, your conclusions are easily deducible. 如果你的前提成立，那么就很容易推断出你的结论了。(pl.) 房屋及其周围的房基地；on the premise of/that... 在……前提下；to make a premise 预述，预设前提。

⑧...as one pattern calling for a coherent causal explanation:
call for 要求，需要。coherent /kəu'hiərənt/ adj. 粘在一起的；连贯的；一致的；符合的: a coherent essay 一篇条理分明的文章。causal /'kɔ:zəl/ adj. 原因的，因果关系的，表示原因或理由的: causal relation 因果关系；a causal relationship between scarcity of goods and higher prices 食品匮乏与高价格的因果关系。

⑨...ever colonially subjugated:
subjugate /'sʌbdʒugeit/ vt. 征服；压服；使屈服，使服从，克制，抑制。

⑩...proto-bureaucratic autocracies: 最初的官僚独裁政府。
proto- /'prəutəu/ comb. form 表示"第一"，"首要"，"原始"，"初"，"母": prototype 原形。autocracy /ɔ:'tɔkrəsi/ n. 独裁政治，专制政治；独裁政府，专制国家。

⑪...trends to produce a conjuncture of:
conjuncture /kən'dʒʌŋktʃə/ n. 事态；局面；危机；时机，紧要关头；结合: at this conjuncture 在这（危急）时刻。

⑫...and mass-incorporating nation-state with enhanced great-power potential in the international arena:
mass-incorporating nation-state 人民参与的多民族国家。incorporate /in'kɔ:pəreit/ v. 包含；加上；吸收；把……合并: His book incorporated his earlier essays. 他的书收录了他早年写的文章。arena /ə'ri:nə/ n. 竞技场；活动场所；活动范围；界: arena of politics 政治舞台，政界；the world as an arena of moral conflict 世界像一个道义冲突的竞争场所。

⑬greatly curtailed:
curtail /kə:'teil/ vt. 缩短；减缩；限制: to curtail public spending 缩减公共支出；curtail a speech 缩短讲话。

⑭the two "polar" cases of my trio: 我这三个国家中两个所谓相反的例子。
polar /'pəulə/ adj. 靠近极地的，靠近北极（或南极）的；正好相反的；有两种相反性质的: polar personalities 相反的个性；Love and hatred are polar feelings. 爱与恨是完全相反的感情。trio /'tri:əu/ n. 三人一组；三个一组；三重唱；三重奏。

⑮...as their contrasting spatiotemporal and cultural settings might suggest:

spatiotemporal /speʃiəu'tempərəl/ adj. 存在于时间和空间的；时空的；与时空有关的。

⑯... determined to keep them segregated in separate type categories.
segregate /'segrigeit/ vt. 分开,隔开；分离：segregate boys and/from girls 把男孩和女孩分开。

⑰... from the juxtaposition of these Revolutions... :
juxtaposition /dʒʌkstəpə'ziʃən/ n. 并置,并列；接近,邻近；交叉重叠法；毗连：juxtaposition of characters 叠字法。

⑱... the breakdown and reconstruction of state administrative and coercive organizations... :
……coercive /kəu'ə:siv/ adj. 强制的，胁迫的；高压的：coercive method/measures 压制方法/手段。

⑲... either to be played down or assumed away by many other comparative analyses：
play down 对……不多重视；贬低：He played down his part in the discovery. 他故意贬低自己在这一发现中所起的作用。

⑳... either bourgeois/proletarian class configurations or patterns of legitimate political authority and the ideological self-conceptions... :
bourgeois/proletarian class configurations 资产阶级或无产阶级的结构形式 bourgeois /'buəʒwɑː/ adj. 中产阶级的；资产阶级的；configuration /kənˌfigju'reiʃən/ n. 构造,结构,配置,外形：aircraft configuration 飞机结构(外形)；atomic configuration 原子组态(排列)；the ideological self-conceptions 意识形态上的自我概念。self-conception /ˌselfkən'sepʃən/ n. 自我概念：An individual's self-conception often differs from the conception others have of him. 一个人的自我概念常同旁人对他的看法不一。

㉑..., we can also attend to the variations... :
attend to 专心、仔细听；注意；处理：attend to your teacher 专心听老师讲课；attend to the advice 重视这个劝告。

㉒In order to help validate the main lines of the argument... :
validate /'vælideit/ vt. 证实；证明正确；使生效，使有法律效力；批准，确认：validate a passport 使护照生效(在护照上签字)；Time validated our suspicion. 时间证实了我们的怀疑。

㉓... the conditions hypothesized to be crucial for producing social-revolutionary situations in France, Russia, and China... :
hypothesized 引导的这个分词短语作定语,修饰 conditions。
hypothesize /hai'pɔθisaiz/ vi.,vt. 假设,假定。

㉔... how the conflicts unleashed in the revolutionary crises... :
unleashed in the revolutionary crises 这个分词短语修饰 conflicts。
unleash /ʌn'liːʃ/ vt. 解开……的皮带(链索)；(喻)释放；放纵；发动：unleash a war 发动战争；unleash one's temper 发脾气。

【 Exercises 】

I. Comprehension Questions

(1) Skocpol's definition of a social revolution is "rapid, basic transformations of society's _____ and _____ structures." (Fill in the blanks.)

(2) At the beginning of this section (hint: in Paragraph 3) Skocpol explains there are obvious similarities between French, Russian and Chinese Revolutions. What are the two similarities she gives?

(3) The author sees these 3 revolutions as all following the same pattern. Which of the following 4 characteristics did they all show?
  A. Breakdown of bureaucratic central state machines of the Old Regimes.
  B. Widespread natural disasters and starvation.
  C. Widespread peasant rebellions.
  D. Attempt to consolidate revolutionary state power by mass-mobilizing political leaderships.

(4) True or False:
Skocpol states that the peasant revolts in France resulted in the French Revolution becoming a liberal parliamentary regime.

II. Points for Discussion

The author says there are similar socio-political features in all three of these revolutions. What are the ones she points out? She goes on to say that these revolutions varied in their particular character. What are these similarities and differences. Choose one of the revolutions and try to project how she might develop the points as she writes the rest of the book. (See paragraphs 7 and 8 for ideas.)

III. Complete the following sentences, using the words or expressions from the passage according to the given meaning in brackets. Changes the form where necessary.

(1) Years of waiting _____ (end in) a tearful reunion.

(2) If she _____ (pay attention to) what her mother told her, she wouldn't be in trouble now.

(3) "Discipline is the soul of an army" was his favorite _____ (a fundamental principle)

(4) Financial Times issued reports on the deteriorating world _____ (a crisis) and the disappointment of earlier hopes.

(5) The doctor _____ (reduce) the serious nature of the patient's illness.

IV. Fill in the gaps with the words or expressions given below. Change the form where necessary.

> premise   rather than   give rise to   segregate
> justify   line   call for   associate
> break out take for granted

(1) The government will find it difficult to _____ the decision to go back on his promise to the public.

(2) The identification of blood groups and the analysis of ink in forged documents can _____ considerable skill.

(3) The government's economic policy _____ increased unemployment, though it is true that it produced a favorable balance of payments in the country's international trade.

(4) The condition portion of a rule that is tested by the inference engine. If the _____ is found to be true, the corresponding action specified in the rule conclusion is taken.

(5) The manager replied that he had issued orders exactly on these _____.

(6) The doctor _____ the child sick with infectious diseases.

(7) There are certain standards of civilized behavior in international relations which it should be possible _____ in the family of nations.

Unit 3

Ancient Greece

9. How the Greek World Grew[1]

Maurice Pope[2]

> 作者是专门研究古希腊的美国考古学家和历史学家。这篇古希腊史的文章应用了该书中斯坦弗瑞奥诺斯(Stavrianos)有关人类文明发展的阶段论。虽然希腊与古希腊文明的核心地带位置相同,但是当代希腊民族已经不再是古希腊人的直接后裔。这篇文章虽然省略了一些对雅典这样的希腊城市国家的深入讨论,但是已勾画出希腊人的世界从最早阶段到最近阶段的轮廓。

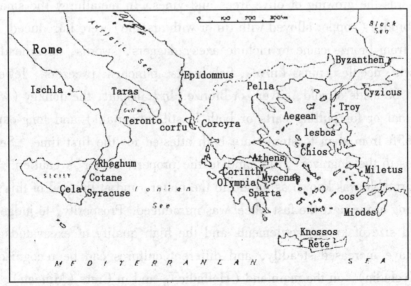

Map of Greece

PRELUDE

Early Times

In very early times hunters and plant-gatherers ranged over the mainland of Greece, and recent excavation in the Franchthi cave overlooking the Gulf of Argos suggests that there may have been a continuity between them and the founders of the Neolithic (New Stone) Age culture[3], which began in Greece around 7000 BC. This age was marked by the introduction of agriculture (cereals and pulses), herding (mainly sheep and goats), and, by 5000 BC, the manufacture of fired clay pottery vessels.[4] Diet was supplemented by hunting and fishing, and the collection of fruit and nuts. Gold, silver, and copper were known and worked from at least 4000 BC, though cutting tools remained predominantly of stone; for small cutting edges these people used obsidian,[5] a black glass-like volcanic rock found on the Aegean island of Melos. Spinning and weaving were among the known crafts. Neolithic settlement was particularly heavy in Thessaly, where the plains favour the cultivation of cereals, but sites occur elsewhere in Greece and not only on the mainland. There was already a village at Knossos in Crete in pre-pottery times, dated by the Carbon 14 method to the end of the seventh millennium: Knossos can claim to be the oldest continuously inhabited site in Europe, and one of the oldest in the world.

The Early Bronze Age in Greece began about 3000 BC. Agriculturally the main innovation was the growing of olive trees and vines. In metallurgy the smelting and casting of bronze (copper alloyed with tin or with arsenic) were introduced, and articles made from bronze came to include axes, daggers, swords, spearheads, saws, chisels, awls, needles, pins, knives, fish-hooks, punches, tweezers.[6] Jewellery and plate might be made of gold, silver, or bronze. In transport, the donkey (whether as a pack animal or for pulling carts or both is still uncertain) and long-oared ships (perhaps 65ft from stem to stern) are both attested for the first time.[7] Seal stones bear witness to the engraver's art[8] and to the property owner's caution. The slow wheel or turntable was known as an aid to the potter, and at the end of this period or the beginning of the next the fast wheel was introduced. Prosperity, to judge from the number and size of known settlements and the high quality of excavated artefacts, seems to have increased steadily, and different cultures can be recognized in the islands (Cycladic), on the mainland (Helladic), and in Crete (Minoan).[9] It is not possible, however, to say who the inhabitants of any of these regions were, or whether they spoke Greek or any language related to it.

The Minoans

The Middle (2200-1500 BC) and the Late (1500-1100 BC) Bronze Age are characterised by the growth of population centres that deserve the name of cities, and by the building of great palaces. Minoan Crete led the way. The palace of Knossos covers some 3 acres of ground, including courtyards, and had an average elevation of two or three storeys.[10] The palaces at Phaistos, Mallia, and Zakro were of comparable dimensions. Minoan palaces existed in smaller towns like Gournia, and a number of sizeable country houses[11] have also been discovered and excavated.

The palaces seem to have played a central part in both the religious and the economic life of Minoan Crete. They contained shrines clearly furnished for ritual use. Bulk granaries were attached to them,[12] and it has been estimated that their storerooms were able to hold as much as 100,000 litters of oil or wine. It is evident that the palaces also promoted workmanship of high quality. Minoan art, delicate, detailed, and equally successful on the small scale and on the large, can claim to rank among the major art-styles of the world.

······

Minoan culture seems to have been remarkably homogeneous throughout Crete.[13] It also extended, either by cultural diffusion or by actual settlement, to the neighboring islands of Cythera, Melos, Kea, Thera (where dramatic discoveries are being made), and Rhodes, to Miletus on the mainland of Asia Minor, and beyond Sicily to the Aeolian Islands in the west. The southern part of the Greek mainland, especially Messenia and the Argolid, was also strongly penetrated by Minoan influence.

The end of this brilliant period of Cretan civilisation came suddenly in the middle of the fifteenth century BC, when the archaeological record tells us of widespread fire and destruction throughout the Minoan world. The cause is uncertain. One theory in vogue[14] is that it was an immediate and dramatic result of the Krakatoa-like explosion of the volcanic island Thera in the central Aegean some 50 miles north of central Crete. The other, less romantic, is that the destruction took place some 50 years after the eruption and was the work of foreign invaders from the Greek mainland. Whichever of these explanations is correct, it is certain that in the following period mainland Greeks occupied Knossos and Khania (in the north-west of Crete) and dominated the rest of the island.

The Mycenaeans[15]

The mainland civilisation of this period is generally called Mycenaean after one of its main centres, Mycenae. Artistically and technologically the Mycenaeans had been very much the pupils of Minoan Crete, and now they became its heirs.[16] On the Levant coast, in Egypt, in south Italy and Sicily, we find Mycenaean traders establishing themselves on the sites of former Minoan trading posts. There was also Mycenaean colonisation, both in the west, as at Scoglio del Tonno near Taranto, and more particularly in the east, where there are some fifteen cities on the Asia Minor coast and the neighbouring islands that can plausibly claim Mycenaean ancestry.[17]

Among the crafts the Mycenaeans took over from the Minoan civilisation was that of writing. ... The script, known as "Linear B," has been deciphered (by Michael Ventris in 1953)[18] and shown to have been used for writing Greek. Unfortunately the tablets[19] are purely administrative or accounting records. They give no historical information about the Mycenaean Greeks' arrival in Greece. ...

The period of Mycenaean glory lasted from about 1500 BC to 1200 BC. It was followed by contraction and decline.

THE DARK AGE

The Extent of the Decline

The Dark Age, as the name given to it implies, is little known. The most striking fact about it is the tremendous reduction in the number of recognised settlements. We can trace about 320 occupied Mycenaean sites of the thirteenth century BC on the Greek mainland, the islands in the Aegean (excluding Crete) and Ionian Seas, and on the west coast of Asia Minor, but for the twelfth century this number drops to about 130, and for the tenth to about forty. These figures are only approximate, since they are founded on surface observation, and they tell us nothing about the size of the settlements or the density of their occupation. Nevertheless such a heavy reduction in the number of observed sites must imply that there was a great fall in population.

There was certainly a great fall in standards. Among the crafts which either declined seriously or disappeared altogether were those of the scribe, the goldsmith, the silversmith, the worker in ivory, the mason and stonecutter,[20] and in some areas the bronze-worker—in short all the arts that had been necessary for the previous palace civilisation.

... Despite the impoverishment[21] and isolation there was one major innovation. This was iron-working. The technology seems to have reached Greece from North Syria via Cyprus about 1050 BC. At this stage iron probably had no advantages over bronze, not even for hardness of cutting edge, but it was available when bronze was not, and ultimately it was to become far more plentiful. There was also one minor innovation of the same date. It was found that the multiple brush, a device which had been known for a very long time, could be attached to a compass and used for tracing concentric circles.[22] This discovery, which was apparently made in Athens and helped in the development there of a new pottery style known to us as Protogeometric,[23] was trivial enough in itself, but it shows that the Dark Age was not so dark that there was a total eclipse of human ingenuity.[24]

The Question of Continuity

One of the most interesting questions about the Dark Age is how far the lines were kept open between the high points of Bronze Age and Classical Greek civilisation. In Crete there was certainly a strong measure of continuity. Minoan traditions in building, pottery, and above all in religious practices continued not only in ancient centres like Knossos but in quite new ones like the mountain village or refuge of Karphi, which only dates from about 1150 BC. Elsewhere there are often gaps. Delos and Delphi, two great religious sanctuaries of classical times, both seem to have been Mycenaean cult-centres too, but on both sites there is only scanty Dark Age pottery,[25] not enough to prove uninterrupted use. At Amyclae in the southern Peloponnese there is a clear gap of 100 years between the latest Mycenaean pottery found in the sanctuary area and the earliest protogeometric; but Hyacinthus[26] was worshipped there in classical times, and Hyacinthus is a name of pre-Greek type. Another motive for colonisation could be land-hunger caused by overpopulation at home. This seems to have been the reason for Thera's colonisation of Cyrene. There were cases of force majeure. The Eretrians, who originally founded Corcyra (Corfu), are said to have been evicted by the Corinthians,[27] and to have gone off and founded Methone in the Gulf of Salonika. Less typical was the case of Taras (Taranto), a Spartan colony. The original colonists were bastards[28], or so the story goes. During a particularly long military campaign, with most husbands away from home, Sparta had found it necessary to take emergency measures to maintain the population. The measures were successful, but when matters returned to normal at the end of the war, civic liabilities were imposed on the irregularly conceived offspring.[29] Not unnaturally, it is said, they resented this, and emigrated to found Taras.

... Colonisation was not universally successful. Colonies were planted in the Balearics, on the south coast of Spain, in Corsica, perhaps in Sardinia, and perhaps on the Tunis coast, but they were all lost before the end of the sixth century, partly to the Etruscans, but mainly to the Carthaginians. Mostly though the colonies thrived, sometimes becoming richer than their mother-cities, and Greek influence spread far inland from them. The tomb of a Celtic princess at Vix on the Seine 100 miles above Paris contained Athenian cups and a bronze vase, probably from Sparta, of large size and fine workmanship. Another bronze vase of Spartan manufacture and early sixth-century date has been found at Grachwyl in Switzerland. At Vettersfelde not far from Berlin a Scythian chief was buried with his personal arms and his horse's equipment decorated with the work of Ionian Greek craftsmen. He had presumably commissioned them at one of Miletus's colonies on the Black Sea. When King Darius of Persia built his new palace at Persepolis, he employed Greek masons and Greek artists. Greek mercenary soldiers[30] were employed in Egypt in both the seventh and sixth centuries BC; they even reached, and defaced with their signatures, the great statues of Rameses at Abu Simbel.[31]

Thus the Greeks, a far from numerous people even by the standards of those times, had made their presence felt over a very wide area of the world while they were still in their archaic age, before the pattern of their civilisation had settled into its definitive form.[32] What we now consider most characteristic ancient Greece—the temples flanked with great marble columns, the lifelike statues, the machinery of democracy, drama, philosophy, history, science, and medicine—was only just emerging or lay still hidden in the future.

Greatest Extent of the Greek World

... The Greek world seemed to have reached its geographical limits, and that might have been so if it had not been for the Persian Empire.

That Empire was created in an astonishing 25 years during which the four major powers of the time were conquered and their territory annexed by Cyrus and his son Cambyses.[33] Media fell in 549, Lydia in 546, Babylon in 538, and Egypt in 525 BC. These conquests, equivalent in scale and speed to those of the Arabs after Mohammed, made Persia the heir of all the major Bronze Age civilisations of the Near East, and the master of the largest empire the world had yet seen. Included in it since 545 BC had been the Greek cities of the Asia Minor coast, but their desire for independence had been naturally kept alive by the existence of the free Greek cities across the water, and even Persia decided to incorporate these too. A preliminary expedition, mounted by Darius, was defeated by the Athenians at Marathon in 490 BC.[34] Ten years later a much larger force under the personal command of the king, Xerxes,[35] crossed the Bosporus to carry out the annexation. The campaign, which included the celebrated battles of Thermopylae, Salamis, and Platea, was always regarded by the later Greeks as their most glorious moment of achievement and as a major turning point in their history. Its immediate result was the total defeat of the invading army. Its long-term effect was to put the hope of revenge and conquest of Persia as a plausible item on the programme of panhellenic (all-Greek) nationalism.[36] The crusade[37] was not to come for 150 years, but when it did, its success was complete.

Alexander of Macedon[38]—Macedon was now the ruling state in Greece -launched his attack on the Persian Empire in 334 BC. During the next ten years he not only defeated the numerically far superior Persian army, but annexed and reorganised the whole of the former Persian empire from Egypt to Afghanistan, and entered India itself. There his troops mutinied[39] and forced him to turn back. But though he died of a fever at Babylon in the next year (323 BC), and though his successors quarrelled and divided his empire into separate kingdoms which continued to quarrel with each other for the best part of the next 300 years, the result of his victories was a massive and enduring extension of the Greek world.

【 Notes 】

①This selection is taken from *The Ancient Greeks: How They Lived and Worked*, Dufour Editions, 1976, pp. 15—29. This history of ancient Greece applies to the Greek world the stage theory of the development of human civilization used in the Stavrianos World History selection in this book. The modern nation of Greece is not a direct, in line descendent of ancient Greece although it does occupy the same peninsula in the eastern Mediterranean Sea that was the core of Greek civilization. This selected passage gives an overview of the Greek world from its earliest phase to later stages. Omitted from this selection is any in depth discussion of the Greek City States, such as Athens, where Greek thought flourished.

Calendar of Dates in Greek Civilization

Neolithic Age	About 7000 BC	
Early Bronze Age	3000 BC	Minoa
Middle Bronze Age	2200—1500 BC	
Late Bronze Age	1500—1100 BC	Mycenea
Dark Ages Archaic	8th to 6th century BC	776 BC First Olympic Games
Classical Greek civilization	6th, 5th, and 4th centuries	Persian threat
Athenian Empire founded	478—477 BC	
Rise of Rome	225—133 BC	

②Maurice Pope is an American archeologist and historian who specializes in ancient Greece.

③the Neolithic (New Stone) Age culture:

Neolithic /niːəuˈliθik/ adj. 新石器时代的: Neolithic villages 新石器时代的村庄。

④...agriculture (cereals and pulses), herding (mainly sheep and goats), and, by 5000 BC, the manufacture of fired clay pottery vessels.

cereal /ˈsiəriəl/ (常用复)禾谷类,(美)(加过工的)谷类食物(麦片粥等): cereal-leguminous crops 豆类作物。pulse /pʌls/ n. 豆,豆类: Pulses are protein foods such as peanuts, beans or peas. 豆是诸如花生、蚕豆和豌豆这样含有蛋白质的食物。fired clay pottery vessels 用黏土烧制的陶器器皿。

⑤...though cutting tools remained predominantly of stone; for small cutting edges these people used obsidian...:

predominantly /priˈdɔminəntli/ adv. 主要地,占主导地位地。obsidian /ɔbˈsidiən/ 黑曜岩(一般为黑色,带状,摔碎时色泽光亮,表面变曲,由火山熔岩迅速凝固而成)。

⑥In metallurgy the smelting and casting of bronze (copper alloyed with tin or with arsenic) were introduced, and articles made from bronze came to include axes, daggers, swords, spearheads, saws, chisels, awls, needles, pins, knives, fish-hooks, punches, tweezers.

metallurgy /meˈtælədʒi/ n. 冶金学;冶金术。smelt /smelt/ vt. (冶)熔炼;提炼;冶炼;熔解:smelt copper 炼铜。alloy /ˈælɔi/ vt. 使成合金,减低成色。alloy...with...:把……与……熔合。n. 合金。arsenic /ˈɑːsənik/ n. (化)砷,砒霜。dagger /ˈdæɡə/ n. 短剑,匕首。chisel /ˈtʃizl/ n. 凿子。awl /ɔːl/ n. 锥子,尖钻。punch /pʌntʃ/ n. 冲压机,冲床,打孔机。tweezers /ˈtwiːzəz/ n. 镊子,小钳。

⑦...and long-oared ships (perhaps 65ft from stem to stern) are both attested for the first time.

oared /ˈɔːd/ adj. 有桨的: two-oared 双桨的。stern /stəːn/ n. 船尾: from stem to stern 从船头到船尾;从头到尾;完全。attest /əˈtest/ vt., vi. 证明;表明: The child's good health attests his mother's care. 这孩子身体健康证实他母亲照料周到。(~ to) 证明;表明: I can attest to the absolute truth of his story. 我可以证实他的话是千真万确的。

⑧Sealstones bear witness to the engraver's art...:

engraver /inˈɡreivə/ n. 雕刻师,雕工。

⑨...in the islands (Cycladic), on the mainland (Helladic), and in Crete (Minoan).

Cycladic /siˈklædik/ adj. 基克拉迪群岛的,(史前青铜时代)基克拉迪文化的。铜器时代希腊文化的基克拉泽斯希腊东南一群岛,位于爱琴海南部。这个名字用于古代,指得洛斯小岛四周的群岛。Helladic /heˈlædik/ adj. 铜器时代的;希腊文化的。Minoan /miˈnəuən/ n. 弥诺斯人,克里特人,古克里特的居民,古克里特人。adj. 弥诺斯文化的,克里特(Crete)文化的,与从公元前3000年到前1100年克里特岛辉煌、先进的青铜文明的。

⑩...and had an average elevation of two or three storeys:

elevation /eliˈveiʃn/ n. 提升;升级;高尚;高雅;小丘;高地;海拔: a city at an elevation of 3,000 feet above sea level 高于海平面3000英尺的一座城市。

⑪a number of sizeable country houses:
sizeable /ˈsaizəbl/ adj. 相当大的;颇为可观的。

⑫Bulk granaries were attached to them…:
bulk /bʌlk/ n. 巨大的体积;大量,大部分;大半: a ship of great bulk 巨大的船。The bulk of the work has been done. 工作大部分已经完成。granary /ˈgrænəri/ 谷仓;粮仓: The Mid-West is the granary of the US. (喻)美国的中西部等于是全国的粮仓。

⑬…remarkably homogeneous throughout Crete:
homogeneous /ˌhɔməuˈgiːniəs/ adj. 同类的;同族的;相似的: a tight-knit, homogeneous society 一个紧密相连的同类社会。

⑭one theory in vogue:
vogue /vəug/ n. 流行: in vogue 流行,时髦; a party game no longer in vogue 不再时髦的集体游戏。

⑮Mycenaean: /ˌmaisiˈniːən/ adj. (希腊古城)迈锡尼的;迈锡尼人的;迈锡尼时代的(约在公元前1500—前1100年);迈锡尼青铜文化的。n. 迈锡尼人;迈锡尼语(指迈锡尼时代的希腊语)。

⑯…and now they became its heirs:
heir /ɛə/ n. 继承人;嗣子: Richard was his father's only heir, as he had no brothers or sisters. 理查德是他父亲的惟一继承人,因为他没有兄弟姐妹。女性为: heiress。

⑰…that can plausibly claim Mycenaean ancestry:
plausibly /ˈplɔːzəbli/ adv. 似真地。

⑱The script, known as "Linear B," has been deciphered (by Michael Ventris in 1953)…:
Linear B /ˈliniəl biː/ (公元前15—前12世纪希腊克里特岛的克诺索斯(Knossos)及希腊大陆上用代表音节的线形符号书写的) B类线形文字。Michael Ventris (1922—1956),英国语言学家,博士,英国古典学会研究员,他译解线形文字(爱琴古文字的一种)成功,认为它是希腊语已知的最早形式。

⑲tablet /ˈtæblit/ n. 刻写板;简。Archaeologists are laboring to decipher clay tablets. 考古学家们正在辛苦地译读土简。

⑳…those of the scribe, the goldsmith, the silversmith, the worker in ivory, the mason and stonecutter…:
scribe /skraib/ n. 抄写员;书记;作者,新闻记者;犹太法律学家。mason /ˈmeisn/ n. 泥瓦匠: The mason filled the joint with mortar. 泥工用灰浆把接缝处嵌平。stonecutter n. 石匠,石工。

㉑impoverishment /imˈpɔvəriʃmənt/ n. 贫穷,穷困。

㉒…used for tracing concentric circles:
concentric /kɔnˈsentrik/ adj. 同中心的,同轴的: be concentric…with 与……同中心; concentric circles 同心圆。

㉓…known to us as Protogeometric…:
protogeometric /ˌprəutəudʒiəˈmetrik/ adj. 原型几何的。

㉔ ...a total eclipse of human ingenuity:

eclipse /ik'lips/ n. 食: lunar eclipse 月食; 失去, 丧失（名声、威望等）: Once a famous actress, she is now in eclipse. 过去她是名演员, 今日已黯然失色。ingenuity /in'dʒi:njəs/ n. 机灵, 独创性, 精巧, 灵活性: a narrative plot of great ingenuity 精彩绝伦的小说情节。

㉕ ...two great religious sanctuaries of classical times, both seem to have been Mycenaean cult-centres too, but on both sites there is only scanty Dark Age pottery...:

sanctuary /'sæŋktjuəri/ n. 圣所, 圣殿; 礼拜堂;（罪犯等的）避难所;（中世纪教堂等特有的）庇护权: take sanctuary 逃入庇护所（请求保护）, 避难。The Buddhist temple was a religious sanctuary 佛教寺庙是宗教的殿堂。cult /kʌlt/ n. 礼拜, 祭仪; 一群信徒, 礼拜式。scanty /'skænti/ adj.（数量）不足的, 少量的: scanty knowledge 知识贫乏; His words were scanty (few). 他话不多。

㉖ Hyacinthus: n.（希神）雅辛托斯（Apollo 所钟爱的美少年, 被 Apollo 误杀后为纪念他使其血泊中长出风信子花）。

㉗ ...are said to have been evicted by the Corinthians...:

evict /i'vikt/ vt. 驱逐; 赶出: If you don't pay your rent you'll be evicted. 你如果不付房租, 就会被赶出去。Corinthian /kə'rinθiən/ adj. 科林斯（人）的;（古希腊）科林斯（式）的; 古雅的; 放荡的; 奢侈的;（古）放荡的。

㉘ bastard: /'bæstə:d/ n. 私生子; 代用品; 劣货: house of bastard design 设计简陋的房子。

㉙ ...civic liabilities were imposed on the irregularly conceived offspring:

civic /'sivik/ adj. 城市的; 市镇的; 公民的: civic duties 公民的义务。liability /laiə'biliti/ n. 责任; 义务; 负债: liability to pay taxes 纳税的义务。offspring /'ɔ:fspriŋ/ n.（单复数同形）儿女, 子孙, 后代; 产物。

㉚ Greek mercenary soldiers...:

mercenary /'mə:sinəri/ adj. 为钱的, 惟利是图的, 贪财的; 被雇佣的: mercenary politicians 惟利是图的政客; a mercenary marriage 买卖式婚姻。

㉛ ...and defaced with their signatures, the great statues of Rameses at Abu Simbel:

deface /di'feis/ vt. 损坏外观; 损毁表面: deface an inscription 磨损碑文。Rameses（拉美西斯二世）, 古埃及第十九王朝法老, 他在位期间大兴土木, 开凿阿布西姆贝尔（Abu Simbel）石庙, 广造巨石雕像。

㉜ ...had settled into its definitive form: 形成既定的形式。

definitive /di'finitiv/ adj. 决定性的; 最后的; 明确的: a definitive edition 定本; the definitive life of Byron 权威性的拜伦传。

㉝ ...and their territory annexed by Cyrus and his son Cambyses:

annex /ə'neks/ vt.（常与 to 连用）附加; 并吞: The city annexed the man's property. 这座城市吞并了这个人的财产。annex a clause to a contract 在合同中附加一条款。Cyrus 居鲁士二世（大帝）, 约公元前 600—前 529。古波斯帝国国王。公元前 550 年发兵灭米堤亚王国, 建立阿契美德尼王朝, 波斯帝国开始。他执行征服扩张政策, 公元前 546 年侵入小亚细亚, 灭吕底亚, 并臣服沿海的希腊各城邦。公元前 538 年, 占领巴比伦城。它的版图包括东起伊朗高原,西至小亚细亚的广大地区。他在作战中被杀,其子冈比西继之。

㉞...mounted by Darius, was defeated by the Athenians at Marathon in 490 BC：
Darius,大流士一世(公元前558—前486)。古波斯帝国国王(公元前522—前486)。疆域东起印度河,西至小亚细亚沿岸,南自埃及(尼罗河第一瀑布),北达欧洲的色雷斯,造成一空前的庞大帝国。大流士一世时期,是波斯帝国的强盛时期。Athenian /ə'θinjən/ adj. 雅典的;雅典人的;雅典文化的。n. 雅典人。

㉟the king, Xerxes：(约公元前519—前465)泽薛西斯一世。古波斯帝国国王(公元前486—前465),大流士一世之子。

㊱...as a plausible item on the programme of panhellenic (all-Greek) nationalism：
plausible /'plɔːzəbl/ adj. 好像有道理的,似乎可能的,似乎真实的,似乎可信的;嘴巧的,善于花言巧语的:a plausible story 好像是真实的故事。panhellenic /ˌpænheˈliːnik/ adj. 泛希腊的;全大学校友会的。

㊲crusade：/kruːˈseid/ n. 十字军东征,宗教战争,改革运动；vi. 加入十字军,投身正义运动。

㊳Alexander of Macedon：亚历山大大帝(公元前356—前323),马其顿国王(公元前336—前323),亚历山大帝国的创立者("大帝")。

㊴There his troops mutinied...：
mutiny /ˈmjuːtini/ n. 兵变,反抗;叛变,造反。v. 叛变,造反,兵变。

【 Exercises 】

I. Comprehension Questions

(1) What place is the oldest known continuously inhabited site in Europe? What and how was this date established? What is the date of this earliest inhabitation? (Hint：Paragraph 1)

(2) Minoa (Crete) saw the growth of cities meaning it had an urban aspect to its civilization. True _____ or False _____?

(3) Iron working came before the Bronze age in Greece. True _____ or False _____?

(4) What was the approximate period of Classical Greece? (Hint：see the paragraph above the heading The Greatest Extent of the World)

(5) 1) Alexander of Macedon (the ruling state of Greece at that time) was defeated by the superior Persian army. True _____ or False _____?

  2) Alexander was the ruler who died young but was responsible for the spread of Greek civilization far into the Middle East even to India. True _____ or False _____

(6) Calendar of the development of Greek Civilanization. From your study of this passage and the endnotes fill in the blanks in this chart.

Question (Find the answers for A, B, C, and D.)

Neolithic Age	**A.**	
B.	3000 BC	Minoa
Middle Bronze Age	2200—1500 BC	
Late Bronze Age	1500—1100	Mycenea
Dark Ages Archaic	8th to 6th century BC	**C.**
D.	6th, 5th, and 4th centuries BC	Persian threat
Athenian Empire founded	478—477 BC	
Rise of Rome	225—133 BC	

II. Points for Discussion

Carefully read the last section, "Greatest Extent of the Greek World." Persia (modern day Iran) and the Greek world were in a continuing struggle. Write a short essay, or make a brief oral presentation, on that struggle and its outcome. Include a description of the Persian empire. Find the name of the first battle where the Athenians defeated the Persians. What events did the Athenians consider the turning point for them? What success did the Greeks led by Alexander of Macedon have.

III. Fill in the gaps with the words or expressions given below. Change the form where necessary.

> elevation   nex   from stem to stern   scanty   crusade
> bulk   civic   mutiny   liability

(1) The business failed because its assets were not so great as its _____.

(2) Their tents were situated at an _____ of 3000 metres.

(3) The great _____ of necessary work can never be anything but painful.

(4) The potato crop was rather _____ this year.

(5) The US President's visit was the most important _____ event of the year.

(6) Don't worry about the liner. It has been refitted _____.

IV. Complete the following sentences with appropriate phrasal verbs formed from the verbs given below.

> attest   go   settle   judge   attach

(1) We can _____ that he was a tall man _____ the finger marks high on the cupboard.

(2) The handwriting expert _____ the genuineness of the signature.

(3) They sold off their house and _____ to live in America with their married daughter.

(4) We'd hardly _____ the children _____ a new school when we were posted to another district and had to uproot(赶出家门) them again.

(5) Too much importance should not be _____ the reports of impending (迫近的) revolution in Ruritania.

Unit 4

China

10. Chinese Economic History in Comparative Perspective[1]

Albert Feuerwerker[2]

> 艾伯特·费尔沃克(Albert Feuerwerker)是密西根大学历史系教授和研究中国经济史的专家。他出版了许多书,并发表了不少有关中国经济史的文章。同时,他还编辑了几部文集。在这篇选文中,他对中国和西方国家以往的经济状况进行了综合的历史比较。

Much ink has been spilled and many pages filled with explanations of economic "backwardness" or "underdevelopment" or "late development" in the non-European world. Even as late as the sixteenth century, China's economy produced for its population a standard of living in no way inferior to that of any other nation in Europe or Asia. Western students of China have asked with some frequency why late imperial China did not therefore "industrialize" or "modernize" as Europe did from the eighteenth century onward and Japan proceeded to do in the late nineteenth and early twentieth centuries. Scholars in the People's Republic of China phrase the equivalent question in terms of a failed or delayed transition from "feudalism" to "capitalism" along the Marxist path of historical progress.

... I would argue that underdevelopment, in fact,... was the "norm" of world history until very recent times. Even today, development is more the exception than the rule.[3] Proponents of economic, cultural, political, social, and other causes of underdevelopment have each found overwhelming evidence[4] for their favored explanations. In fact, any one of these factors is sufficiently important to prevent a premodern economy from developing into a modern one. ... Of course I do not mean that there was no economic growth before industrialization of the modern variety. The necessary distinction is between growth of total production and growth of production per capita, which I call respectively "premodern economic growth" and "modern economic growth."

... We know a great deal about the enormous obstacles to moving from the framework of premodern growth to that of modern growth. Despite a century of study and research economic historians are much less certain about how the process of modern economic growth got started... in the seventeenth and eighteenth centuries. And we are least of all informed about the history and dynamics of premodern economies per se[5], apart from the question of their not being transformed into modern economies.

......

Let me restate this admittedly broad comparison between Western Europe from the Fall of Rome to the seventeenth century and China from the Han dynasty to the mid Ch'ing: premodern economic growth interacting with demographic changes in China over this millennium and a half produced overall, ... on average, a perceptibly higher level of material culture than that enjoyed by most of Europe before 1700.[6] There were two foundations for this achievement: first, the productive technology (mainly agricultural because that was the principal industry, but including other economic sectors as well) that was elaborated in Sung China and adopted over the next thousand years; second, the social, political, and economic institutions (also perfected in the Sung period, even though originating much earlier) that facilitated... China's extraordinary premodern economic growth[7]...

In contrasting China with Europe what is most striking is that the potentialities of the Sung traditional technology and institutions in China were not exhausted until the nineteenth and twentieth centuries. These institutions, even when in decline, could feed, clothe, house, govern, edify,[8] and amuse China's large and rapidly growing population. In contrast, agricultural and other technology in late medieval and early modern Western Europe does not seem to have advanced much beyond the best performance of the Roman Empire...

... Significant changes in both the technology and the organization of Western European agriculture (still the major "industry") began to appear from the seventeenth century onward. The production potentialities of these changes... were not fully realized for more than two centuries. This process of realization included the geographic extension of cultivated land, technological "deepening," and major social reorganization... The new mixed farming and crop rotation practices were first effectively employed in the light soil areas of southern England, where they resulted in increased production not only per unit of land but also per worker. From England the improved agriculture spread gradually over the Western European mainland. Paralleling this diffusion, but occurring mainly in the nineteenth century and later, we can note the systematic application of chemical and biological science to horticultural problems[9] as well as the increased mechanization of the principal agricultural processes.

The social changes that accompanied these economic developments were enormous. In England hundreds of "enclosure acts" ended the old village system of common lands and served to concentrate land in the hands of the large landowners, who let it out to the most efficient farmers. This development and the introduction of crop rotations marked the end of the necessity to maintain fallow land.[10] The enclosures also increased agricultural efficiency by reducing the size of the peasant labor force while raising production. On the European continent serfdom came to an end as absolute monarchs in search of increased revenues sought to raise agricultural output by reducing the feudal privileges of the nobles, who obstructed productivity, and by increasing the incentives for peasant producers to make greater productive efforts.[11]

An agricultural revolution is probably not a necessary and distinct phase of economic development prior to modern industrialization. But concurrent agricultural transformation[12] seems to have been essential in order to release manpower for industry, feed the growing cities, and supply raw materials for manufacture... Although the full realization of the new agricultural technology required centuries, its consequences were already evident when eighteenth-century Europe confronted the Chinese empire of the Ch'ing.

The onset of fundamental change[13] in Western Europe was not matched in China, which remained largely in the mold that had been set in the Sung dynasty and refined in succeeding dynasties...

Stagnation or "homeostasis" in China,[14] however, was in part the product of a demographic and institutional stability—even rigidity—that blocked further technological and economic development. The possibilities of the traditional technology were not exhausted before the twentieth century in China, and therefore there were fewer incentives for the internal self-regulation of population growth in the Ch'ing dynasty than was the case in early modern Europe or Tokugawa Japan.

One of the sad ironies of modern Chinese history is that when the necessity and, at last, the possibility of developing and adapting the new European production technologies arrived, it occurred simultaneously with the advent of a... hinese demographic cycle—one in which the rate of population increase reached or exceeded for a time 2 percent per annum. This pattern is typical in what we call the developing countries and is the consequence of a large fall in mortality without any significant decline in fertility.[15] The difficulties of achieving sustained modern economic growth in the People's Republic of China since 1949 in the face of such overwhelming population pressure is self-evident.

... Before concluding, I would like to consider two further matters, namely, social and political institutions, and the international environment. Both premodern and modern economic growth in Europe and China were of course shaped by their differences in these two areas as well...

Although the third European demographic-economic cycle was one of modern economic growth, the comparable Chinese cycle definitely was not. The institutional structures of traditional Chinese society—its political, legal, kinship,[16] and educational formations, among others—had not obstructed and perhaps had even facilitated premodern economic growth from the Sung dynasty to the eighteenth century. Chinese performance during this period was at least as successful as in contemporary Europe. Certainly the acceleration of traditional growth in the seventeenth and eighteenth centuries argues against the received view in China today that late imperial "feudal autocracy"[17] was the major obstacle to economic performance and that it prevented China from following the Marxist path to capitalism and beyond. But Chinese political institutions... unlike those of early modern Europe, seem to have contributed little if anything toward modern economic growth.

I would argue that a situation in which there are several competing polities (such as the state-building monarchies of early modern Europe) is much more conducive than a unified empire (as in Ming and Ch'ing China) to the development and implementation of the critical abstractions and institutions of law and property of the kind that facilitated Europe's modern economic growth[18]...

For all its bureaucratic sophistication[19] the Chinese empire never undertook several basic policies that would have aided economic development. It never developed a funded national debt that untied wealth from the land, it never promulgated comprehensive codes of business law[20] nor created judicial institutions that were devoted to maintaining property rights, and it never developed insurance schemes that could have been used to reduce commercial risk. Before the nineteenth century there was little need—that is, no credible domestic or foreign challenge—for the Ch'ing emperors and the bureaucratic elite that served them to follow the path of the Houses of Stuart, Bourbon, and Habsburg and their administrators, who built the modern European nation-states and favored economic enterprise in exchange for the financial resources to pursue their competitive struggles.[21] The Chinese rulers already possessed "all under Heaven," and they could not be aware of how parochial that conceit would soon become.[22] By the nineteenth century Ch'ing decline and China's unprecedented population growth,[23] its ignorance of the West, and the simultaneous European assault on Ch'ing sovereignty all helped insure Chinese frustration and "failure" to develop the infrastructures necessary for modern economic growth,[24] even when the pressing need for such infrastructures became painfully clear.

The protection of property, the reduction of risk, and the facilitation of capital mobility[25] are all important concerns, but they do not address the critical question of how new technical and organizational knowledge (without which modern economic growth cannot occur) was itself discovered and applied in the seventeenth, eighteenth, and nineteenth centuries in Europe. The production of knowledge is dependent in large part on the "knowledge institutions" of a society... Why, for example, does the remarkable technological, institutional, and ideological creativity of Sung China appear to have exhausted itself and not to have been renewed before the twentieth century?

Before modern times, then, we can "award" technological and institutional leadership to China and demographic flexibility to Western Europe. In the early modern world scientific and technological discovery advanced in Europe but not in China. Institutional innovation swept over Europe, but China offered the sacred "virtue" of its emperor to all who came from afar[26] and sought to be civilized.

The international context also favored Western Europe while it moved from premodern to modern economic growth... Europe, by exploiting... the New World and its markets as well as those of Africa and Asia, made the outside world a participant in the beginning of its modern economic growth. For China, Europe before the nineteenth century was mainly a curiosity and the source of substantial local trading profits. Afterward, Europe (and America and Japan) brought China political loss—

abridgment of sovereignty and cultural denigration.[27] These losses were serious forms of damage in a zero-sum game,[28] where for every "winner" there must also be a "loser." But the economic shock of foreign trade, investment, and technology transfer—and the special privileges foreign businesses enjoyed in China that were protected by political concessions—was simultaneously an opportunity. In principle, unlike the political realm of unequal treaties and extraterritoriality[29] (whereby Westerners in China were subject only to Western law), the economic realm was an arena where there could be more than one winner.

In the last decades of the twentieth century China is importing Western technology and making its own growing contributions to its economic development... China has undertaken a major effort to limit its population expansion and has achieved considerable success, at least in urban areas. Institutional innovations in the areas of law, contracts, property rights, and so forth (which would have been unthinkable in the days of Chairman Mao) are proceeding apace.[30] Foreign trade turnover[31] continues to grow, and China's links to the world are being continually enlarged in every realm. If, as I have implied, these are the critical variables[32] for the achievement of modern economic growth, that long-delayed transition is now beginning to be realized in China.

【 Notes 】

①This selection is taken from "Chinese Economic in Comparative Perspective" in *Heritage of China: Contemporary Perspective on Chinese Civilization* edited by Paul S. Ropp, University of California Press, 1990, pp. 224—225, 235—241. It is a general historical comparison of economic aspects of China and Western European countries in the past.

②Albert Feurerwerker (1927—) is Professor of History at the University of Michigan and a specialist in the economic history of China. He has published numerous books and articles on China's economic history and edited several collections, including (with John King Fairbank) volume 13 of the *Cambridge History of China*.

③Even today, development is more the exception than the rule.
　　more...than... 与其说是……不如说是……: He is more diligent than clever. 与其说他聪明,不如说他勤奋。

④Proponents of economic, cultural, political, social, and other causes of underdevelopment have each found overwhelming evidence. 说明经济、文化、政治、社会和其他方面不发展原因的人个个都找到了充分的证据。
　　proponent /prə'pəunənt/ n. 提议者;建议者;支持者;辩护者。each adv. 各个,每个:

The children each have a pencil. 孩子们个个有一支铅笔。

⑤per se /pɜː'sei/ adv. 本身；就其本身而论：Natural environment cannot per se cause forms of culture. 自然环境本身并不能产生各种文化形式。

⑥Let me restate this admittedly broad comparison between Western Europe from the Fall of Rome to the seventeenth century and China from the Han dynasty to the mid Ch'ing：premodern economic growth interacting with demographic changes in China over this millennium and a half produced overall, ... on average, a perceptibly higher level of material culture than that enjoyed by most of Europe before 1700.

interact /ɪntər'ækt/ vi. 相互作用，相互影响；交相感应，反应：interact on 作用，影响，制约，配合；interact with 与……相合：More than a dozen variable factors could interact, with their permutations running into the thousands. 一打以上的可变因素可以相互作用，使它们的排列成千上万。millennium /mɪ'lenɪəm/ n. (-nia) 一千年；未来的太平盛世,幸福时代。

⑦...that facilitated China's extraordinary premodern economic growth：

facilitate /fə'sɪlɪteɪt/ vt. 使容易；使便利：It would facilitate matters if you were more co-operative. 要是你再合作些，事情就会变得更容易。The broken lock facilitated my entrance into the empty house. 坏了的门锁使我毫不费力地进入那所空房子。

⑧edify：/'edɪfaɪ/ vt. 教育（启发，熏陶）edifying books 有启发性的书。

⑨...the systematic application of chemical and biological science to horticultural problems...：

horticultural /hɔːtɪ'kʌltʃərəl/ adj. 园艺的。

⑩...the necessity to maintain fallow land：

fallow /'fæləʊ/ adj. 休闲中的（田地）；n. 休闲地；休耕法：Summer fallow is the best method of destroying weeds. 夏季休耕是消灭杂草的最好办法。

⑪On the European continent serfdom came to an end as absolute monarchs in search of increased revenues sought to raise agricultural output by reducing the feudal privileges of the nobles, who obstructed productivity, and by increasing the incentives for peasant producers to make greater productive efforts.

serfdom /'sɜːfdəm/ n. 农奴身份，农奴境遇。revenue /'revɪnjuː/ n. 收入,国家的收入，税收。incentive /ɪn'sentɪv/ n. 刺激；鼓励；动机。adj. 刺激性的，鼓励性质的，诱发的：be an incentive to further study 鼓励进一步研究；incentive wage（增产）奖励工资。

⑫But concurrent agricultural transformation...：

concurrent /kə'kʌrənt/ n. 直流；同向。

⑬The onset of fundamental change...：

onset /'ɒnset/ n. 攻击；开始：the onset of a cold 感冒初起；at very onset 刚一开始。

⑭Stagnation or "homeostasis" in China...：

stagnation /stæɡ'neɪʃən/ n. 停滞(性)；萧条；迟钝：economic stagnation 经济停滞。homeostasis /ˌhəʊmiəʊ'steɪsɪs/ n. 系统(动态)平衡；一个系统中的输入和输出恰好平衡，以至系统没有变化的一种动态性的状态：ecological homeostasis 生态内稳定（现象）。

⑮...the consequence of a large fall in mortality without any significant decline in fertility:
mortality /mɔː'tæliti/ n. 死亡人数；死亡率：greatly reduce the mortality from tuberculosis 使结核病的死亡率大大降低。fertility /fəː'tiliti/ n. 肥沃；丰饶；多产；繁殖；生殖力：the fertility of imagination 想像力丰富；world fertility 世界生育率。

⑯...its political, legal, kinship...:
kinship /'kinʃip/ n. 亲属关系；相似。

⑰"feudal autocracy"：autocracy /ɔː'tɔkrəsi/ n. 专制制度；独裁制度；专制国家。

⑱I would argue that a situation in which there are several competing polities (such as the state-building monarchies of early modern Europe) is much more conducive than a unified empire (as in Ming and Ch'ing China) to the development and implementation of the critical abstractions and institutions of law and property of the kind that facilitated Europe's modern economic growth. 这个长句是一个主从复合句。在谓语 argue 后由 that 引导的宾语从句中，主语 a situation 与谓语 is 被 in which 引导的定语从句分隔开了。在形容词短语 conductive to 中，形容词 conducive 与介词 to 被 than 引导的比较状语从句分隔开了。由 that 引导的定语从句 that facilitated Europe's modern economic growth 修饰 property of the kind。
polity /'pɔliti/ n. 政治组织，国家组织，政治，政体。abstraction /æb'strækʃən/ n. 抽象；抽象观念：The idea of redness is an abstraction. 红色概念是一种抽象概念。

⑲For all its bureaucratic sophistication...:
sophistication /səfisti'keiʃən/ n. 完善度，技巧；强词夺理，诡辩；混合。

⑳...it never promulgated comprehensive codes of business law...:
promulgate /'prɔməlgeit/ vt. 宣布，颁布，公布(法令等)；传播；宣传；散播。

㉑Before the nineteenth century there was little need—that is, no credible domestic or foreign challenge—for the Ch'ing emperors and the bureaucratic elite that served them to follow the path of the Houses of Stuart, Bourbon, and Habsburg and their administrators, who built the modern European nation-states and favored economic enterprise in exchange for the financial resources to pursue their competitive struggles. 在这个长句中，破折号之间的部分起解释作用，把主语部分 little need 与 for the Ch'ing emperors...分隔开了。that 引导的定语从句修饰 elite。who 引导一个非限定定语从句，修饰 the Houses of Stuart, Bourbon, and Habsburg and their administrators。
credible /'kredəbl/ adj. 可信的，可靠的：credible witness 可信的证人。elite /ei'liːt, i'liːt/ n. 精英；精华；中坚：the ruling elite were powerful 占统治地位的精英很强大。

㉒...how parochial that conceit would soon become:
parochial /pə'rəukiəl/ adj. 教区的；受限制的；狭隘的；狭小的(思想、兴趣等)：parochial outlook 狭隘的眼界。conceit /kən'siːt/ n. 自负；自夸；骄傲自大；自高自大(亦作：conceitedness)：No one admires a man who is full of conceit. 没有人喜欢一个十分自负的人。

㉓...China's unprecedented population growth:
unprecedented /ʌn'presidəntid/ adj. 空前的；没有前例的：The enemy bombardment caused

unprecedented death and destruction in the country. 敌人的狂轰滥炸在这个国家造成了空前的死亡和破坏。

㉔ ...and the simultaneous European assault on Ch'ing sovereignty all helped insure Chinese frustration and "failure" to develop the infrastructures necessary for modern economic growth：
simultaneous /saiml'teinjəs, siml'teinjəs/ adj. 同时的;同步的：The two simultaneous shots sounded like one. 同时发出的两声枪响听起来像一声。sovereignty /'sɔvrinti/ n. 君权,统治权,主权;主权国家：China's sovereignty and territorial integrity must not be infringed. 中国的主权和领土完整决不允许侵犯。infrastructure /infrə'strʌktʃə/ n. 基础;基础结构[设施]（尤指社会、国家赖以生存和发展的，如道路、学校、电厂、交通、通讯系统等）：economic infrastructure 经济基础结构部门;physical infrastructure 物质基础设施。

㉕ ...and the facilitation of capital mobility...：
facilitation /fəsili'teiʃən/ n. 简易化,助长。

㉖ from afar：afar /ə'fɑː/ adv. 由远方;在远处;到远方;from afar 自远方,远道,从远处。

㉗ ...abridgment of sovereignty and cultural denigration：
abridgment /ə'bridʒmənt/ n. 删节;缩短;节本;摘要;剥夺;削减：abridgment of expenses 削减费用。denigration /deni'greiʃən/ n. 抹黑,贬低,诋毁。

㉘ zero-sum：赌赛胜负双方一方得益引起另一方损失的,得失所系的:zero-sum games 得失所系的赌赛。

㉙ extraterritoriality：/ˌekstrəˌteritɔːri'æliti/ n. 治外法权

㉚ apace：/ə'peis/ adv. 快速地,急速地

㉛ foreign trade turnover：对外贸易额。
turnover /'tɔːnəuvə/ n. 翻覆,翻折;半圆卷饼;流通量,营业额;周转：export turnover 出口交易额;commodity (goods) turnover 商品流转。

㉜ variable /'veəriəbl/ n. [数]变数,可变物,变量

【 Exercises 】

I. Comprehension Questions

(1) The author outlines several different propositions often advanced about China's economic position in the modern world. Which of the following is not what he gives?

   A. The question is asked—why did late imperial China not develop or modernize as the West and Japan did?

   B. The proposition scholars in the People's Republic of China put forth was that China was very slow to develop and modernize because of the delayed transition from "feudalism" to "capitalism" found in their Marxist idea of historical progress.

   C. Another view of the cause of China's slow entry into the modern world is over population in the 19th century and increased poverty and lack of capital accumulation.

   D. Another proposition is that actually China's slow entry into the modern world is the "norm" in world history until recent times and even today. This view distinguished between a country's total production and production per capital so as not to give large countries an advantage over small countries when comparing.

(2) In the pre 18th century world, if we compare Western Europe and the Chinese Empire Europe had a higher level of material culture than China. True _____ or False _____?

(3) What were the two foundations of Chinese premodern economic growth and high material culture before 1700? (Hint: look for the answer in paragraph 4.)

(4) True or False
   1) Europe's agriculture and institution in the early modern period did not advance beyond the best performance of the Roman Empire.
   2) Significant agricultural change in Europe began in the 19th century.
   3) Use of improved agricultural technology is necessary to have more manpower available for industry.
   4) Stagnation in China blocked technological and economic development. This was also related to the lack of regulation of population growth in the Qing (Ch'ing) period.
   5) The author thinks great population growth in the PRC after 1949 was not a negative influence in sustained economic growth.

II. Points for Discussion

After careful consideration do you think Feuerwerker's analysis of the historical reasons for China's lagging behind the world economy in the 20th century are valid? First summarize his reasons and then explain why you think they are valid if you agree. If you disagree explain your position, citing historical evidence.

III. Complete the following sentences with the words or expressions from the passage given below. Change the form where necessary.

apart from   award   in decline   unprecedented   sweep over
consequence   in exchange   elite   phase

(1) In addition to notions of social equality there was much emphasis on the role of _____ and of heroes within them?

(2) The early 1990's finds an _____ tide of rural workers flooding into big cities in China.

(3) The government _____ that they would build a new highway to the mountain.

(4) It has been observed that unemployment, quite _____ exerting financial pressures, brings enormous psychological troubles.

(5) Uncontrollable anger _____ Jim when he learned how Mary had been treated.

(6) Martin Ruther King Jr. _____ the peace Nobal Prize of 1964 for advocating nonviolence policy in the movement for civil rights.

(7) Not only in medicine, but in other professions as well, practitioners may find themselves repeatedly in difficulty where serious _____ seem avoidable only through deception.

IV. **Translate the following sentences into English, using the words and phrases given below.**

more... than   simultaneous   each   edify   facilitate

(1) 纯科学家与应用科学家之间的所谓区别，与其说是真的，不如说是表面的。
(2) 一切事物都是互相联系又互相作用的。这件事几乎是与那件事同时发生的。
(3) 已有三个人靠着别人的心脏活了七年。
(4) 建议青年学生们读一些陶冶性情的书籍，以提高自己的心智。
(5) 新的地下铁路将为去城市各处提供方便。

11. Chinese Science Explorations of an Ancient Tradition[1]

Nathan Sivin[2]

> 内森·席文(Nathan Sivin)是宾夕法尼亚大学中国文化和科学史的教授。他出版了有关中国科学史等多方面的著作。其中包括与李约瑟合著的《中国古代科学文化史》第五卷第四部分。这篇文章选自席文向非专业的西方读者介绍中国的文集。这篇文章让读者对中国的传统科学基本范畴有所了解。
>
> 席文著作中的一个观点是早期的中国科学思想基于生活的整体方式和假设人、自然和天是紧密相连，不可分割的。这种思想使得科学技术的传统连绵不断，一直持续到中国帝王时代的最后几个世纪，这在世界上是无与伦比的。

Although every culture must experience much the same physical world, each breaks it up into manageable segments in very distinct ways... at the most general level of science (natural philosophy, it used to be called) certain basic concepts became established because of their very general usefulness in making nature comprehensible. In Europe after Aristotle's time among the most important of these notions were the Four Elements of Empedocles and the qualitative idea of a proper place[3] that was part of the definition of each thing. In ancient China the most common tools of abstract thought were the Yin-Yang and Five Phases concepts, implying as they did a dynamic harmony compounded out of the cyclical alternation of complementary energies. Today scientists use a much wider range of well-defined concepts, embracing space, time, mass, energy, and information.

Thus the fields of science in a given culture are determined by the application of these general concepts, suitably refined, reinterpreted if necessary, and supplemented by more special concepts, to various fields of experience, demarked as the culture chooses for intrinsic and extrinsic reasons to demark them.[4]

......

Then what fields of science did the Chinese themselves organize in the course of conceptualizing the phenomenal world? I would propose more or less the following list of major disciplines:

1. Medicine (I), which included theoretical studies of health and disease (i ching, and so on), therapeutics (i fang, and so on), macro-biotics (yang sheng) or the theory and practice of longevity techniques, sexual hygiene (fang chung, on the whole an aspect of macro-biotics), pharmacognosy (pen-ts'ao), and veterinary medicine (shou I).[5] Pharmacognosy, the study of materia medica, incorporated a large part of early knowledge of natural history as well as approached to biological classification... Acupuncture,[6] which has recently been seized upon by the mass media in their endless quest for novel misinformation,[7] was (and still is) on the whole only a minor branch of therapeutics.

2. Alchemy (fu-lien, and so on), the science of immortality,[8] which overlapped greatly in practice with medical macro-biotics. Immortality was thought of, in fact, as the highest kind of health. The two major divisions were "external alchemy" (wei tan) and "internal alchemy" (nei tan). In the former, immortality drugs were prepared by techniques largely based on the natural processes by which minerals and metals were believed to mature within the earth, but in the laboratory they were carried out on a telescoped scale of time.[9] A year of cyclical treatment by the alchemist might correspond to a cosmic cycle of 4320 years. In internal alchemy, by a different sort of analogy the interior of the adept's body became the laboratory and the "cyclical maturation of the elixir" was carried out by meditation,[10] concentration, breath control, or sexual disciplines.

3. Astrology (t'ien-wen), in which anomalous celestial and meteorological phenomena[11] were observed and interpreted in order to detect defects in the political order. This science was based on a close correspondence between the cosmic and political realms. In the "field allocation" (fen yeh) theory of the second century BC, this was an actual mapping of sections of the sky upon political divisions of the civilized world. In astrology the Emperor was the mediator between the orders of nature and humanity. Like a vibrating dipole, the ideal monarch drew his charisma[12] from

the eternal order of the cosmos, radiating it in turn to inspire virtue—defined implicitly as values oriented toward hierarchical order[13]— in society. Because of his centrality, the harmony of above and below depended critically upon the Emperor's ability to maintain his ritual and moral fitness. Omens[14] in the sky were thus an early warning that his responsibility as Son of Heaven needed to be taken more seriously.

4. Geomancy[15] (feng-shui), the science of "wind and water," which determines the auspicious placement of houses and tombs with respect to features of the landscape. While alchemy uses the yin-yang, Five Phases, and other concepts mainly to study the temporal relations[16] involved in maturing the Great Work, geomancy adapts them predominantly to topological configurations.[17] Geomancy has been shrugged off as mere superstition, but perhaps more to the point is the rationale[18] it provides for expressing the status or wealth of a family in terms of control of its physical environment in life and death. Nevertheless geomancy, which has no Occidental counter-part, is much more than an arbitrary excuse for demonstrating social clout.[19] Geographers have found it intrinsically[20] interesting as the world's only time-proven theoretical approach to the aesthetics of land use. In other words, it succeeds consistently in producing sites that... are beautiful...

5. Physical studies (wu li). The shape of this composite field has more in common with that of Greek or Islamic natural philosophy than with that of post-Newtonian physics. In general this is the area in which fundamental concepts were adapted and applied to explain particular physical phenomena, as well as chemical, biological, and psychological phenomena that were not distinguished or were thought to be closely related. We can distinguish three overlapping exploratory approaches, which at various times and in various circumstances served much the same function in Chinese thought as elementary physics today—as well as other functions with which modern physics does not concern itself. Their free use of numerology should not obscure their essentially qualitative character.[21]

The two major early approaches to the theoretical principles behind the events of nature might be called "mutation studies" and "resonance studies."[22] The first uses the conceptual apparatus of the commentaries to the *Book of Changes*, and is in general as concerned with the social and political spheres as with nature. The second, which unlike the others has been studied from the viewpoint of the history of science, has its own literature, going back to the second century B. C. The resonance (hsiang lei) treatises[23] elaborate the notion that physical interactions are prompted by or controlled by categorical associations and correspondences, set out in terms of yin-yang and the Five Phases. The third approach is "correspondence studies" (ko chih, ko wu), which attained prominence much later as part of the program of Chu Hsi (1130—1200) and other Neo-Confucian philosophers. This tendency brought to bear on interesting natural phenomena not only the more sophisticated concepts of the Neo-Confucians but their concern for the didactic applications of their insights,[24] for they were committed to the integration of nature, society, and the individual psyche. The term wu li (literally, "the pattern-principles of the phenomena") was ultimately redefined to become the standard equivalent in modern Chinese for "physics."

In addition to these qualitative sciences there were others concerned with number and its applications:

6. Mathematics (suan), which was on the whole numerical and algebraic in its approach rather than geometric, and oriented toward practical application rather than toward exploration of the properties of number and measure for their own sake. The search for the deeper meaning and implication of number seems to have remained within the province[25] of what we would call numerology.

7. Mathematical harmonics[26] (lu or lu lu...) was perhaps the field in which mathematics and numerology were applied in closest combination. It arose from discoveries about the simple numerical relations between sound intervals, which had also suggested to the Pythagoreans that the basis of regularity in nature was numerical. In China the relations explored were mainly those of the dimensions of resonant pipes. The importance of music in ceremonial[27] made harmonics part of the intellectual trappings of imperial charisma. This tied it to other kinds of ritually oriented charisma, guaranteed it sponsorship, protected its study, and petrified it institutionally.[28]...... Attempts were made, for instance, to use the standard pipes as basic measures of length, capacity, and (indirectly) weight.

8. Mathematical astronomy (li or li fa) was, especially in early times, thought of as closely related to harmonics. In some of the dynastic histories the state of the two fields is surveyed in a single Treatise on Harmonics and Calendrical Astronomy [Lu li chih]. Astrology and astronomy,[29] on the other hand, were treated separately except in the first of the histories (Shih chi, ca. 90 BC)... It is perhaps most useful to think of mathematical astronomy as aimed at making celestial phenomena predictable and thus removing them from the realm of astrology, which interpreted the ominous significance of unpredictable phenomena. The ties of both... to ritual thought

and institutions, which depend in their essence upon precedent, often tended to blur the boundary[30] by retaining astrological significance for phenomena that astronomers had learned to predict. The sky's eternal changes, especially the fine variations underlying the gross regularities of the solar and lunar motions, prompted the most sophisticated technical developments of which Chinese mathematics was to prove capable.

This crude topography of the Chinese sciences can at least serve to remind us of a truth that we easily forget when we focus our attention narrowly on the anticipations of modern chemistry, physics, biology, and so on... Although many Chinese concepts and attitudes can be found in science today... the disciplines in which they were originally embedded were drastically different from our own in aim, approach, and organization.

【 Notes 】

① This selection is taken from "Chinese Science: Explorations of an Ancient Tradition" in *The Chinese: Adapting the Past, Building the Future*, edited by Robert F. Dernberger, et al, Center for Chinese Studies, University of Michigan, 1986, pp. 617—622. This excerpt is from a short essay written to introduce a non-specialist Western audience to China. Here the reader is given an overview of the basic categories in traditional Chinese science. One of Sivin's points in his work is that basic to early Chinese scientific thought is a holistic approach to life and the assumption that people, nature, and the heavens are inseparably connected. Until the last centuries of Imperial China, Chinese thought had a continuous and coherent tradition of science and technology that was unparalleled in the world.

② At the time this article was written Nathan Sivin was Professor of Chinese Culture and the History of Science at the University of Pennsylvania. He has published widely on the history of Chinese science including, with Joseph Needham, volume 5, part 4 of *Science and Civilisation in China*.

③ ... after Aristotle's time among the most important of these notions were the Four Elements of Empedocles and the qualitative idea of a proper place...:
Aristotle /ˈærɪstɒtl/ n. 亚里士多德（古希腊大哲学家，科学家）。Empedocles /emˈpedəkliz/ 恩培多克勒(490 BC—430 BC)，古希腊哲学家、诗人、医生，持物活论观点，认为万物皆由火、水、土、气四种元素组成，动力是爱和憎，爱使元素结合，恨使元素分离。qualitative /ˈkwɒlɪtətɪv/ adj. 性质的；定性的：a qualitative analysis 定性分析。

④ ... demarked as the culture chooses for intrinsic and extrinsic reasons to demark them: demark /dɪˈmɑːk/ vt. 区别，区分。as 是连接词，引导一个时间状语从句。intrinsic /ɪnˈtrɪnsɪk/

adj. 固有的;本身的;内在的: The intrinsic value of a coin is the value of the metal it is made of. 一枚钱币的内在价值是造这枚钱币的金属的价值。extrinsic /eks'trinsk/ adj. 外界的(常与 to 连用)外在的;非固有的。

⑤...therapeutics (i fang, and so on), macro-biotics (yang sheng) or the theory and practice of longevity techniques, sexual hygiene (fang chung, on the whole an aspect of macro-biotics), pharmacognosy (pen-ts'ao), and veterinary medicine (shou I):

therapeutics /θerə'puːtiks/ n. 治疗学,疗法。longevity /lɔn'dʒeviti/ n. 长命,寿命;供职期限,资历。hygiene /'haidʒiːn/ n. 卫生学;保健法;卫生: personal hygiene 个人保健。pharmacognosy /fɑːmə'kɔgnəsi/ n. (研究天然药物的)生药学。veterinary /'vetərinəri/ n. 兽医。adj. 医牲畜的,兽医的。

⑥acupuncture:/'ækjupʌŋktʃə/ n. 针刺疗法。v. 施行针刺疗法。

⑦novel misinformation: 新颖的误传。

misinformation /'misinfə'meiʃən/ n. 误报,误传。

⑧Alchemy (fu-lien, and so on), the science of immortality,...:

alchemy /'ælkimi/ n. 炼金术,魔力。immortality /imɔː'tæləti/ n. 不死(永生,永远性);不朽,不朽的声名。

⑨...on a telescoped scale of time: 按缩短了的时间比例。

telescope vt., vi. 使叠缩;缩短,精简:He telescoped 150 years of history into one lesson. 他把 150 年的历史浓缩在一课之内。

⑩...the interior of the adept's body became the laboratory and the "cyclical maturation of the elixir" was carried out by meditation,...:

the interior of the adept's body 高手的体内。adept /'ædəpt/ n. 内行,熟手,名家: an adept at chess 一位象棋名手; adj. (与 at, in 连用)熟练的;精通的。"cyclical maturation of the elixir"完成炼长生不老药的周期。elixir /i'liksə/ n. 炼金药,长生不老药(= elixir of life),仙丹妙药。meditation /medi'teiʃən/ n. 熟虑;(尤指宗教的)默想;沉思;[pl.]冥想录: He is deep in meditation. 他陷入沉思中。

⑪...anomalous celestial and meteorological phenomena...: 天空和气候不规则的现象。

anomalous /ə'nɔmələs/ adj. 不规则的;异常的;反常的。celestial /si'lestiəl/ adj. 天的;天上的;天空的;天体的: The sun, the stars, and the moon are celestial bodies. 太阳、星星、月亮都是天体。

⑫Like a vibrating dipole, the ideal monarch drew his charisma....:

dipole /'daipəul/ n. (物)偶极子;(化)偶极:偶极天线。charisma /kə'rizmə/ n. -mas 或 -mata 领袖人物的超凡魅力;神授的能力。

⑬defined implicitly as values oriented toward hierarchical order:

implicitly /im'plisitli/ adv. 含蓄地,暗中地。hierarchical /haiə'rɑːkikəl/ adj. 分等级的。

⑭omen:/'əumen/ n. 预兆,征兆: a bad omen 坏兆头; a good omen 好兆头; vt. 预示,有……的前兆:The clouds were an omen of bad weather coming. 这些云预示着坏天气即将来临。

⑮geomancy：/ˈdʒiːəmænsi/ n. 泥土占卜（抓沙撒地，按其所成像以断吉凶）；风水。

⑯the temporal relations：

temporal /ˈtempərəl/ adj. （表示）时间的，时态的；世俗的；现世的：temporal and spatial boundaries 时间和空间的界限；the temporal possessions of the Church 教堂拥有的世俗的财产。

⑰topological configurations：地质结构。

topological /tɔpəˈlɔdʒikəl/ adj. 地质学的；拓扑学的。

⑱rationale：/ræʃəˈnɑːl/ n. 基本原理；基本理论，理论基础；原理的说明或解释。

⑲which has no Occidental counterpart, is much more than an arbitrary excuse for demonstrating social clout：

occidental /ɔksiˈdentəl/ n. 欧美人，西方人；adj. 西洋的，西方的。counterpart /ˈkauntəpɑːt/ n. 副本，极相似的人或物，配对物：Night really has no counterpart to the day's sun since moonlight is only reflected light. 实际上，黑夜并不是白天太阳的配对物，因为月光只不过是反射光。arbitrary /ˈɑːbitrəri/ adj. 任意的，武断的，独裁的，专断的：an arbitrary interpretation 武断的解释。clout /klaut/ n. 敲打，轻叩；破布；影响；引力。

⑳intrinsically /inˈtrinsikli/ adv. 固有地，本质地，内在地

㉑Their free use of numerology should not obscure their essentially qualitative character.

numerology /njuːməˈrɔlədʒi/ n. （根据出生日期等数字来解释人的性格或占卜祸福的）数字命理学。obscure /əbˈskjuə/ vt. 使暗；遮掩；使难理解，搞混；使不分明；使失色：His success obscured his failures. 他的成功使他的失败显得微不足道。

㉒"mutation studies" and "resonance studies"：

mutation /mjuːˈteiʃən/ n. 变化；（生）突变；变异，突变种；新种：true point mutation 真点突变。resonance /ˈrezənəns/ n. 共鸣，谐振，共振；回声；反响：atomic resonance 原子共振。

㉓treatises：/ˈtriːtiz/ n. 论文，论述。

㉔the didactic applications of their insights：运用他们的洞察力启发人们。

didactic /diˈdæktik/ adj. 教诲的，教训的；说教的：a didactic(al) manner 启发人的态度。

㉕province：n. （知识、研究的）范围，部门：the province of science 科学领域。

㉖mathematical harmonics：

harmonics /hɑːˈmɔniks/ n. 和声学。

㉗ceremonial：/seriˈməuniəl/ n. 仪式

㉘and petrified it institutionally：从机构上把它固定下来了。

petrify /ˈpetrifai/ vt. 使石（质）化；使坚硬；使僵硬；使麻木；使僵化；使失去活力；使发呆；使迟钝。

㉙astrology and astronomy：占星学和天文学。

astrology /əˈstrɔlədʒi/ n. 占星术，占星学（以观测天象来预卜人间事务的一种方术）。

㉚...which depend in their essence upon precedent, often tended to blur the boundary...：动词短语中，depend 与 upon 被介词短语 in their essence 分隔开了。

precedent /pri'sidənt/ n. 先例。

【 Exercises 】

I. Comprehension Questions

(1) Nathan Sivin says in paragraph one that in the general level of science in different cultures in the world certain basic concepts were established due to their usefulness in making human relations understandable. True _____ ? False _____ ?

(2) If your answer to No. 1 was that the statement was false how would you correct the statement?

(3) According to the author Chinese thought held that there were five general fields of science. What were they?

(4) Chinese mathematics was technically the most sophisticated in the study of the regularities of the motions of the sun and moon (See paragraph 8). True _____ ? False _____ ?

(5) Fengshui is geomancy. True _____ ? False _____ ?

(6) "Geographers have found it [geomancy] intrinsically interesting as the world's only time-proven theoretical approach to the aesthetics of land use." In this sentence Sivin's idea is that the _____ of land use are theoretically assisted and explained by geomancy.
  A. economics
  B. beauty and ugliness
  C. planning

II. Points for Discussion

(1) Considering the basic concepts in traditional Chinese science outlined by this author which would you consider the most relevant to the life of the common people and which were particularly important to the ruling elite and the Emperor?

(2) In the last paragraph the author points out that the thought categories of traditional Chinese science were very different from modern scientific thought in aim, approach and organization. Find two comparative examples to illustrate this great difference and explain the difference.

III. Complete the following sentences with appropriate forms of words or expressions from the passage according to the given meaning in brackets.

(1) The article _____ (include) many important points of the government reconstruction plan.

(2) It was clear that these were vital decisions that _____ (affect) the happiness of everybody.

(3) All the evidence showed that Russia does not have that kind of _____ (influence) in the Far East any more?

(4) She reached her decision only after much _____ (serious thought) .
(5) Why wasn't the convention _____ (condense) into three days? Time is running out.

IV. **Fill in blanks with the appropriate forms of the words and expressions listed below.**

correspond to	commit	obscure	compound
arbitrary	shrug off	extrinsic	counterpart
approach	in turn	seize upon	intrinsic

(1) We _____ a new plan from parts of several former plans.
(2) Recovering the stolen radio was _____ to the main purpose of catching the thief.
(3) The foreign minister is the _____ of the secretary of state.
(4) Recent successes _____ the fact that the company is still in trouble.
(5) What makes it rather disturbing was the _____ circumstances both of my arrest and my subsequent fate in court.
(6) Life becomes possible only when food is converted into energy, which _____ is used to seek more food to grow, to reproduce and to survive.
(7) He had a way of _____ criticism as though it were beneath his notice.
(8) The witness's account _____ fairly closely to the policeman's observations.

Unit 5

Japan

12. Ideology and Imperial Japan[1]

Carol Gluck[2]

> 卡罗尔·格拉克(Carol Gluck)是纽约哥伦比亚大学日本史的教授。她被公认为研究日本近代史的权威人士。这篇文章选自格拉克所撰写的关于明治晚期意识形态思想史的《日本的当代谜团:明治时代晚期的思想意识形态》中第一章"意识形态和日本帝国"。这本书分析了1890至1915年间日本国民价值观的形成和传播,这个时期促进了导致第二次世界大战的极端民族主义。格拉克教授认为,这个过程比起原来所设想的要复杂得多。她不同意19世纪90年代的明治政府把天皇制度强加在日本人民头上这种普遍看法。她的研究结果表明,天皇制度随着不同的时期对复杂的社会有不同的解释,主要取决于当时人民的需求和一些特殊的事件。

I Although no society is innocent of collective notions about itself, some countries have made more of ideology than others. From the time Japan began its deliberate pursuit of "civilization" in the mid-nineteenth century, ideology appeared as a conscious enterprise, a perpetual civic concern, an affair, indeed, of state. Even as the exigencies of institutional transformation were met[3] in the years following the Restoration of 1868, Japanese leaders expressed their sense that institutions alone were insufficient to secure the nation. It was not enough that the polity be centralized, the economy developed, social classes rearranged, international recognition striven for—the people must also be "influenced," their minds and hearts made one.

In 1869, one year after the abolition of feudal rule, traveling missionaries were sent to the countryside to proselytize for the new imperial state.[4] In 1881, a bureaucrat whose own illustrious career[5] was devoted to drafting government legislation, including the Constitution, declared the most urgent national business to be "not government ordinances,[6] but inspiration." While the interest of those in power clearly lay in persuading the population "to yield as the grasses before the wind,"[7] the opposition and others outside the political sphere were no less concerned with their own efforts to arouse the universal sentiment of the people.[8] From the 1880s through the first fifteen years of the twentieth century, Japanese sought first to conceive and then to inculcate an ideology[9] suitable for modern Japan.

This proved no easy task. Although many believed in the desirability—and indeed the efficacy—of national exhortation,[10] few agreed on its substance. The state missionaries in 1869 had briefly propagated Shinto as the Great Way of the new era;[11] the legal bureaucrat in 1881 preferred Chinese and German learning as the vessels of inspiration. In the eighties and nineties some suggested imperial loyalty and filial piety,[12] others, the Japanese aesthetic tradition, still others, sociology. In the early 1900s empire abroad and agrarian values at home were offered as the proper content for civic edification.[13] In Japan, as elsewhere, the process of establishing a national ethos in a changed and changing social setting was a trial-and-error affair.[14] Ideologies of the sort imperial Japan produced were neither created ex nihilo nor adopted ready-made.[15] Without a text or a revelation to serve as a canonical source, views of state and society evolved fitfully, often inconsistently, into changing amalgams of past and present, near and foreign.[16] This fitful and inconsistent process—the making of late Meiji ideology—is the subject of this book.

II In both Japanese and Western writing it is often a disagreeable subject, since it quickly brings to mind Japan of the late 1930s and early 1940s. During those years of militarism and war, the Japanese were said to be imbued with the notion[17] that Japan was the land of the gods, inhabited by a people uniquely superior in the world, who lived together, the whole nation as a single family, under the benevolent guidance of a divine emperor.[18] This picture of a society mobilized by its mythology in service to the national cause was the backdrop against which the subject of tennosei ideorogii, the ideology of the emperor system, was articulated in the early postwar period.[19] In 1945 and 1946 the Japanese sought to understand the constellation of forces[20] that had brought Japan to war, because they felt, as did their American occupiers, that the past was the obstacle to the future. In order for postwar Japan to begin anew, the first reckoning would be with history.[21] In this turbulent intellectual context attention soon centered on the nature and origins of the prewar emperor system. From Douglas MacArthur[22] to the Japan Communist Party, commentators attempted to identify the elements that had been responsible for the events of Japan's dark years.

Ideology figured prominently in almost every rendering.[23] MacArthur described the Japanese as having been made "abject slaves"[24] to "mythological fiction," and the Occupation attempted to liberate them from "an ideology which contributed to their war guilt, defeat, suffering, privation, and present deplorable condition."[25] Maruyama Masao began his famous essay of 1946 with a similar reference to enslavement, war, and an ideology which "succeeded in spreading a many-layered, though invisible, net over the Japanese people," who had yet to be freed of its hold. Other Japanese felt the same way, some to a visceral extent.[26] One writer recalled his chest constricting at the mention of the word "emperor"; the sight of the flag sent spine-chilling tremors through him.[27] The recommended treatment for his "tennosei neurosis" consisted of an aggressive pursuit of the ideas of the emperor system until they plagued him,[28] and the country, no longer. Along with the generals, the bureaucrats, the industrialists, and the landlords, ideology assumed a place on the newly compiled list of prewar forces whose power had to be both examined and purged.[29]

In the years since tennosei ideomogy first appeared on Japan's post-war intellectual agenda, differences of interpretation have generated lively dispute among Japanese historians. But as with so many other issues that were defined in the gripping atmosphere[30] just after the war, the essential nature of the problem has not changed. The outlines of the argument are these: tennosei ideology was the product of the modern emperor system, of the period from 1890, when the Meiji Constitution established the new political structures of modern Japan, until 1945, when these structures collapsed with the surrender. The Meiji government is described as having developed this ideology to legitimate itself and support its modernizing programs. That is, the oligarchs,[31] the bureaucrats, and their ideologues, realizing that some explanation was necessary to secure the cooperation of the people through the rigors of economic development and international expansion, created a state orthodoxy[32] around the figure of the emperor and then imposed it upon the people. The orthodoxy was rigid and flexible at the same time. While its rigidity worked to prevent effective opposition by equating dissent with disloyalty, its vagueness enabled it to adapt its injunctions to different needs,[33] so that sacrifice in war and savings accounts in peace could both be justified in terms of the same national myths. By moralizing and mystifying the nature of the state, politics was depoliticized.[34] All that was required of the citizen was loyal and willing submission, and this he is said to have given as a result of an indoctrination[35] that began in his elementary school years and extended eventually into almost every quarter of his social life. In one of the most common phrases, the people were "shackled" (sokubaku),[36] and any efforts to escape were met first with intensified propaganda in the years after World War I, and then with increasingly repressive measures that culminated in police control of thought in the 1930s.[37]

For most Japanese writers tennosei ideology represents both internal psychological constriction and external political submissiveness in prewar Japanese society. Not only did ideological orthodoxy help ultranationalism and militarism to prevail, but, like the war itself, it represents a blight[38] on Japan's modern experience from which the nation has not fully recovered, even today. The metaphors have changed: what Maruyama called an invisible net became in Irokawa Daikichi's work "an enormous black box into which the Japanese people unknowingly walked." But many of the scholars who study tennosei ideology still do so for therapeutic reasons: they intend to explore whatever national conditions and predispositions[39] enabled the ideology to take hold in the prewar years, and thus prevent its consequences from occurring again. It is for this same reason that Japanese intellectuals keep vigilant watch over what are called "tennosei issues" in Japanese politics today. Whether it is the proposal to revive kigensetsu, the anniversary of the legendary founding of the empire and a prewar national holiday, or the move to reinstate government funds for Yasukuni, the shrine of the war dead and an important religious link in the prewar state orthodoxy—any suggestion of ideological recidivism[40] arouses protest and concern.

Tennosei ideology, defined and established as a scholarly subject in the months after the war, is thus as much a part of postwar intellectual history as it is a reference to the late Meiji period (1890—1912) during which the ideology gradually emerged. But the view from 1945 backward across the decades conferred on the prewar myths a substantiality[41] that they did not possess in the earlier period. The suppression of the late thirties and wartime years had so solidified the civic dogma[42] that it was naturally assumed to have been cohesive, purposive, and effective from the start. Meiji ideology, or for that matter any ideology that stops short of totalitarianism, would not likely have manifested such characteristics in its formative stages,[43] if indeed it ever did.

For ideology, like history, is less thing than process.

III

Before the process can be described, some definition of ideology is required, even if a brief and eclectic[44] one. From the theoretical possibilities available to the late twentieth century student of ideology, I draw the outlines of my subject from an approach common to recent anthropological, sociological, and post-Marxist analyses of the relation between ideas and society. For the anthropologist Clifford Geertz,[45] ideology renders social life significant for those who must live it; by both describing and prescribing, ideology provides "maps of problematic social reality" without which the societal arrangement would seem meaningless and the individual's place in it unclear. Any impression that such maps correspond in some geodetic way to the social topography of a given period,[46] however, is misleading. Ideologies not only reflect and interpret the social realities that sustain them; they also, in Berger and Luckmann's term, construct those realities and remain in constant dialectical relationship with them. ... Since different people construe their world differently, there is always a multiplicity[47] of ideological formations within a society. ... Finally, though one speaks of ideological discourse as if it were singular and static,[48] it is in fact a plural and dynamic field of ideas and practices "within which there are not only continuities and persistent determinations but also tensions, conflicts, resolutions and irresolutions, innovations and actual changes."

[These ideas of ideology] ... have in common certain emphases that are shared here as well. Each considers ideology an essential social element, "not an aberration or a contingent excrescence of History."[49] All societies, in short, produce ideologies which in turn help to reproduce the social order. These definitions thus avoid the common, but restrictive, equation of ideology with a systematic and manipulative political program. They further refrain from substituting terms like "belief system" or "national myth" in the hope that ideology by any other name would be a different matter. ... [Both] Japanese and Western writers retain the post-Marxist concern with the social determination of ideas, insisting that ideological formations be tied to the social groups that produce and are produced by them. Despite the abstraction of the terms, ideology does not march disembodied[50] through time, but exists in a concrete and particular social history that has not only dates but also names and faces.

Defined in this way, the subject under consideration here is the interpretation of the political and social world as the articulate elite lived it—or imagined they lived it—in late nineteenth and early twentieth century Japan. Since it is the eventually dominant versions that concern us, the focus is on the establishment and the ascendant social orders that constituted the ideological mainstream of the late Meiji period. Shared ascendancy notwithstanding,[51] they were a diverse lot, whose efforts display no sign of a calculated or consistent ideological vision, but splinter instead into a jumble of contending positions.[52] Often self-appointed to the task, they attempted to formulate views of state and society that they themselves could believe in, and then to persuade others to believe in them as well. Not cynical propagandists, they believed utterly in their depictions.[53] The maps they redrew, partly along old, partly along new contours,[54] were also, perhaps primarily, for themselves. Not theorists either, they addressed themselves to the people, interested less in argument than in suasion[55] and its power to create kokumin (citizens, or countrymen) of them. Moralists, certainly, they were at home in the hortatory mode, which seemed at once comfortingly Confucian[56] and, in the light of the latest Western treatises on moral education, also reassuringly European. They tackled large issues, defining the meaning of law, the place of politics, the role of the new middle class. They attended to details, the proprieties of imperial ceremony, the reading habits of youth, the extravagance of gold-rimmed spectacles.[57] Impelled almost always by an acute sense of crisis,[58] they prefaced their formulations with dramatic expressions of concern with the present state of social or national affairs. In the gap between what they said—the prefectural governors in 1890 deploring the lack of a unifying moral standard[59]—and what they meant—fearing that the advent of party politics in the first election would unseat them—lay a welter of purposes and cross-purposes[60] in the midst of which different groups and their different views contended.

【 Notes 】

①This selection is from the first chapter, "Ideology and Imperial Japan," in *Japan's Modern Myth: Ideology in the Late Meiji Period*, Princeton University Press, 1985, pp. 3—9. The book analyses the formulation and communication of national civic values in Japan between 1890 and 1915. This was a time which was to contribute to the ultra-nationalism that led to World War II. Professor Gluck's argument that this process was more diverse than previously thought is a new interpretation of the political views in imperial Japan. She disagrees with the widely held view that the emperor system had been imposed on the Japanese people by the Meiji government in the 1890's, finding rather that it varied from time to time as an expression of a complex society, depending on the needs of the people and of particular events in time.

②Carol Gluck (1941—) is Professor of Japanese History at Columbia University, New York and a widely recognized authority on modern Japan.

③... the exigencies of institutional transformation were met... :
exigency /ˈeksidʒənsi/ n. 紧急,危急,迫切;(常用复)迫切的需要;苛求;紧急事件: in this extreme exigency 在这危急关头; meet the exigency of 应付……紧急需要。

④... to proselytize for the new imperial state:
proselytize /ˈprɔsilitaiz/ vt. 改变宗教;改变党籍; vi. 改变宗教,改党;变节。

⑤illustrious: /iˈlʌstriəs/ adj. 杰出的;著名的;光荣的;辉煌的,有光泽的: illustrious accomplishments 杰出成就; illustrious acts 光荣的行为。

⑥ordinance: /ˈɔːdinəns/ n. 法令;条例;布告;训令;传统的风俗习惯: an Imperial ordinance(英)敕令。

⑦While the interest of those in power clearly lay in persuading the population "to yield as the grasses before the wind"... : 虽然这些掌权人的兴趣明显地在于要说服公众服从,就像风一吹草就低头一样。

⑧... to arouse the universal sentiment of the people: 唤起全体人民的感情。
sentiment /ˈsentimənt/ n. 感情;情绪;情操;柔情,温情;脆弱的感情: There's no place for sentiment in business. 做生意不能感情用事。general sentiment 一般意见,舆论。

⑨... to inculcate an ideology... :
inculcate /inˈkʌlkeit/ vt. 谆谆教诲(劝导): inculcate a doctrine in a person's mind 把某一教义(或学说)反复讲述灌输到某人头脑中; inculcate the young with a sense of duty 向年轻人灌输责任感。

⑩... and indeed the efficacy—of national exhortation... :
efficacy /ˈefikəsi/ n. (= efficacity) 效力(益,能)。new efficacy 新增效益。exhortation /egzɔːˈteiʃən/ n. 劝告,讲道词,训词;vt. 规劝,告诫,勉(激)励,敦促;倡导: exhort sb. to do sth. 劝某人做某事。

⑪... propagated Shinto as the Great Way of the new era:
Shinto /ˈʃintəu/ n. 日本之神道教,1945 年前为日本国教。

⑫... imperial loyalty and filial piety: 对帝国虔诚的效忠。
filial /ˈfiliəl/ adj. 子女的,孝顺的: filial respect 对父母的孝敬。piety /ˈpaiəti/ n. 虔诚,孝行。

⑬... as the proper contect for civic edification:
civic /ˈsivik/ adj. 市的,市民的,公民的。edification /edifiˈkeiʃən/ n. (尤指道德或精神方面的)教诲,启迪,熏陶。

⑭... the process of establishing a national ethos in a changed and changing social setting was a trial-and-error affair:
ethos /ˈiːθəs/ n. 气质,道义,民族精神;社会思潮,风气: cultural ethos 文化精华。trial-and-error adj. 反复实验的;n. 尝试—错误,试错法;反复实验。

⑮ ...neither created ex nihilo nor adopted ready-made：既不是无中生有地创造一种东西,也不是接受一种现成的东西。

ex nihilo /eksˈnaihiləu/（拉）从无,出于无。

⑯ Without a text or a revelation to serve as a canonical source, views of state and society evolved fitfully, often inconsistently, into changing amalgams of past and present, near and foreign.

revelation /reviˈleiʃən/ n. 显示,揭露；被揭露的事；新发现；启示,揭示：revelations about her past 关于她过去情况的泄露。canonical /kəˈnɔnikəl/ adj. 规范的；按照教规的；见于宗教经典的；权威的,权威性的；教士的,牧师的。amalgam /əˈmælgəm/ n. 混合物；汞合金：an amalgam of strength, reputation, and commitment to ethical principles 力量、名誉和坚信民族信念的结合体。

⑰ ...to be imbued with the notion...：

imbue /imˈbju:/ vt.（与 with 连用）（用感情）充满；灌输；影响：be imbued with new ideas 受新思想的影响。

⑱ ...under the benevolent guidance of a divine emperor：

benevolent /biˈnevələnt/ adj. 慈善的；善意的；行善的；仁爱的,仁慈的：her benevolent smile 她那和蔼可亲的微笑。divine /diˈvain/ adj. 神的；上帝的；天赐的；非常非常好的；极好的：a divine emperor 天皇；divine songs 圣歌；divine intelligence 非凡的才能。

⑲ This picture of a society mobilized by its mythology in service to the national cause was the backdrop against which the subject of tennosei ideorogii, the ideology of the emperor system, was articulated in the early postwar period. 在这个复合句中,主句中的主语 this picture 和谓语 was 被介词短语 of a society mobilized by its mythology in service to the national cause 分隔开了。against which 引导了一个定语从句,修饰 backdrop,意思是在这种背景的陪衬下。tennosei ideorogii 是法语同位语, the ideology of the emperor system 解释了作为同位语的它的意思,即天皇制度的意识形态。

backdrop /ˈbækdrɔp/ n. 背景幕,(事件的)背景。

⑳ ...the constellation of forces...：

constellation /kɔnstəˈleiʃən/ n.［天］星群,星座；灿烂的一群；荟萃群集或会合,尤指杰出的人或物：a constellation of demands ranging from better food to improved health care 一系列从更好的食物到改善的医疗保健的不同要求。

㉑ ...to begin anew, the first reckoning would be with history：

anew /əˈnju:/ adv. 再,重新：start anew 重新开始。reckoning /ˈrekəniŋ/ n. 计算；估计：Short reckoning makes long friends. 好兄弟勤算账。

㉒ Douglas MacArthur：麦克阿瑟(1880—1964),美国五星级上将。1945 年 9 月 2 日在东京湾主持日本投降仪式。1945—1951 年间,以盟军最高司令官的身份执行占领日本的任务。

㉓ rendering：/ˈrendəriŋ/ n. 翻译；表现,描写；表演：He gave a splendid rendering of the song. 他这首歌唱得好极了。

㉔ "abject slaves"：

107

abject /ˈæbdʒekt/ adj. 卑鄙的；下贱的；不幸的；可怜的：an abject liar 卑鄙的说谎者；abject poverty 一贫如洗。

㉕ ...privation, and present deplorable condition：
privation /praiˈveiʃən/ n. （生活必需品的）匮乏；穷困；艰难：Without heat or food he suffered privation. 既没有暖气，又没有食物，他吃尽了苦头。deplorable /diˈplɔːrəbl/ adj. 可悲的，令人遗憾的；极糟糕的：in deplorable order 极杂乱；deplorable housing conditions in the inner city 城市里面糟糕的住房条件。

㉖ ...to a visceral extent：
visceral /ˈvisərəl/ n. 内脏的；出自内心的；内心深处的；深奥的；本能的：visceral needs 本能的需要。

㉗ ...spine-chilling tremors through him：
spine-chilling adj. 令人毛骨悚然的。tremor /ˈtremə/ n. 震动；地震；震颤；颤抖；抖动：felt a tremor of joy 感到一阵欣喜。

㉘ ...for his "tennosei neurosis" consisted of an aggressive pursuit of the ideas of the emperor system until they plagued him...：
neurosis /njuəˈrəusis/ n. (-ses) 神经官能症；精神神经病。plague /pleig/ vt. 折磨，使苦恼，使得灾祸：He was plagued by his strange ideas until he went crazy and died. 他受到各种奇奇怪怪想法的折磨，直到发疯和死亡。

㉙ ...whose power had to be both examined and purged：
purge /pəːdʒ/ vt. 清洗；洗涤；Try to purge your spirit of hatred. 尽量涤净你灵魂中的仇恨。（常与 of, from 连用）整肃；排除异己；清除（坏人）。

㉚ the gripping atmosphere：
gripping /ˈgraipiŋ/ adj. 引起人注意的；吸引人的：a gripping novel 引人入胜的小说。

㉛ the oligarchs：oligarch /ˈɔligɑːk/ n. 寡头政治的执政者（支持者）：a financial oligarch 金融寡头。

㉜ ...through the rigors of economic development and international expansion, created a state orthodoxy...：
rigor /ˈrigə/ n. 严峻；严肃；严厉；（法律等的）严格执行；严密；艰苦；困苦；（常用复）（气候等的）凛烈：with the utmost rigor of the law 最严格地依法（办理等）。orthodoxy /ˈɔːθədɔksi/ n. 信奉正教；正教，正统学说。

㉝ ...by equating dissent with disloyalty, its vagueness enabled it to adapt its injunctions to different needs...：
equate /iˈkweit/ vt. （常与 to, with 连用）使相等：You can't equate his poems with his plays. 你不能把他的诗跟剧本相提并论。dissent /diˈsent/ n. 异议；不同意；意见不一致；vi. （常与 from 连用）持异议；不同意；意见不一致：He and I dissented from each other in choosing a suitable candidate. 他和我在选择适当的人选这个问题上意见不一致。injunction /inˈdʒʌŋkʃən/ n. 命令，责戒，训谕；（律）指令，禁令。

㉞ ...politics was depoliticized：

depoliticize /diːpəˈlitisaiz/ vt. 使非政治化, 使不受政治影响（亦作: depoliticise）: depoliticize foreign aid 使外援非政治化。

㉟ as a result of an indoctrination:
indoctrination /inˌdɔktriˈneiʃən/ n. 教导, 教化; vt. （在基础知识方面）指导, 教授, 灌输以某种学说或信仰: The writer wants to indoctrinate the readers with the idea. 作者想把这种想法灌输给读者。

㊱ …"shackled" (sokubaku):
shackle /ˈʃækl/ vt. 束缚; 桎梏; 上镣铐。

㊲ … with increasingly repressive measures that culminated in police control of thought in the 1930s:
repressive /riˈpresiv/ adj. 压抑的, 压制的。

㊳ …, it represents a blight…:
blight /blait/ n. 枯萎病; 不良影响, 打击; 杂乱; 市容杂乱的地区; 受挫, 被损毁的状态: the blight of litter on the beach 杂乱不堪的海滩; Bankruptcy was the blight of the family. 破产毁坏了这一家。

㊴ …for therapeutic reasons: they intend to explore whatever national conditions and predispositions…:
therapeutic /θerəˈpjuːtik/ adj. 治病的; 治疗术的; 治疗学的: a therapeutic agent; therapeutic exercises 治疗剂; 治疗练习。predisposition /priːdispˈsiʃən/ n. 倾向, 素质; 癖性（to）: natural predisposition 先天素质。

㊵ …or the move to reinstate government funds for Yasukuni, the shrine of the war dead and an important religious link in the prewar state orthodoxy—any suggestion of ideological recidivism…:
reinstate /ˈriːinsteit/ vt. 使恢复原状（原位）; 使恢复（权利等）; 使恢复健康; 修补, 修理: be reinstated in an office (to return some privilege) 复职（恢复特权）。recidivism /riˈsidivizəm/ n. 累犯。

㊶ …conferred on the prewar myths a substantiality…:
confer /kənˈfəː/ vt. (conferred; conferring) 授予, 颁予（称号、学位等）; 赋予; 使具有（性能）: confer a medal /title on/ upon sb. 授与某人以勋章（称号）: conferred an honorary degree on her 授予她荣誉学位; vi. confer with sb. on /about sth. 与某人协商（商议）某事。substantiality /səbˌstænʃiˈæliti/ n. 实在性, 实质性, 实体。

㊷ …had so solidified the civic dogma…:
solidify /səˈlidifai/ vt. 使凝固; 使硬; 使结晶; 使团结一致; 充实, 巩固: solidify one's knowledge 充实学识。dogma /ˈdɔgmə/ n. 教条; 信条: Church dogma 宗教信条。

㊸ …that stops short of totalitarianism, would not likely have manifested such characteristics in its formative stages…:
totalitarianism /təuˌtutæliˈteəriənizm/ n. 极权主义。manifest /ˈmænifest/ vt. 显示, 表明, 指明; 证明; (manifest oneself) 使显现, 使显露: He doesn't manifest much interest in his

studies. 他表现出对学业没多大兴趣。formative /ˈfɔːmətiv/ *adj.* 格式化的；影响形成的；影响发展的：the formative stages of a plot 情节的发展阶段。

㊹eclectic：eclectic /ekˈlektik/ *adj.* 折中的，折中学派的；*n.* 折中主义者，折中派的人。

㊺Clifford Geertz：格尔茨(1926—)美国文化人类学学者，也是一名重要的修辞家以及符号人类学和释义人类学的倡导者。

㊻... correspond in some geodetic way to the social topography of a given period...：
geodetic /dʒiːəˈdetik/ *adj.* 大地测量学的；大地线的；(最)短程线的。topography /təˈpɔgərəfi/ *n.* 地形学；地形；地势。

㊼... there is always a multiplicity...：
multiplicity /mʌltiˈplisiti/ *n.* 大数目；多种多样；繁多：the multiplicity of architectural styles on that street 那条街上建筑风格多种多样。

㊽static /ˈstætik/ *adj.* 静止的，静态的；呆板的；乏味的

㊾... "not an aberration or a contingent excrescence of History"：
aberration /æbəˈreiʃən/ *n.* 脱离常轨规；失常：a mental aberration 精神失常。events that were aberrations from the norm 不合常规的事件。contingent /kənˈtindʒənt/ *adj.* (常与 on, upon 连用)偶然的；偶发性的；附带的；可能发生的；可能的；或有的：a contingent event 意外事件；a contingent fund 应急费用。excrescence /iksˈkresns/ *n.* 多余物，长出物，赘疣，瘤：glacier excrescence 冰川上的隆起。

㊿... ideology does not march disembodied...：
disembodied /disimˈbɔdid/ *adj.* 无实体的；空洞的；空虚的：Disembodied voices could be heard in the darkness. 在黑暗中听见了人声，却看不见人影。

(51)Shared ascendancy notwithstanding, ...：
ascendancy /əˈsendənsi/ *n.* 优势；权势；主权；支配地位：get the ascendancy over 占优势；对……占支配地位。
notwithstanding /nɔtwiθˈstændiŋ/ *prep.* 虽然，尽管；*adv.* 尽管，还是；*conj.* 虽然，尽管。

(52)... but splinter instead into a jumble of contending positions：
splinter /ˈsplintə/ *vt.*, *vi.* (使)裂成碎片，(使)分裂：Opinions are splintered now. 现在意见纷纭。jumble /ˈdʒʌmbl/ *n.* 一堆；一团糟；混杂(混乱的)一团(一堆)；杂乱：jumble sale 旧杂货拍卖。contend /kənˈtend/ *vi.* (常与 with 连用)竞争；争取：to contend for a prize 为奖品而竞争；争论；辩论；声称：The man contends that it was not his fault. 那人争辩说这不是他的过错。

(53)depiction /diˈpikʃən/ *n.* 描写，叙述

(54)contours /ˈkɔntuə/ *n.* 轮廓；外形；周线；海岸线；等高线；a contour map 等高线地图。

(55)suasion /ˈsweiʃən/ *n.* 劝告，说服：moral suasion 道义上的劝告。

(56)... in the hortatory mode, which seemed at once comfortingly Confucian...：
hortatory /ˈhɔːtətəri/ *adj.* 督促的；劝告的；激励的：a hortatory speech 激励性演讲。comfortingly /ˈkʌmfətiɔŋli/ *adv.* 安慰地；令人鼓舞地。Confucian /kənˈfjuːʃ(ə)n/ *adj.* 孔子学说的，儒学的；*n.* 儒家学者。

(57)They attended to details, the proprieties of imperial ceremony, the reading habits of youth, the extravagance of gold-rimmed spectacles.

attend to 专心，注意，照顾；倾听，留心；关心。propriety /prə'praiəti/ *n.* 礼节；规矩；行为规范：observe the proprieties 遵守礼节；依照社交惯例。extravagance /ik'strævəgəns/ *n.* 奢侈，铺张，过度，放纵的言行。gold-rimmed spectacles 金玳瑁框眼镜。

(58)Impelled almost always by an acute sense of crisis...:

impel /im'pel/ *vt.* (-ll-) 推进；驱使：He said he had been impelled to crime by poverty. 他说他被穷困所逼而犯罪。acute /ə'kjuːt/ *adj.* 敏锐的；灵敏的；剧烈的；严重的：an acute sense of smell 灵敏的嗅觉；an acute lack of research funds 研究经费的严重短缺。

(59)... the prefectural governors in 1890 deploring the lack of a unifying moral standard...:

prefectural /priː'fektʃuərəl/ *adj.* 地方官的。deplore /di'plɔː/ *vt.* 悲悼，痛惜；悔恨；指责：deplore one's faults 悔恨失误。

(60)... would unseat them—lay a welter of purposes and cross-purposes...:

unseat /'ʌn'siːt/ *vt.* 使(从马背或自行车上)摔下来；罢免，免去……席位：He was unseated at the General Election and lost his seat in the House of Commons. 他在大选中落选，失去了下议院席位。welter /'weltə/ *n.* (与 of 连用)杂乱无章；混乱；翻腾；起伏：a welter of words 乱七八糟的词句。cross-purpose *n.* 相反的目的，不一致的目的。

【Exercises】

I. Comprehension Questions

(1) After the Restoration of 1868 (the Meiji Restoration) Japanese leaders thought the ideology of the state was not as essential to accomplishing the changes underway as institutions, the economy, and international recognition. True ________? False ________?

(2) The purpose of the book Carol Gluck is writing is to ________.

A. identify the true nature of the Meiji era ideology.

B. investigate the process of the production of the Meiji ideology

(3) Professor Gluck thinks that tennosei ideology (Emperor ideology) ________

A. was completely established in the Meiji period (1868—1912) and never changed

B. did not appear until after World War II

C. began in the Meiji era and flourished during World War II, then ceased to exist in post-war Japan

D. was a part of the Japanese post World War II period thinking as well as the Meiji and pre WW II thinking but changed in nature through time (See all of Section II and especially the last paragraph.)

(4) The author is very interested in what ideology is and how it works in relation to society.

After a long discussion giving examples from Clifford Geertz, and Berger and Luckmann (See the first paragraph of Section III) she writes that—the influence of Marxism led to the denial of the idea that social groups produced and are produced by ideology. Is this statement of her idea true or false _____?

II. Points for Discussion

(1) Using Gluck's ideas about the relation of ideology and society, was it inevitable that Japanese nationalism went in the direction it did by the 1930's? Explain your opinion with illustrations from your knowledge of Japanese culture and society. What different directions might the Japanese social order have taken, keeping in mind the relation of society and ideology and the existence of the Emperor ideology?

(2) What other countries show a strong historical relationship between ideology and society? Explain your opinion using a historians approach.

(3) From Gluck's discussion of tennosei ideology in the late 19th and early 20th centuries write out and explain your own definition, keeping in mind the Japanese historical experience, of the Japanese Emperor ideology in the 20th century.

III. Complete the following sentences with words or expressions from the passage similar in meaning to the words in brackets.

(1) _____ (speak clearly) your words carefully so that everyone in the room can understand you.

(2) As you knew, my finances were in a _____ (bad) state of neglect.

(3) Her husband was captured and sent to an unknown prison camp somewhere, but years of waiting _____ (result in) a tearful reunion.

(4) Though we had a firm belief that the economy was booming, the contradiction _____ (demonstrate) itself in the employment situation.

(5) Winston S. Churchill pointed out that Germany only awaited trade revival to gain an immense mercantile _____ (superiority).

(6) It is clear that the _____ (outline) of the Atlantic coast of America is very irregular.

(7) Her grandmother still has very _____ (sharp) hearing, though she is eighty years old.

IV. Complete the following sentences with the words or expressions from the passage given below. Change the form where necessary.

inculcate	backdrop	privation	by trial and error
constellation equate	lay in confer	imbue	deplore
serve as	contend	impel	take hold
visceral	justify	blight	confer

(1) We have learned to _____ students with love of knowledge _____.

112

(2) A president should _____ with a sense of responsibility for the nation.

(3) The important events at the beginning of the century provided the _____ for his novel.

(4) The symposium was attended by a _____ of artists and writers.

(5) _____ of the company of all other human beings is a serious hardship.

(6) The scientific approach to life is not really appropriate to states of _____ anguish.

(7) Nowadays, many people _____ passing examinations with being educated.

(8) Sudden loss of fortune came as a _____ to his hopes of going abroad.

(9) This was a carefully worded statement that _____ an aura of credibility onto the administration's actions

(10) The official in the tax office _____ that the shopkeeper was innocent.

(11) We were _____ by circumstances to take a stand. I doubt the propriety of doing so.

(12) Henry A. Kissinger said that somehow they had to master events, not simply _____ them.

Unit 6

South Asia

13. On Some Aspects of the Historiography of Colonial India[1]

Ranajit Guha[2]

> 雷纳吉特·古哈(Ranajit Guha)是居住在澳大利亚堪培拉的印度历史学家和政治经济学家。他是《从属阶层的研究:南亚历史和社会》的主编。这一套书至少有五卷,于1982年在德里首次出版。他收集、出版了大量从非上层和非殖民主义观点来描写印度的著作。
>
> 在研究印度的过程中,研究从属阶层的历史学家认为,历史不仅是上层,而且也是从属阶层所创造的。从属阶层这个词在字典中的含义是低层的,而在这些著作中,按照阶级、世袭地位、年龄、性别、官职,作者用这个词表明了南亚社会从属阶层的特点。

1. The historiography of Indian nationalism has for a long time been dominated by elitism—colonialist elitism and bourgeoisnationalist elitism.[3] Both originated as the ideological product of British rule in India, but have survived the transfer of power and been assimilated to neocolonialist and neonationalist forms of discourse in Britain and India respectively.[4] Elitist historiography of the colonialist or neocolonialist type counts British writers and institutions among its principal protagonists,[5] but has its imitators in India and other countries too. Elitist historiography of the nationalist or neonationalist type is primarily an Indian practice.

2. Both these varieties of elitism share the prejudice that the making of the Indian nation and the development of the consciousnessnationalism which informed this process were exclusively or predominantly elite achievements. In the colonialist and neocolonialist historiographies these achievements are credited to British colonial rulers, administrators, policies, institutions and culture; in the nationalist and neonati-

onalist writings to Indian elite personalities, institutions, activities and ideas.

3. The first of these two historiographies defines Indian nationalism primarily as a function of stimulus and response. Based on a narrowly behaviouristic approach this represents nationalism as the sum of the activities and ideas[6] by which the Indian elite responded to the institutions, opportunities, resources, etc. generated by colonialism. There are several versions of this historiography, but the central modality[7] common to them is to describe Indian nationalism as a sort of "learning process" through which the native elite became involved in politics by trying to negotiate the maze[8] of institutions and the corresponding cultural complex introduced by the colonial authorities in order to govern the country. What made the elite go through this process was, according to this historiography, no lofty idealism addressed to the general good of the nation but simply the expectation of rewards in the form of a share in the wealth, power and prestige created by and associated with colonial rule; and it was the drive for such rewards with all its concomitant play of collaboration and competition[9] between the ruling power and the native elite as well as between various elements among the latter themselves. which, we are told, was what constituted Indian nationalism.

4. The general orientation of the other kind of elitist historiography is to represent Indian nationalism as primarily an idealist venture in which the indigenous elite led the people from subjugation to freedom.[10] It upholds Indian nationalism as a phenomenal expression of the goodness of the native elite with the antagonistic aspect of their relation to the colonial regime made, against all evidence, to look larger than its collaborationist aspect, their role as promoters of the cause of the people than that as exploiters and oppressors, their altruism and self-abnegation than their scramble for the modicum of power and privilege granted by the rulers in order to make sure of their support for the Raj.[11] The history of Indian nationalism is thus written up as a sort of spiritual biography of the Indian elite.

5. What, however, historical writing of this kind cannot do is to explain Indian nationalism for us. For it fails to acknowledge, far less interpret, the contribution made by the people on their own, that is, independently of the elite to the making and development of this nationalism. In this particular respect the poverty of this historiography is demonstrated beyond doubt by its failure to understand and assess the mass articulation of this nationalism except, negatively, as a law and order problem, and positively, if at all, either as a response to the charisma of certain elite leaders

or in the currently more fashionable terms of vertical mobilization by the manipulation of factions.[12] The involvement of the Indian people in vast numbers, sometimes in hundreds of thousands or even millions, in nationalist activities and ideas is thus represented as a diversion from a supposedly "real" political process, that is, the grinding away of the wheels of the state apparatus and of elite institutions geared to it, or it is simply credited, as an act of ideological appropriation, to the influence and initiative of the elite themselves.[13]

6. This inadequacy of elitist historiography follows directly from the narrow and partial view of politics to which it is committed by virtue of its class outlook. In all writings of this kind the parameters of Indian politics are assumed to be or enunciated as[14] exclusively or primarily those of the institutions introduced by the British for the government of the country and the corresponding sets of laws, policies, attitudes and other elements of the superstructure. Inevitably, therefore, a historiography hamstrung by such a definition can do no more than to equate politics with the aggregation of activities and ideas of those[15] who were directly involved in operating these institutions, that is, the colonial rulers and their *élèves*—the dominant groups in native society. To the extent that their mutual transactions were thought to be all there was to Indian nationalism, the domain of the latter is regarded as coincident with that of politics.[16]

7. What clearly is left out of this unhistorical historiography is the politics of the people. For parallel to the domain of elite politics there existed throughout the colonial period another domain of Indian politics in which the principal actors were not the dominant groups of the indigenous society or the colonial authorities but the subaltern classes and groups constituting the mass of the labouring population and the intermediate strata in town and country, that is, the people.[17] This was an autonomous domain for it neither originated from elite politics nor did its existence depend on the latter. It was traditional only in so far as its roots could be traced back to precolonial times, but it was by no means archaic in the sense of being outmoded.[18] Far from being destroyed or rendered virtually ineffective, as was elite politics of the traditional type by the intrusion of colonialism, it continued to operate vigorously in spite of the latter, adjusting itself to the conditions prevailing under the Raj and in many respects developing entirely new strains in both form and content. As modern as indigenous elite politics, it was distinguished by its relatively greater depth in time as well as structure.

8. One of the more important features of this politics related precisely to those aspects of mobilization which are so little explained by elitist historiography. Mobilization in the domain of elite politics was achieved vertically whereas in that of subaltern politics this was achieved horizontally. The instrumentation of the former was characterized by a relatively greater reliance on the colonial adaptations of British parliamentary institutions and the residua of semifeudal political institutions of the precolonial period;[19] that of the latter relied rather more on the traditional organization of kinship and territoriality or on class associations, depending on the level of the consciousness of the people involved. Elite mobilization tended to be relatively more legalistic and constitutionalist in orientation, subaltern mobilization relatively more violent. The former was, on the whole, more cautious and controlled, the latter more spontaneous. Popular mobilization in the colonial period was realized in its most comprehensive form in peasant uprisings.

9. In spite of [the diversity of its social composition] one of its invariant features was a notion of resistance to elite domination. This followed from the subalternity common to all the social constituents of this domain and as such distinguished it sharply from that of elite politics.

10. Yet another set of the distinctive features of this politics derived from the conditions of exploitation to which the subaltern classes were subjected in varying degrees as well as from its relation to the productive labour of the majority of its protagonists, that is. workers and peasants, and to the manual and intellectual labour respectively of the nonindustrial urban poor and the lower sections of the petty bourgeoisie. The experience of exploitation and labour endowed this politics with many idioms, norms and values[20] which put it in a category apart from elite politics.

11. These and other distinctive features helped to demarcate the domain of subaltern politics from that of elite politics.[21] The coexistence of these two domains or streams was the index of an important historical truth,. that is, the failure of the Indian bourgeoisie to speak for the nation. There were vast areas in the life and consciousness of the people which were never integrated into their hegemony.[22] The structural dichotomy that arose from this is a datum of Indian history of the colonial period,[23] which no one who sets out to interpret it can ignore without falling into error.

12. Such dichotomy did not, however, mean that these two domains were hermetically sealed off from each other[24] and there was no contact between them. On the

contrary, there was a great deal of overlap arising precisely from the effort made from time to time by the more advanced elements among the indigenous elite, especially the bourgeoisie, to integrate them. The braiding together of the two strands of elite and subaltern politics led invariably to explosive situations[25] indicating that the masses mobilized by the elite to fight for their own objectives managed to break away from their control and put the characteristic imprint of popular politics on campaigns initiated by the upper classes.

13. However, the initiatives which originated from the domain of subaltern politics were not, on their part, powerful enough to develop the nationalist movement into a fullfledged struggle[26] for national liberation. The outcome of it all was that the numerous peasant uprisings of the period, some of them massive in scope and rich in anticolonialist consciousness, waited in vain for a leadership to raise them above localism and generalize them into a nationwide antiimperialist campaign. Much of the sectional struggle of workers, peasants and the urban petty bourgeoisie either got entangled in economism or, wherever politicized, remained, for want of a revolutionary leadership, far too fragmented to form effectively into anything like a national liberation movement.[27]

14. It is the study of this historic failure of the nation to come to its own, a failure due to the inadequacy of the bourgeoisie as well as of the working class to lead it into a decisive victory over colonialism and a bourgeois democratic revolution of either the classic nineteenth century type under the hegemony of the bourgeoisie or a more modern type under the hegemony of workers and peasants, that is, a "new democracy" it is the study of this failure which constitutes the central problematic of the historiography of colonial India. There is no one given way of investigating this problematic. Let a hundred flowers blossom and we don't mind even the weeds. We are also convinced that elitist historiography should be resolutely fought by developing an alternative discourse based on the rejection of the spurious and unhistorical monism[28] characteristic of its view of Indian nationalism and on the recognition of the coexistence and interaction of the elite and subaltern domains of politics.

A note on the terms "elite," "people," "subaltern," etc. as used above:

The term "elite" has been used in this statement to signify dominant groups, foreign as well as indigenous. The dominant foreign groups included all the nonIndian, that is, mainly British officials of the colonial state and foreign industrialists, merchants, financiers, planters, landlords and missionaries.

The dominant indigenous groups included classes and interests operating at two levels. At the allIndia level they included the biggest feudal magnates, the most important representatives of the industrial and mercantile bourgeoisie and native recruits to the uppermost levels of the bureaucracy.

At the regional and local levels they represented such classes and other elements as were either members of the dominant allIndia groups included in the previous category or if belonging to social strata hierarchically inferior to those of the dominant allIndia groups still acted in the interests of the latter and not in conformity to interests corresponding truly to their own social being.

The terms "people" and "subaltern classes" have been used as synonymous throughout this note. The social groups and elements included in this category represent the demographic difference between the total Indian population and all those whom we have described as the "elite". Some of these classes and groups such as the lesser rural gentry, impoverished landlords, rich peasants and uppermiddle peasants who "naturally" ranked among the "people" and the "subaltern", could under certain circumstances act for the "elite" and therefore be classified as such in some local or regional situations an ambiguity which it is up to the historian to sort out on the basis of a close and judicious reading of his evidence .

【 Notes 】

①This selection is from "On Some Aspects of the Historiography of Colonial India" in *Selected Subaltern Studies*, edited by R. Guha and G. C. Spivak, Oxford University Press, 1988, pp. 37—44. The Subaltern Studies Collective, founded in 1982, began with the goal of creating a critique of the existing colonialist and nationalist perspectives in the historiography of colonized countries. The most well known members Ranajit Guha, Gayatri Spivak, and Partha Chatterjeewere instrumental in establishing what is now known as Postcolonial Studies. The essays written by the collective scholars moved from the early interest of subaltern history in peasant revolts and popular insurgency to the study of the more complex processes of domination and subordination in many of the changing institutions and practices in modern times.

Focusing on India, the Subaltern Studies historians show that history is made by the subaltern classes as well as the elite. "Subaltern", according to the dictionary, means "of inferior rank." It is used in these writings to indicate the characteristics of subordination in South Asian society in terms of class, caste, age, gender and office. These historians were particularly influenced by the Italian Marxist historian and theoretician, Antonio Gramsci, who developed the idea of subalternity.

②Ranajit Guha is an Indian historian and political economist living in Canberra, Australia and now retired. He is the editor of a series of at least five volumes, Subaltern Studies: Writings in South Asian History and Society, which began to appear in Delhi in 1982. He gathered, through his editorship of the series, a collective of historians who write about India from a nonelitist, noncolonialist viewpoint.

③The historiography of Indian nationalism has for a long time been dominated by elitismcolonialist elitism and bourgeoisnationalist elitism. 在这个简单句中, for a long time 把谓语部分 has 与 been dominated 分隔开了。elitismcolonialist elitism and bourgeoisnationalist elitism 高人一等的殖民者统治论和资产阶级民族主义者统治论。

④...assimilated to neocolonialist and neonationalist forms of discourse in Britain and India respectively:
assimilate /ə'simileit/ vt. 吸收, 消化; 使同化(into, with); 使相似, 使相同, 使成一样; 把……比作(to, with): assimilate life to a dream 把人生比作梦。discourse /'diskɔ:s/ n. 演说; 演讲; 谈话; 论文。

⑤...among its principal protagonists...:
protagonist /prəu'tægənist/ n. (戏剧, 故事, 小说中的)主角, 领导者; 提倡者; 支持者: the protagonists of big business 大企业的首脑人物; The negative protagonists in the play inspire hate in me. 该剧中的反面角色激起我心中的仇恨。

⑥Based on a narrowly behaviouristic approach this represents nationalism as the sum of the activities and ideas...:
behaviouristic /beheivjə'risitik/ adj. 行动主义的。the sum (and substance) of 要点, 要义, 精义; 概略: the sum of this book 这本书的要点。

⑦modality /məu'dæliti/ n. 形式, 形态, 特征。

⑧maze /meiz/ n. 迷宫; 错综复杂的曲径: a maze of government regulations 纷乱的政府条例; a maze of thoughts 千思万绪; a maze of narrow winding streets 迂曲的街道。

⑨...with all its concomitant play of collaboration and competition...: 利用伴随在协作和竞争中而产生的一切作用。
concomitant /kənkɔmi'tənt/ adj. 相伴的, 伴生、附随的: concomitant circumstances 伴随的情况。

⑩from subjugation to freedom: 从被征服到获得自由。
subjugation /sʌbdju'geiʃən/ n. 镇压, 平息, 征服。

⑪It upholds Indian nationalism as a phenomenal expression of the goodness of the native elite with the antagonistic aspect of their relation to the colonial regime made, against all evidence, to look larger than its collaborationist aspect, their role as promoters of the cause of the people than that as exploiters and oppressors, their altruism and selfabnegation than their scramble for the modicum of power and privilege granted by the rulers in order to make sure of their support for the Raj. 这个长句是个主从复合句。made 引导出的分词短语一直到句末 the Raj, 修饰 the colonial regime。在这个短语中, against all evidence 是插入语; made to look larger

than... 使其看起来比... 更重要; made their role as... than... 使他们的作用是……而不是……; granted by... 这个分词短语修饰 power and privilege。
antagonistic /æntæg'nistik/ *adj.* 对抗性的; 敌对的。altruism /'æltruizəm/ *n.* 利他主义。abnegation /æbni'geiʃən/ *n.* 放弃; 克制。scramble /'skræmbl/ *n.* 攀登; 爬; 抢夺, 争夺: scramble for power and wealth 争权夺利。modicum /'mɔdikm/ *n.* 少量: a modicum of sleep 小睡。Raj /rɑːdʒ/ *n.* 统治; 支配。

⑫ ...either as a response to the charisma of certain elite leaders or in the currently more fashionable terms of vertical mobilization by the manipulation of factions. 或者作为对某些高层领导超凡魅力的反响或者用现在更时髦的话来说,通过操纵派系斗争来直接鼓动。
manipulation /mənipʃuleiʃən/ *n.* 处理, 操作, 操纵, 被操纵。

⑬ The involvement of the Indian people in vast numbers, sometimes in hundreds of thousands or even millions, in nationalist activities and ideas is thus represented as a diversion from a supposedly "real" political process, that is, the grinding away of the wheels of the state apparatus and of elite institutions geared to it, or it is simply credited, as an act of ideological appropriation, to the influence and initiative of the elite themselves. 这个长句是一个并列句。or 后面是第二个分句。在第一个分句中,主语部分 The involvement... in nationalist activities and ideas 被定语 of the Indian people in vast numbers, sometimes in hundreds of thousands or even millions 分隔开了。在第二个分句中,谓语部分 is simply credited ... to the influence and initiative of the elite themselves 被作为插入语的介词短语 as an act of ideological appropriation 分隔开了。
grind away 磨掉(光); the state apparatus 国家机构; credit...to... 把……归功于; 把某数记入某人账户: He is credited with the invention. 那发明该归功于他。Please credit my account with $1000. 请将1000美元存入我的账户。

⑭ ...the parameters of Indian politics are assumed to be or enunciated as...:
parameter /pə'ræmitə/ *n.* 参数, 参量; 〈口〉起限定作用的因素: policy parameter 政策参数。all the parameters of shelter — where people will live, what mode of housing they will choose, and how they will pay for it 住宿的所有限制因素——人们住在哪里、他们将选择什么样的住房式样以及他们如何付房钱。enunciate /i'nʌnsieit/ *v.* 阐明, 清晰发言, 宣布, 发表(学说等): enunciate views 发表见解; enunciate a doctrine. 阐述一个信条。

⑮ ...a historiography hamstrung by such a definition can do no more than to equate politics with the aggregation of activities and ideas of those...:
hamstring /'hæmstriŋ/ *vt.* 割断……的腿筋; 使残废; 减弱……的活动能力; 使无效; 破坏。equate /i'kweit/ *vt.* 使相等, 等同(常与 to, with 连用) 使相等: You can't equate his poems with his plays. 你不能把他的诗跟剧本相提并论。aggregation /ægri'geiʃən/ *n.* 聚集; 集合; 总计; 集合体: urban aggregation 城市聚集。

⑯ To the extent that their mutual transactions were thought to be all there was to Indian nationalism, the domain of the latter is regarded as coincident with that of politics. 对印度的民族主义来说,他们共同处理事务被认为是至关重要的。本土社会统治集团的势力范围被认为相

当于政治势力范围。这是一个主从复合句,为了强调程度状语,把 to the extent that... nationalism 提到了句首。

transaction /træn'zekʃən/ n. 办理;处理;执行;事务,业务,交易:commercial transaction 商业行为;a rich sense of the transaction between writer and reader 作者与读者之间丰富的意识交流。coincident /kəu'insidənt/ adj. 一致的,符合的,巧合的:testimony that was coincident with the actual facts. 与事实相符合的证据。

⑰ ... were not the dominant groups of the indigenous society or the colonial authorities but the subaltern classes and groups constituting the mass of the labouring population and the intermediate strata in town and country, that is, the people.

the indigenous society 本土社会;subaltern classes 下层阶级;subaltern /'sʌbəltən/ adj. 下的,副的,次的;intermediate strata 中间阶层。intermediate /intə'miːdiət/ adj. 中间的;居中的:an intermediate stage 中间阶段。strata /'streitə/ (stratum 的复数) n. 层,地层。

⑱ ... archaic in the sense of being outmoded:
archaic /ɑ'keiik/ adj. 古代的;过时的:an archaic bronze statuette. 一种相当古老的青铜小雕像;archaic laws 已不使用的法律。outmode /aut'məud/ vt. 使不流行;vi. 变旧,变不流行:Equipment becomes outmoded quicker than hairdos. 机械的型式比女人的发式过时得更快。

⑲ ... the residua of semifeudal political institutions of the precolonial period:殖民地时期以前半封建制度政治机构的残余。

residua /ri'zidjuə/ n. 残余物;残基;残渣:solid residue 固体残渣。

⑳ The experience of exploitation and labour endowed this politics with many idioms, norms and values...:这种被剥削和出卖劳动力的经历赋予这种政治许多习惯用语、行为规范以及价值观念。

endow /in'dau/ vt. 捐赠;资助:endow a hospital 捐助一所医院。endow with 赋予;天赋:be endowed with genius 有天才。She is endowed with great writing ability. 她具有杰出的写作天赋。

㉑ ... helped to demarcate the domain of subaltern politics from that of elite politics:促成把上层政治和下层政治的范围区分开了。

demarcate /di'mɑːkeit/ vt. 定界线;划界;定范围;区分;分开:demarcate categories 区分类别。

㉒ ... which were never integrated into their hegemony:
integrate /'intigreit/ vt. 使成整体,使一体化,结合;求……的积分:integrate theory with practice 使理论与实践相结合。

㉓ The structural dichotomy...:
dichotomy /dai'kɔtəmi/ n. 两分,二分法,分裂:the dichotomy of the one and the many 一个人与许多人的二分法。

㉔ ... hermetically sealed off from each other...:严密地互相封锁。
hermetically /həː'metikli/ adv. 密封地;炼金术地。

㉕The braiding together of the two strands of elite and subaltern politics led invariably to explosive situations... :

braiding /ˈbreidiŋ/ *n.* 编织物；缏饰。strand /strænd/ *n.* 绳，线；海滨，河岸。explosive /iksˈpləusiv/ *adj.* 会爆炸的；激起感情的：The question of race today is an explosive one. 种族问题在今天是一个会引起激烈争论的问题。

㉖a fullfledged struggle：成熟的斗争。

fullfledged /ˈfulˈfledʒd/ *adj.* 成熟的；完全有资格的：a fullfledged lawyer 完全合格的律师。

㉗Much of the sectional struggle of workers, peasants and the urban petty bourgeoisie either got entangled in economism or, wherever politicized, remained, for want of a revolutionary leadership, far too fragmented to form effectively into anything like a national liberation movement. 这个句子的主、谓语部分是：Much of the sectional struggle... either got entangled in economism or remained far too fragmented. 其他短语把句子的这些主要部分分隔开了。

entangle /inˈtæŋgl/ *vt.* 使缠上，纠缠，卷入，使混乱：The ropes were entangled so I was not able to untie the parcel. 绳子缠在一起了,所以我没能解开包裹。be entangled in 陷入（困境）卷入；牵连；缠住：A sparrow became/got entangled in the net/wire. 一只麻雀给缠在网/铁丝网里了。

㉘the spurious and unhistorical monism：

spurious /ˈspjuəriəs/ *adj.* 伪造的，假造的，欺骗的；似是而非的；谬误的：a spurious eye 假眼。monism /ˈmɔnizəm/ *n.* （哲）一元论。

【Exercises】

I. Comprehension Questions

(1) Ranajit Guha _____ (A. agrees or B. disagrees) that Indian nationalism historically was dominated by elitism, either colonialist or bourgeois elitism. (See paragraph 16.) Before answering this question read carefully the note on Elitism at the end of the selection.

(2) In Guha's opinion what was the most important source of Indian nationalism? (See paragraph 6.)

   A. The People.

   B. The colonialist elite (British and influenced by Britain).

   C. The bourgeois (Indian) elite.

(3) Guha emphasizes that the writing of Indian history (historiography) leaves out _____. (See paragraph 8.)

   A. the story of the British in India

   B. the politics of the Indian people

   C. the role of the Indian elite.

(4) Who are the "subaltern classes"?
   A. The poorest and untouchable strata.
   B. The lower level of civil servants in the government.
   C. The dominant group of the native society.
   D. The mass of the laboring population and the intermediate level of society in town and country.

(5) Subaltern politics in India mobilized people horizontally, not vertically, according to Guha. (See paragraph 9.) If this is true which of the following would not occur in subaltern politics?
   A. Peasant uprisings.
   B. Use of parliamentary organizations.
   C. Kinship and territorial organization.

(6) According to the Subaltern School of historiography the Indian bourgeoisie failed to speak for the nation. True _____? False _____?

II. Points for Discussion

(1) What does Guha say is the biggest problem in Indian historiography of the colonial period? (See paragraph 15.) Is Guha mainly interested in opposing elite historiography or does he have a more general purpose? If the latter, what would his history of India look like?

(2) Do you think the same approach can be used in the historiography of China? If you applied his ideas to the writing of Chinese history what would it look like? Would it be different from the histories written in China now?

III. Complete the following sentences with appropriate forms of words or expressions from the passage according to the given meaning in brackets.

(1) She was a good singer and nature _____ (provide) her with a beautiful singing voice.

(2) Mrs Pankhurst was one of the chief _____ (an advocate) of women's rights.

(3) Actors learn how _____ (pronounce) clearly in the theatrical college.

(4) If he had a _____ (a small amount) of sense, he wouldn't do such a foolish thing.

(5) When she knew she would be dismissed she was lost in the _____ (confusion) for several hours.

IV. Complete the following sentences with the words or expressions from the passage given below. Change the form where necessary.

intermediate	derived from	integrate	in the form of
gear	generalize	assimilate	demarcate
rely on	transaction	equate	

(1) The U. S. A. _____ people from many European countries.
(2) The teachers are trying _____ all the children into society.
(3) Nowadays, many people _____ passing examinations with being educated.
(4) As we all know that gray is _____ between black and white.
(5) All _____, from banking to shopping, will be performed electronically.
(6) Wild animals survive from year to year by eating as much as they can during times of plenty usually _____ fat.
(7) Individuals landing on another coast or another continent would find the society they reached _____ the same time of day as at home.
(8) Most industry within Cornwall can be _____ to produce only modest growth.
(9) The MayDay ceremonies are said to be _____ the fertility rites of the Ancient Britons.

Unit 7

Islamic World

14. Muhammad and the Appearance of Islam[1]

Albert Hourani[2]

> 艾伯特·豪勒尼(1915—1993)生于英格兰曼彻斯特,是研究和解析伊斯兰世界的杰出历史学家。他是牛津大学圣安东尼学院名誉退休教授。在《阿拉伯各国人民史》这本书中,他综合了讲阿拉伯语的伊斯兰世界各国的珍贵历史。他从伊斯兰教的兴起一直写到今日。这本书全面纵览了阿拉伯人12个世纪的历史和文化。他还描述了这一文明的方方面面。其中包括大清真寺的美丽壮观、教育的重要性、阿拉伯的科学成就、内部冲突、普遍的贫困、妇女的作用以及当代巴勒斯坦问题等。

By the early seventh century in the Middle East there existed a combination of a settled world which had lost something of its strength and assurance, and another world on its frontiers which was in closer contact with its northern neighbours and opening itself to their cultures. The decisive meeting between them took place in the middle years of that century. A new political order was created which included the whole of the Arabian peninsula, the whole of the Sasanian lands, and the Syrian and Egyptian provinces of the Byzantine Empire; old frontiers were erased and new ones created.[3] In this new order, the ruling group was formed not by the peoples of the empires but by Arabs from western Arabia, and to a great extent from Mecca.[4]

Before the end of the seventh century, this Arab ruling group was identifying its new order with a revelation given by God to Muhammad, a citizen of Mecca, in the form of a holy book, the Qur'an: a revelation which completed those given to earlier prophets or messengers of God and created a new religion, Islam, separate from Judaism and Christianity.[5]

The most obscure part of the life of Muhammad, as the biographers narrate it, is the early one. They tell us that he was born in Mecca, a town in western Arabia, perhaps in or near the year 570. His family belonged to the tribe of Quraysh, although not to its most powerful part. Members of the tribe were traders, who had agreements with pastoral tribes around Mecca[6] and also relations with Syria as well as south-western Arabia. They are also said to have had a connection with the sanctuary of the town, the Ka'ba,[7] where the images of local gods were kept. Muhammad married Khadija, a widow engaged in trade, and looked after her business for her. Various anecdotes recorded by those who later wrote his life portray a world waiting for a guide and a man searching for a vocation.[8] A seeker after God expresses his wish to be taught: "O God, if I knew how you wished to be worshipped I would so worship you, but I do not know." Jewish rabbis, Christian monks and Arab soothsayers predict[9] the coming of a prophet: a monk, met by Muhammad on a trading journey to southern Syria, "looked at his back and saw the seal of prophethood between his shoulders." Natural objects saluted him: "Not a stone or tree that he passed but would say, 'Peace unto you, O apostle of God!'"[10]

He became a solitary wanderer among the rocks, and then one day, perhaps when he was about forty years old, something happened: some contact with the supernatural, known to later generations as the Night of Power or Destiny.

......

From this time Muhammad began communicating to those who adhered to him a succession of messages which he believed to have been revealed by an angel of God. The world would end; God the all-powerful, who had created human beings, would judge them all; the delights of Heaven and the pains of Hell were depicted in vivid colours.[11] If in their lives they submitted to God's Will, they could rely on His mercy when they came to judgement; and it was God's Will that they should show their gratitude by regular prayer and other observances, and by benevolence[12] and sexual restraint. The name used for God was "Allah,"[13] which was already in use for one of the local gods (it is now also used by Arabic-speaking Jews and Christians as the name of God). Those who submitted to His Will came eventually to be known as Muslims;[14] the name for their religion, Islam, is derived from the same linguistic root.[15]

Gradually there gathered around Muhammad a small group of believers: a few young members of the influential families of Quraysh, some members of minor families, clients of other tribes who had placed themselves under the protection of Quraysh, and some craftsmen and slaves. As support for Muhammad grew, his relations with the leading families of Quraysh became worse. They did not accept his claim to be a messenger of God, and they saw him as one who attacked their way of life. "O Abu Talib," they said to his uncle, who was his protector among them, "your nephew has cursed our gods, insulted our religion, mocked our way of life,[16] and accused our forefathers of error." His situation grew worse when his wife Khadija and Abu Talib died in the same year.

As his teaching developed, its differences from accepted beliefs became clearer. The idols of the gods[17] and ceremonies connected with them were attacked; new forms of worship were enjoined, in particular regular communal prayer,[18] and new kinds of good works. He placed himself more explicitly[19] in the line of prophets of the Jewish and Christian tradition.

Finally his position became so difficult that in 622 he left Mecca for an oasis settlement 200 miles to the north, Yathrib, to be known in future as Madina.[20] The way had been prepared by men from Yathrib who had come to Mecca for trade. They belonged to two tribes and needed an arbiter in tribal disputes;[21] having lived side by side with Jewish inhabitants of the oasis, they were prepared to accept a teaching expressed in terms of a prophet and a holy book. This move to Madina, from which later generations were to date the beginning of the Muslim era, is known as the hijira: the word has not simply the negative meaning of a flight from Mecca, but the positive one of seeking protection by settling in a place other than one's own. In later Islamic centuries, it would be used to mean the abandonment of a pagan or wicked community[22] for one living in accordance with the moral teaching of Islam...

From Madina, Muhammad began to gather a power which radiated throughout the oasis and the surrounding desert. He was soon drawn into an armed struggle with Quraysh, perhaps for control of the trade-routes, and in the course of the struggle the nature of the community was shaped. They came to believe that it was necessary to fight for what was right: "when Quraysh became insolent towards God and rejected His gracious purpose.[23] He gave permission to His apostle to fight and protect himself." They acquired the conviction that God and the angels were fighting on their side, and accepted calamity[24] when it came as a trial by which God tested believers.

It was in this period of expanding power and struggle that the Prophet's teaching took its final form. In the parts of the Qur'an which are thought to have been revealed then, there is a greater concern with defining the ritual observances of religion[25] and with social morality, the rules of social peace, property, marriage and inheritance. In some regards specific injunctions are given,[26] in others general principles...

The development of the Prophet's teaching may have been connected with changes in his relations with the Jews of Madina. Although they had formed part of the original alliance, their position became more difficult as Muhammad's claim for his mission expanded. They could not accept him as a genuine messenger of God within their own tradition, and he in turn is said to have accused them of perverting the revelation given to them:[27] "you have concealed what you were ordered to make plain." Finally some of the Jewish clans were expelled and others killed.

It may have been a sign of the breach with the Jews[28] that the direction which the community faced in prayer was changed from Jerusalem to Mecca..., and a new emphasis was placed on the line of spiritual descent which bound Muhammad to Abraham.[29] The idea that Abraham was the founder of a high monotheistic faith and of the sanctuary at Mecca already existed;[30] now he was seen as neither a Jew nor a Christian, but the common ancestor of both, and of Muslims too. This change was also connected with a change in Muhammad's relations with Quraysh and Mecca. A kind of reconciliation of interests[31] took place. The merchants of Mecca were in danger of losing their alliances with tribal chiefs and their control of trade, and in the city itself there was a growing number of adherents to Islam; an agreement with the new power would remove certain dangers, while the community of Muhammad for its part could not feel safe so long as Mecca was hostile, and it needed the skills of the Meccan patricians.[32] Since the haram[33] at Mecca was thought to have been founded by Abraham, it could be accepted as a place to which pilgrimage was allowed, although with a changed meaning.

By 629 relations had become close enough for the community to be permitted to go to Mecca on pilgrimage, and next year the leaders of the city surrendered it to Muhammad, who occupied it virtually without resistance and announced the principles of a new order: "every claim of privilege or blood or property is abolished by me except the custody[34] of the temple and the watering of the pilgrims."

Madina still remained his capital, however. There he exercised authority over his followers less by regular government than by political manipulation and personal ascendancy; of the several marriages he made after Khadija's death, some, although not all, were contracted for political reasons. There was no elaborate administration or army, simply Muhammad as supreme arbiter with a number of deputies, a military levy of believers,[35] and a public treasury filled by voluntary gifts and by levies on tribes which submitted. Beyond the towns, Muhammad's peace stretched over a wide area. Tribal chiefs needed agreements with him because he controlled the oases and markets. The nature of the agreements varied; in some cases there was alliance and renunciation of conflict, in others acceptance of the prophet-hood of Muhammad,[36] the obligation of prayer and the regular giving of financial contributions.

In 632 Muhammad made his last visit to Mecca, and his speech there has been recorded in the traditional writings as the final statement of his message: "know that every Muslim is a Muslim's brother, and that the Muslims are brethren";[37] fighting between them should be avoided, and the blood shed in pagan times should not be avenged;[38] Muslims should fight all men until they say, "There is no god but God."

Later that year he died. He left more than one legacy. First was that of his personality as seen through the eyes of his close companions. Their testimony, handed down mainly by oral transmission, did not assume its definite shape until much later, and by that time it was certainly swollen by accretions, but it seems plausible to suggest[39] that from an early time those who had known and followed Muhammad would have tried to model their behaviour upon his...

If an image of Muhammad was gradually elaborated and transmitted from one generation to another, so was that of the community he founded. As pictured by later ages, it was a community which revered the Prophet[40] and held his memory dear, trying to follow his path and strive in the way of Islam for the service of God. It was held together by the basic rituals of devotion, all of which had a communal aspect: Muslims went on pilgrimage at the same time, fasted throughout the same month and united in regular prayer, the activity which marked them off most clearly from the rest of the world.[41]

Above all, there was the legacy of the Qur'an, a book which depicts in language of great force and beauty the incursion of a transcendent God, source of all power and goodness, into the human world.[42] He has created the revelation of His Will through a line of prophets sent to warn men and bring them back to their true selves as grateful and obedient creatures, God's judgement of men at the end of time, and the rewards and punishments to follow from it.

Orthodox Muslims[43] have always believed that the Qur'an is the Word of God, revealed in the Arabic language through an angel to Muhammad, at various times and in ways appropriate to the needs of the community. Few non-Muslims would entirely accept this belief... Those who are divided by [this difference of belief] can agree on certain questions which might legitimately be asked about the Qur'an.

First is the question of when and how it took its final form. Muhammad communicated the revelations to his followers at various times, and they recorded them in writing or kept them in their memories. Most scholars would agree that the process by which different versions were collected and a generally accepted text and arrangement established did not end until after Muhammad's death... Some Muslim sects[44] have accused others of inserting into the text material not derived by transmission from the Prophet.

A more important question is that of the originality of the Qur'an. Scholars have tried to place it in the context of ideas current in its time and place. Undoubtedly there are echoes in it of the teaching of earlier religions: Jewish ideas in its doctrines; some reflections of eastern Christian monastic piety in the brooding on the terrors of judgement and the descriptions of Heaven and Hell (but few references to Christian doctrine or liturgy); Biblical stories in forms different from those of the Old and New Testaments; an echo of the Manichaean idea of a succession of revelations given to different peoples.[45] There are also traces of an indigenous tradition: the moral ideas in some ways continue those prevalent in Arabia, although in others they break with them; in the early revelations the tone is that of the Arabian soothsayer, stammering out his sense of an encounter with the supernatural.[46]

... Some non-Muslim scholars... have drawn [the] conclusion: that the Qur'an contains little more than borrowings from what was already available to Muhammad in that time and place. To say this, however, is to misunderstand what it is to be original: whatever was taken over from the religious culture of the age was so rearranged and transmuted that, [47]for those who accepted the message, the familiar world was made anew.

【 Notes 】

①This selection is from "A New Power in an Old World" in *A History of the Arab Peoples*, Belknap Press of Harvard University Press, 1991, pp. 14—21. In *A History of the Arab Peoples* Hourani's subject is a valuable synthesis of the history of the Arabic speaking parts of the Islamic world He starts with the rise of Islam and includes up to the present day. The book gives a panoramic view of twelve centuries of Arab history and culture. He writes about all aspects of this civilization including the beauty of the Alhambra and the great mosques, the importance of education, the achievements of Arab science and also the internal conflicts, widespread poverty, the role of women, and the contemporary Palestinian question.

② Albert Hourani (1915—1993), born in Manchester, England, a distinguished historian and interpreter of the Islamic world, was Emeritus Professor, St. Antony's College, Oxford University.

③ ...the whole of the Sasanian lands, and the Syrian and Egyptian provinces of the Byzantine Empire; old frontiers were erased and new ones created:
Sasanian /sæˈseiniən/ n. & adj. = Sassanid（公元 226—651 年间波斯的）萨桑王朝的君主。萨桑王朝的；萨桑王朝特点的：Sasanian metalwork 萨桑王朝时代的金属制品。Syrian /ˈsiriən/ adj. 叙利亚的；叙利亚人的；叙利亚语的。n. 叙利亚人；叙利亚语。the Byzantine /biˈzəntian/ Empire 拜占庭帝国（即东罗马帝国）。erase /iˈreiz/ vt. 擦掉，抹掉：The recording can be erased and the tape used again. 录音可以抹去，磁带可以再用。

④ Mecca /ˈmekə/ n. (= Makkah, Mekka) 麦加（沙特阿拉伯西部，穆罕默德诞生地，伊斯兰教第一圣地）；（常作 mecca）朝拜的地方，圣地；仰慕的目标；发源地，急欲前往的地方：a mecca for tourists 旅游者们的游览胜地。

⑤ Before the end of the seventh century, this Arab ruling group was identifying its new order with a revelation given by God to Muhammad, a citizen of Mecca, in the form of a holy book, the Qur'an: a revelation which completed those given to earlier prophets or messengers of God and created a new religion, Islam, separate from Judaism and Christianity. 在 7 世纪结束以前，这一阿拉伯统治集团逐步认可上帝以圣书的形式给予一麦加公民穆罕默德的启示是一种新规则。这本圣书就是可兰经。它囊括了上帝给予早期先知者的所有启示，并创建了一种新宗教，也就是与犹太教和基督教分开的伊斯兰教。
revelation /reviˈleiʃən/ n. 显露；泄露：revelations about her past 泄露有关她过去的情况。[R-]〈圣经〉启示录(= Revelations)。
Muhammad /muˈhæməd/ （约 570—632）伊斯兰教创始人穆罕默德。
Qur'an /Kɔːˈræn/ n. = Koran (Arab) n. （伊斯兰教）可兰经。prophets /ˈprɔfit/ n. [pl.] 犹太诸圣徒，先知；（新思想的）提倡者，宣扬者；预言家；预言者；a weather prophet 气象预报员；（前面与 the 连用）（伊斯兰教创始人）穆罕默德：Mohammed is the prophet of the Muslims. 穆罕默德是穆斯林的先知。[pl.]（圣经·旧约）预言书（女性 prophetess）。
Islam /ˈizlɑːm/ n. 伊斯兰教（在中国旧称回教，清真教）；伊斯兰教徒；伊斯兰教国家。
Judaism /ˈdʒuːdeiizm/ n. 犹太教。Christianity /kristiˈæniti/ n. 基督教。

⑥ ...pastoral tribes around Mecca:
pastoral /ˈpɑːstərəl/ adj. 田园生活的；田园风光的；宁静的；乡村生活的；多草的（土地）；适于牧畜的（草地）；牧师的：pastoral poetry 田园诗。

⑦ the sanctuary of the town,

132

the Ka'ba：克尔白神庙，麦加大清真寺（又译"禁寺"），世界各地穆斯林视之为人间最神圣的处所。

⑧Various anecdotes recorded by those who later wrote his life portray a world waiting for a guide and a man searching for a vocation. 在这个句子中，主语 anecdotes 和谓语 portray 被 recorded by 这个分词短语分隔开了。

anecdote /'ænikdəut/ n. 轶事，逸话，奇闻；短而有趣的故事；[pl.] 秘史。portray /pɔː'trei/ vt. 画（人物，风景），画（肖像）；描绘；描写；描述；（戏）扮演；饰演：What idea did King Lear portray? 李尔王描述了什么思想？vocation /vəu'keiʃən/ n. 职业；行业；天职；使命：commercial vocation 商务行业。

⑨Jewish rabbis, Christian monks and Arab soothsayers predict：

rabbi /'ræbai/ 拉比（指犹太教负责执行教规，律法并主持宗教仪式的人员或犹太教会众领袖）；大师，夫子。monk /mʌŋk/ n. 修道士，僧侣。soothsayer /'suːθseiər/ n. 预言者；占卜者。

⑩O apostle of God! 上帝的使徒。

apostle /ə'pɔsl/ n. （基督的）使徒；（早期的）基督教传教者。

⑪... the delights of Heaven and the pains of Hell were depicted in vivid colours：天堂的光辉以及地狱的痛苦已经用不同的色彩生动地描绘出来了。

depict /di'pikt/ vt. 画，刻画；描写，描绘，叙述：depict the horrors of war 描述战争的恐怖。

⑫benevolence /bi'nevələns/ n. 仁爱，善心；慈善；善行，捐款。

⑬Allah /'ælə/ n. （伊斯兰教的）阿拉，真主：Allah is Allah. 真主之外无真主。

⑭Muslim /'muzlim,' mʌzləm/ n. 伊斯兰教徒；穆斯林。

⑮... the name for their religion, Islam, is derived from the same linguistic root：他们的宗教名称伊斯兰教从语言学的角度来说，也出自同一词根。

linguistic /liŋ'gwistik/ n. & adj. 词的；语言的；语言学（的）

⑯... mocked our way of life：mock /mɔk/ vt., vi. （常与 at 连用）嘲笑；嘲弄：He went to church only to mock. 他到教堂去只是为了嘲弄宗教。

⑰The idols of the gods：

idol /'aid(ə)l/ n. 神像；偶像；宠爱物；崇拜对象：make an idol of sb/sth 崇拜（迷信）某人（某物）。

⑱regular communal prayer：例行的团体祈祷。

communal /'kɔmjun(ə)l/ adj. 公社的；社区的；公有的；团体的：communal marriage 群婚。

⑲explicitly /iks'plisitli/ adv. 明白地，明确地。

⑳... left Mecca for an oasis settlement 200 miles to the north, Yathrib, to be known in future as Madina：

oasis /əu'eisis/ n. (pl. -ses)（沙漠中的）绿洲；（不毛之地中的）沃洲；宜人的地方；慰藉物：an oasis of serenity amid chaos 闹中取静的避风港。Madina：麦地那。

㉑an arbiter in tribal disputes:部落争端的仲裁人。

arbiter /ˈɑːbitə(r)/ n. 仲裁人,公断人;裁决人,决定者;判优器,判别器。dispute /disˈpjuːt/ n. 争论;辩论:deputy chief arbiter 代理总裁判 We had a dispute about how much money he owes me. 我们就他欠我多少钱一事进行了一番争论。

㉒...the abandonment of a pagan or wicked community:

abandonment /əˈbændənmənt/ n. 放弃:abandonment of a right 弃权。pagan /ˈpeigən/ n. 没有宗教信仰的人;异教徒。wicked /wikid/ adj. 邪恶的;不道德的;恶劣的;绝妙的:wicked cruelty 伤天害理的暴行;wicked deeds 恶劣的行为。

㉓...became insolent towards God and rejected His gracious purpose:

insolent /ˈinsələnt/ adj. 粗野的;无礼的。gracious /ˈgreiʃəs/ adj. 亲切的;高尚的:She welcomed her guests in a gracious manner. 她亲切地欢迎了客人。

㉔..., and accepted calamity:

calamity /kəˈlæmiti/ n. 灾难,不幸事件:War is a frightful calamity. 战争是可怕的灾难。

㉕the ritual observances of religion:所遵守的宗教仪式。

ritual /ˈritʃuəl/ n. 典礼,(宗教)仪式,礼节;adj. 典礼的,(宗教)仪式的:the ritual of an inauguration 就职典礼。observance /əbˈzəːvəns/ n. (法律、习俗等的)遵守,奉行;(对节日的)纪念,庆祝;宗教仪式:the observance of the King's birthday 国王祝寿大典。

㉖In some regards specific injunctions are given:

in some regards 在某些方面(从某种意义上来说)。

injunction /inˈdʒʌkʃən/ n. 命令,责戒,训谕;(律)指令,禁令。

㉗...to have accused them of perverting the revelation given to them:

pervert /pə(ː)ˈvəːt/ vt. 使堕落;滥用;误解;曲解;使反常;颠倒:pervert the truth 颠倒是非;an analysis that perverts the meaning of the poem 曲解这首诗含义的分析。

㉘a sign of the breach with the Jews:违背犹太人意愿的一个标志。

breach /briːtʃ/ n. 破坏,违反,违背,不履行;(对他人权利等的)侵犯;(友好关系的)破裂,绝交,毁约;不和;缺口;裂口;伤口:breach of discipline 违反纪律;breach of promise 不履行诺言。

㉙...the line of spiritual descent which bound Muhammad to Abraham:结合穆罕默德和亚伯拉罕而一脉相承的宗教领袖。

line 家族的世代,家系:a line of kings 历代国王。bind...to...:把……和……结合起来。Abraham /ˈeibrəhæm/ n. (圣经)亚伯拉罕(相传为希伯来人的始祖)。

㉚The idea that Abraham was the founder of a high monotheistic faith and of the sanctuary at Mecca already existed. 在这个分句中,主语 the idea 与谓语 existed 被 that 引导的同位语从句分隔开了。

monotheistic /ˌmɔnəuθiːˈistik/ adj. 一神论的

㉛A kind of reconciliation of interests:一种利益的调和。

reconciliation /ˌrekənsiliˈeiʃən/ n. 和解,调和,顺从。

㉜patrician /pəˈtriʃən/ n. (古罗马的)贵族;(中世纪意大利的)显贵;(罗马帝国的)地方

官；贵族；有教养的人

㉝haram /'hɛərəm/ n. (=harem)(伊斯兰教徒)女眷居住的内室,闺房,(伊斯兰教徒的)女眷

㉞custody /'kʌstədi/ n. 监督；监视；保护；监护,看守；拘留,监禁：child custody 儿童保护。His car was held in the custody of the police. 他的汽车被警察扣压。

㉟..., simply Muhammad as supreme arbiter with a number of deputies, a military levy of believers：只有穆罕默德作为最高的仲裁者,带有许多代理人和招募由信徒组成的军队。deputy chief arbiter 代理总裁判。levy /'levi/ n. 征税；征募 vt. 征收(捐税,罚款等)；强索；(动员人力、物力)发动(战争)；征集(兵员)：levy a fine [tax] on sb 向某人征收罚金[税款]。

㊱renunciation of conflict, in others acceptance of the prophet-hood of Muhammad：renunciation /rinʌnsi'eiʃən/ n. 放(抛、废)弃；弃权；拒绝,否认；克制；克己；出家 the renunciation of all earthly pleasures. 抛弃所有的世俗享乐。prophet-hood 先知书的作者。

㊲brethren /'breðrən/ n. 兄弟；教友；会友：dearly beloved brethren 亲爱的兄弟们。

㊳...and the blood shed in pagan times should not be avenged：avenge /ə'vendʒ/ vt. 为……复仇；向……报仇：avenge a murder 惩罚谋杀者。The prince was determined to avenge his father, the King. 王子下决心要替父王报仇。

㊴...it was certainly swollen by accretions, but it seems plausible to suggest：accretion /æ'kri:ʃən/ n. 自然增加；增加之物；增值：Accretion of wealth means accumulation of riches. 财产的增加意味着财富的积累。plausible /'blɔ:zəbl/ adj. 似乎合理的；似乎可能的；善言能辩的；能说会道的。

㊵...a community which revered the Prophet：revere /ri'viə/ vt. 尊敬,崇敬：revere virtue 崇敬美德；People revere the general. 人们对那将军甚表尊敬。

㊶...fasted throughout the same month and united in regular prayer, the activity which marked them off most clearly from the rest of the world：在同一个月把斋,定期在一起祈祷,这些活动把他们与世界上其他人群明显地区分开来了。
fast vi. 绝食, 斋戒：If the patient is fasting he is allowed nothing to eat 如果病人禁食,不允许他吃东西。mark off 用界线隔开；(名单上)做上表示已做完的记号。

㊷..., a book which depicts in language of great force and beauty the incursion of a transcendent God, source of all power and goodness, into the human world：经书用铿锵有力和优美的语言描写了超越宇宙的上帝,使一切力量和美德的源泉进入到人类世界。
在 which 引导的定语从句中,主要成分为：which depicts the incursion...。
incursion /in'kə:ʃən/ n. 侵入, 侵略；袭击；(河水等)流入；进入：homes damaged by the incursion of floodwater 被涌入的洪水破坏的房屋。transcendent /træn'sendənt/ adj. 出类拔萃的, 超群的；卓越的；超越宇宙的。

㊸Orthodox Muslims：正统的穆斯林。
orthodox /'ɔ:θədɔks/ adj. 正统的；正派的；传统的；习俗的：orthodox ideas 正统观念。

an orthodox view of world affairs 对于世事的传统看法。

㊹some Muslim sects: sect /sekt/ n. 派别,宗派,派系。

㊺Undoubtedly there are echoes in it of the teaching of earlier religions: Jewish ideas in its doctrines; some reflections of eastern Christian monastic piety in the brooding on the terrors of judgement and the descriptions of Heaven and Hell (but few references to Christian doctrine or liturgy); Biblical stories in forms different from those of the Old and New Testaments; an echo of the Manichaean idea of a succession of revelations given to different peoples. 这个句子虽然很长,却是一个简单句。主句的意思是"毫无疑问,可兰经反映了不少比较早的宗教教义"。主句中的主语部分是 echoes in it of the teaching of earlier religions, 冒号后是由分号连接的四个同位语,进一步说明了早期宗教教义包涵的内容。

monastic /mə'næstik/ n. 僧侣,修道士;adj. 修道院的;僧侣的。brood /bruːd/ vt. 孵(卵),孵出;沉思;筹划:For years he brooded about taking vengeance. 多年来他一直在盘算报仇。vi. 孵卵;忧郁地想;(云,雾等)低覆,笼罩(over, on):The fog seemed like a ghost brooding over the village. 雾笼罩这个村庄。liturgy /'litə(ː)dʒi/ n. 圣餐仪式,礼拜仪式。Manichaean /mæni'kiːən/ n. 摩尼教徒;(宗教或哲学上的)二元论者。adj. 摩尼教的,摩尼教徒的。

㊻... in the early revelations the tone is that of the Arabian soothsayer, stammering out his sense of an encounter with the supernatural: 早期启示录中的语气就是阿拉伯预言者断断续续讲叙遇到神时有所领悟的语气。

stammer /'stæmə/ vi., vt. 口吃,结结巴巴地说:stammer (out) a few words 结结巴巴地说出几个字;He stammered most when he was nervous 他一紧张往往口吃。

㊼... so rearranged and transmuted that...: 经过重新整理和转化,其结果是。

transmute /trænz'mjuːt/ vt. 使变形(质,化);使……转化:We can transmute water power into electrical power. 我们能将水力变成电力。

【 Exercises 】

I. **Comprehension Questions**

(1) According to Hourani's account, which of the following were characteristics of Muhammad?

 A. He came from a trading tribe.

 B. He was born in the city of Mecca.

 C. His family had no connection with the local gods.

 D. He married a woman who was involved with trade.

 E. When he was forty he became a wanderer in the desert rocks and an angel of God talked to him.

(2) The Arabic language word for God is "Allah," used by Arabic speaking Muslims, Jews and Christians to name, in each case, their God. True _____ ? False _____ ?

(3) Khadija was Muhammad's _____.
   A. mother
   B. wife
(4) The Hijira was _____. (See paragraph 8.)
   A. a journey Muhammad took to Jerusalem
   B. a journey Muhammad took to leave Mecca and seek protection in a place that was not his own
   C. a trip he took to buy camels in the desert to trade with the tribe of Quraysh in Mecca
(5) Abraham, the major founding figure in the Old Testament of the Jewish and Christian Bible, is known by Muslims as the ancestor of only the Muslims, according to Hourani. True _____? False _____?

II. Points for Discussion
(1) According to the author, what are the questions that can be asked about the sacred book of Islam, the Qur'an? (See the last four paragraphs.)
(2) What is Albert Hourani's opinion on the question of whether the Qur'an was original or only borrowed from other writings of Muhammad's period?

III. Complete the following sentences with appropriate forms of words or expressions from the passage according to the given meaning in brackets.
(1) Although he failed in the maths test, it was wrong _____ (laugh at) his efforts.
(2) She was injured in the accident and unconsciousness _____ (wipe out) the details of it from her memory.
(3) I write only in my spare rime, so I think teaching is my _____ (profession) and writing is my avocation.
(4) They didn't get along well together. A trivial misunderstanding caused a _____ (gap) between them.
(5) It is obvious that a hurricane would be a _____ (a disaster) for this low-lying coastal region.

IV. Complete the following sentences with the words or expressions from the passage given below. Change the form where necessary.

take over	pervert	extent	adhere to	dispute
transmute	levy	connect	idol	authority
accuse of	revere	belong	derive	

(1) The members of the town council _____ for hours about whether to build a new museum.
(2) Computers process data to create the information that at least one third of the population _____ every sort of holy man.

137

(3) I _____ on many writers for my essential conception of American culture.

(4) The clever criminal _____ his talents and he was in jail because he got into trouble with the law.

(5) The tendency to _____ what has become customary into what has been divinely ordained.

(6) Can you imagine the football player is the _____ of many young people?

(7) He has been _____ many things in his life, but never of theft.

(8) To a certain _____, I am responsible for breaking the glass case. It's not solely Tom's fault.

(9) The story the film is based on _____ an old legend.

V. Translate the following sentences into English.

(1) 孩子年幼时，做父亲的有监护的责任。(custody)

(2) 他迫使自己断断续续讲出自己的懊悔。(stammer)

(3) 她的真实性格对我是一个新发现。(revelation)

(4) 他惩处了凶手，为母亲报了仇。(avenge)

(5) 堤防保护低地免于海水流入。(incursion)

Unit 8

Sub-Saharan Africa

15. Africa after Independence[1]

Paul Bohannan and Philip Curtin[2]

> 保罗·波汉南(Paul Bohannan)于 1920 年出生在美国内布拉斯加。他是一位人类学家,曾在牛津大学、普林斯顿大学任教,后来在芝加哥西北大学任教,并领导人类学系发展了非洲人种学。以后他到加州大学圣巴巴拉分校执教,1987 年作为人类学荣誉教授退休。
>
> 菲力普·克庭(Philip Curtin)是一位专门研究非洲、大西洋跨文化贸易史的历史学家。克庭最近的研究已经由以欧洲为中心的历史转向研究不同文化间的贸易关系。这两位学者通过自己的著作在研究非洲人如何看待现代化这个根本问题上都占有一席之地。

Modernization and Nation-Building

One of Africa's fundamental problems has to do with its reaction to "modernization"—a term used here simply to mean getting the benefits of industrialization for African use. African leaders have sought these benefits—though the extent of economic development over the past quarter century is not a true measure of the effort. They use air-conditioned cars, have their offices in skyscrapers, and all too often they keep their spare cash in Swiss bank accounts. Even from the fundamentalist mosques, the call for prayer comes from a public address system in the mosque tower.[3] But the tools of industrial technology can mask the cultural reality, and African leaders do not want to copy everything the West has to offer.

They also appeal to values of an African past. Leopold Senghor of Senegal wrote about negritude as an abstract quality that permeates African thought, art, and achievement.[4] But he wrote in superb French, not in Serer, his home language. Kwame Nkrumah of Ghana[5] also had a lot to say—in English—about African philosophy and the "african personality." Julius Nyerere gave himself the Swahili title of mwalimu or teacher and tried to reorganize Tanzania's rural life[6] along lines dictated by ujamaa, an African sense of community. Joseph Mobutu changed his name to Mobutu Sese Seko, changed his country's name from the Congo to Zaire,[7] and insisted that his fellow countrymen also change their names to "authentic" African forms and wear a cut of suit not in the precise fashion of the Western world. Some of this window-dressing no doubt represents a genuine effort to get back to values, real or imagined, of Africa as it was before the conquest, but the myth of the noble African lurks there as well.[8]

In fact, the living traditions of African culture do not have to be recovered. They were never lost—modified to make innovation possible, but not lost. This is the case in the most modern-looking situation in such matters as marriage customs, family affairs, treatment of children and the way children are trained to treat adults. In the villages, a whole body of custom lives on. It controls relations between families, control over the land, and worship of the gods (including the Christian/Muslim god). Even in adapting some practices for modern life, some possibilities feel "right" and others feel "wrong" and are likely to be rejected.

This sense of "rightness" attaches less easily to the new life of rural migrants in the slums that surround all African cities. And it never attached very easily to the colonial state. The post-colonial state inherited that weakness and added new weakness on its own. The state is rarely perceived as an institution to which every person should owe his ultimate loyalty. It demands taxes and it gives back benefits like schools, roads, medical care (sometimes), and jobs. It is the focus of political life, but it is not the focus of a sentiment that could be called patriotism. Other institutions than the state are the first source of group loyalty. Even urban Africans tend to keep the foci of loyalty[9] they had in the village—loyalty often based on age and kinship, secondly on common language and common standards of behavior. In the competition with others from other rural areas, the play of these loyalties can appear as "tribalism."[10] When an individual acts for his group, in competition with other groups, it can look to outsiders like favoritism, if not corruption.

Yet neither the post-colonial state nor its colonial predecessor provided people with the kind of emotional support that might have been reciprocated by ultimate loyalty[11]—by feelings the West represents with words like "patriotism." This is not to argue that patriotism is a "good thing," in all circumstances, but African loyalties, since independence as before, have gone in other directions. This has had a enormous influence on what the state can and cannot do. Of. the various calls for traditional values, Mobutu's call for authenticity in Zaire[12] is a clear case of trying to redirect older loyalties to the state. There is no evidence so far that it worked very well.

Political Order and Disorder

Many of Africa's economic shortcomings after independence can be traced directly or indirectly to political conditions. These conditions, in turn, depend in large measure on underlying culture and on the history of the colonial period. To say that the colonial powers failed to prepare Africa for independence is to state the obvious. But it is important to remember that they did not intend Africa to become independent in the 1960s. Even the most enlightened administrators of the 1930s would hardly have expected independence before the end of the century; most would have put it later still; and some would have said "never." Independence was a surprise, when it came peacefully. Even two decades of conscious preparation might well have brought quit different results, but the colonial powers were not allowed that much time.

The lack of preparation shows in a number of important ways. On the British side, the long-term colonial policy for tropical Africa called for Indirect Rule, rule through the chiefs. In the event, the organized groups that demanded an end to European rule demanded an end to chiefly rule as well. Some of the bloodiest struggles during and after decolonization were on precisely this issue. The anti-Arab revolt on Zanzibar and the peasant risings in Rwanda and Burundi come immediately to mind,[13] though they were not alone. The people the British had been grooming to take over—though in the far more distant future—were not, therefore the ones who actually came to power.

In addition, neither France, Belgium, nor Britain, made a serious effort to prepare Africa for electoral democracy. For the French colonies, the Senegalese communes had a long electoral experience, but the new electoral freedom under the Framework Law brought only one election before independence was declared. For the Belgian Congo, the only national! election was the one that led directly to independence. In the British sphere, what electoral politics had existed was limited to the old port towns and a very limited electorate. In tropical Africa generally, some politicians had secured electoral victories before independence, but virtually no one had left office even after an electoral defeat. Politicians were therefore loath to leave office,[14] suspecting (quite correctly) that their successors would never give them another chance.

A third source of non-preparation for independence was the colonial treatment of the military. The conquest of Africa had been carried out largely by African troops under European officers. Africans had fought in two world wars, but almost no public attention was paid to the place of the military under the newly independent governments. It was as though the colonial administrators and the rising African politicians shared a belief that the armies would behave under their new officers just as they had under the old.

The colonial powers made the military problem more serious by the way they recruited their armies. Both the French and British had a theory that certain peoples, whom the British called "martial races" were better soldiers than other colonial people. The so-called martial races tended to be people away from the core area of colony, often from its poorest sections. These were, after all, the places where soldiers could be recruited for little pay. Sometimes, as with Gurkhas from Nepal, the British even recruited their armies from outside the empire. In East Africa, some of the earliest British forces were from the Sudan, recruited there by purchase well before the British had conquered the Sudan. Later on, in Ghana, Nigeria, and Uganda, the recruits (though not necessarily the local officers) were drawn from the comparatively impoverished northern territories.[15] The importance in the longer run was that such soldiers tended to have ties to others from their home districts, to their fellow soldiers, and to their officers at times, but rarely to the civilians or the people of the core area of the colonial state.

At independence, the initial forms of government were universally democratic, and, almost as universally, they did not stay that way. One of the first steps was to shift power to a strong president, replacing as chief executive officer the prime minister responsible to a [Westminster model] parliamentary body. Ghana became independent in 1957. By 1960, President Kwame Nkrumah secured a new constitution which gave the president the right to veto any legislation,[16] to pass laws without calling on parliament for approval, and to control the budget. A common [third] step was to set up a one-party state. In Ghana in 1964, Nkrumah made his Convention People's Party the sole legal party. In theory, important decisions would be reached by democratic means, but within the single party, not outside it. In 1966, Ghana reached a fourth stage: the military seized control of the country while Nkrumah was overseas. Supreme power then passed to a group of officers that called itself the National Liberation Council.

These stages—from the Westminster model, to a powerful presidency, to a one-party state, to a military dictatorship—were not universal, but they were common enough to represent a process. Some stopped short at the stage of one-party state. Several one-party states were remarkably stable, and some of their leaders remained in office from independence into the 1980s—Kenneth Kaunda in Zambia, Sékou Touré in Guinea-Conakry, Félix Houphouet Boigny in the Ivory Coast, or Julius Nyerere in Tanzania.[17] In other cases, the party went on in power, though the leader may have died, like Jomo Kenyatta of Kenya[18] in 1978, or resigned, like Leopold Senghor of Senegal in 1980.

The more usual pattern, however, was to move on to military dictatorship. That political form was dominant in sub-Saharan Africa[19] in the mid-1980s. Of the 45 states in Africa and the off-shore islands, more than half were under military rule, though the nature of the military control varied considerably. Ghana and Uganda have become what are sometimes called "praetorian" states[20]—the military units that determined who ruled in ancient Rome. Governments changed, but only when one military group overthrew its military predecessors. Other military regimes called themselves socialist with more or less Marxist-Leninist trappings, like Madagascar, Benin,[21] and the Congo Republic. Others had built an originally military source of power into something that resembled a one-party, non-parliamentary state, like Mobutu Sese's Seko's Zaire. Others regarded themselves as interim regimes,[22] ready to pass control over to a new civilian government when circumstances warranted—like Nigeria.

One final category of government went well beyond the usual rules of military take-over. In the late 1960s and the 1970s, Africa had a few governments whose record for tyranny was among the worst in the post-war world—though less cruel than that of either Stalin's Soviet Union or Hitler's National Socialist Germany. These were Equatorial Guinea under Macias Nguema from 1968; Jean Bedel Bokassa of the Central Africa Republic from 1965, which he renamed the Central African Empire;

and Idi Amin in Uganda from 1971.[23] This phase has apparently passed for tropical Africa. These three worst tyrants were all deposed in 1978; leaving only South Africa as the most systematically repressive government in sub-Saharan Africa.[24]

The most tragic of the three was Uganda, if only because the country had a record of rapid modernization and great expectations at the time of independence. Part of the background was a conflict between the previously dominant Ganda people[25] near the capital, and their neighbors. Milton Obote[26] became the first President, mainly with non-Ganda support. He was not generally popular, and he quickly suspended the constitution and created a one-party state. His lack of support made it all the easier for the army to revolt under Idi Amin, whose followers were mainly badly-educated soldiers from the poverty-stricken north. Most were Muslim, though the majority of Uganda was Christian. They set out to rule Uganda like a conquered country, being credited with killing more than 100,000 people before they were driven from power by a Tanzanian invasion in 1978. But the fall of the tyrant was only the beginning of a process of rebuilding a stable and prosperous country.

【Notes】

①This selection is from "Africa after Independence" in *Africa and Africans*, 3rd Edition, Waveland Press, 1988, pp. 384—386, 393—397. The authors are both interested in economic aspects of the African past. In this book they take the position a basic problem in African countries has been how Africans react to modernization.

②Paul Bohannan (1920—) was born in Nebraska, USA. He is an anthropologist who taught at Oxford University, England, at Princeton University, and later at Northwestern University in Chicago. There he led the anthropology department in developing African ethnography. Later he moved to the University of California at Santa Barbara, where he retired as an Emeritus Professor of Anthropology in 1987.

Philip Curtin is a noted American historian specializing particularly in African, Atlantic, and cross cultural trade history. He is a former President of the American Historical Society. Curtin's recent research moves attention away from a Europe centered history to study trading relationships between cultures.

③Even from the fundamentalist mosques, the call for prayer comes from a public address system in the mosque tower. 甚至从原教旨主义者的清真寺发出的要大家去祈祷的号召都是通过清真寺顶塔的播音系统发出的。

the fundamentalist mosques 原教旨主义者的清真寺。fundamentalist /fʌndə'mentəlist/ n. 原教旨主义者。mosque /mɔsk/ n. 清真寺:They go to the mosque to pray once a week. 他

们每周到清真寺去祈祷一次。public address system 播音系统。

④Leopold Senghor of Senegal wrote about negritude as an abstract quality that permeates African thought, art, and achievement.

Leopold Senghor 桑戈尔(1906-10-09—)诗人、政治家、塞内加尔总统(1960—1980),主张"非洲社会主义"的温和派。Senegal /ˌseniˈɡɔːl/ n. [国名]塞内加尔(西非国家)。negritude /ˈneɡritjuːd/ n. 黑人文化传统的认同,对黑人文化传统的自豪感。permeate /ˈpəːmieit/ vt. 渗入,透过;穿过;弥漫,充满;普遍(及):Water will permeate blotting paper. 水能渗透吸水纸。Our thinking is permeated by our historical myths. 我们的历史神话渗透着我们的思想。

⑤Kwame Nkrumah of Ghana:恩克鲁马(1909-09—1972-04-27),加纳民族领袖,领导黄金海岸脱离英国的独立运动,在加纳成为新国家后执政,从1957年独立起他领导该国家直至1966年被政变推翻。

Ghana /ˈɡɑːnə/ n. 加纳。

⑥Julius Nyerere gave himself the Swahili title of mwalimu or teacher and tried to reorganize Tanzania's rural life...:

Julius Nyerere 尼雷尔(1922-03—),坦噶尼喀独立后的第一任总统(1961),新成立的坦桑尼亚国家的第一任总理(1964),非洲统一组织主要领导人之一。Swahili /ˈswɑːhili/ n. 斯瓦希里人(语)。Tanzania /tɑːnzɑːˈniə/ n. 坦桑尼亚(东非国家)。

⑦Joseph Mobutu changed his name to Mobutu Sese Seko, changed his country's name from the Congo to Zaire...:蒙博托将他的名字改为 Mobutu Sese Seko, 又将国名由刚果改为扎伊尔。

Joseph Mobutu 蒙博托(1939-10-14—1997-09-07),扎伊尔(Zaire)共和国(原比属刚果 Belgian Congo)总统(1965—1997)。

⑧..., but the myth of the noble African lurks there as well:

lurk /ləːk/ v. 埋伏;潜伏:There is a suspicious man lurking in the shadows. 有一可疑的人躲在阴暗中。

Some anxiety still lurked in her mind. 她心里还暗暗地有点不放心。

⑨to keep the foci of loyalty:保持这种忠诚的关系。

foci /ˈfəusai/ (focus 的复数) 焦距,配光。

⑩...the play of these loyalties can appear as "tribalism":这种忠诚所起的作用表现为部落文化。

tribalism /ˈtraibəlism/ n. 部落制,部落的特征,部落文化。

⑪...that might have been reciprocated by ultimate loyalty:最后可能都获得互相绝对忠诚的报答。

reciprocate /riˈsiprəkeit/ v. 互给,酬答,互换,报答:reciprocate favors 互相帮助;He reciprocated my good wishes. 他答谢了我的祝福。

⑫Mobutu's call for authenticity in Zaire:

authenticity /ˌɔːθenˈtisiti/ n. 确实性,真实性;纯正性:the authenticity of an anecdote 一则

轶事的真实性；equal authenticity 同等效力。

call for *n. &v.* 要求，需要；提倡，取；接；为……叫喊：There is no call for us to adjust the price. 我们无需调整价格。He asked me to call for him at four o'clock in the afternoon. 他要我下午四点钟来接他。to call for bid 招标。The occasion calls for a cool head. 这种场合需要冷静的头脑。

⑬The anti-Arab revolt on Zanzibar and the peasant risings in Rwanda and Burundi come immediately to mind：

Zanzibar /zænzi'bɑː/ *n.* 桑给巴尔岛(坦桑尼亚东北部)；桑给巴尔(非洲坦桑尼亚的一部分)。Rwanda /ru'ændə/ *n.* 卢旺达(非洲国家)。Burundi /bu'rundi/ *n.* 布隆迪(非洲国家)。

come to mind 出现于某人的脑海中。"Have you any suggestion?" "Nothing immediately comes to mind.""你有什么建议？""一下子想不出什么来。"

⑭Politicians were therefore loath to leave office：

loath /ləuθ/ *adj.* 不情愿的，勉强的(to do; that)：be loath for him to go 不愿意他去；nothing loath 很愿意，很高兴。

I am loath to go on such short notice. 我不愿这么急急忙忙就走。

⑮Later on, in Ghana, Nigeria, and Uganda, the recruits (though not necessarily the local officers) were drawn from the comparatively impoverished northern territories.

Nigeria /nai'dʒiəriə/ *n.* 尼日利亚(非洲中西部国家)。Uganda /ju(ː)'gændə/ *n.* 乌干达(东非国家)。impoverish /im'pɔvəriʃ/ *vt.* 使贫困，使枯竭：an impoverished writer 穷困潦倒的作家；impoverish natural resources 耗尽自然资源；impoverish the soil by overuse 过度耕作而使土壤变得贫瘠。

⑯right to veto any legislation：否决任何立法的权利。

veto /'viːtəu/ *vt.* 否决，禁止：veto a bill 否决一项议案。

⑰—Kenneth Kaunda in Zambia, Sékou Touré in Guinea-Conakry, Félix Houphouet Boigny in the Ivory Coast, or Julius Nyerere in Tanzania：

Kenneth Kaunda，卡翁达(1924-04-28—)，赞比亚政治家，领导赞比亚于1964年获得独立，并担任该国总统直至1991年。Guinea /'gini/ *n.* 几内亚。Conakry /'kɔnəkri/ *n.* 科纳克里(几内亚首都)。Ivory Coast /'aivərikəust/ 象牙海岸(非洲)，1986年以后，全称科特迪瓦共和国；Félix Houphouet Boigny 乌佛埃·博瓦尼是科特迪瓦民主党的创造者，自1960年国家独立至1990年他去世为止，一直任科特迪瓦国家总统。Julius Nyerere，尼雷尔(1922-03—)，坦噶尼喀独立后的第一任总理(1961)，新成立的坦桑尼亚国家的第一任总统(1964)，非洲统一组织的主要领导人之一。

⑱Jomo Kenyatta of Kenya：Jomo Kenyatta 肯雅塔(约1894—1978-08-22)，原名 Kamau Ngengi，非洲政治家、民族主义者，肯尼亚独立后首任总理(1963—1964)、总统(1964—1978)。

⑲sub-Saharan /sʌbsə'hɑːrən/ *adj.* (非洲)撒哈拉沙漠以南的。

⑳"praetorian" states：禁卫军国家。

praetorian /priːˈtɔriən/ adj. 执政官的，禁卫队的：the praetorian guards 罗马禁卫军。

㉑... with more or less Marxist-Leninist trappings, like Madagascar, Benin：
trappings /ˈtræpiŋz/ n. 服饰，马饰。Madagascar /mædəˈgæskə/ n. 马达加斯加岛（非洲岛国）。Benin /bəˈnin/ 贝宁（非洲国家）。

㉒Others regarded themselves as interim regimes...：另一些则认为他们自己是临时政权。
interim /ˈintərim/ adj. 暂时的；临时的：an interim government 过渡政府；an interim agreement 一项临时协议。

㉓These were Equatorial Guinea under Macias Nguema from 1968; Jean Bedel Bokassa of the Central Africa Republic from 1965, which he renamed the Central African Empire; and Idi Amin in Uganda from 1971.
Equatorial Guinea 赤道几内亚（西非国家）。Macias Nguema 恩奎马（1924—1979）1968年赤道几内亚宣布独立后，他是独裁总统，实行恐怖统治，造成国内经济混乱，因而在1979被推翻，后被处死。Jean Bedel Bokassa 博卡萨（1921-02-22—   ），后改名为 Eddine Ahmed Bosassa，非洲军事领袖、中非共和国总统（1966—1967），自称中非帝国皇帝（1977—1979），1980年缺席被判处死刑，1987年判定犯有杀害学童罪和其他罪行，随后死刑被减轻，并于1993年获释。Idi Amin 阿明，乌干达军官、总统（1971—1979）。

㉔These three worst tyrants were all deposed in 1978; leaving only South Africa as the most systematically repressive government in sub-Saharan Africa.
depose /diˈpəuz/ vt. 免职，废（王位）；作证：The king was deposed by his people. 那位国王被人民罢免（废除）。

㉕Ganda people：干达人。又称巴干达人或瓦干达人。居住在乌干达中南部维多利亚湖以北和西北地区。干达人是乌干达人数最多的民族，居住地区富饶肥沃。1966—1993年数百年的君主制被废除，1993年卡巴卡（国王）复位，但权力已大大削弱。

㉖Milton Obote：奥博特（1924-12-28—   ），乌干达政治家、总理（1962—1970）和两任总理（1966—1971，1980—1985）。

【 Exercises 】

I. Comprehension Questions

(1) When the authors say a basic issue in African countries is how Africans react to modernization do they mean that _____.

   A. Africans don't like to drive cars and work in modern industry
   B. Africans don't want to lose their values from the past
   C. the people reject modernization?

(2) In the villages custom controls relations between families, control over the land, and worship of the gods (including the tribal gods)... (See paragraph 3). True _____? False _____? If true describe the tribal belief in gods. If false correct the incorrect section of this sentence.

(3) In the following list which are weaknesses of the post-colonial African state? (See paragraph 4)

A. It is the central focus of political life but does not have the strong loyalty of the people.
B. It is the focus of patriotism.
C. Other institutions than the state are the main focus of individual and group loyalty.
D. Loyalty is often based on age, kinship, common language and tribalism.

(4) Match the rulers or ruling groups in List A with the type of government in List B that describes the way they governed: (See last 5 paragraphs.)

List A:
① Idi Amin, Uganda
② Jomo Kenyatta, Kenya
③ Julius Nyerere, Tanzania
④ Mobuto Sese Seko, Zaire
⑤ Kwame Nkrumah, Ghana
⑥ National Guard Council, Ghana

List B:
a. Stable one-party state
b. Military dictatorship
c. Tyranny
d. One party non-parliamentary state, with military power base

II. Points for Discussion

The authors state: "Many of Africa's economic shortcomings after independence can be traced directly or indirectly to political conditions." Considering what you have learned in this selection about the failure of the colonial powers to prepare these countries for independence and the post-independence governments that developed up to the 1980's when the book was published, project how these African political regimes would have shaped and controlled the economies of the areas they were ruling.

III. Complete the following sentences with the words or expressions from the passage given below. Change the form where necessary.

permeate	focus	have to do with	in the long run	act on its own
attach	loath	interim	call for	live on
lurk	set out	cut		

(1) The identification of blood groups and the analysis of ink in forged documents can _____ considerable skill.

(2) He wanted me to tell you that the full report wasn't ready yet, but you could see the _____ report.

(3) The conversation was mainly _____ exchange of students between the two countries.

(4) Our thinking is _____ by our historical myths. In the same way we sometimes place in the past, that which is occurring in the present.

(5) The main credit for the party's electoral success _____ to the coolness and confidence of its leader.

(6) The villagers reported that the tiger from the zoo was still _____ close to, so it was better fo stay at home.

(7) The Mexican peasant _____ to burn an acre of woodland in order to plant his maize.

(8) I was hungry to death. When he suggested a meal, I was nothing _____.

(9) It pays to buy the coat of high quality, but I don't like the _____ of the coat.

(10) You may make grades by studying only before examinations, but you will succeed _____ only by studying hard every day.

IV. Translate the following sentences from English to Chinese.

(1) But the tools of industrial technology can mask the cultural reality, and African leaders do not want to copy everything the West has to offer.

(2) The living traditions of African culture are not lost. This is the case in the most modern-looking situation in such matters as marriage customs, family affairs, treatment of children and the way children are trained to treat adults.

(3) The state is rarely perceived as an institution to which every person should owe his ultimate loyalty.

(4) Africans had fought in two world wars, but almost no public attention was paid to the place of the military under the newly independent governments.

(5) These conditions, in turn, depend in large measure on underlying culture and on the history of the colonial period.

Unit 9

Europe

16. From Balance of Power to World Politics[1]

Geoffrey Barraclough[2]

> 吉奥佛雷·巴勒克拉夫(Geoffrey Barraclough,1908—1985)在英国历史学家中被认为是研究近代历史的栋梁。他毕业于牛津大学。由于他激进的历史观点,在20世纪40到60年代间,他的知名度已经相当高。由于反对20世纪初期和中期以欧洲为中心的传统历史学,他从一位研究中世纪的历史学家转变成为了研究现代史的历史学家。他观点和方法的改变为第二次世界大战前期通史的定位做出了范例。1957年,他被委派为伦敦大学国际历史学教授。他是20世纪提倡打破旧习的历史学家,对欧洲文明的历史时期及边界划分,以及撰写普通史的方法和意义都特别感兴趣。他坚持谈论世界史转折点的问题。在这篇文章里,他论述了近代世界史上最重要的转折点。

For anyone looking down on the world of 1960 and comparing it with the world of 1870 or 1880, nothing will probably be more striking than the change which has taken place in the structure of international relations [in the world]... The structure of great power politics, and its modalities, in the age of Khrushchev were essentially different from those of the age of Bismarck.[3] Instead of by a concert of powers, we were confronted by two great super-powers, the Soviet Union and the United States, whose pre-eminence was based on their quasi-monopoly of nuclear weapons and of the delivery systems for launching nuclear weapons; and although Russia has one foot in Europe, it is significant that both super powers are great continent-spanning federal states, neither of which can realistically be classed as European.[4] Thus in the space of half a century a multilateral system of equilibrium centred upon Europe had been displaced by a system of global bipolarity between the two great extra-European powers,⁵ the United States, and the Soviet Union.

......

The rise of the United States, and parallel with it, the rise of Russia to world-power were in fact the decisive events in a new period in world politics...

......

It is therefore no exaggeration to say that the entry of the United States into the war in 1917 was a turning-point in history: it marked the decisive stage in the transition from the European age to the age of world politics. It is a turning-point in another way also. After the Bolshevik revolution in Russia in November 1917 the division of the world into two great rival power blocks, inspired by apparently irreconcilable ideologies, took tangible shape.⁶ Though it was something like two years before President Wilson identified himself with the anti-Bolshevik crusaders in the west, he and Lenin were aware from the start that they were competing for the suffrage of mankind, and it was to prevent Lenin gaining a monopoly of the blueprints for the post-war world that, in January 1918, Wilson issued his famous Fourteen Points.⁷ "Either Wilson or Lenin," wrote the French socialist, Albert Thomas: "either Democracy or Bolshevism. ... A choice must be made." But, in spite of their rivalry, Wilson and Lenin had one thing in common: their rejection of the existing international system. Both rejected secret diplomacy, annexations,⁸ trade discrimination; both cut loose from the balance of power; both denounced the "dead hand of the past."⁹ They were "the champion revolutionists of the age," "the prophets of a new international order."

Here was a decisive break. Although at a later date both the Soviet Union and the United States were to revert in practice to the old methods of power politics, by then the revolutionary principles enunciated by Wilson and Lenin¹⁰ had done their work. From the beginning of 1917 the conflict among the European powers was transformed from a war of limited objectives into a world-wide revolutionary and ideological struggle. The war aims of England, France, Czarist Russia,¹¹ and Italy, as formulated in the secret treaties, had assumed that the war would lead to the re-establishment of a European balance of power without markedly disturbing the domestic status quo in and of the major belligerent nations.¹² After the Russian revolution and the entry of the United States into the war this assumption ceased to hold good. Lenin and Trotsky,¹³ counting on universal revolution, refused to accept the permanence of a system of independent self-balancing states; Wilson had no faith in the mechanism, traditional in Europe since the defeat of the French revolution, through which the powers conducted their affairs by adjusting the claims of sovereign states against each other as they arose; and all three planned to end the balance of power, not to restore it. Thus the continuity in mood, procedures, and objectives of nineteenth century diplomacy was irretrievably disrupted.[14] One of the most momentous developments of the war was the simultaneous emergence of Washington and Petrograd[15] as two rival centres of power, both of which abandoned the old diplomacy and its ruling concept, the balance of power.

The character of this revolution has often been misjudged. Historians have for the most part attributed Wilson's rejection of the concept of balance of power to an utopian moralism, for which he has been both praised and condemned. In reality, as an acute observer has remarked, it was due less to any alteration in ethical standards than to a shift in the centre of power. Wilson and Lenin were no less realists than Clemenceau, Sonnino, or Lloyd George;[16] but the realities they had to deal with were different. From the point of view of the United States, the policy of territorial adjustments, annexations and compensations on which European statesmen relied, was of little consequence in the sense that it would neither increase American security nor improve its strategic position; and Wilson was right when he perceived, as Lenin also perceived, that the new diplomacy—the diplomacy of appeals to the people over the heads of politicians—would serve his purpose better in a rapidly changing world. The entry of the United States into the war meant, therefore, not—as allied statesmen deceived themselves into thinking—simply the mobilization at the crucial moment of another all-powerful belligerent, the addition of a decisive counter on the existing political chessboard; on the contrary, it meant the appearance on the scene of a power which had, for historical reasons, scant interest in the old European political system, which was not prepared to underwrite the European balance of power, and which had almost irresistible means, in the state of exhaustion to which the European powers on both sides had been reduced, of enforcing its point of view.[17]

When revolutionary Russia, under Lenin and Trotsky, embarked on a parallel course, the breach with the past became irrevocable.[18] The Bolsheviks also repudiated the old system of balance of power.[19] So far as the security of Russia was at stake, they sought it not, as Stalin was to do in 1939, 1944 and 1945, by piecemeal territorial annexations—the Baltic states, East Prussia, Bukovina, etc.—but through world revolution.[20] By 1915 Lenin was convinced that the power of Europe was on the wane. The war, he believed, would give a decisive impetus not only to the ripening of a revolutionary crisis in Europe,[21] but also to the development of extra-European centres of power and to a colonial awakening which would decisively weaken the European countries that had hitherto been dominant. Like Wilson, in short, but from a very different starting-point, Lenin moved under the impact of war—a world war which involved India, China, Japan, the Arab world, and the United States—from a European to a global view of international politics, which he set out to embody in Bolshevik doctrine and strategy. In many ways the most significant feature both of Wilson's programme and of Lenin's is that they were not European-centred but, world-embracing: that is to say, both set out to appeal to all peoples of the world, irrespective of race and colour.[22] Both implied a negation of the preceding European system; whether it was confined to Europe, or whether it spread (as it had done during the preceding generation) over the whole world. And both quickly fell into bitter competition. Lenin's summons to world revolution called forth, as a deliberate counter-stroke, Wilson's Fourteen Points, the solidarity of the proletariat and the revolt against imperialism were matched by self-determination and the century of the common man.[23] These were the slogans under which a new international system, different in all its basic tenets, took over from the old, and which preclude the view, still occasionally propounded, that it was merely "the same system of states in a new phase of its development."[24]

In this way, to the divergence of political interests which had begun to affect Russo-American relations at the close of the nineteenth century was added a deep ideological cleavage,[25] and each side set up a banner around which to gather its forces. The reversal that followed—the withdrawal of the United States into isolation, the weakening of Soviet Russia under the stress of civil war—does not detract from the importance of this turning-point.[26] It allowed Japan under Tojo to make, and Germany under Hitler to renew, its bid for a place among the world-powers;[27] but the result was to establish the primacy of the Soviet Union and the United States[28] even more definitely than before.

After 1945 the division of the world between Russia and America went on apace.[29] It would doubtless be a mistake to regard the resulting cleavage of the world into two conflicting power blocks as final; but in spite of a neutralist group attached to neither side. and in spite of differences between Russia and China, on the one side, and between the United States and its associates in western Europe, on the other, it is the situation with which we are confronted today. Much has been written in recent years of the dissolution of the monolithic blocks[30] which dominated the world for a decade after 1947. The fact remains that the Soviet Union and the United States are so far ahead of the rest of the world in nuclear weapons, and the resources to construct nuclear weapons. that no other country is in a position to challenge their preponderance within a foreseeable future.[31] Even if "bipolarity," which stamped its imprint on the period after the Second World War, may now be passing, it is evident that any new multipower system will be fundamentally different, in its structure and in its modalities. from the "classical" one.

【 Notes 】

①This selection is from "From the European Balance of Power to the Age of WorldPolitics" in *An Introduction to Contemporary History*, Penguin Books, 1978, pp.93—122. Barraclough, an iconoclast among mid 20th century historians, was particularly interested in questions of periodization and the boundaries of European civilization, of methodology and the meaning of universal history. He insisted on addressing the question of turning points in world history and the problem of whether there was a European civilization. In this selection he deals with the issue of the most important turning point in modern world history.

②Geoffrey Barraclough (1908—1985) is considered, among British historians, as one of the pillars of modern historical studies. A graduate of Oxford University and although trained as a classical scholar of medieval Germany, his rise to prominence in the 1940's to 60's was because of his radical views on history. Transformed from a medievalist into a contemporary world historian, he revolted against the Eurocentrism of the conventional history of the early and mid 20th century. Barraclough's change of view and methodology exemplified the reorientation of historiography in the post World War II period. In 1957 he was appointed as Professor of International History at the University of London.

③... and its modalities, in the age of Khrushchev were essentially different from those of the age of Bismarck:
modality /məu'dæliti/ n. 模式，形态，样式，仪式。Khrushchev /kruʃtʃɔf/ 赫鲁晓夫（1894—1971），苏共中央第一书记（1953—1964），部长会议主席（1958—1964），后被苏共中央全会解除党内外职务（1964）。Bismarck /'bizmɑːk/ 俾斯麦（Otto von, 1815—1898），德国政治家，德意志帝国第一任首相。

④Instead of by a concert of powers, we were confronted by two great super-powers, the Soviet Union and the United States, whose pre-eminence was based on their quasi-monopoly of nuclear weapons and of the delivery systems for launching nuclear weapons; and although Russia has one foot in Europe, it is significant that both super powers are great continent-spanning federal states, neither of which can realistically be classed as European. 我们面临着两个超级大国，苏联和美国，而不是各国力量的协调。这两个国家在显赫之前就部分地垄断核武器以及它的发射系统。虽然俄国有一只脚插在欧洲，但是，有一点是很重要的，即两个超级大国都是幅员广阔的联邦国家，实际上，没有一个国家能划分在欧洲。

concert 一致，和谐：in concert 一致；共同：acted in concert on the issue 和……采取一致步骤。eminence /ˈeminəns/ n. 卓越，显赫，著名：a position of eminence 显赫的地位；a man of eminence 名人；rose to eminence as a surgeon 成为一位杰出的外科医生。

⑤...a multilateral system of equilibrium centred upon Europe had been displaced by a system of global bipolarity between the two great two extra-European powers...：以欧洲为中心的多国平衡制已经被把欧洲排除在外的两个超级大国间的全球两极制所取代。

multilateral /ˌmultiˈlætərəl/ adj. 多边的，多国的：multilateral trade agreements 多边贸易协定。equilibrium /ˌiːkwiˈlibriəm/ n. 平衡，平静，均衡：the equilibrium of demand and supply 供求均衡；be in equilibrium with 与……平衡。bipolarity /ˌbaipəuˈlærəti/ n. 两极，双极。

⑥...blocks, inspired by apparently irreconcilable ideologies, took tangible shape：很明显，由于两种不可调和的意识形态所形成的两大阵营实际上已经形成。

irreconcilable /iˈreknsailbl/ adj. 不能和解的；矛盾的：be irreconcilable to / with sb. 同某人势不两立，不可调和的；irreconcilable enemies 不能和解的敌人；irreconcilable as fire and water 如水火不相容。tangible /ˈtændʒəbi/ adj. 可触摸的，有形的；确实的：tangible asset 有形财产；tangible evidence 确凿的证据；the tangible benefits of the plan 该项计划带来的实际益处。

⑦Though it was something like two years before President Wilson identified himself with the anti-Bolshevik crusaders in the west, he and Lenin were aware from the start that they were competing for the suffrage of mankind, and it was to prevent Lenin gaining a monopoly of the blueprints for the post-war world that, in January 1918, Wilson issued his famous Fourteen Points. 这个长句是一个并列复合句。在第一个分句中，he and Lenin were aware from the start 是主句，Though 引导一个让步状语从句，that 引导一个状语从句。在第二个分句中，主句是 it was to prevent Lenin gaining a monopoly of the blueprints for the post-war world，it 是形式主语，that 引导一个主语从句。

President Wilson (1856-12-18—1924-02-03)，威尔逊是第 28 任美国总统，1918 年 1 月他提出"公正和持久和平"的 14 点和平纲领。Bolshevik /ˈbɔlʃivik/ n. 布尔什维克。crusader /kruːˈseidə/ n. 十字军战士；改革者：a dry crusade（美）禁酒运动。suffrage /ˈsʌfridʒ/ n. 投票权；选举权：universal suffrage 普选权。monopoly /məˈnɔpəli/ n. 垄断，垄断者；专利权，专利事业：monopoly capital 垄断资本，独占资本。

⑧annexation /ˌænekˈseiʃən/ n.（常与 by 或 to 连用）附加；合并，吞并：the annexation of Texas to the United States 得克萨斯州并入美国。

⑨...both cut loose from the balance of power; both denounced the "dead hand of the past"：双方都摆脱了国家间的平衡，双方都公开指责过去的旧势力。

cut loose (from) a. 割断（船）的缆绳：The thief hastily cut the boat loose from its anchor. 小

155

偷匆忙地割断了船上的缆绳；b. 把……解救出来：cut the driver loose from the wreck of his car 把司机从他汽车的废墟中解救出来 ；c.（从束缚等中）解放出来,摆脱(from, of)；结束对……的控制：This country cut the colony loose a year ago. 一年前,这个国家结束了对这块殖民地的统治。

denounce /di'nauns/ vt. 公开指责,公然抨击,谴责：denounce a treaty 通知废止条约。

dead hand 旧势力,(喻)不散的阴魂。

⑩the revolutionary principles enunciated by Wilson and Lenin：

enunciate /i'nʌnsieit/ v. 阐明,清晰发言：enunciate views 发表见解。

⑪Czarist Russia：沙皇俄国。

⑫...without markedly disturbing the domestic status quo in and of the major belligerent nations：而不明显地扰乱国内的现状以及主要交战国的现状。

status quo /steitəs'kwəu/ n.（拉丁语）现状：to maintain the status quo 维持现状。belligerent /bi'lidʒərənt/ adj. 好战的,交战国的,交战的：belligerent powers 交战国。

⑬Trotsky /'trɔtski/ n. 托洛茨基（俄国革命领导者）。

⑭...was irretrievably disrupted：

irretrievably /iri'triːvəbli/ adv. 不能挽回地,不能补救地。disrupt /disrʌpt/ vt. 使混乱；使瓦解：The quarrels of the different political parties seemed likely to disrupt the state. 各政党的争执可能导致国家分裂。

⑮Washington and Petrograd：华盛顿和彼得格勒。

Petrograd /'petrəugræd/ 彼得格勒（苏联西北部港市）。

⑯Clemenceau, Sonnino, or Lloyd George：

Clemenceau 克列孟俊（1841-09-28—1929-11-34）,法国政治家、新闻记者、第三共和国总理,为第一次世界大战协约国的胜利和《凡尔赛和约》的签订做出重要贡献。

Sonnino 桑尼诺（1847-03-11—1922-11-24）,意大利政治家。

⑰The entry of the United States into the war meant, therefore, not—as allied statesmen deceived themselves into thinking—simply the mobilization at the crucial moment of another all-powerful belligerent, the addition of a decisive counter on the existing political chessboard; on the contrary, it meant the appearance on the scene of a power which had, for historical reasons, scant interest in the old European political system, which was not prepared to underwrite the European balance of power, and which had almost irresistible means, in the state of exhaustion to which the European powers on both sides had been reduced, of enforcing its point of view. 因此,正如盟国的政治家们所认为的那样,美国参战意味着不只是在关键时刻动员了另一个全能的参战国,而是在现存的政治棋盘上加上一个筹码,这是自欺欺人；事实正好相反,它意味着一个强国登台了,由于历史的原因,它对欧洲古老的政治制度没有太多的兴趣,也没有打算承诺欧洲国家的平衡,而当欧洲各国交战双方都已筋疲力尽时,它几乎以不可抗拒的方式强迫推行它的观点。

这个长句是由分号连接的并列复合句。第一个分句是一个简单句,therefore 和 as allied statesmen deceived themselves into thinking 把谓语动词 meant 和它的宾语部分 not simply the mobilization at the crucial moment of another all-powerful belligerent, the addition of a decisive counter on the existing political chessboard 分隔开了。第二个分句是一个复合句。主句是 it meant the appearance on the scene of a power，带有四个由 which 引导的定语从句，前面三个修饰 a power，第四个从句和被修饰的部分 in the state of exhaustion to which the European powers on both sides had been reduced 把 means of enforcing its point of view 分隔开了。

on the scene 出现；登场：Came on the scene just when we needed him. 在我们需要他的时候，他出现了。

scant /skænt/ vt. 限制；节省；减少；藐视；忽略：Don't scant the butter when you make a cake. 做糕饼时不要吝惜奶油。underwrite /ˈʌndərait/ vt. 签在……下，给……保险，签名，承保；承担赔偿责任：underwrite a theatrical production 承担戏院演出责任。

⑱When revolutionary Russia, under Lenin and Trotsky, embarked on a parallel course, the breach with the past became irrevocable.
embark /imˈbɑːtk/ v.（常与 on, in 连用）开始；从事：embark upon a new business undertaking 着手一项新的商业；使……上船或飞机：stopped to embark passengers 停止使乘客登船或飞机。breach /britʃ/ v.（常与 of 连用）违背；不履行；破坏：breach an agreement 违反协议。Your company are in breach of the contract. 你们公司违反了合同。irrevocable /iˈrevəkəbl/ adj. 不能改变的；不能取消的：irrevocable yesterday 不能唤回的昨天。

⑲...repudiated the old system of balance of power：拒绝权利平衡的老制度。
repudiate /riˈpjuːdieit/ vt., vi. 拒绝；断绝关系：repudiate offers of friendship 拒绝友谊；repudiate a bribe 拒绝受贿；否定；驳倒：repudiate a charge of murder 否认谋杀案的指控；repudiate a debt 赖债。

⑳So far as the security of Russia was at stake, they sought it not, as Stalin was to do in 1939, 1944 and 1945, by piecemeal territorial annexations—the Baltic states, East Prussia, Bukovina, etc., —but through world revolution. 只要俄罗斯的安全濒临危险，他们就会像斯大林在1939、1944和1945年打算做的那样去寻求安全，但不是通过兼并像东普鲁士、布科维纳那样零散的一块块土地，而是通过世界革命的方式。
at stake 濒临危险；得失攸关。repudiate /riˈpjuːdieit/ vt., vi. 拒绝；断绝关系。Bukovina /buːkəˈviːnə/ 布科维纳（欧洲东部一地区）。on(in) the wane（月）正在亏缺中；衰落（减少）中。

㉑...would give a decisive impetus not only to the ripening of a revolutionary crisis in Europe：
impetus /ˈimpitəs/ n. 冲力，推动力；刺激：Her speech gave an impetus to my ideas. 她的讲话激发了我的思绪。The approaching deadline gave impetus to the investigation. 即将到来的最后期限推动了谈判。ripen /ˈraipən/ vt., vi.（使）成熟。

㉒irrespective of race and colour：无论种族和肤色。
irrespective /irisˈpektiv/ adj.（与 of 连用）不顾……的；不考虑……的；不论……的：irrespective of the consequences 不顾后果。

㉓Lenin's summons to world revolution called forth, as a deliberate counter-stroke, Wilson's

Fourteen Points, the solidarity of the proletariat and the revolt against imperialism were matched by self-determination and the century of the common man. 列宁召唤世界革命招致威尔逊有的放矢的反击,威尔逊接着提出了十四点和平纲领,列宁号召无产阶级团结起来反对帝国主义与自主和平民的世纪是相适应的。

summons /ˈsʌmənz/ n. 召集,召唤,号召,鼓起,振作:At death's summons each must go. 死神有召,无可违抗。call forth 唤起;振起;引起;招致:a love song that calls forth sad memories 一首引起我悲伤回忆的爱情歌曲。

㉔These were the slogans under which a new international system, different in all its basic tenets, took over from the old, and which preclude the view, still occasionally propounded, that it was merely "the same system of states in a new phase of its development." 在这个长句中,主句是 These were the slogans;under which 和 which 引导两个并列的定语从句,修饰 slogans;that 引导 propounded 的宾语从句。

tenet /ˈtenit/ n. 信念;信条;教义;主义:basic tenets 基本原则。preclude /priˈkluːd/ v. (与 from 连用)避免;排除;阻止;妨碍:to preclude all doubts 排除一切疑虑。The flood precluded him from coming 他因洪水不能来了。it 指的是 a new international system。

㉕In this way, to the divergence of political interests which had begun to affect Russo-American relations at the close of the nineteenth century was added a deep ideological cleavage...:这个句子中,主语部分和谓语部分的词序有倒置现象,正常的词序是 In this way, a deep ideological cleavage was added to the divergence of political interests which had begun to affect Russo-American relations at the close of the nineteenth century.

divergence /daiˈvəːdʒəns/ n. 分歧,意见分歧。cleavage /ˈkliːvidʒ/ n. 分裂;裂缝;分解;裂开。

㉖does not detract from the importance of this turning-point:并没有减弱这一转折点的重要性。detract /diˈtrækt/ vi. (与 from 连用)减损;去掉;诽谤;贬低;毁损:to detract from one's merit 贬低某人的功绩。

㉗It allowed Japan under Tojo to make, and Germany under Hitler to renew, its bid for a place among the world-powers...:这使得东条英机统治下的日本在世界强国中争得了一席,希特勒统治下的德国又恢复了世界强国地位。

Tojo Hifrki 东条英机(1884-12-30—1948-12-23),日本军人和政治家,第二次世界大战大部分期间任首相(1941—1944),后来作为战犯受审判并被处决。

bid /bid/ n. 出价;投标;招标:Bids for building the bridge were invited. 应邀参加建造那座桥梁的投标。make a bid for 在拍卖中出价钱,投标;试图得到(名望、恩宠)。

㉘to establish the primacy of the Soviet Union and the United States:建立苏联和美国的首席地位。

primacy /ˈpraiməsi/ n. 首位;首要;首席:the primacy of the deed over word and thought 行动胜过言语和思想;primacy of planning 计划优先原则。

㉙...the division...went on apace:分歧迅速继续扩大。

apace /əˈpeis/ adv. 飞快地,迅速地:The hours and days speed apace. 时日过得飞快。

㉚Much... of the dissolution of the monolithic blocks：有关两大阵营解体的不少情况。dissolution /ˌdisə'liuʃən/ n. 分解；分裂；腐朽；解体；解散；解除：the dissolution of Parliament 国会解散。monolithic /ˌmɔnə'liθik/ adj. 巨石的；巨大而屹立的；单一的；统一的：the monolithic buildings 高耸的建筑；a single monolithic party 统一不分派别的政党。

㉛to challenge their preponderance within a foreseeable future：preponderance /pri'pɔndərəns/ n. 优势，占优势。foreseeable /fɔː'siːəbl/ adj. 可预知的，能预测的，能看透的。

【Exercises】

I. Comprehension Questions

(1) In what two ways does this author think the entry of the United States into World War I was a turning point in modern history? (See paragraph 2.)

(2) According to Barraclough, what did Woodrow Wilson and Lenin have in common?

(3) This author does not think World War II was a major turning point in history. True or False? Explain your choice.

(4) In this selection what does "new diplomacy" mean? Choose the best answer from the following:

 A. Diplomacy backed by military strength.

 B. Diplomacy appealing to the people over the heads of the politicians.

 C. Territorial adjustment, annexation, and compensation negotiated by diplomats to produce a balance of power among nations.

(5) What did Wilson's Fourteen Points stand for? Choose as many of the following as you think are correct.

 A. The century of the common man.

 B. World revolution.

 C. Self-determination.

 D. Solidarity of the proletariat.

 E. Balance of power among nations.

II. Points for Discussion

(1) In your opinion as an historian, in relation to Europe and to the United States what role have the Asian nations played in each of the following time periods: the middle of the 20th century, the end of the 20th century and the beginning of this, the 21st century. Pick out the most important characteristics of each of these three periods and contrast them for similarities and differences.

(2) What does Barraclough mean by "world politics" in your view? Distinguish this concept from "national politics." Give several illustrations from the twentieth century of "world politics."

III. Complete the following sentences with appropriate forms of words or expressions from the passage according to the given meaning in brackets.

(1) Chaucer not only came to doubt the worth of his extraordinary body of work, but _____ (reject) it.

(2) He grew so enthusiastic about our prospects that he began to speculate on the _____ (the ceremonial forms) of signing.

(3) The girl left home and _____ (become independent) from her parents' control.

(4) An accident of the collision of a truck with a train has _____ (throw into disorder) railway services into and out of the city.

(5) One feels between them an accumulation of gentleness and strength, a _____ (harmony) of energies.

(6) What do you think of the fact that modesty _____ (prevent) me from accepting the honor?

IV. Complete the following sentences with the words or expressions from the passage given below. Change the form where necessary.

| confront | monopoly | belligerent | on the contrary | due to | bid |
| call forth | attributed | sense | irrespective | | in short |

(1) Mike wants to sell his farm, and he has already had two large _____ for it.

(2) A university education shouldn't be the _____ of the minority whose parents are rich.

(3) They send information every week, _____ of whether it's useful or not.

(4) The boys found it hard to get along with Tom, because he always said some very _____ things.

(5) His untimely death _____ at least in part to overwork and lack of exercises.

(6) _____, studies show that an overwhelming majority of patients do want to be told the truth, even about grave illness.

(7) But you do not own the beefsteak in the most important _____ until you consume it and get it into your bloodstream.

(8) When the accident was _____ with the evidence of half a dozen witnesses, he broke down and confessed.

Unit 10

Russia and the Soviet Union

17. A Geographical Note[1]

Nicholas V. Riasanovsky[2]

> 尼古拉·里尔萨诺夫斯基(Nicholas V. Riasanovsky,1923—)自1957年至今是加利福尼亚伯克利大学名誉教授。他是一位重要的美国、俄罗斯历史学家。他先后在莫斯科、赫尔辛基、列宁格勒、巴黎和伦敦的斯拉夫研究中心工作,曾经是斯拉夫研究美国协会的主席。他撰写的《俄罗斯历史》首次于1963年出版,1984年第四次再版。这是一本既有条不紊又具有权威性的标准教科书,但是它没有包含1989年苏联解体后的这段历史。

THE RUSSIAN EMPIRE,[3] and more recently the Union of Soviet Socialist Republics, represents a land mass of over eight and one-half million square miles, an area larger than the entire North American continent. To quote the leading Russian encyclopedia: "The Russian empire, stretching in the main latitudinally, occupies all of eastern Europe and northern Asia,[4] and its surface constitutes 0.42 of the area of these two continents. The Russian empire occupies 1/22 part of the entire globe and approximately 1/6 part of its total land surface."

Yet, this enormous territory exhibits considerable homogeneity.[5] Indeed, homogeneity helps to explain its size. The great bulk of Russia is an immense plain -at one time the bottom of a huge sea -extending from central and even western Europe deep into Siberia. Although numerous hills arid chains of hills[6] are scattered on its surface, they are not high enough or sufficiently concentrated to interfere appreciably with the flow of the mighty plain, the largest on the entire globe.[7] The Ural mountains themselves, ancient and weather-beaten, constitute no effective barrier between Europe and Asia, which they separate; besides, a broad gap of steppe land[8] remains between the southern tips of the Ural chain and the Caspian and Aral seas. Only in vast northeastern Siberia, beyond the Enisei river, does the elevation rise considerably and hills predominate. But this area, while of a remarkable potential, has so far remained at best on the periphery of Russian history.[9] Impressive mountain ranges are restricted to Russian borders or, at the most, borderlands. They include the Carpathians to the southwest, the high and picturesque Caucasian chain in the south between the Black Sea and the Caspian, and the mighty Pamir, Tien Shan, and Altai ranges further east along the southern border.

Rivers flow slowly through the plain. Most of them carry their waters along a north-south axis and empty either into the Baltic and the Arctic Ocean or into the Black and the Caspian seas. In European Russia, such rivers as the Northern Dvina and the Pechora flow northward, while others, notably the Dniester, the Bug, and the larger Dnieper, Don, and Volga proceed south. The Dnieper and the Don empty into the Black Sea, the Volga into the Caspian. Siberian rivers, the huge Ob and Enisei, as well as the rapid Lena, the Indigirka, and the Kolyma, drain into the Arctic Ocean. The exception is the Amur, which flows eastward, serves during much of its course as the boundary between Russia and China, and empties into the Strait of Tartary. South of Siberia in Russian Central Asia both the Amu Daria and the Syr Daria flow northwestward to the Aral Sea, although the former at one time used to reach the Caspian. These rivers and their tributaries, together with other rivers and lakes, provide Russia with an excellent system of water communication. The low Valdai hills in northwestern European Russia represent a particularly important watershed, for it is there that the Dnieper and the Volga, as well as the Western Dvina and the Lovat, have their sources.

But while Russia abounds in rivers and lakes, it is essentially a landlocked country. By far its longest coastline opens on the icy Arctic Ocean. The neighboring seas include the Baltic and the Black, both of which must pass through narrow straits, away from Russian borders, to connect with broader expanses of water, and the Caspian and the Aral, which are totally isolated. The Aral Sea is also entirely within Russian territory, and it has been listed with such major Russian lakes as Ladoga and Onega in the European part of the country, Balkhash in Central Asia, and the huge and extremely deep Lake Baikal in Siberia. The Russian eastern coastline too is subject to cold and inclement weather, except for the southern section adjacent to the Chinese border.[10]

Latitude and a landlocked condition largely determine Russian climate, which can be best described as severely continental. Northern and even central Russia are on the latitude of Alaska, while the position of southern Russia corresponds more to the position of Canada in the western hemisphere than to that of the United States. The Gulf Strain, which does so much to make the climate of western and northern Europe milder, barely reaches one segment of the northern coastline of Russia. In the absence of interfering mountain ranges, icy winds from the Arctic Ocean sweep across European Russia to the Black Sea. Siberian weather, except in the extreme southeastern corner, is more brutal still. In short, although sections of the Crimean littoral can be described as the Russian Riviera,[11] and although sub-tropical conditions do prevail in parts of the southern Caucasus, the over-whelming bulk of Russian territory remains subject to a very severe climate. In northern European Russia the soil stays frozen eight months out of twelve. Even the Ukraine[12] is covered by snow three months every year, while the rivers freeze all the way to the Black Sea. Siberia in general and northeastern Siberia in particular belong among the coldest areas in the world. The temperature at Verkhoiansk[13] has been registered at as low as $-90°$ F. Still, in keeping with the continental nature of the climate, when summer finally comes—and it often comes rather suddenly—temperatures soar. Heat waves are common in European Russia and in much of Siberia, not to mention the deserts of Central Asia which spew sand many miles to the west.[14]

Climate determines the vegetation that forms several broad belts extending latitudinally across the country. In the extreme north lies the tundra, virtually uninhabited frozen waste of swamps, moss, and shrubs covering almost per cent of Russian territory. South of the tundra stretches the taiga, a zone of coniferous forest, merging with and followed by the next zone, that of mixed forest.[15] The two huge forested belts sweep across Russia from its western boundaries to its eastern shoreline and account for over half of its territory. Next comes the steppe, or prairie, occupying southern European Russia and extending into Asia up to the Altai mountains. Finally, the southernmost zone, that of semi-desert and desert, takes in most of Central Asia. Being very wide if considerably shorter than even the steppe belt, it occupies somewhat less than one-fifth of the total area of the country.

One important result of the climate and of this pattern of vegetation in Russia has been a relative dearth of first-rate agricultural land.[16] Only an estimated one million square miles out of an area more than eight times the size are truly rewarding to the tiller[17] of the soil. Other sections of the country suffer from the cold and from insufficient precipitation,[18] which becomes more inadequate as one progresses east. Even the heavy snowfalls add relatively little moisture because of the rapid melting and the quick run-off of water in the spring. In Central Asia farming depends almost entirely on irrigation. The best land in Russia, the excellent black soil of the southern steppe offers agricultural conditions comparable to those on the great plains of Canada rather than those in warmer Iowa or Illioois. Russia, on the other hand, is fabulously rich in forests,[19] more so than any other country in the world. And it possesses a great wealth and variety of natural resources, ranging from platinum to oil[20] and from coal to gold. On the whole, however, these resources remained unused and even unexplored for a very long time.

Ever since Herodotus historians[21] have been fascinated by the role of geographic factors in human history. Indeed the father of history referred to the broad sweep of the southern Russian steppe and to the adaptation of the steppe inhabitants, the Scythians,[22] to their natural environment in his explanation of why the mighty Persians could not overcome them. Modern historians of Russia, including such leading Russian scholars as Kliuchevsky and especially his teacher S. Soloviev, as well as such prominent Western writers as Kerner and Sumner,[23] have persistently emphasized the significance of geography for Russian history. Even if we reject the rigid determinism implicit in some of their views and refuse to speculate on such nebulous and precarious topics as the Russian national character[24] and its dependence on the environment -speculations in which Kliuchevsky and others engaged in a fascinating manner—some fundamental points have to be made.

For instance, it appears certain that the growth of the Russian state was affected by the geography of the area: a vast plain with very few natural obstacles to expansion. This setting notably made it easier for the Moscow state to spread across eastern Europe. Beyond the Urals, the Russians advanced all the way to the Pacific, and even to Alaska and California, a progression paralleled only by the great American movement west. As the boundaries of the Russian empire ultimately emerged, they consisted of oceans to the north and east and, in large part, of seas, high mountains, and deserts to the south; only in the west, where the Russians merged with streams of other peoples, did the border seem unrelated to geography. The extremely severe climate contributed to the weakness of the tribes scattered in northern European Russia and of the various inhabitants of Siberia, leading to their utter inability to stem the Russian advance. Whereas the Russians could easily expand, they were well protected from outside attack. Russian distances brought defeat to many, although not all, invaders, from the days of the Persians and the Scythians to those of Napoleon and Hitler.

Occupied territory had to be governed. The problem of administering an enormous area, of holding the parts together, of coordinating local activities and efforts remained a staggering task for those in power, whether Ivan the Terrible, Nicholas I, or Stalin.[25] And the variety of peoples on the great plain was bound to make such issues as centralization and federation all the more acute. One can appreciate, if not accept, the opinion of those thinkers, prominent in the Enlightenment and present in other periods, who related the system of government of a country directly to its size and declared despotism to be the natural form of rule in Russia.[26]

The magnificent network of Russian rivers and lakes also left its mark on Russian history. It is sufficient to mention the significance of the Dneiper for Kievan Russia,[27] or of the Volga and its tributaries for the Moscow state. The landlocked position of the country and the search for an access to the waterways of the world made the Russians repeatedly concerned with the Baltic, the Black Sea, and the Straits.[28] Climate and vegetation basically affected the distribution of people in Russia and also their occupations. The poor quality of much agricultural land has led to endemic suffering among Russian peasants and has taxed the ingenuity of tsarist ministers and Khrushchev alike.[29] Russian natural resources, since they began to be developed on a large scale, have added immeasurably to Soviet strength. Both the wealth of Russia and the geographic and climatic obstacles to a utilization of this wealth have perhaps never stood out so sharply as in the course of present efforts to industrialize eastern Siberia.

The location of Russia on its two continents has had a profound impact on Russian history. The southern Russian steppe in particular served for centuries as the highway for Asiatic nomads to burst into Europe.[30] Mongol devastation was for the Russians only the most notable incident in a long series,[31] and it was followed by over two hundred years of Mongol rule. In effect, the steppe frontier, open for centuries, contributed hugely to the miniaturization of Russian society,[32] a trend reinforced by the generally unprotected and fluid nature of the western border of the country. But proximity to Asiatic lands led also to some less warlike contacts; furthermore, it enabled Russia later in turn to expand grandly in Asia without the need first to rule the high seas. Recently the Eurasian school of historians, represented in the English language especially by Vernadsky, has tried to interpret the entire development of Russia in terms of its unique position in the Old World.

Russian location in Europe may well be regarded as even more important than its connections with Asia. Linked to the West by language, religion, and basic culture, the Russians nevertheless suffered the usual fate of border peoples: invasion from the outside, relative isolation, and retardation.[33] Hence, at least in part, the efforts to catch up, whether by means of Peter the Great's reforms or the Five-Year Plans.[34] Hence also, among other things, the interminable[35] debate concerning the nature and the significance of the relationship between Russia and the West.

As the examples above, which by no means exhaust the subject, indicate, geography does affect history, Russian history included. It has been noted that the influence of certain geographic factors tends to be especially persistent. Thus, while our modern scientific civilization does much to mitigate the impact of climate,[36] a fact brilliantly illustrated in the development of such a northern country as Finland, so far we have not changed mountains into plains or created new seas. Still, it is best to conclude with a reservation: geography may set the stage for history; human beings make history.

【 Notes 】

①This selection is from *A History of Russia*, 4th Edition, Oxford University Press, 1984, pp. 2—10. This 4th Edition of *A History of Russia*, published in 1984, updated the book, originally published in 1963. A standard textbook for the study of Russian history, it is considered authoritative and balanced but does not cover the period after the collapse of the Soviet Union in 1989.

②Nicholas V. Riasanovsky (1923—), Professor Emeritus, has taught at the University of California at Berkeley since 1957. He is one of the foremost American Russian historians. He has worked in Centers of Slavic Studies in Moscow, Helsinki, Leningrad, Paris and London and is a past president of the American Association for the of Slavic Studies.

③本文第二、三段中所出现的地点、山脉和河流的汉语名称(生词)：
Siberia /saiˈbiəriə/ 西伯利亚；the Ural /ˈjuərəl/ mountains 乌拉尔山脉；the Caspian /ˈkæspiən/ 里海；the Aral /ˈærəl/ sea 咸海；the Enisei river 叶尼塞河；the Carpathians /kɑːˈpeiθjənz/ 喀尔巴阡山脉；the Caucasian /kkɔːˈkeiziən/ chain 高加索山系；the Black Sea 黑海；the Pamir 帕米尔高原；the Altai /ælˈtai/ 阿尔泰山；the Baltic /ˈbɔːltik/ 波罗

的海; the Northern Dvina 北德维纳河; the Pechora 北潮拉河; the Dniester /ˈdnjestə/ 德涅斯特河; the Bug 巴格河; the Dnieper 第聂伯河; the Don /dɔn/ 顿河; the Volga /ˈvɔlgə/ 伏尔加河; the Ob /əub/ 鄂毕湾; the Lena 勒拿河; the Indigirka 印迪吉尔卡河; the Kolyma 科累马河; the Amur 黑龙江河; the Strait of Tartary 鞑靼海峡; the Amu Daria 阿姆河; the Syr Daria 锡尔河; the Valdai hills 阿尔泰山; the Western Dvina 西德维纳河; the Lovat 涅瓦河; Ladoga Lake 拉多加湖; Onega Lake 奥涅加湖; Balkhash Lake 巴尔喀什湖; Baikal Lake 贝加尔湖; the Crimean /kraiˈmiən/ adj. 克里米亚半岛的: Crimean War 克里米亚战争(1853—1856年英、法、土等与俄国之战)。

④The Russian empire, stretching in the main latitudinally, occupies all of eastern Europe and northern Asia...: 俄罗斯帝国从纬度方向延伸,基本上占据了东欧和北亚。

 in the main 大体上;基本上;就一般而论。latitudinally /lætiˈtjuːdinəli/ adv. 向纬度方向。

⑤Yet, this enormous territory exhibits considerable homogeneity. 然而,这块幅员辽阔的土地却表现出了相当大的同一性。

 homogeneity /ˌhɔməudʒeˈniːiti/ n. 同种;同质;同性;(数)齐性,均匀性: absolute homogeneity 绝对齐性; chemical homogeneity 化学均匀性。

⑥arid chains of hills: 贫瘠的一个个山系。

 arid /ˈærid/ adj. 干旱的;贫瘠的,荒芜的;枯燥无味的: Desert lands are arid. 沙漠地区是草木不生的。a technically perfect but arid musical performance 一场技术上完美但枯燥的音乐演出。

⑦..., they are not high enough or sufficiently concentrated to interfere appreciably with the flow of the mighty plain, the largest on the entire globe. 这些山系不够高也不够集中,对世界上最大的一泻千里的大平原影响不大。

 appreciably /əˈpriːʃəb(ə)li/ adv. 略微,有一点;相当地(可观地)。

⑧a broad gap of steppe land: 广阔的大草原。

 steppe /ˈstep/ n. 干草原;疏树大平原: the Steppes(尤指东南欧或西伯利亚的)大草原;吉尔吉斯(Kirghiz)大草原; desert steppe 沙漠草原。

⑨on the periphery of Russian history: 在俄罗斯历史的范围。

 periphery /pəˈrifəri/ n. 外围;界限;周边;外围设备: fibre periphery 纤维周边,纤维外缘。

⑩... is subject to cold and inclement weather, except for the southern section adjacent to the Chinese border. 除了接近中国边界的南部地区,气候也多是严寒的。

 inclement /inˈklemənt/ adj. 恶劣的,严寒的,狂风暴雨的(天气): inclement weather 险恶的天气。adjacent /əˈdʒeisənt/ adj. 相邻的,邻近的: be adjacent to 接近。

⑪... although sections of the Crimean littoral can be described as the Russian Riviera...:
the Crimean Littoral 克里米亚沿海地区。littoral /ˈlitərəl/ n. 沿海地,沿海地区: the littoral province 沿海省份(地区); a littoral property 海岸所有权。Riviera /riviˈeərə/ 里维埃拉(南欧沿地中海一地区),在法国东南部和意大利西北部,是假日游憩胜地。

⑫the Ukraine /ju(ː)ˈkrein/ n. [国名]乌克兰。

⑬Verkhoiansk /vjekəˈjænisk/ Range：维尔霍扬斯克山脉（苏联西北利亚东北部）。

⑭... which spew sand many miles to the west. 沙漠把沙子向西喷射出数十英里。
　　spew /spjuː/ vt.,vi. 涌出；喷出；渗出：a volcano spewing out lava 喷出熔岩的火山；Water spewed slowly from the soil. 水慢慢从土中渗出。

⑮South of the tundra stretches the taiga, a zone of coniferous forest, merging with and followed by the next zone, that of mixed forest.
　　tundra /ˈtʌndrə/ n. 苔原，冻土地带。taiga /ˈteigə/ n. 针叶树林地带。coniferous /kəuˈnifərəs/ adj. 松类的，结球果的。

⑯a relative dearth of first-rate agricultural land：相对来说，缺少第一流的耕地。
　　dearth /dəːθ/ n. 缺乏；饥荒：a dearth of food 粮食缺乏；in time of dearth 饥荒时候。

⑰tiller /ˈtilə/ n.（=farmer）耕作者，农夫；耕作机具：land to the tiller 耕者有其田。

⑱Other sections of the count suffer from the cold and from insufficient precipitation. 其他考虑的因素是受到寒冷和降雨量不足的损害。
　　precipitation /prisipiˈteiʃən/ n. 急躁；仓促；降（雨）量；雨量；沉淀；沉淀作用：annual precipitation 年降水量；acid precipitation 酸雨。

⑲... is fabulously rich in forests...：森林资源极大丰富。
　　fabulously /ˈfæbjuləsli/ adv. 难以置信地，惊人地。

⑳... variety of natural resources, ranging from platinum to oil：从白金到石油的各种自然资源。
　　platinum /ˈplætinəm/ n. 白金，铂。

㉑Herodotus historians：希罗多德派历史学家。
　　Herodotus /hiˈrɔdətəs/ n. 希罗多德（公元前5世纪希腊历史学家，有历史之父之称）。

㉒the Scythians /ˈsiðiən/ adj. 锡西厄的；锡西厄人的；锡西厄语的。n. 锡西厄人；锡西厄语。

㉓...,including such leading Russian scholars as Kliuchevsky and especially his teacher S. Soloviev, as well as such prominent Western writers as Kerner and Sumner...：
Kliuchevsky 克柳切夫斯基（1841-01-28—1911-05-25），生在俄罗斯奔萨省沃滋涅先斯科耶，死在莫斯科，俄国历史学家，他对有关社会问题的探讨和俄国历史的研究、生动有趣的著作以及讲课风格使他成为当时最杰出的学者之一；1879年成为莫斯科大学历史学教授，曾出版讲义卷（1904—1910）。
Kerner 克尔纳（1786-09-18—1862-02-21），德国诗人和唯灵主义作家，与诗人乌兰德共同创立晚期浪漫主义诗人的所谓"士瓦本派"。
Sumner 萨姆纳（1840-10-30—1910-04-12），美国社会学家和经济学家，一生写有很多文章，宣传社会达尔文主义。

㉔... the rigid determinism implicit in some of their views and refuse to speculate on such nebulous and precarious topics as the Russian national character...：
implicit /imˈplisit/ adj. 暗含的,含蓄的：an implicit threat 暗示的恐吓；无疑的,绝对的：implicit belief 绝对相信。nebulous /ˈnebjuləs/ adj. 含糊的,模糊的；暧昧的：a nebulous idea 一个模糊不清的观念；云雾状的：a nebulous liquid 云雾状的液体。precarious /priˈkɛəriəs/ adj. 不安全的；危险的；臆断的；基于不稳定的前提的：a precarious argu-

ment 立论不稳的议论；a precarious posture 不安全的姿势；precarious footing on the ladder：在梯子上没站稳。

㉕ ... remained a staggering task for those in power, whether Ivan the Terrible, Nicholas I, or Stalin：对于这些掌权人来说，无论是伊凡（俄国沙皇）、暴君尼古拉一世还是斯大林，……仍然是一个庞大的任务。

staggering /ˈstæɡəriŋ/ adj. 难以置信的；惊愕的：a staggering problem 难题；The cost is staggering. 费用大得惊人。Ivan 伊凡，六位莫斯科大公及俄国沙皇之名。

Nicholas I 尼古拉一世（1796-07-06—1855-03-02），俄国皇帝（1825—1855），通常被认为是独裁者的典型。

Stalin 斯大林（姓氏；Joseph Vissarionovitch, 1879—1953, 苏联党和国家领导人）。

㉖ ... declared despotism to be the natural form of rule in Russia：宣称专制是俄罗斯统治的自然形式。

despotism /ˈdespətizm/ n. 专制，暴政；专制统治。

㉗ ... the significance of the Dneiper for Kievan Russia ...：第聂伯河对俄罗斯基辅地区的意义。

Kievan /ˈkiːjefən/ adj. 基辅的（基辅是乌克兰的首都）。

㉘ the straits 海峡（指连接黑海与地中海的水道，由达达尼尔海峡与博斯普鲁斯海峡组成，旧时也指直布罗陀海峡）。

㉙ ... has taxed the ingenuity of tsarist ministers and Khrushchev alike：让沙皇的大臣以及赫鲁晓夫一样都用尽心机。

tsarist /ˈtsɑːrist/ adj. 沙皇的（专制的）。tax one's ingenuity 用尽心机。

㉚ ... served for centuries as the highway for Asiatic nomads to burst into Europe：几世纪都作为亚洲的游牧民涌向欧洲的通道。

nomad /ˈnəumæd/ n. 游牧部落的人，流浪者，游牧民；adj. 游牧的。

㉛ Mongol devastation was for the Russians only the most notable incident in along series ...：蒙古人的侵入对俄国人来说只是一系列事件中最明显的一个。

devastation /ˌdevəsˈteiʃən/ n. 荒废；[pl.] 劫后余迹：forest devastation 森林破坏；森林荒废。notable /ˈnəutəbl/ adj. 值得注意的；显著的；显要的；优越的：Sled dogs are notable for their stamina. 雪橇狗以它们的忍耐力而著称。

㉜ the miniaturization of Russian society：俄罗斯社会的小型化。

miniaturization /ˌminiətʃəraiˈzeiʃən/ n. 小型化。

㉝ invasion from the outside, relative isolation, and retardation：外界的侵入、相对闭塞和落后。

retardation /ritɑːˈdeiʃən/ n. 延迟，阻滞；延迟程度，妨碍量：mental retardation 智力迟钝。

㉞ whether by means of Peter the Great's reforms or the Five-Year Plans：无论是通过彼得大帝的改革还是多个五年计划的实施。

Peter the Great 彼得大帝（1672-06-09—1725-02-08），俄国沙皇（1682年起），1721年起为皇帝，是俄国最伟大的政治家、组织家和改革家之一。由于他，俄国成了强大的国家，从此以后,没有他的同意,欧洲的任何重大问题都是不能解决的。他在国内改革方面取得的成就是先前任何一位主张革新的人也不敢设想的。the Five-Year Plans 五年计划。斯大林于1928年主张通过连续几个五年计划实现由国家组织的工业化。

㉟interminable /inˈtəːminəbl/ *adj.* 无终止的,没完没了的

㊱to mitigate the impact of climate:

mitigate /ˈmitigeit/ *vt.* 减轻严重性;缓和,减低(坏处、伤害等): mitigate pain (suffering, grief, anger, harm)减缓疼痛(痛苦、忧伤、愤怒、伤害); Nothing could mitigate the cruelty with which she had treated him. 她对他太残暴了,实在是罪无可恕。

【 Exercises 】

I. Comprehension Questions

(1) The Russian Empire and the recent Soviet Union were not as large as North America. This statement is True _____ or False _____?

(2) Which of the following geographical features are the main characteristics of most of Russia?

    A. Mountainous terrain.

    B. Rolling hills and valleys.

    C. A great plain.

    D. Arid desert land.

(3) Most rivers in Russia _____.

    A. flow north to the Arctic Ocean

    B. empty into the Atlantic or Pacific Ocean

    C. flood every year and cause great erosion

    D. flow along a North-South axis

(4) Choose from the following list the most important conditions that determine Russia's continental climate.

    A. Near the equator.

    B. Subject to constant trade winds.

    C. Latitude position on the globe.

    D. Subject to monsoon winds.

    E. Land locked.

    F. In a rain belt.

(5) What proportion of Russian land is high grade agricultural land?

    A. 1/8.

    B. 1/2.

    C. 1/4.

    D. 1/20.

(6) What are Russia's most important natural resources? Identify four that Riasanovsky lists.

(7) What country shows us that modern scientific civilization can overcome the affect of climate?

II. Points for Discussion

(1) According to the author, what are the reasons that geographic features have been extremely important in the Russian past? Find as many examples as you can to answer this question.

(2) Which conditions do you think have been the most important in the past?

(3) What do these geographic conditions and Russia's location suggest will be Russia's relationship with Asian countries, and European countries in the future?

III. Complete the following sentences with the words or expressions from the passage given below. Change the form where necessary.

> rigid   impact   contribute to   in turn   serve
> interlude   take in   by no means   interminable   mitigate
> catch up   may well   in terms of   in particular

(1) We have watered down a _____ training until we now have an educational diet in many of our public high schools that nourishes neither the classes nor the masses.

(2) The judge said that nothing could _____ the cruelty with which the stepmother had treated the girl.

(3) Kerensky has a place in history, of a brief _____ between despotisms.

(4) We had seen mountains before, but we had never experienced anything even remotely like that initial _____ of the Tetons.

(5) While there were ten or twelve of these "teams" that worked together, one _____ was known for its perfect coordination and lightning-like efforts.

(6) Each of us wants to feel he or she has the ability to do something that is meaningful and that _____ as a tribute to our inherent abilities.

(7) Armed with such a precept, a number of doctors may slip into deceptive practices that they assume will "do no harm" and _____ help their patients.

(8) Forensic science _____ criminology, which covers the causes of crime.

(9) I had _____ problems with my last computer; it never worked well.

Unit 11

United States

18. George Washington and the Enlightenment[1]

Garry Wills[2]

> 加里·威尔斯(Garry Wills)是美国知名的文化历史学家,也是一位受欢迎的作家。他于1961年获得耶鲁大学博士学位,现在是伊里诺斯州西北大学的兼职教授。在他的乔治·华盛顿传记研究中,他认为乔治·华盛顿确实很伟大,因为他代表了英雄的政治领导者的启蒙运动理想。他向读者展示了美国殖民者在军事上打败了英国军队以后,在这一关键时刻,华盛顿是怎样以自己的风格和行动建立起了稳定的国家政府,领导人民进入一个崭新的世纪。他通过自己辞位所让出的政权使得过去的殖民者有可能接受宪法,从而建立起稳定团结的联邦政府,也就是今天的美国。

Excerpts from the Introduction

Washington eludes us,[3] even in the city named for him.... Washington's faceless Monument tapers off from us however we come at it[4]—visible everywhere, and perfect; but impersonal, uncompelling.... The classical control of the exterior hides a varied and spontaneous interior—an image of the puzzle that faces us, the early popularity of someone lifted so high above the populace. The man we can hardly find was the icon our ancestors turned to[5] most easily and often. We are distanced from him by their generosity, their willingness to see in him something almost more than human.

......

Before there was a nation—before there was any symbol of that nation (a flag, a constitution, a national seal)—there was Washington. Even when, in the course of revolutionary events, a flag did appear, and a Constitution, they did not have a long tradition behind them, to halo them with sacred memories.[6] But Washington was still there, steadying the symbols, lending strength to them instead of drawing it from them.

......

More than most men, this man was what he meant to his contemporaries. If he played a necessary role at the birth of our republic, it is important for us to assess the expectations of his audience, along with his willingness consciously to meet those expectations. That means we must understand the Enlightenment's conception of political heroism. ... The way Washington conceived his task, and went about it, was tempered from the outset by the responses he hoped to elicit from his countrymen.[7] His life verged on legend,[8] even as he lived it, because he had models he was trying to live up to; and he came close enough for others to accept him as a literal fulfillment of the age's aspirations.[9] This was nowhere more true than in the three great moments which seemed, for his contemporaries, to sum up his life—the resignation of his commission as Commander in Chief, his sponsorship of the new Constitution in 1787, and his surrender of the presidency by a farewell address. It was in the performance of these acts that Washington became "larger than life," since each seemed to revive the ancient republic that men were yearning for. My book will consider each of those three acts, and the symbols through which early Americans tried to express their significance.

Excerpts from Chapter 1

HE WAS A VIRTUOSO of resignations.[10] He perfected the art of getting power by giving it away. He tried this first, unsuccessfully, as a young colonel of militia[11]—but then only as a gesture from hurt pride. He was still learning that mere power to refuse is real, but limited. The power would later be refined, as would the gestures—when he learned the creative power of surrender.

Unlike other officers in the Revolution, he did not resign or threaten to resign when baffled of honor or advantage[12] (GW 10. 4- 63). He did not want to cheapen the currency; he would not anticipate his promised abdication at war's end.[13] His whole war service was urged forward under the archway of two pledges—to receive no pay, and to resign when independence was won. He was choreographing his departure with great care.[14] It was an act of pedagogical theater;[15] and the world applauded.

He tells us later what care he took to underline the meaning of his act. Pressed to rejoin the struggle for a stronger union in 1787, he wrote John Jay[16] that he had escaped from that "sea of troubles":

> Nor could it be expected, that my sentiments and opinion would have much weight on the minds of my Countrymen; they have been neglected, tho'[17] given as a last legacy in the most solemn manner (GW 27. 503).

He is referring to the circular letter sent to the governors of all thirteen states, during the summer of 1783, in which he announced his forthcoming resignation and coupled it with a plea for a more vigorous central government. He wanted the resignation at Annapolis[18] to be seen as lending moral force to the arguments he had advanced to the governors.

He gave the matter careful thought, with an eye to timing as well as content.[19] He would stage his lesson to men's eyes,[20] not merely address their minds. The job he had given himself required great tact,[21] an awareness of others' sensibilities, and an assurance that he was not overstepping his authority. The circular letter itself must be carefully phrased, and the situation of the Army had to be presented in just the right way. Washington had addressed circular letters to the governors during the war, but these were respectful pleas that the will of Congress be done in meeting particular crises. Besides, while the war was being actively waged, Washington had to be guarded in his language, since the posting of so many copies of a single letter made it probable that one or more would fall into enemy hands (GW 25. 188). Now he meant to advance a proposal of his own, and one that fell more within the political than the military sphere.

He would not have undertaken this risky act were it not for his sense of the crisis that would follow on a victory; and he coupled the recommendation with his own pledge to resign not only his military commission but all future public office, lest the argument be read as a way of promoting his career. The resignation would give him moral standing for the circular letter. As he put it later to Governor Harrison of Virginia, a strengthened government would not directly profit him:

> For my own part, . altho'[22] I am returned to, and am now mingled with the class of private citizens, and like them must suffer all the evils of a Tyranny, or of too great an extension of federal powers, I have no fears arising from this source (GW 27. 306).

The same argument formed the basis of his appeal to the governors:

> I will therefore speak to your Excellency, the language of freedom and of sincerity, without disguise; I am aware, however, that those who differ from me in political sentiment, may perhaps remark, I am stepping out of the proper line of my duty, and they may possibly ascribe to arrogance or ostentation, what I know is alone the result of the purest intention, but the rectitude of my own heart, which disdains such unworthy motives, the part I have hitherto acted in life, the determination I have formed, of not taking any share in public business hereafter, the ardent desire I feel, and shall continue to manifest, of quietly enjoying in private life, after all the toils of war, the benefits of a wise and liberal Government, will, I flatter myself, sooner or later convince my Countrymen, that I have no sinister views in delivering with so little reserve, the opinions contained in this Address (GW 26.486—87). [23]

The other factor requiring delicacy on Washington's part was the situation of the Army. It was an excruciating task[24] for Washington to maintain morale and discipline during the two years of "phony peace"[25] that stretched from the battle at Yorktown to the departure of British troops from American soil. Washington could not relax so long as there was any possibility of a breakdown in the treaty negotiations—something that seemed quite possible after De Grasse, the victor at Yorktown, was himself defeated by Admiral Rodney off the island of Dominica, removing British fears for their hold on Jamaica.[26] Washington was forced to treat all rumors of an early peace as tricks of the enemy, attempts to make the American Army disband[27] before the British had departed (GW 25.267—68). But this, in turn, made it look as if he were clinging to power at the very moment when he was hoping to surrender it. Meanwhile, officers and men were looking toward their future, with a growing suspicion that Congress would not or could not honor the promises by which they had been recruited. Even where this discontent did not lead to actual or threatened mutiny,[28] it threatened the public good will, the pride in the fighting forces, on which Washington hoped to base his plea for a union that would reflect the continental consciousness forged within his Army.[29] As civilian-military tension mounted, Washington felt that the chance to use victory as the basis for a stable political order was slipping away from him. The wearisome time of neither peace nor war[30] tried his patience as sorely as military setbacks ever had: "The predicament in which I stand, is as critical and delicate as can well be conceived" (GW 25.186).

After Yorktown, Washington had briefly hoped that he could, for the first time in the war, leave winter camp to visit Mount Vernon. But he soon realized that his presence was still called for. Complaints in the Army "will oblige me to stick very close to the Troops this Winter (1782) and to try like a careful physician to prevent if possible the disorders getting to an incurable height" (GW 25.270). Despite all his efforts, mutinous talk grew in the Army, fostered by Washington's old rival, Horatio Gates,[31] who was with him at the winter camp in Newburgh. What made the matter doubly ticklish[32] was the fact that some members of Congress, who desired the stronger union that Washington was sponsoring, thought they could advance their cause by playing on the Army's grievances,[33] on the inability of the central government to address its complaints. Nothing could stand at a greater distance from Washington's moral argument for increased authority than any attempt to seize power, or to form it on a military basis.

Washington sent uncharacteristically stern warnings to Alexander Hamilton, letting him know that he realized what Hamilton and Robert Morris were up to.[34] They must be brought to realize that "the Army (considering the irritable state it is in, its sufferings and composition)[35] is a dangerous instrument to play with" (GW 26.293). Washington's political wisdom shows clearly in the urgency of these warnings (ibid. 208,213). Since Washington would be obliged to oppose the schemers, he let them know in advance that their meddling "might create such divisions in the Army as would weaken, rather than strengthen the hands of those who were disposed to support Continental measures"[36] (ibid. 324). Washington's work to establish the principle of civilian supremacy is usually based on the rebuke to the officers at Newburgh.[37] At least as important were these earlier warnings sent to the schemers in Congress.

When that has been said, however, one must admire the tact with which he handled the discontented officers. Scheduling his own special meeting, preempting the anonymous[38] call to consider revolt, he praised the Army for its standard of public service. Though he knew the role General Gates was playing, he let Gates assume the chair before his arrival, and pretended that the anonymous letter came from an "outside agitator,"[39] since it was so obviously below the honor of those assembled before him. Skillfully, Washington took the call to mutiny as a great opportunity for the men to display, in dramatic terms, their public virtue (The assembly hall in which he spoke had been nicknamed by the Army "the Temple of Virtue"):

> You will give one more distinguished proof of unexampled patriotism and patient virtue, rising superior to the pressure of the most complicated sufferings; and you will, by the dignity of your Conduct, afford oc-

casion for Posterity to say,[40] when speaking of the glorious example you have exhibited to Mankind, "had this day been wanting, the World had never seen the last stage of perfection to which human nature is capable of attaining" (ibid. 227).

Though Freeman argues that the rhetoric is Jonathan Trumbull's, the psychological tactics are characteristically Washingtonian, and the only draft we have of the address is the one he wrote in his own large hand, so he would have no trouble reading it. Washington's intimate participation in the composition of the address is indicated by a reference to one of his favorite lines from his favorite play, Addison's Cato:[41] "In the mild lights of calm philosophy" (ibid. 226).

Only when Washington tried to read an excerpt from a congressional dispatch[42] did the most famous moment occur, that touch of theater with which he drew out his new pair of glasses and adjusted them to read. The necessity for the glasses was unfeigned; he had recently thanked David Rittenhouse, the mechanical genius of Philadelphia, for grinding their lenses:

> The Spectacles suit my Eyes extremely well, as I am persuaded the reading glasses also will when I get more accustomed to the use of them. At present I find some difficulty in coming at the proper Focus; but when I do obtain it, they magnify properly and show objects very distinctly which at first appear like a mist blended together and confused (ibid. 137).

It is not his use of the glasses that reduced some in his audience to tears, but the words he spoke while getting the congressional document at the right distance to focus on its contents: "Gentlemen, you must pardon me. I have grown grey in your service and now find myself growing blind" (Freeman 5.435).

Actually, the crowning touch of theater was given when Washington folded up the letter and left the hall, signaling by his manner that it was unthinkable anyone would defend the anonymous call to mutiny—despite the fact that Gates still sat in the chair as the highest ranking officer after Washington. He had gauged his men well.[43] Though Timothy Pickering[44] tried to turn the gathering's mind back to the anonymous address, he was silenced by a motion of thanks for General Washington's intervention. The impact of Washington's appearance was registered by one of those present, Samuel Shaw:

> On other occasions, he had been supported by the exertions of an Army and the countenance of his friends;[45] but in this he stood single and alone. There was no saying where the passions of an Army, which

were not a little inflamed, might lead; but it was generally allowed that longer forbearance was dangerous, and moderation had ceased to be a virtue. Under these circumstances he appeared, not. at the head of his troops, but as it were in opposition to them; and for a dreadful moment the interests of the Army and its General seemed to be in competition. He spoke—every doubt was dispelled, and the tide of patriotism rolled again in its wonted course[46] (ibid. 436).

Washington, as usual, gave the credit for this outcome to his men. He had a gift for shaming them into actions above themselves and then praising what he had made them become. In forwarding to Congress the respectful petition[47] drawn up in consequence of the meeting he had called, Washington wrote:

> The result of the proceedings of the grand Convention of the Officers, which I have the honor of enclosing to your Excellency for the inspection of Congress, will, I flatter myself, be considered as the last glorious proof of patriotism which could have been given by Men who aspired to the distinction of a patriot Army; and will not only confirm their claim to the justice, but will increase their title to the gratitude of their Country (GW 26. 229).

There is no mention of his own address at the meeting. He would erase, if he could, all memory of division between himself and other officers; he goes on, in this letter, to advocate the officers' cause as ardently as any of the mutineers could have wished. The ranks were reunited.

But not everywhere. When a Pennsylvania garrison broke out in mutiny,[48] Washington sent picked troops to break their revolt . and, at the same time, wrote Congress to defend the Army's honor:

> I feel an expressible satisfaction, that even this behaviour cannot stain the name of the American Soldiery; it cannot be imputable to,[49] or reflect dishonour on the army at large; but on the contrary, it will, by the striking contrast it exhibits, hold up to public view the other Troops, in the most advantageous point of light. ...for when we consider that these Pennsylvania Levies[50] who have now mutinied, are Recruits and Soldiers of a day, who have not borne the heat and burden of the War, and who can have in reality very few hardships to complain of, and when we at the same time recollect, that those Soldiers who have lately been furloughed from this Army, are the Veterans who have patiently endured hunger, nakedness and cold, who have suffered and bled without a murmur, and who with perfect good order have retired to their homes, without the settlement of their Accounts or a farthing of money[51] in their pockets, we shall be as much astonished at the virtues of the latter, as we are struck with horror and detestation [52] at the proceedings of the former (GW 27. 33).

Having kept the Army (for the most part) virtuous in the eighteenth-century sense—i. e., public-spirited—he must now defend that virtue. Only then, appealing to the national gratitude, could he make his plea for a closer expression of national spirit within the government itself.

The timing of the plea was important. It should not be issued till victory was assured and the tasks of waging war had been eased. But if Washington waited till the signing of the definitive treaty (which came in September of 1783), or the departure of the British (which came in November), or his own actual resignation (on December 23), his message might be overlooked in the hubbub of celebration[53] and emotional relief. So, after careful drafting, he sent out his circular letter early in June, when word of the treaty was anxiously awaited but debate about its terms could not begin. For Washington, his "Legacy" (as the letter was soon being called) and his resignation were two aspects of a single process, moving from the events at Newburgh through the dispatching of the letter, culminating[54] in the resignation, at Annapolis, in December. It had been a tortuous course to steer, and he saw his project threatened all along: yet he maneuvered his way at last to the fulfillment of his pledge.

【 Notes 】

①This selections is from *George Washington and the Enlightenment*, Robert Hale, 1984, pp. xix—xxv, 3—10. In Garry Will's biographical study of George Washington, the author sees Washington as truly great because he represented the Enlightenment ideal of heroic political leadership. The Enlightenment was the European intellectual movement of the 17th and 18th centuries that had great influence on revolutions around the world including the American Revolution. Central to Enlightenment thought were the use and honoring of reason, the power by which man understands the universe and improves his own condition. The goals of rational man were considered to be knowledge, freedom, and happiness. Wills shows the reader that during the critical period of crisis after the American colonists' military victory over the British Army at the Battle of Yorktown before there was a stable national government in place, by his own manner and actions George Washington led his people into the new era. The power that he gained by resigning made possible the adoption of the Constitution by the former colonists and the establishment of a stable united federal government—now known as the United States of America.

②Garry Wills, a well known American cultural historian and popular author who received his Ph. D. from Yale University in 1961 is an adjunct professor at Northwestern University in Evanston, Illinois. His many books include studies about many public figures in the United States such as Richard Nixon, Abraham Lincoln, the Kennedy family, and Ronald Reagan. He has also written on religion in America. His latest work, *Negro President: Jefferson and the Slave*

Power (2003) is a provocative look at how Jefferson's presidency related to the power of the states that had slave holders.

③Washington eludes us...：华盛顿,我们理解不了他。

elude /i'luːd/ vt. 逃避；逃脱；记不起；使人不解：The fox succeeded in eluding the hunters. 狐狸成功地逃脱了猎人的追捕。Your name eludes me. 你的名字我想不起来了。a metaphor that eluded them 他们理解不了的隐喻。

④Monument tapers off from us however we come at it：无论我们怎么走近纪念碑,它都巍峨耸立,逐渐变成尖顶。

taper /'teipə/ vt., vi. (常与 off 连用)逐渐尖细,使逐渐尖细：taper a stick to a point 使木棍的末端逐渐尖细成为尖头。The storm finally tapered off. 风暴渐渐平息下去。come at 到达,找到,发现：Put the food where the cat can't come at it. 把食物放在猫够不着的地方。It is always difficult to come at the truth. 发现真理总是困难。

⑤the icon our ancestors turned to：我们的祖先所向往的偶像。

icon /'aikən/ n. 图标,肖像,偶像：He is a pop icon designed and manufactured for the video generation. 他是音像时代里设计和造就出来的流行音乐偶像。

⑥to halo them with sacred memories：神圣的记忆像光环一样环绕着他们。

halo /'heiləu/ vt. 使有晕轮,围以光环；vi. 成晕轮。

⑦...was tempered from the outset by the responses he hoped to elicit from his countrymen：

temper vt., vi. 锻炼：soldiers who had been tempered by combat 经过战斗锻炼的士兵们；调整,使协调：The sea tempers the climates. 海洋调节气候。temper strong drinks with water 用水将烈酒冲淡。from the outset 从一开始。

elicit /i'lisit/ vt. 得出,引出,抽出,引起。

⑧His life verged on legend：他的一生近乎于传奇。

verge /'vəːdʒ/ v. (与 on, upon 连用)将近,接近；处在……的边缘,向……倾斜：verge on complete failure 濒于全面失败；Her land verges on the neighboring township. 她的土地与邻镇相连。

⑨...for others to accept him as a literal fulfillment of the age's aspirations：其他人毫无夸张地认为他是实现那个时代所渴望的代表。

aspiration /ˌæspə'reiʃən/ n. 热望,渴望。

⑩a virtuoso of resignations：辞退的艺术大师。

virtuoso /ˌvəːtju'əuzəu/ n. (pl. -sos 或 -si) 艺术名家,艺术大师；音乐演奏名家：a virtuoso performance 名师演奏。

⑪as a young colonel of militia：

colonel /'kəːnl/ n. 上校。militia /mi'liʃə/ n. 预备役部队。

⑫...when baffled of honor or advantage：当他要获得荣誉和取得进展为难时。(从句中 he was 省略。)

baffle /'bæfl/ vt. 困惑,阻碍,为难：This puzzle baffles me. 这个谜使我困惑不解。

⑬...he would not anticipate his promised abdication at war's end：他并没有期望承诺战争结

束时辞职。

abdication /ˌæbdɪˈkeɪʃən/ n. 弃权，让位，辞职。

⑭He was choreographing his departure with great care. 他极其小心谨慎地设计他如何辞退。
choreograph /ˈkɔ(ː)rɪəɡrɑːf/ vt. 为(芭蕾舞或诗歌等)设计舞蹈动作；精心策划；设计：choreograph a ballet 为一出芭蕾舞剧设计舞蹈动作。

⑮It was an act of pedagogical theater: 这是一场具有教育意义的戏。
pedagogical /ˌpedəˈɡɔdʒɪkəl/ adj. 教育学的，教学法的。

⑯John Jay: 杰伊(1745-12-12—1827-05-17)美国的缔造者之一，在法律和外交方面均曾做出贡献。

⑰tho': though

⑱Annapolis /əˈnæpəlɪs/ n. 安纳波利斯(美国马里兰州首府)。

⑲with an eye to timing as well as content:
with an eye to 着眼于：He redecorated the room with an eye to its future use as a nursery. 他从新装饰这间屋子时着眼于将来用它作保育室。

⑳...stage his lesson to men's eyes: 他把他的教导展示给大家看。stage vt. 展现，呈现：The market staged a mild recovery. 市场有复苏的迹象。

㉑...required great tact:
tact /tækt/ n. 机智；老练，圆滑：He showed tact in dealing with difficult customers. 他在应付难对付的顾客时表现老练。A minister of foreign affairs who lacks tact is a dangerous man. 一个缺乏机智的外交部长是个很危险的人物。

㉒altho: although

㉓I will therefore speak... in this Address. 这一段引言是一个并列复合句。分号前是一个分句，分号后是另一个分句。
your (his, her) Excellency 阁下："The King will see you now, your Excellency." "阁下，国王现在要接见您。"
ascribe /əsˈkraɪb/ vt. (常与to连用)归于，归因于：She ascribed difficulties to overspending. 她把困难归因于费用超支太大。He ascribed his failure to objective conditions. 他把失败归咎于客观条件。ostentation /ˌɔstenˈteɪʃən/ n. 卖弄，夸耀，摆阔，风头主义。rectitude /ˈrektɪtjuːd/ n. 正直，公正，清廉，笔直；disdain /dɪsˈdeɪn/ vt. 轻视；蔑视；不屑：A great man should disdain flatterers. 伟大的人物应鄙视献媚者。I would certainly disdain to live in such tiny flats. 我当然不愿意住在这样小的单元房里。ardent /ˈɑːdənt/ adj. 热心的；热情的：an ardent lover of art 酷爱艺术的人；ardent supporter 热心的支持者。toil /tɔɪl/ n. 苦工，难事；劳苦，辛苦：be taken (caught) in the toils 落网，上圈套，被迷住；toil and moil 做苦工，辛辛苦苦地工作；The book is a toil to read. 这本书读起来真费劲。sinister /ˈsɪnɪstə/ adj. 险恶的：a sinister beginning 不吉祥的开端；sinister storm clouds. 预示暴风雨降临的不祥之云。

㉔an excruciating task: 极艰巨的任务。
excruciating /ɪksˈkruːʃieɪtɪŋ/ adj. 极痛苦的，折磨人的：wrote with excruciating precision 高

度精确地写出。

㉕during the two years of "phony peace": 假和平的两年中。
phony /'fəuni/ 假(冒)的,伪造的,不值钱的: a phony writer 空头作家; a phony credit card 伪造的信用卡。

㉖... after De Grasse, the victor at Yorktown, was himself defeated by Admiral Rodney off the island of Dominica, removing British fears for their hold on Jamaica. De Grasse 支持美国的法国海军指挥官。
victor /'viktə/ n. 胜利者;征服者;战胜者。Yorktown /'jɔːktaun/ n. 约克镇(美国弗吉尼亚州东南部城镇)。Admiral Rodney 英国军官。Dominica /dɔmi'niːkə/ n. 多米尼加(西印度群岛岛国)。Jamaica /dʒə'meikə/ n. 牙买加,牙买加甜酒。

㉗to make the American Army disband:
disband /dis'bænd/ v. 解散,裁减。

㉘actual or threatened mutiny:
mutiny /'mjuːtini/ n. 兵变,反抗;叛变。

㉙the continental consciousness forged within his Army: 在他的军队中铸造出来的觉悟。
continental /ˌkɔnti'nentl/ n. (独立战争中的)美国军人。forge /fɔːdʒ/ vi. 打(铁),锻制;锻炼;编造(故事等);伪造(文书等): forge an anchor 锻造铁锚; forge a signature 伪造签名。

㉚The wearisome time of neither peace nor war...:
wearisome /'wiərisʌm/ adj. 令人厌烦的;使人疲倦的,乏味的。

㉛Horatio Gates 盖茨(1728—1806-04-10),美国独立战争时期一位英国出生的美国将领。

㉜What made the matter doubly ticklish...:
ticklish /'tikliʃ/ adj. 难以处理的,棘手的,不好对付的(事);怕痒的,易痒的(人): a ticklish matter 一件棘手的事。

㉝by playing on the Army's grievances:
play on 利用;发展: Politicians often win votes by playing on electors' distrust of the party in power. 政治家们常常利用选民对在野党的不信任来获得选票。The plan can be defeated if you play on its weaknesses. 如果你让弱点任其发展,这个计划可能实现不了。
grievance /'griːvəns/ n. 不满;不平;冤情;抱怨;牢骚: to have a grievance against sb 抱怨某人。

㉞Washington sent uncharacteristically stern warnings to Alexander Hamilton, letting him know that he realized what Hamilton and Robert Morris were up to.
uncharacteristically stern warnings 难得有的严厉警告。
Alexander Hamilton 汉密尔顿(1755—1804),参加制宪会议(1787)的纽约州代表,系列文章《联邦党人》的主要作者,美国首任财政部长(1789—1795),他极力主张在美国建立强大的中央政府,他的经济、政治、军事和外交纲领都有一个明确的目标,即建立一个强大的美利坚合众国。
Robert Morris 莫里斯(1734-04-31—1806-05-08),美国商人、银行家,以美国独立战争

(1775—1783)的财政家知名。be up to：忙于的；密谋的：What have you been up to？你近来在忙些什么？The children are always getting up to mischief. 孩子们老是在捣蛋。

㉟the Army (considering the irritable state it is in, its sufferings and composition)：军队(考虑一下它容易激怒的状况、它所吃的苦痛以及它的结构)。

irritable /'iritəbl/ *adj.* 易怒的；易激怒的：She was irritable when she was unhappy. 她不高兴时，容易发脾气。

㊱Since Washington would be obliged to oppose the schemers, he let them know in advance that their meddling "might create such divisions in the Army as would weaken, rather than strengthen the hands of those who were disposed to support Continental measures." 既然华盛顿被迫反对这些提出设计方案的人，他就事先让他们知道，他们的干预可能在军队中造成分裂，结果不是加强，而是削弱打算支持大陆会议的人们。

schemer /'skiːmə/ *n.* 设计者，计划者；阴谋家。meddle /'medl/ *v.* 干预；干涉：Don't meddle in my affairs. 别干预我的事情。

Continental measures (Congress)：大陆会议(1774—1789)，美国独立战争时期殖民地各州(美国前身)人民的代表机构；会议代表为各州人民说话并采取集体行动。这一名词特指1774年、1775—1781年分别召开的第一届、第二届大陆会议。

㊲Washington's work to establish the principle of civilian supremacy is usually based on the rebuke to the officers at Newburgh：

supremacy /sju'preməsi/ *n.* 地位最高的人；至高，无上；霸权：naval supremacy 制海权；海上霸权；male supremacy 大男子主义者。rebuke /ri'bjuːk/ *n.* & *vt.* 指责；非难；谴责：give (administer) a rebuke 谴责；rebuke him strongly for his negligence 严斥他的疏忽；His industry rebukes me. 他的勤劳使我感到惭愧。

㊳preempting the anonymous call：取代了匿名号召。

preempt /pri(ː)'empt/ *vt.* 以优先购买权取得；(为取得先买权)预先占据(公地)；优先于或支配：A special news program preempted the scheduled shows. 特别的新节目取代预定计划的表演。

㊴outside agitator：外部的煽动者。

agitator /'ædʒiteitə/ *n.* 鼓动者；煽动者；搅拌器：air-driven agitator 风动搅拌器。

㊵... afford occasion for Posterity to say：为子孙后代提供机会来说……

posterity /pɔs'teriti/ *n.* (集合名词)后裔，子孙；后代，后世：go down to posterity (=go down to history) 传至后代，载入史册；Everything he writes is consigned to posterity. 他所写的一切都是为了后代。

㊶Freeman 弗里曼，美国记者、编辑。Jonathan Trumbull 特郎布尔，美国诗人、法学家。Addison's Cato：艾迪生(1672-05-01—1719-06-17)，英国散文家、诗人、剧作家和政治家。他写了杰出的悲剧《卡托》，在所办刊物《旁观者中》把期刊散文的艺术发展到完美的境地，成为英语散文最有影响的大师之一。

㊷a congressional dispatch：代表大会的急件。

dispatch /di'spætʃ/ *n.* 派遣；发送；急件；新闻电讯；迅速结束；急于：He conclude the negotiation with dispatch. 他迅速结束谈判。a Xinhua News Agency dispatch from Beijing (on) Oct. 1 新华社北京10月1日电。*vt.* dispatch a business 速办公务。

㊸He had gauged his men well. 他对手下的人了如指掌。

gauge /geidʒ/ *vt.* (用计量器)计量,度量; 估量;评价;判断: I tried to gauge how many people were there. 我想估计出那儿有多少人。(亦作: gage) How would you gauge his conduct? 你对他的品行作何评价? *n.* on-off gauge 开关测量计。

㊹Timothy Pickering 皮克林(1745-07-17—1809-01-29),美国独立时期的军官,联邦党政治家,曾在美国最初两届内阁中任职(1795—1800),政治声誉颇佳。

㊺... supported by the exertions of an Army and the countenance of his friends: 靠军队的努力和朋友的支持。

exertion /igˈzəːʃən/ *n.* 努力, 尽力;行使, 运用: increased exertion 加倍努力。countenance /ˈkauntinəns/ *n.* 面容;面部表情; 赞同;支持;赞助: a sad countenance 愁容; Father refuses to give countenance to your plans. 父亲对你们的计划不予支持。

㊻in its wonted course: 在它惯有的过程中。

wonted /ˈwəuntid/ *adj.* (仅作定语用)习惯的; 平常的, 照常的: with his wonted patience 像他平常那样耐心地; return at one's wonted hour 在惯常的时刻回来。

㊼petition /piˈtiʃən/*n.* 请愿, 请愿书, 诉状: forward a petition 转递请愿书; The villagers all signed a petition asking for a hospital to be built. 村民们都在请愿书上签名要求建一所医院;*v.* 请求, 恳求, 请愿。

㊽When a Pennsylvania garrison broke out in mutiny...: 当宾夕法尼亚的一驻军发生叛乱时。

garrison /ˈgærisn/ *n.* 卫戍部队, 驻军, 卫戍地, 要塞: garrison town 有军队驻防的城镇; *vt.* 守卫;驻守: The soldiers garrisoned the town. 士兵驻守过这座城市。

㊾be imputable to:

imputable /imˈpjuːtbl/ *adj.* 可归罪的, 可使负责的(to): imputable oversights 情有可原的疏忽;No blame is imputable to him. 他无任何责任。

㊿levy /ˈlevi/ *n.* 征税, 派款; 征收额; 征集; 征募兵额

(51)a farthing of money: 一点儿钱。

farthing /ˈfɑːðiŋ/ *n.* <英>1/4 旧便士, 英国最小的钱币; 极少量, 一点儿: not worth a farthing 毫无价值, 一文不值; 毫无用处。

(52)horror and detestation:

detestation /ˌdiːtesˈteiʃən/ *n.* 深恶, 痛恨, 讨厌; 极讨厌的东西: regard with great detestation 非常讨厌。

(53)in the hubbub of celebration: 在庆祝的欢呼声中。

hubbub /ˈhʌbʌb/ *n.* 吵闹声, 呐喊声, 叫嚷声。

(54)culminate /ˈkʌlmineit/ *v.* 达到顶点; 告终(in): culminate in 以……而终结, 以……而达到顶峰, (结果)竟成: The tower culminates in a 40-foot spire. 这塔的顶端是一个40英尺高的塔尖。Years of waiting culminated in a tearful reunion. 多年的等待最终以含泪团聚而结局。

【 Exercises 】

I. Comprehension Questions

(1) According to this historian's interpretation, what were the three great moments in Washington's life that summed up the importance of his whole life? (See paragraph 3.)

(2) In Will's view why were Washington's resignations so effective? (See paragraph 4.)

(3) Washington was paid a large salary while he was commander of the Continental Army. True or False?

(4) Washington resigned as commander of the armies and asked the governors of the individual colonies to establish a weak central government. True or False?

(5) General Horatio Gates was trying to encourage mutiny in the Continental Army by circulating an anonymous letter among the soldiers calling them to revolt against their commanders. True or False?

(6) How did Washington handle the call to the soldiers to mutiny?

II. Points for Discussion

George Washington is called the "Father of the Country" in the United States. Using what you have learned from this passage summarize in English his characteristics and actions that contribute to this view of him. If you disagree and think his actions and characteristics described here would have a negative effect on a leader's ability to lead his people explain your ideas.

III. Complete the following sentences with the words or expressions from the passage given below. Change the form where necessary.

tact	dispose	puzzle	elicit	address
live up to	disdain	irritable	sentiment	cling to
ardent	toil	sum up		

(1) After much questioning among the people concerned, the headmaster at last _____ the truth about the incident.

(2) The _____ hope for the future brought my grand parents through all the sufferings during the war.

(3) We admired him because he had a _____ that would preserve him from flagrant (严重的) error in any society.

(4) Mrs Grey _____ to answer her husband's rude remarks, because he was _____ and sometimes jabbed (戳) his stick into his servant's face.

(5) I am _____ to agree with you as far as the selection of the location of the new town is concerned.

(6) A bit of the blackest and coarsest bread is the sole recompense and the sole profit attac-

hing to so difficult a _____.

(7) He is a man of integrity and he never fails to _____ our trust and expectations.

(8) The Big Horn canyons were incredible, with four and five distinct layers of pine trees somehow _____ the steep, rocky walls.

IV. **Complete the following sentences with appropriate forms of words or expressions from the passage according to the given meaning in brackets.**

(1) I saw the film long time ago and the actor's name _____ (escape) me for the moment.

(2) The examination question _____ (bewilder) me completely and I couldn't answer it, which resulted in my failure.

(3) The longest heat wave in 50 years caused drought, power shortages and loss of life. This trouble _____ (need or deserve) quick action by the government.

(4) In our own day we are used to hearing the traditional _____ (complaints): " I can't wait for my vacation," " I wish I could stay home today," etc.

(5) By _____ (make use of) the old lady's fears, the criminals were able to persuade her to give them her money.

(6) Rudely, he _____ to me (move so as to face) and refused to say anything further.

Unit 12

Environmental History

19. Silent Spring[1]

Rachel Carson[2]

> 雷切尔·卡森(Rachel Carson, 1907—1964)是美国生物学家,她有关环境污染以及海洋自然史的著作使她知名度很高。1951 年出版的《环绕我们的海洋》一书获得了美国国家图书奖。1962 年出版的《寂静的春天》在世界范围内唤起了人们对环境污染危险性的意识。这本书为 20 世纪环境史、农业史以及科学史都提供了第一手的资料。本文选自《寂静的春天》,这是一篇有关在美国和世界范围内建立和发展环境保护最重要和最具有影响力的文章。

The history of life on earth has been a history of interaction between living things and their surroundings. To a large extent, the physical form and the habits of the earth's vegetation and its animal life have been molded by the environment. Considering the whole span of earthly time, the opposite effect, in which life actually modifies its surroundings, has been relatively slight. Only within the moment of time represented by the present century has one species—man—acquired significant power to alter the nature of his world.

During the past quarter century this power has not only increased to one of disturbing magnitude[3] but it has changed in character. The most alarming of all man's assaults upon the environment is the contamination of air, earth, rivers, and sea with dangerous and even lethal materials.[4] This pollution is for the most part irrecoverable; the chain of evil it initiates not only in the world that must support life but in living tissues is for the most part irreversible.[5] In this now universal contamination of the environment, chemicals are the sinister[6] and little-recognized partners of radiation in changing the very nature of the world—the very nature of its life. Strontium 90, released through nuclear explosions into the air, comes to earth in rain or drifts down as fallout, lodges in soil, enters into the grass or corn or wheat grown there, and in time takes up its abode in the bones of a human being, there to remain until his death.[7] Similarly, chemicals sprayed on croplands or forests or gardens lie long in soil, entering into living organisms, passing from one to another in a chain of poisoning and death. Or they pass mysteriously by underground streams until they emerge and, through the alchemy of air and sunlight, combine into new forms that kill vegetation, sicken cattle, and work unknown harm on those who drink from once pure wells...

It took hundreds of millions of years to produce the life that now inhabits the earth—eons of time[8] in which that developing and evolving and diversifying life reached a state of adjustment and balance with its surroundings. The environment, rigorously[9] shaping and directing the life it supported, contained elements that were hostile as well as supporting. Certain rocks gave out dangerous radiation; even within the light of the sun, from which all life draws its energy, there were short-wave radiations with power to injure. Given time—time not in years but in millennia—life adjusts, and a balance has been reached. For time is the essential ingredient; but in the modem world there is no time.

The rapidity of change and the speed with which new situations are created follow the impetuous and heedless pace of man[10] rather than the deliberate pace of nature. Radiation is no longer merely the background radiation of rocks, the bombardment of cosmic rays, the ultraviolet of the sun that have existed before there was any life on earth; radiation is now the unnatural creation of man's tampering with the atom.[11] The chemicals to which life is asked to make its adjustment are no longer merely the calcium and silica and copper and all the rest of the minerals washed out of the rocks and carried in rivers to the sea; they are the synthetic creations of man's inventive mind, brewed in his laboratories, and having no counterparts in nature.[12]

To adjust to these chemicals would require time on the scale that is nature's; it would require not merely the years of a man's life but the life of generations. And even this, were it by some miracle possible, would be futile, for the new chemicals come from our laboratories in an endless stream; almost five hundred annually find their way into actual use in the United States alone.[13]...

Among them are many that are used in man's war against nature. Since the mid-1940's over 200 basic chemicals have been created for use in killing insects, weeds, rodents, and other organisms described in the modern vernacular as "pests";[14] and they are sold under several thousand different brand names.

These sprays, dusts, and aerosols are now applied almost universally to farms, gardens, forests, and homes... Can anyone believe it is possible to lay down such a barrage of poisons[15] on the surface of the earth without making it unfit for all life?...

The whole process of spraying seems caught up in an endless spiral.[16] Since DDT was released for civilian use, a process of escalation has been going on in which ever more toxic materials must be found.[17] This has happened because insects, in a triumphant vindication of Darwin's principle of the survival of the fittest,[18] have evolved super races immune to the particular insecticide used, hence a deadlier one has always to be developed—and then a deadlier one than that. It has happened also because, for reasons to be described later, destructive insects often undergo a "flareback," or resurgence,[19] after spraying, in numbers greater than before. Thus the chemical war is never won, and all life is caught in its violent crossfire.[20]

Along with the possibility of the extinction of mankind by nuclear war, the central problem of our age has therefore become the contamination of man's total environment with such substances of incredible potential for harm—substances that accumulate in the tissues of plants and animals and even penetrate the germ cells to shatter or alter the very material of heredity[21] upon which the shape of the future depends.

......

All this is not to say there is no insect problem and no need of control. I am saying, rather, that control must be geared to realities, not to mythical situations, and that the methods employed must be such that they do not destroy us along with the insects.

The problem whose attempted solution has brought such a train of disaster in its wake is an accompaniment of our modern way of life.[22] Long before the age of man, insects inhabited the earth-a group of extraordinarily varied and adaptable beings. Over the course of time since man's advent,[23] a small percentage of the more than half a million species of insects have come into conflict with human welfare in two principal ways: as competitors for the food supply and as carriers of human disease.

Disease-carrying insects become! important where human beings are crowded together, especially under conditions where sanitation is poor, as in time of natural disaster or war or in situations of extreme poverty and deprivation. Then control of some sort becomes necessary. It is a sobering fact, however, as we shall presently see, that the method of massive chemical control has had only limited success, and also threatens to worsen the very conditions it is intended to curb.[24]

Under primitive agricultural conditions the farmer had few insect problems. These arose with the intensification of agriculture—the devotion of immense acreages to a single crop. Such a system set the stage for explosive increases in specific insect populations. Single-crop farming does not take advantage of the principles by which nature works; it is agriculture as an engineer might conceive it to be. Nature has introduced great variety into the landscape, but man has displayed a passion for simplifying it. Thus he undoes the built-in checks and balances by which nature holds the species within bounds. One important natural check is a limit on the amount of suitable habitat for each species.[25] Obviously then, an insect that lives on wheat can build up its population to much higher levels on a farm devoted to wheat than on one in which wheat is intermingled with other crops[26] to which the insect is not adapted.

. . . . . .

Another factor in the modern insect problem is one that must be viewed against a background of geologic and human history: the spreading of thousands of different kinds of organisms from their native homes to invade new territories. This worldwide migration has been studied and graphically described by the British ecologist Charles Elton[27] in his recent book The Ecology of Invasions...

The importation of plants is the primary agent in the modern spread of species, for animals have almost invariably gone along with the plants, quarantine being a comparatively recent and not completely effective innovation.[28] The United States Office of Plant Introduction alone has introduced almost 200,000 species and varieties of plants from all over the world. Nearly half of the 180 or so major insect enemies of plants in the United States are accidental imports from abroad, and most of them have come as hitchhikers on plants.

In new territory, out of reach of the restraining hand of the natural enemies that kept down its numbers in its native land, an invading plant or animal is able to become enormously abundant. Thus it is no accident that our most troublesome insects are introduced species.

These invasions, both the naturally occurring and those dependent on human assistance, are likely to continue indefinitely. Quarantine and massive chemical campaigns are only extremely expensive ways of buying time. We are faced, according to Dr. Elton, "with a life-and-death need not just to find new technological means of suppressing this plant or that animal"; instead we need the basic knowledge of animal populations and their relations to their surroundings that will "promote an even balance and damp down[29] the explosive power of outbreaks and new invasions."

Much of the necessary knowledge is now available but we do not use it. We train ecologists in our universities and even employ them in our governmental agencies but we seldom take their advice. We allow the chemical death rain to fall as though there were no alternative, whereas in fact there are many, and our ingenuity could soon discover many more[30] if given opportunity.

Have we fallen into a mesmerized state that makes us accept as inevitable that which is inferior or detrimental,[31] as though having lost the will or the vision to demand that which is good? Such thinking, in the words of the ecologist Paul Shepard, "...Why should we tolerate a diet of weak poisons, a home in insipid surroundings,[32] a circle of acquaintances who are not quite our enemies, the noise of motors with just enough relief to prevent insanity?[33] Who would want to live in a world which is just not quite fatal?"

. . . . . .

It is not my contention that chemical insecticides must never be used. I do contend that we have put poisonous and biologically potent chemicals indiscriminately into the hands of persons largely or wholly ignorant of their potentials for harm. We have subjected enormous numbers of people to contact with these poisons, without their consent and often without their knowledge. If the Bill of Rights contains no guarantee that a citizen shall be secure against lethal poisons distributed either by private individuals or by public officials, it is surely only because our forefathers, despite their considerable wisdom and foresight, could conceive of no such problem.

I contend, furthermore, that we have allowed these chemicals to be used with little or no advance investigation of their effect on sod, water, wildlife, and man himself. Future generations are unlikely to condone our lack of prudent concern for the integrity of the natural world[34] that supports all life.

There is still very limited awareness of the nature of the threat. This is an era of specialists, each of whom sees his own problem and is unaware of or intolerant of the larger frame into which it fits. It is also an era dominated by industry, in which the right to make a dollar at whatever cost is seldom challenged. When the public protests, confronted with some obvious evidence of damaging results of pesticide applications, it is fed little tranquilizing pills of half truth. [35] We urgently need an end to these false assurances, to the sugar coating of unpalatable facts. [36] It is the public that is being asked to assume the risks that the insect controllers calculate. The public must decide whether it wishes to continue on the present road, and it can do so only when in full possession of the facts. In the words of Jean Rostand, "The obligation to endure gives us the right to know."

【 Notes 】

①This selection is an excerpt from *Silent Spring* (Houghton Mifflin, 1962, pp. 5—13), one of the most important and influential texts in the modern establishment and growth of American and worldwide environmental protection. This book is a primary source in 20th century environmental history, agricultural history and in the history of technology.

A major problem area of modern technological society is the preservation of a healthy environmental balance. Carson saw that great increases in population and in the intensity of industrialization are promoting a worldwide ecological crisis. This included the dangers involved in destruction of the equatorial rain forests, the careless exploitation of minerals by open-mining techniques, and the pollution of the oceans by radioactive waste and of the atmosphere by combustion products. It was the danger of indiscriminate use of pesticides such as DDT after World War II that first alerted opinion in advanced Western countries to the delicate nature of the world's ecological system. Carson presented this problem in a strong appeal in Silent Spring that was widely read and discussed by many people.

②Rachel Carson (1907—1964) was an American biologist well known for her writings on environmental pollution and the natural history of the sea. Carson received her M. A. from Johns Hopkins University in 1932 and did postgraduate research at Woods Hole Marine Biological Laboratory in Maine. A deep interest in wildlife from her childhood led Carson to a long career with the U. S. Bureau of Fisheries, later the U. S. Fish and Wildlife Service. In 1951 she published *The Sea Around Us*, which won the National Book Award. Her prophetic book, *Silent Spring* (1962), created a worldwide awareness of the dangers of environmental pollution.

③one of disturbing magnitude: 一种相当大的困扰。

magnitude /ˈmægnitiuːd/ n. 大小，数量，巨大，广大，量级: of the first magnitude 头等重要的。The magnitude of the epidemic was frightening. 这种流行病传播的范围之大令人恐惧。

④The most alarming of all man's assaults upon the environment is the contamination of air, earth, rivers, and sea with dangerous and even lethal materials. 在这个简单句中，主语是 alarming, 而谓语是 is。

assault /əˈsɔːlt/ n. 攻击，袭击；v. 袭击: make a surprise assault on 对……进行突然袭击。

contamination /kkən¸tæmi'neiʃən/ n. 玷污，污染，污染物：contamination of the river by industrial waste 工业垃圾造成的河流污染；ideological contamination 精神污染。lethal /'li:θəl/ adj. 致命的；n. 致死因子：a lethal dose 致死(药)量；accusations lethal to the candidate's image 对候选人形象极其有害的谴责。

⑤irreversible /iri'və:səbl/ adj. 不能撤回的，不能取消的：irreversible cycle 不可逆循环；an irreversible momentum toward open revolution 朝向公开革命不可逆转的势头。前缀 ir- 带有否定意义，又如：irrecoverable /iri'kʌvəbl/ adj. 不能恢复的；不能挽回的；不能治好的：irrecoverable time 不能挽回的时间；irrecoverable losses 无法弥补的损失。

⑥sinister /'sinist/ adj. 不吉的；不祥的；凶恶的。

⑦Strontium 90, released through nuclear explosions into the air, comes to earth in rain or drifts down as fallout, lodges in soil, enters into the grass or corn or wheat grown there, and in time takes up its abode in the bones of a human being, there to remain until his death. 这个句子虽然长，却是一个简单句。主语是 Strontium 90，分词短语 released through nuclear explosions into the air 修饰主语。谓语由五个动词短语构成(comes …; drifts…; lodges…; enters…; takes up…)。动词不定式短语 there to remain… 作状语。
strontium 90 锶 90(核爆炸时释放的放射性物质)。abode /ə'bəud/ n. 住所，住处：take up one's abode 居住，住进；定居。

⑧eons of time：eon /'i:ən/ n. (=aeon)世，纪，代，无限长的时代，永世：Eons passed before life existed on the earth. 经过数不清的年代以后，地球上才有人类。

⑨rigorously /'rigərəsli/ adv. 严格地；严肃地；严厉地，严密地；精确地

⑩the impetuous and heedless pace of man：人类没有注意到的猛烈速度。
impetuous /im'petjuəs/ adj. 激烈的，猛烈的；激动的；冲动的：impetuous rush of water 奔腾急流。heedless /'hi:dlis/ adj. 不注意的，不留心的；不谨慎的(of)。

⑪Radiation is no longer merely the background radiation of rocks, the bombardment of cosmic rays, the ultraviolet of the sun that have existed before there was any life on earth; radiation is now the unnatural creation of man's tampering with the atom. 在这个句子中，分号相当于 and 或 but，意思是辐射不再仅只是……，而现在是……。bombardment of cosmic rays 宇宙射线的辐射。
bombardment /bɔm'bɑ:dmənt/ n. 炮击；轰击；碰撞；辐射：a noise of heavy bombardment 猛烈的炮击声。cosmic /'kɔzmik/ adj. 宇宙的：cosmic speed 宇宙速度(物体摆脱地球引力所需之速度)；cosmic year 宇宙年(约等于两亿年)。ultraviolet /ʌltrə'vaiəlit/ adj. 紫外线的，紫外的；n. 紫外线辐射：ultraviolet light 紫外线光。tamper /'tæmpə/ vi. (与 with 连用)擅改；篡改：tamper with history 篡改历史。Don't tamper with my feelings. 不要随意拿我的感情开心。

⑫… brewed in his laboratories, and having no counterparts in nature.
brew /bru:/ vt., vi. 酿造(啤酒)；酝酿；孕育：A storm was brewing. 暴风雨即将来临。As you brew, so you must drink. (谚)自作自受；自食其果。There is something brewing. 眼看就要出什么乱子。counterpart /'kauntpɑ:t/ n. 非常相似的人(或物)；(法)副本。

⑬And even this, were it by some miracle possible, would be futile, for the new chemicals come from our laboratories in an endless stream; almost five hundred annually find their way into actual use in the United States alone. 这是一个并列主从复合句。在第一个分句中，主语 this 与谓语部分 would be futile 被非真实条件从句 were it by some miracle possible 分隔开了；were 移动到句首，if 省略。

futile /ˈfjuːtail/ adj. 琐细的，无用的，无效果的，(人)没有出息的: a futile attempt 无效的尝试; He is a futile sort of person. 他是一个没有用的人。

⑭...rodents and other organisms described in the modern vernacular as "pests": 啮齿动物和其他用现代术语所描写的"害虫"一类的生物。

rodent /ˈrəudənt/ n. 啮齿动物。vernacular /vəˈnækjulə/ n. 本国语；方言；术语，行话；俗话；动植物的俗名(别于学名): in the legal vernacular 在法律术语中。

⑮to lay down such a barrage of poisons: 倾倒这样一些有毒的物质。

lay down (开始)建造: lay down a new ship 建造新船。barrage /ˈbærɑːʒ, bəˈrɑːʒ/ n. 掩护炮火；(指说话或写作)倾泻: an umbrella barrage 防空火网; a barrage of questions 连珠炮似的问题。

⑯...seems caught up in an endless spiral: be caught up in sth 被卷入或陷入某事。She was caught up in the anti-nuclear movement. 她投入反核运动。

⑰...a process of escalation has been going on in which ever more toxic materials must be found: a process of escalation 自动调整的过程。escalation /ˌeskəˈleiʃən/ n. 自动调整；不断增加；逐步上升: tariff escalation 关税升级，滑动税率。toxic /ˈtɔksik/ adj. 毒的；中毒的；有毒的: a toxic drug 毒药。

⑱...in a triumphant vindication of Darwin's principle of the survival of the fittest: 作为达尔文适者生存原则的一个成功例证。

triumphant /traiˈʌmfənt/ adj. 胜利的；成功的；凯旋的；得意洋洋的；(因胜利而)狂欢的。vindication /ˌvindiˈkeiʃən/ n. 辩护，辩明，拥护，证明。

⑲undergo a "flareback," or resurgence: 经历了"回击"又再兴起。

flareback /ˈfleəbæk/ n. 炮尾焰(火炮炮尾后曳的火焰)；短暂而意外地重新出现；激烈的反驳；回击: a flareback of bad publicity 对错误舆论的回击。resurgence /riˈsəːdʒəns/ n. 复兴；再起: a resurgence of nationalist feeling 民族意识的复兴。

⑳...and all life is caught in its violent crossfire: 所有的生命都逃不过这场化学战争的激烈交火。

crossfire /ˈkrɔsˌfaiə/ n. 交叉火力，困境: soldiers caught in crossfire 被交叉火力击倒的士兵。

㉑even penetrate the germ cells to shatter or alter the very material of heredity: 穿透细菌的细胞而损害或改变了遗传物质本身。

shatter /ˈʃætə(r)/ vt., vi. 使粉碎，使破碎；损坏；摧毁；损害: The glass shattered when I dropped it. 我把玻璃摔成了碎片。Our hopes were shattered. 我们的希望破灭了。heredity /hiˈrediti/ n. 遗传；遗传性；遗传特征: social heredity 社会遗传。

㉒The problem whose attempted solution has brought such a train of disaster in its wake is an accompaniment of our modern way of life. 试图解决问题的办法随后带来了一系列的灾难，由

此产生的这个问题随同我们的现代生活方式一起出现。

in its wace 接踵而至;在……之后;痕迹,踪迹: The truck left clouds of dust in its wake. 车后扬起了一阵尘土。

㉓advent /'ædvənt/ n. 到来;来临;降临: Since the advent of jet aircraft, travel has been speeded up. 自从喷气式飞机出现以来,旅行的速度大为提高。

㉔the very conditions it is intended to curb: 打算用这种方法控制的这种状况。

curb /kə:b/ vt. 抑制;控制;勒住(马);给(马)装上马勒链: curb one's anger 抑制愤怒。

㉕a limit on the amount of suitable habitat for each species: 把每一物种的栖息地限制在适当的范围。

habitat /'hæbitæt/ n. (动、植物的)产地,栖息地: human habitat 人类生活环境;complex habitat 复合生境。

㉖…wheat is intermingled with other crops: 小麦与其他农作物混合种植。

intermingle /ˌintə(:)'miŋgl/ vt. 使混合;使掺和;vi. (与……)混合(with): intermingle with each other 互相来往。

㉗Charles Elton: 埃尔顿(1900-03-29 英国利物浦—1991-05-01 牛津郡牛津),全名 Charles Sutherland Elton,英国生物学家,因制订了现代动物生态学的基本原则而闻名,他出版了不少著作,1958 年出版了《动、植物入侵的生态学》一书。

㉘quarantine being a comparatively recent and not completely effective innovation: 这是一个独立结构。

quarantine /'kwɔrəntiːn/ n. 检疫,隔离,(政治或商业上的)封锁;vt. 检疫;使在政治或商业上孤立: import quarantine 进口检疫; a diplomatic quarantine 外交上的隔绝; be in quarantine 被隔离检疫。

㉙damp down: 弄熄;使窒息: You'd better damp (down) the fire before leaving. 你最好在离开以前用灰把火封上。

㉚…, and our ingenuity could soon discover many more:

ingenuity /ˌindʒi'njuːti/ n. 机灵,独创性,精巧,灵活性。

㉛Have we fallen into a mesmerized state that makes us accept as inevitable that which is inferior or detrimental…? 在这个句子中,由于动词 accept(makes 的宾语补足语)的宾语 that 后面有一个定语从句 which is inferior or detrimental 作为修饰语,词序 accept that… as inevitable 可变为 accept as inevitable that which…。

mesmerize /'mezməraiz/ 给……施行催眠术,迷惑;吸引: get mesmerized by family computer 为游戏机所迷。 He could mesmerize an audience by the sheer force of his presence. 他只要一出场,观众就为之倾倒。 detrimental /ˌdetri'mentl/ adj. 有害的,伤害的: be detrimental to 对……不利的, 对……有害的(to)。

㉜a home in insipid surroundings: 在枯燥无味环境中的家。

insipid /in'sipid/ adj. 乏味的;枯燥的 insipid food 淡而无味的食品; insipid conversation 乏味的谈话。

㉝the noise of motors with just enough relief to prevent insanity: 使你勉强能忍受住而不至于发

疯的汽车噪音。

insanity /in'sæniti/ n. 精神错乱，疯狂，愚顽：manic-depressive insanity 躁狂抑郁性精神病，躁郁病。

㉞ ... are unlikely to condone our lack of prudent concern for the integrity of the natural world：不太可能宽恕我们由于缺少谨慎的态度而使自然界受到损害。

condone /kən'dəu/ vt. 原谅；宽容；宽恕；不咎（罪过）：condone a person's faults 宽恕某人的过失；good qualities that condone his many shortcomings 可以弥补他许多缺点的优点。

㉟ ..., it is fed little tranquilizing pills of half truth：提供不出只有一半是事实的镇静剂。

tranquilize /'træŋkwilaiz/ v. 使……平静；使……变安静：Nothing contributes so much to tranquilize the mind as a steady purpose. 没有任何东西像坚定的目标一样能使头脑平静。

㊱ ... end to..., to the sugar coating of unpalatable facts：去掉令人不愉快事实的那层糖衣。

unpalatable /ʌn'pælətəbl/ adj. 不合口味的，没味的；令人不快的：an unpalatable meal 平淡无味的一顿饭；unpalatable truths 令人不快的事实。

【Exercises】

I. Comprehension Questions

(1) When single-crop farming developed _____.

  A. it showed that man was taking advantage of nature's principles

  B. man did not understand the built-in checks and balances of nature

  C. it decreased the number of insects in a farmland area

(2) Historically the importation of plants to an area has _____.

  A. decreased the number of the plants' natural enemies in the area

  B. never carried hitchhiking insects and animals into the area

  C. meant that imported plants drove out native plants and flourished because they had no natural enemies in the area

(3) True or false questions：

  1) Interaction between living things and their natural surroundings has not been important in the history of life on earth. True _____ or False _____ ?

  2) According to Carson man's power over the environment in the 20th century has increased the pollution of the earth's air and water. True _____ or False _____ ?

(4) Carson's intended audience is _____.

  A. scientists

  B. every man on the street

  C. intellectuals

(5) Which of the following is not the man-made pollution that Carson was concerned about? Strontium 90 radiation, Chemicals sprayed on crops, ultraviolet sunlight, cosmic rays, DDT, human disease spread by travelers.

II. **Points for Discussion**

Discuss this excerpt from *Silent Spring* from these two aspects of its historical significance:

(1) What Carson says regarding what has happened to physical environments on earth through the passage of time.

(2) The significance of her book in environmental, agricultural and technological history.

Include your ideas about how this book may have indirectly (or directly) affected events in China that pertain to the environment.

III. **Complete the following sentences with appropriate forms of words or expressions from the passage according to the given meaning in brackets.**

(1) They transferred from the south to the north and established their permanent _____ (dwelling) there.

(2) The outcome of the conflict _____ (destroy) our dreams of peace and prosperity.

(3) In order to take possession of all the wealth belonging to his family he tried to _____ (interfere in a harmful manner) the decedent's will.

(4) All his attempts to unlock the car were _____ (in vain), because he was using the wrong key.

(5) He was put in jail last month, because he _____ (devise) a plot to overthrow the government.

(6) There are many strange words in the _____ (the professional term) of the lawyers, which makes it difficult for us to learn.

IV. **Complete the following sentences with the words or expressions from the passage given below. Change the form where necessary.**

immune	quarantine	impetuous	curb	gear
heredity	damp	down	shatter	passion
advent	undo	keep down	mesmerize	

(1) Do you think it is true that youngsters are usually more _____ than old people?

(2) Modern medical search results have proved that some diseases are present by _____.

(3) Now, with the _____ and popularity of the home computer, its advantages and disadvantages have been a subject of discussion.

(4) The little country girl stood by the road, _____ at the speed of cars racing past.

(5) The city government of Beijing has had daily reports of SARS cases, _____ buildings and hospitals, and a public education program.

(6) The government seems to be making little effort to _____ the cost of living _____ and prices have gone up by fifteen per cent in the last year.

(7) The party spirit was considerably _____ by the news that all heave had been stopped.

Unit 13

The Practice of Historical Studies: Footnotes, Endnotes and Bibliographies[1]

20. Chicago Manual of Style[2]

> 《芝加哥格式指南》对美国学者、出版者以及要写作和出版的人来说,是一本必不可少的工具指南书。各个领域的学者、作者和出版者都把它当作一本附有范例的写作规范书来使用。

Note Documentation Systems[3]

Almost every work that is neither fiction nor an account based on personal experience relies in part on secondary sources (other publications on the same or related subjects) or on primary sources (manuscript collections, archives, contemporary accounts, diaries, books, personal interviews, and so on). Ethics, as well as the laws of copyright, require authors to identify their sources, particularly when quoting directly from them. Conventions and practices for thus documenting a text have long varied from discipline to discipline, from publisher to publisher, and from journal to journal. Increasingly, however, the old distinctions are becoming blurred as scholars cross disciplinary lines and as publishers, more than ever concerned about the balance sheet, urge conciseness and practicality over scholarly indulgence in documentation.[4]

Two basic documentation systems, each favored by different groups of scholars, will be presented in this manual. One of these systems, often referred to as the documentary-note or humanities style and still favored by many in literature, history, and the arts, provides bibliographic citations in notes. Documentary notes of this sort may or may not be accompanied by a bibliography. The other system, long used by those in the physical and natural sciences and now gaining adherents in the social sciences and humanities, is known as the author-date system. Sources are cited in the text, usually in parentheses, by author's last name and the date of publication. These short author-date citations are then amplified in a list of references, where full bibliographic information is given. The author-date system of citation will be presented in the next chapter. The advantages of the author-date system are its brevity[5] and clarity. Its use for the more esoteric[6] source citations, however, is somewhat cumbersome. The humanities system is not so succinct[7] as the author-date style, but it does offer its own forms of condensation, and it is probably more accommodating to a book with many esoteric sources.

Documentation by Footnotes

Notes documenting the text, and corresponding to reference numbers in the text, are properly called footnotes when they are printed at the foot of the page and notes or endnotes (sometimes backnotes) when they are printed at the back of the book, at the end of a chapter, or at the end of an article in a journal... Notes should be numbered consecutively,[8] beginning with 1, throughout each chapter or article...

Note reference numbers. The superior numerals[9] used for note reference numbers in the text should follow any punctuation marks except the dash, which they precede. The numbers should also be placed outside closing parentheses.

"This," George Templeton Strong wrote approvingly, "is what our tailors can do."

(In an earlier book he had said quite the opposite.)

Documentation: Endnotes versus Footnotes

An advantage of endnotes over footnotes is that the length of each note is not a great concern, since notes and text need not be juggled[10] about to make them fit on the same printed page. The author may therefore include in the notes such things as lists, poems, and discursive adjuncts to the text[11]. It is desirable, however, that the note section not overbalance the text.

When preparing endnotes, which the reader must find at the end of the text rather than at the bottom of the page, the author accustomed to using footnotes will need to keep certain differences in mind:

1. Material necessary for understanding the argument should be included in the text rather than placed in the note, where the incurious may miss it.

2. The name of the author and the title of the work ought to be included in the first note citation to it, even if one or both have been mentioned in the text. Such repetition is unnecessary in a footnote.

Bibliographies

A list of books and other references used by an author in a scholarly work may be titled Bibliography, Select or Selected Bibliography, or, if it includes only works referred to in the text, Works Cited, Literature Cited, or References; other appropriate titles are not ruled out.

A bibliographical list is best placed at the end of the book, before the index. Lists are sometimes placed at the ends of the chapters to which they apply, particularly in textbooks and in multiauthor books when there are to be offprints.[12]

A bibliography appended to a scholarly work rarely includes all works available in the field. When it is desirable, in the author's opinion, to mention the principle of selection,[13] a note may precede the list. Similarly, a list of abbreviations used in text and bibliography may precede the entries, just as an abbreviation list may accompany a note section. It is not necessary to list standard abbreviations of journal titles.

Note systems of documentation do not in themselves require bibliographies, because full bibliographical details can be given in a note accompanying the first reference to a work. In a work containing many citations in notes, however, a bibliography in addition to the notes is a most useful device for the reader and an economical one for the author and publisher: the reader not only can locate each source readily but can also see at a glance the sources the author has relied on or has selected as most germane[14] to the subject. When the book does include many citations in notes, full particulars for each source need appear only in the bibliography[15]; citations in the notes may thus be considerably shortened or abbreviated. Various forms such a bibliography may take are, a straight alphabetical list; a list divided into sections according to kinds of material, subject matter, or other appropriate categories; an annotated bibliography;[16] a bibliographical essay. Author's preference, nature of the material, and convenience to the reader should dictate the form to be used.

【 Notes 】

①This selection is from *Chicago Manual of Style*: *The Essential Guide for Writers, Editors, and Publishers 14th Edition, Edition, University of Chicago Press*, 1993, p.493, 494, 505, 513, 514. The Manual is used by research scholars, writers, and publishers in all fields as a rule book and model with examples. Major topics included, for example, are: manuscript preparation and copy editing, style, production, and printing.

②*Chicago Manual of Style* is considered the essential reference and guide tool for scholars, editors and all involved in writing and publishing in the United States. It was originally begun as a Style Book about 1900 and soon was published as *the Manual of Style* by the University of Chicago Press.

③documentation /ˌdɔkjumenˈteiʃən/ *n.* 证明文件，文献或参考资料：a book with full documentation 引证详尽的书。

④Increasingly, however, the old distinctions are becoming blurred as scholars cross disciplinary lines and as publishers, more than ever concerned about the balance sheet, urge conciseness and practicality over scholarly indulgence in documentation. 在这个长句中，两个 as 分别引导了两个时间状语从句。
blur /bləː/ *vt.* (-rred, rring) (视线、感觉)模糊不清；弄脏，玷污：Mist blurred the hills. 大雾弥漫，群山隐隐。cross 作为动词，表示超越，交叉。over 关于，对于：cry over split milk 后悔不及。mourn over one's death 哀悼某人去世。

⑤brevity /ˈbreviti/ *n.* (时间)短暂，(讲话、文章等)简短

⑥esoteric /esəuˈterik/ *adj.* 深奥的：esoteric source citations 引用深奥的原始资料。cumbersome /ˈkʌmbəsəm/ *adj.* 讨厌的；麻烦的；笨重的。

⑦succinct /səkˈsiŋkt/ *adj.* 简洁的；紧身的；压缩在小范围内的：a succinct reply 简明扼要的回答；a succinct style 简洁的风格。

⑧consecutively /kənˈsekjutivli/ *adv.* 连贯地，连续地

⑨superior numerals. 上标。

⑩juggle /ˈdʒʌgl/ *vt.* 耍弄，歪曲，篡改；同时做使(如两种以上活动等)同时保持运作或进展：managed to juggle a full-time job and homemaking 设法在持家的同时做一份全职工作；*vi.* 玩戏法，欺骗，篡改；juggle the true and false 颠倒真假；juggle the accounts 窜改账目。

⑪discursive adjuncts to the text: 与原文关系不大的附属注释。
discursive /disˈkəːsiv/ *adj.* 散漫的，东拉西扯的，离题的；(哲)推论的。adjunct /ˈædʒʌŋkt/ *n.* 附属物，附件，配件，添加剂：This is an adjunct of bodies. 这是物体的一个附属属性。This is an adjunct to the verb. 这是动词的一个修饰语。

⑫Lists are sometimes placed at the ends of the chapters to which they apply, particularly in textbooks and in multiauthor books when there are to be offprints. 参考书目有时放在与书目有关的章节后面，教科书和多作者的书要作为选印本时，尤其如此。
apply to... 有关系；涉及：This applied to us as much as to them. 这对我们和他们同样有关

系。offprint /'ɔfprint/ *n.* 选印本。

⑬When it is desirable, in the author's opinion, to mention the principle of selection...:按照作者的观点,当需要提及选择书目的原则时……

在这个从句中,主语 to mention the principle of selection 被插入语 in the author's opinion 与形式主语 it 和谓语部分 is 分隔开了。

⑭germane /dʒə'mein/ *adj.* (议论等)切题的,关系密切的;(比喻等)恰当的,贴切的(to): a remark hardly germane to the question 与问题关系不大的话。

⑮full particular for each source reed appear only in the bibliography:

particular *n.* 一项、一点、一条、一个单独项、事实或细节;特例:correct in every particular 每一个细节都正确。常用 particulars 表示详情、细节情报或消息的一项或细节:The police refused to divulge the particulars of the case. 警察拒绝透露案件的详情。What particulars were ambushed behind these generalizations? 这些一般结论背后隐含着什么特殊情况呢? in particular 特殊地;尤其。

bibliography /bibli'ɔgrəfi/ *n.* 书目参考文献,志学书籍学。

⑯annotated /'ænəuteitid/ *adj.* 有评注的,有注解的

【Exercises】

I. Comprehension Questions

(1) According to the *Manual of Style* what are the two types of sources for written works?

(2) What are the essential parts of the author-date citation system?

(3) Where are the endnotes placed and what is the advantage of endnotes over footnotes?

(4) Which kind of notes are used in this book?

(5) What is a bibliography and what are the advantages of including a bibliography in addition to notes?

II. Complete the following sentences, using the words or expressions from the passage according to the given meaning in brackets. Change the form where necessary.

(1) He _____ (depend on) the train to take me to and from work each day.

(2) She _____ (recognize) the man as her attacker with the help of the police officer.

(3) He will _____ (provide) me with the use of his house, while he is abroad.

(4) Since we _____ (refuse to consider) the possibility of buying a new car, we must get the old one fixed.

(5) As we knew, he had already entered into _____ (a detail of information) of the affair in his notebook.

III. Fill in the gaps with the words or expressions given below. Change the form where necessary.

concern	vary	append to	known as
refer to	in addition to	to accompany	correspond

(1) Reactions to the news that a new oil terminal is to be built _____ from bitterness and hostility to cautious optimism.
(2) _____ such subjects, the department also taught mathematics and geography.
(3) The items contained in the parcel do not _____ to those on the list that accompanied it.
(4) The activity inside the Labour Party became _____ the Left Wing Movement.
(5) Political terrorism continued as a major subject of public _____.

IV. **Translate the following from English into Chinese.**
(1) primary sources
(2) superior numerals
(3) the laws of copyright
(4) scholarly works
(5) social sciences and humanities
(6) the physical and natural science
(7) Increasingly, however, the old distinctions are becoming blurred as scholars cross disciplinary lines and as publishers, more than ever concerned about the balance sheet, urge conciseness and practicality over scholarly indulgence in documentation.
(8) In a work containing many citations in notes, however, a bibliography in addition to the notes is a most useful device for the reader and an economical one for the author and publisher: the reader not only can locate each source readily but can also see at a glance the sources the author has relied on or has selected as most germane to the subject.

Supplementary Reading Materials

Section 1   Europe

21. The Fundamental Characteristics of European Feudalism[1]
Marc Bloch

The simplest way will be to begin by saying what feudal society was not. Although the obligations arising from blood-relationship played a very active part in it, it did not rely on kinship alone. More precisely, feudal ties proper were developed when those of kinship proved inadequate. ... Feudalism coincided with a profound weakening of the State, particularly in its protective capacity. But much as feudal society differed from societies based on kinship as well as from those dominated by the power of the State, it was their successor and bore their imprint. For while the characteristic relationships of personal subjection retained something of the quasi-family[2] character..., a considerable part of the political authority exercised by innumerable petty chiefs had the appearance of a usurpation[3] of "regalian" rights.

European feudalism should therefore be seen as the outcome of the violent dissolution of older societies. It would in fact be unintelligible without the great upheaval of the Germanic invasions which, by forcibly uniting two societies originally at very different stages of development, disrupted both of them and brought to the surface a great many modes of thought and social practices of an extremely primitive character. It finally developed in the atmosphere of the last barbarian raids. It involved a far-reaching restriction of social intercourse, a circulation of money too sluggish[4] to admit of a salaried officialdom, and a mentality attached to things tangible and local. When these conditions began to change, feudalism began to wane.

It was an unequal society, rather than a hierarchical one—with chiefs rather than nobles; and with serfs[5], not slaves. If slavery had not played so small a part, there would have been no need for the characteristically feudal forms of dependence, as applied to the lower orders of society. In an age of disorder, the place of the adventurer was too important, the memory of men too short, the regularity of social classifications too uncertain, to admit of the strict formation of regular castes.

Nevertheless the feudal system meant the rigorous economic subjection of a host of humble folk to a few powerful men. Having received from earlier ages the Roman villa (which in some respects anticipated the manor) and the German village chiefdom, it extended and consolidated these methods whereby men exploited men, and combining inextricably the right to the revenues from the land with the right to exercise authority, it fashioned from all this the true manor of medieval times. And this it did partly for the benefit of an oligarchy of priests and monks whose task it was to propitiate[6] Heaven, but chiefly for the benefit of an oligarchy of warriors.

As even the most perfunctory[7] comparative study will show, one of the most distinctive characteristics of feudal societies was the virtual identity of the class of chiefs with the class of professional warriors serving... as heavily armed horsemen. ... Of the societies where an armed peasantry survived, some knew neither vassalage nor the manor, while others knew them only in very imperfect forms...

In feudal society the characteristic human bond was the subordinate's link with a nearby chief. From one level to another the ties thus formed—like so many chains branching out indefinitely—joined the smallest to the greatest. Land itself was valued above all because it enabled a lord to provide himself with "men" by supplying the remuneration[8] for them. We want lands, said in effect the Norman lords who refused the gifts of jewels, arms, and horses offered by their duke. And they added among themselves: "It will thus be possible for us to maintain many knights, and the duke will no longer be able to do so."

It remained to devise a form of real property right suitable for the remuneration of services and coinciding in duration with the personal tie itself. From the solution which it found for this problem, Western feudalism derived one of its most original features. While the "men of service" who surrounded the Slav princes continued to receive their estates as outright gifts, the fief of the Frankish vassal, after some fluctuations of policy, was in theory conceded[9] to him only for the term of his life. For among the highest classes, distinguished by the honourable profession of arms, relationships of dependence had assumed, at the outset, the form of contracts freely entered into between two living men confronting one another. From this necessary personal contact the relationship derived the best part of its moral value. Nevertheless at an early date various factors tarnished the purity of the obligation: hereditary[10] succession, natural in a society where the family remained so strong; the practice of enfeoffment which was imposed by economic conditions and ended by burdening the land with services rather than the man with fealty; finally and above all, the plurality of vassal engagements. The loyalty of the commended man remained, in many cases, a potent factor. But as a paramount social bond designed to unite the various groups at all levels, to prevent fragmentation and to arrest disorder, it showed itself decidedly ineffective.

Indeed in the immense range of these ties there had been from the first something artificial. Their general diffusion in feudal times was the legacy of a moribund[11] State—that of the Carolingians—which had conceived the idea of combating social disintegration by means of one of the institutions born of that very condition. The system of superposed protective relationships was certainly not incapable of contributing to the cohesion of the State: witness, the Anglo-Norman monarchy. But for this it was necessary that there should be a central authority favoured, as in England, not only by the fact of conquest itself but even more by the circumstance that it coincided with new material and moral conditions. In the ninth century the forces making for disintegration were too strong.

In the area of Western civilization the map of feudalism reveals some large blank spaces—the Scandinavian peninsula, Frisia, Ireland. Perhaps it is more important still to note that feudal Europe was not all feudalized in the same degree or according to the same rhythm and, above all, that it was nowhere feudalized completely. In no country did the whole of the rural population fall into the bonds of personal and hereditary dependence. ... The concept of the State never absolutely disappeared, and where it retained the most vitality men continued to call themselves "free," in the old sense of the word, because they were dependent only on the head of the people or his representatives. Groups of peasant warriors remained in Normandy, in the Danelaw, and in Spain. The mutual oath, strongly contrasting with the oaths of subordination, survived in the peace associations and triumphed in the communes. No doubt it is the fate of every system of human institutions never to be more than imperfectly realized. Capitalism was unquestionably the dominant influence on the European economy at the beginning of the twentieth century; yet more than one undertaking continued to exist outside it.

Returning to our feudal map, ... it is not difficult to recognize the regions where the regularizing influence of the Carolingians had been most far-reaching and where also the mingling of Romanized elements and Germanic elements······had most completely disrupted the structure of the two societies and made possible the growth of very old seeds of territorial lordship and personal dependence.

A Cross-Section of Comparative History

A subject peasantry; widespread use of the service tenement (i.e. the fief) instead of a salary, which was out of the question; the supremacy of a class of specialized warriors; ties of obedience and protection which bind man to man and, within the warrior class, assume the distinctive form called vassalage; fragmentation of authority—leading inevitably to disorder; and, in the midst of all this, the survival of other forms of association, family and State, of which the latter, during the second feudal age, was to acquire renewed strength—such then seem to be the fundamental features of European feudalism. Like all the phenomena revealed by that science of eternal change which is history, the social structure thus characterized certainly bore the peculiar stamp of an age and an environment. Yet..., it is by no means impossible that societies different from our own should have passed through a phase closely resembling that which has just been defined. If so, it is legitimate to call them feudal during that phase. ... The work of comparison... is facilitated by the existence of excellent studies which already bear the hall-mark of the soundest comparative method.

In the dark ages of Japanese history we dimly perceive a society based on kinship groups, real or fictitious. Then towards the end of the seventh century of our era, under Chinese influence a system of government is founded which strives (exactly as the Carolingians did) to maintain a kind of moral control over its subjects. Finally, about the eleventh century, the period begins which it has become customary to call feudal and whose advent seems... to have coincided with a certain slackening[12] of commercial activity. Here, therefore, as in Europe, 'feudalism' seems to have been preceded by two very different forms of social organization... [and] was profoundly influenced by both. The monarchy, though it had less connection than in Europe with the feudal structure proper—since the chains of vassalage terminated before reaching the Emperor—subsisted, in law, as the theoretical source of all power; and there also the fragmentation of political authority, which was fostered by very old habits, was held to be a consequence of encroachments[13] on the State.

Above the peasantry a class of professional warriors had arisen. It was in these circles that ties of personal dependence developed, on the model furnished by the relations of the armed retainer with his chief; they were thus... marked by a much more pronounced class character than European "commendation." They were hierarchically organized, just as in Europe; but Japanese vassalage[14] was much more an act of submission than was European vassalage and much less a contract. It was also more strict, since it did not allow plurality of lords. As these warriors had to be supported they were granted tenements closely resembling the fiefs of the West. Sometimes even, ... the grant was purely fictitious and involved in fact lands which had originally belonged to the patrimony of the pretended recipient. These fighting-men were naturally less and less willing to cultivate the soil... The vassals therefore lived mainly on the rents from their own tenants. There were too many of them, however—far more, apparently, than in Europe—to admit of the establishment for their benefit of real manors, with extensive powers over the people. Few manors were created, except by the baronage and the temples, and being widely scattered and having no demesne, they recalled the embryonic[15] manors of Anglo-Saxon England rather than those of the really manorialized regions of the West. Furthermore, on this soil where irrigated rice-fields represented the prevailing form of agriculture, the technical conditions were so different from European practice that the subjection of the peasantry assumed correspondingly different forms.

... This outline... enables us to reach a fairly firm conclusion. Feudalism was not "an event which happened once in the world." Like Europe—though with inevitable and deep-seated differences—Japan went through this phase. Have other societies also passed through it? And if so, what were the causes, and were they perhaps common to all such societies? It is for future works to provide the answers.

【 Notes 】

This Selection is from Marc Bloch, *Feudal Society*, Volume 2: *Social Classes and Political Organization*, translated by L. A. Manyon, University of Chicago Press, 1961, pp. 443—447.

Marc Bloch (1886—1944), born in Lyon, France, was Professor of Medieval History at the University of Strasbourg and later Chairman of Economic History at the Sorbonne in Paris. He served in the French Resistance during World War II and was executed by the Germans in 1944. Feudal Society from which this excerpt comes is considered to be a basic work on European feudalism. Bloch was a founder of the influential Annales School, a major force in Western historiography, which stresses social and economic structure in the long view of civilizations. French rural history was Bloch's special field of interest. Fernand Braudel is another important Annales historian.

【 New Words 】

① feudalism /ˈfjuːdəlizəm/ n. 封建主义，封建制度
② quasi-family /ˈkwɑːzi(ː)ˈfæmili,ˈkweisai-/ n. 准家庭
③ usurpation /ˌjuːzəːˈpeiʃən/ n. 篡夺
④ sluggish /ˈslʌgiʃ/ adj. 行动迟缓的
⑤ serf /səːf/ n. 农奴，奴隶
⑥ propitiate /prəˈpiʃieit/ v. 向（上帝）赎罪；劝解
⑦ perfunctory /pəˈfʌŋktəri/ adj. 马马虎虎的
⑧ remuneration /riˌmjuːnəˈreiʃən/ n. 报酬
⑨ concede /kənˈsiːd/ vt. 勉强，承认，退让；vi. 让步
⑩ hereditary /hiˈreditəri/ adj. 世袭的，遗传的
⑪ moribund /ˈmɔ(ː)ribribʌnd/ n. 垂死的人；adj. 垂死的
⑫ slacken /ˈslækən/ v. 松弛，放慢，减弱，减少，减缓
⑬ encroachments /inˈkrəutʃmənt/ n. 侵蚀，侵犯
⑭ vassalage /ˈvæsəlidʒ/ n. 家臣身份，隶属
⑮ embryonic /ˌembriˈɔnik/ adj. 萌芽的，初期的

22. The Coming of the French Revolution

The ultimate cause of the French Revolution of 1789 goes deep into the history of France and of the western world. At the end of the eighteenth century the social structure of France was aristocratic[1]. It showed the traces of having originated at a time when land was almost the only form of wealth, and when the possessors of land were the masters of those who needed it to work and to live. It is true that in the course of age-old struggles (of which the Fronde, the last revolt of the aristocracy, was as recent as the seventeenth century) the king had been able gradually to deprive the lords of their political power and subject nobles and clergy[2] to his authority. But he had left them the first place in the social hierarchy[3]. Still restless at being merely his "subjects," they remained privileged persons.

Meanwhile the growth of commerce and industry had created, step by step, a new form of wealth, mobile or commercial wealth, and a new class, called in France the bourgeoisie[4], which since the fourteenth century had taken its place as the Third Estate in the General Estates of the kingdom. This class had grown much stronger with the maritime discoveries of the fifteenth and sixteenth centuries and the ensuing exploitation[5] of new worlds, and also because it proved highly useful to the monarchical state in supplying it with money and competent officials. In the eighteenth century commerce, industry and finance occupied an increasingly important place in the national economy. It was the bourgeoisie that rescued the royal treasury in moments of crisis. From its ranks were recruited[6] most members of the liberal professions and most public employees. It had developed a new ideology which the "philosophers" and "economists" of the time had simply put into definite form. The role of the nobility had correspondingly declined; and the clergy, as the ideal which it proclaimed lost prestige, found its authority growing weaker. These groups preserved the highest rank in the legal structure of the country, but in reality economic power, personal abilities and confidence in the future had passed largely to the bourgeoisie. Such a discrepancy[7] never lasts forever. The Revolution of 1789 restored the harmony between fact and law. This transformation spread in the nineteenth century throughout the west and then to the first whole globe, and in this sense the ideas of 1789 toured the world.

But this deeper cause of the French Revolution does not explain all its distinctive features. In England, though there have been political revolutions, social evolution has gone on in relative calm. The French Revolution was realized by violence. On the Continent, in the nineteenth century, the transformation was first precipitated[8] by the Napoleonic armies, and thereafter carried through more by governments than by the peoples themselves. In France the Third Estate liberated itself. Hence the older aristocracy long preserved more wealth and influence in other countries than in France. These special features of the Revolution in France arose from its immediate causes, and especially from the collapse of the central power which in other countries was able to keep events under control.

There would have been no French Revolution—such as actually took place—if the king, "handing in his resignation," had not convoked[9] the Estates-General. The immediate cause lay in a government emergency for which Louis XVI could find no other solution. But the Third Estate was by no means the first to profit from the emergency, contrary to the general opinion, taken over from the Revolutionists themselves, who declared adnauseam[10] that "the people rose up and overthrew despotism and aristocracy." No doubt it did end that way. But the people were not the original motive force. The bourgeoisie, having no legal means of expression, was in no position to force the king to appeal to the nation. Still less were the peasants and working classes. The privileged groups did have the necessary means: the clergy in its Assembly, the nobility in the Parliaments and Provincial Estates. It is these bodies that forced the king's hand. "The patricians began the Revolution," wrote Chateaubriand; "the plebeians[11] finished it." The first act of the Revolution, in 1788, consisted in a triumph of the aristocracy, which, taking advantage of the government crisis, hoped to reassert itself and win back the political authority of which the Capetian dynasty had despoiled[12] it. But, after having paralyzed the royal power which upheld its own social preeminence[13], the aristocracy opened the way to the bourgeois revolution, then to the popular revolution in the cities and finally to the revolution of the peasants—and found itself buried under the ruins of the Old regime...

【 Notes 】

This Selection is from Georges Lefebvre, "Introduction" to *The Coming of the French Revolution*, translated by R. R. Palmer, (First published in French in 1939) Princeton University Press, 1967, pp. 1—3.

Georges Lefebvre (1874—1959) was a Marxist historian who specialized in social history. A major historian of the French Revolution, he interpreted the Revolution as caused by social strains and economic deprivation. The Revolution itself was a turning point in the formation of the modern world, announcing the principle of the sovereignty of the people or nation and Lefebvre's work is considered a classic in its history. His viewpoint has been opposed by Francois Furet, another major French historian, who sees the Revolution as a victory of the rationalism of the Enlightenment over social interests.

【 New Words 】

①aristocratic /ˌæristəˈkrætik/ adj.　贵族的，贵族化的，贵族政治的
②clergy /ˈklɜːdʒi/ n.　（集合称）圣职者，牧师，僧侣，神职人员
③hierarchy /ˈhaiərɑːki/ n.　统治集团，等级制度，特权阶级
④bourgeoisie /ˌbuəʒwɑːˈziː/ n.　资产阶级
⑤exploitation /ˌeksplɔiˈteiʃən/ n.　开发，开采；剥削；自私的利用；宣传，广告
⑥recruit /riˈkruːt/ vt., vi.　使恢复，补充，征募新兵；n. 新兵，新会员
⑦discrepancy /disˈkrepənsi/ n.　相差，差异；矛盾
⑧precipitate /priˈsipiteit/ vt.　猛抛；使陷入；促成；使沉淀
⑨convoke /kənˈvəuk/ vt.　召集
⑩adnauseam /ˌædˈnɔːziæm/ n.　令人作呕地，讨厌地
⑪plebeian /pliˈbiːən/ n.　平民，庶民；adj. 平民的，卑俗的
⑫despoil /disˈpɔil/ vt.　夺取，掠夺
⑬preeminence /priː(ː)ˈeminəns/ n.　卓越

213

Section 2 Latin America

23. Latin America since 1800
Richard J. Walter

As with most fields of historical study. there has been an enormous expansion of scholarly works on Latin America in recent decades. perhaps more than in most fields. This scholarly boom on Latin America since 1800 however. is related, directly and indirectly. to a particular historical event: the Cuban Revolution of 1959. That Revolution. in its infancy when the last Guide appeared. stimulated first a notable outpouring of materials on the event itself and on the previously little-studied (by non-Cuban historians) Cuba. While scholars and policymakers struggled to understand the background, significance, and consequences of the Revolution, the challenge posed by a communist Cuba allied with the Soviet Union led the United States government and major foundations to direct unprecedented attention and resources to Latin American studies in general. Generous grants[1] were provided to bolster[2] and expand graduate programs and Latin American institutes at leading universities with longstanding academic strengths in the area and helped create centers of study in other institutions that previously had shown little concern for the nations south of the border. As a result. the 1960s became something of a golden age for Latin American studies. and while support and attention have ebbed and flowed since then. much of that momentum has carried through to the early 1990s.

This generous support produced a bumper crop of graduate students and future historians, most of whom received extensive training in languages, were exposed to advanced techniques in the social sciences, and had the opportunity to spend long periods in Latin American countries to conduct their field research. There, they were joined by scholars of earlier generations, who also benefited from this new surge of interest. As the decade ended and into the following years, a number of former Peace Corps[3] volunteers entered the ranks of Latin American historians, bringing to their work the special perspective gained from several years of living and working at the grassroots level in the region. Moreover, as Latin America became an area of increasing national and international interest, talented journalists added their experiences and insights to the growing historiography of the area. A number of the new historians were women, and their ranks swelled substantially in the 1970s and 1980s.

Generally, the new scholars of the post-1959 generation took a more critical view of Latin

American history than had their predecessors. Influenced by the events in Cuba and later the Vietnam War, they were particularly skeptical[4] of and often opposed to U. S. policy in the region. While this critical view is seen most clearly in the study of diplomatic history and inter-American affairs, it is also visible in examinations of Latin American societies themselves. Moving away from an emphasis on individuals and events, historians of Latin America increasingly focused on the social classes and forces, economic structures, and political institutions that perpetuated[5] and reinforced authoritarian governments and blocked progressive change. In the process, they reversed the tendency noted by H. Cline in his introduction to the 1961 Guide "to eschew narrative or analysis of the recent past. " As the material listed below amply shows, the post-World War II history of Latin America has received and continues to receive considerable scholarly emphasis.

Another important result of the U. S. boom in Latin American studies was the creation in 1965 of a national and international organization, the Latin American Studies Association. Historians played a leading role in the creation of the association and made up a large part of its constituency. Nonetheless, it drew members from a wide variety of fields, reflecting the growing interdisciplinary nature of the study of the region. One of the first major activities of the association was the production of a new journal, the Latin American Research Review, which contained essays on the state of research in various areas and provided practical advice on such matters as access to holdings of archives and documentary collections in the United States and abroad, the development of new research methodologies, the status of ongoing studies, and suggestions for future work.

The 1960s also saw a considerable expansion in publication opportunities for research in the field. University and commercial presses developed special series for Latin American studies and generally expanded their lists of Latin American titles. Finally, in addition to the Latin American Research Review, new journals such as the Journal of Interamerican Studies and World Affairs, Latin American Perspectives, and the Journal of Latin American Studies established themselves as important outlets[6] for scholarly publication.

Since the 1960s, scholarly interests in Latin America frequently paralleled U. S. policy interests. There was a dramatic increase, for example, in studies on countries such as Brazil[7] and Chile[8], that, like Cuba, experienced in the 1960s and 1970s important political changes with major implications for and involvement with U. S. foreign policies. A similar trend occurred for Central American countries in the 1980s. Two important countries with somewhat lower policy profiles, Argentina[9] and Mexico, continued to draw consistent scholarly attention. Work on the Andean republics (Venezuela, Colombia, Ecuador, Peru, and Bolivia) and Paraguay and Uruguay[10] grew, but overall these nations received less attention than others.

As in most fields of historical research, Latin Americanists adopted diverse[11] and changing approaches to their material and subject matter. In the late 1960s and early 1970s, many fell under the sway[12] of dependency theory and focused on the relationship between individual Latin American nations or the region as a whole and the capitalist world system centered in the United

215

States and western Europe. In the 1970s and 1980s, other scholars took issue with the dependency theory, often producing lively intellectual exchanges. Latin Americanists, clearly influenced by larger scholarly trends in the United States and Europe, adopted many of the techniques and approaches of the social sciences to their own efforts. They concentrated more on social and economic groups and forces than had previously been the case and emphasized the historical role of those left out of many prior accounts—black slaves, Indian peasants, immigrant and migrant workers, and women. Increasingly, historians drew on sources such as census manuscripts, local legal records, government economic reports, and election results and applied sophisticated quantitative methods to determine or to speculate on the historical trends and consequences they represented. Family history, labor history, women's history, and history of popular culture, among other topics, became important subspecialties.

For the most part, throughout the period since the 1960s, the majority of Latin American historians of the postindependence years have continued to focus their efforts and develop their special expertise on individual countries. In some instances, they sought to narrow the focus even more to particular cities, regions, provinces, or states. This trend has been most notable in work on Brazil and Mexico, where research on state histories has produced important results and provided building blocks for more synthetic[13] national histories. Others have developed a larger regional perspective on issues related to institutions, such as the military, or particular groups, such as workers, women, students, and peasants. A number of scholars have used a regional comparative approach to highlight similarities and differences between and among the various Latin American countries or to compare the Latin American historical experience with that of nations outside the region. Perhaps the best example of such efforts has been the impressive and growing literature on black slavery in Latin America, often compared with the development of that institution in the United States.

As historical specialties and expertise have grown, attempts to bring diverse perspectives to bear on a common theme or issue have been facilitated by frequent scholarly conferences, a rare occurrence before the 1960s. These conferences, most often held in the United States or in Latin America and frequently attended by scholars from around the world, in turn often have resulted in valuable collaborative publications, a practice that seems likely to continue.

【 Notes 】

Richard J. Walter, "Latin America since 1800" in *American Historical Association's Guide to Historical Literature*, Mary Beth Norton, general editor, New York: Oxford University Press, 1995, pp. 1199—1201.

Richard Walter is Professor of History at Washington University in St. Louis. He specializes in the history of Argentina. This selection by Walter, Section Editor for Latin America, from the 2 volume reference work *The American Historical Association's Guide to Historical Literature*, is from the introduction to the "Latin America since 1800" section. The purpose of the Guide, a major reference work for all historians, is "the selection and listing, with appropriate commentary, of the finest and most useful books and articles available from every field of historical scholarship." Revised and enlarged from time to time, the Guide arranges by specialized topics and geographical regions of the world citations of works published, principally in English. The whole Guide aims 1) to provide entry for scholars into a field, 2) to give information about the most important works in the field and 3) to cite differing viewpoints and interpretations. For any readers who want to know the secondary literature in a particular historical field this is an invaluable reference tool.

【 New Words 】

①grant /'grɑːnt/ n. 赠款;津贴,专用拨款
②bolster /'bəulstə/ v. 支持; n. 垫子
③corps /kɔː/ n. 军团,技术兵种,特殊兵种
④skeptical /'skeptikəl/ adj. 怀疑性的,好怀疑的;<口>无神论的
⑤perpetuate /pə(ː)'petjueit/ vt. 使永存,使不朽
⑥outlet /'autlet, -lit/ n. 出口,出路
⑦Brazil /brə'zil/ n. 巴西
⑧Chile /'tʃili/ n. 智利(南美洲西南部的一个国家,首都是圣地亚哥 Santiago)
⑨Argentina /ˌɑːdʒən'tiːnə/ n. 阿根廷(南美洲国家)
⑩Uruguay /ˌuruː'gwai/ n. 乌拉圭
⑪diverse /dai'vəːs/ adj. 不同的,变化多的
⑫sway /swei/ v. 摇摆,摇动
⑬synthetic /sin'θetic/ adj. 合成的,人造的,综合的

217

Section 3 United States

24. The Cuban Missile Crisis
Graham T. Allison

The Cuban missile crisis was a seminal[1] event. History offers no parallel to those thirteen days of October 1962, when the United States and the Soviet Union paused at the nuclear precipice.[2] Never before had there been such a high probability that so many lives would end suddenly. Had war come, it could have meant the death of 100 million Americans, more than 100 million Russians, as well as millions of Europeans. Beside it, the natural calamities and inhumanities of earlier history would have faded into insignificance. Given the odds on disaster—which President Kennedy estimated as "between one out of three and even" —our escape seems awesome[3]. This event symbolizes a central, if only partially "thinkable," fact about our existence. Although several excellent accounts are now available, the missile crisis remains, as Harold Mac mill an has observed, a "strange and still scarcely explicable affair." Even the central questions have eluded satisfactory answers :

Why did the Soviet Union place strategic offensive missiles in Cuba? For what purpose did the Russians undertake such a drastic, risky departure from their traditional policy? Given the repeated American warnings that such an act would not be tolerated, how could Khrushchev have made such a major miscalculation ?

Why did the United States respond with a naval quarantine of Soviet shipments to Cuba? Was it necessary for the United States to force a public nuclear confrontation ? What alternatives were really available? What danger did the Soviet missiles in Cuba pose[4] for the United States? Did this threat justify the President's choice of a course of action that he believed entailed[5] a 33 to 50 percent chance of disaster? Did that threat require more immediate action to disable the Soviet missiles in Cuba before they became operational?

Why were the missiles withdrawn? What would have happened if, instead of withdrawing the missiles, Khrushchev had announced that the operational Soviet missiles would fire if fired upon ? Did the "blockade" work, or was there an "ultimatum" or perhaps some "deal"? Why did the Soviets remove the missiles rather than retaliate[6] at other equally sensitive points —Berlin, for example?

What are the "lessons" of the missile crisis? What does this event teach us about nuclear confrontations? What does it imply about crisis management and government coordination? Is this a model of how to deal with the Soviet Union?

Satisfactory answers to these questions await information that has not yet come to light and more penetrating analysis of available evidence. This study provides new information about the missile crisis and a more powerful analysis of some aspects of it. But the missile crisis also serves here as grist[7] in a more general investigation. This study proceeds from the premise that satisfactory answers to questions about the missile crisis wait for more than information and analysis. Real improvement in our answers to questions of this sort depends on greater awareness of what we (both laymen and professional analysts) bring to the analysis. When answering questions like "Why did the Soviet Union place missiles in Cuba ?" what we see and judge to be important and accept as adequate depends not only on the evidence but also on the "conceptual lenses" through which we look at the evidence. Another purpose of this study is therefore to explore some of the fundamental yet often unnoticed choices among the categories and assumptions that channel our thinking about problems like the Cuban missile crisis.

The General Argument

When we are puzzled by a happening in foreign affairs, the source of our puzzlement is typically a particular outcome: the Soviet emplacement of missiles in Cuba, the movement of U. S. troops across the narrow neck of the Korean peninsula, the Japanese attack on Pearl Harbor. These occurrences raise obvious questions: Why did the Soviet Union place missiles in Cuba? Why did U. S. troops fail to stop at the narrow neck in their march up Korea ? Why did Japan attack the American fleet at Pearl Harbor? In pursuing the answers to these questions, the serious analyst seeks to discover why one specific state of the world came about—rather than some other.

In searching for an explanation, one typically puts himself in the place of the nation, or national government, confronting a problem of foreign affairs, and tries to figure out why he might have chosen the action in question. Thus, analysts have explained the Soviet missiles in Cuba as a probe of American intentions. U. S. troops marched across the narrow neck in Korea because American objectives had escalated[8] as a consequence of easy victories in the South. The attack on Pearl Harbor is explained as Japan's solution to the strategic problem posed by U. S. pressure in the Far East.

In offering (or accepting) these explanations, we are assuming governmental behavior can be most satisfactorily understood by analogy with the purposive acts of individuals. In many cases this is a fruitful assumption. Treating national governments as if they were centrally coordinated, purposive individuals provides a useful shorthand for understanding problems of policy. But this simplification—like all simplifications—obscures as well as reveals. In particular, it obscures the persistently neglected fact of bureaucracy: the "maker" of government policy is not one calculating decisionmaker but is rather a conglomerate[9] of large organizations and political actors. What this fact implies for analysts of events like the Cuban missile crisis is no simple matter: its implications concern the basic categories and assumptions with which we approach events.

More rigorously, the argument developed in the body of this study can be summarized in three propositions:

1. Professional analysts of foreign affairs (as well as ordinary laymen) think about problems of foreign and military policy in terms of largely implicit conceptual models that have significant consequences for the content of their thought.

In thinking about problems of foreign affairs, professional analysts as well as ordinary laymen proceed in a straightforward, informal, non theoretical fashion. Careful examination of explanations of events like the Soviet installation of missiles in Cuba, however, reveals a more complex theoretical substructure. Explanations by particular analysts show regular and predictable characteristics, which reflect unrecognized assumptions about the character of puzzles, the categories in which problems should be considered, the types of evidence that are relevant, and the determinants of occurrences. The first proposition is that bundles of such related assumptions constitute basic frames of reference or conceptual models in terms of which analysts and ordinary laymen ask and answer the questions: What happened? Why did it happen? What will happen? Assumptions like these are central to the activities of explanation and prediction. In attempting to explain a particular event, the analyst cannot simply describe the full state of the world leading up to that event. The logic of explanation requires that he single out the relevant, important determinants of the occurrence. Moreover, as the logic of prediction underscores, he must summarize the various factors as they bear on the occurrence. Conceptual models not only fix the mesh of the nets that the analyst drags through the material in order to explain a particular action; they also direct him to cast his nets in select ponds, at certain depths, in order to catch the fish he is after.

2. Most analysts explain (and predict) the behavior of national governments in terms of one basic conceptual model, here entitled Rational Actor or "Classical" Model (Model 1).

In spite of significant differences in interest and focus, most analysts and ordinary laymen attempt to understand happenings in foreign affairs as the more or less purposive acts of unified national governments. Laymen personify rational actors and speak of their aims and choices. Theorists of international relations focus on problems between nations in accounting for the choices of unitary rational actors. Strategic analysts concentrate on the logic of action in the absence of an actor. For each of these groups, the point of an explanation is to show how the nation or government could have chosen to act as it did, given the strategic problems it faced. For example, in confronting the problem posed by the Soviet installation of strategic missiles in Cuba, the Model I analyst frames the puzzle: Why did the Soviet Union decide to install missiles in Cuba? He then fixes the unit of analysis: governmental choice. Next, he focuses attention on certain concepts: goals and objectives of the nation or government. And finally, he invokes certain patterns of inference:[10] if the nation performed an action of this sort, it must have had a goal of this type. The analyst has "explained" this event when he can show how placing missiles in Cuba was a reasonable action, given Soviet strategic objectives. Predictions about what a nation will do or would have done are generated by calculating the rational thing to do in a certain situation, given specified objectives.

3. Two alternative conceptual models, here labeled an Organizational Process Model (Model II) and a Governmental I (Bureaucratic) Politics Model (Model Ill),... provide a base for improved explanations and predictions.

Although the Rational[11] Actor Model has proved useful for many purposes, there is powerful evidence that it must be supplemented, if not supplanted,[12] by frames of reference that focus on the governmental machine—the organizations and political actors involved in the policy process. Model I's implication that important events have important causes, Le.,[13] that monoliths[14] perform large actions for large reasons, must be balanced by the appreciation that (1) monoliths are black boxes covering various gears and levers in a highly differentiated decision making structure and (2) large acts result from innumerable and often conflicting smaller actions by individuals at various levels of bureaucratic organizations in the service of a variety of only partially compatible conceptions of national goals, organizational goals, and political objectives. Model I's grasp of national purposes and of the pressures created by problems in inter national relations must confront the intra national[15] mechanisms from which governmental actions emerge.

Recent developments in organization theory provide the foundation for the second model, which emphasizes the processes and procedures of the large organizations that constitute a government. According to this Organizational Process Model, what Model I analysts characterize as "acts" and "choices" are thought of instead as outputs of large organizations functioning according to regular patterns of behavior. Faced with the problem of Soviet missiles in Cuba, a Model II analyst frames the puzzle : From what organizational context and pressures did this decision emerge? He then fixes the unit of analysis: organizational output. Next, he focuses attention on certain concepts : the strength, standard operating procedures, and repertoires of organizations. And finally, he invokes certain patterns of inference: if organizations produced an output of this kind today, that behavior resulted from existing organizational features, procedures, and repertoires.[16] A Model II analyst has "explained" the event when he has identified the relevant Soviet organizations and displayed the patterns of organizational behavior from which the action emerged. Predictions identify trends that reflect established organizations and their fixed procedures and programs.

The third model focuses on the politics of a government. Events in foreign affairs are understood, according to this model, neither as choices nor as outputs. Rather, what happens is characterized as a resultant[17] of various bargaining games among players in the national government. In confronting the problem posed by Soviet missiles in Cuba, a Model III analyst frames the puzzle: Which results of what kinds of bargaining among which players yielded the critical decisions and actions? He then fixes the unit of analysis: political resultant. Next, he focuses attention on certain concepts: the perceptions, motivations, positions, power, and maneuvers of the players. And finally, he invokes certain patterns of inference: if a government per-formed an action, that action was the resultant of bargaining among players in games. A Model III analyst has "explained" this event when he has discovered who did what to whom that yielded the action in question. Predictions are generated by identifying the game in which an issue will arise, the relevant players, and their relative power and skill.

A central metaphor illuminates the differences among these models. Foreign policy has often been compared to moves and sequences of moves in the game of chess. Imagine a chess game in which the observer could see only a screen upon which moves in the game were projected, with no information about how the pieces came to be moved. Initially, most observers would assume—as Model I does—that an individual chess player was moving the pieces with reference to plans and tactics toward the goal of winning the game. But a pattern of moves can be imagined that would lead some observers, after watching several games, to consider a Model II assumption: the chess player might not be a single individual but rather a loose alliance of semi-independent organizations, each of which moved its set of pieces according to standard operating procedures. For example, movement of separate sets of pieces might proceed in turn, each according to a routine, the king's rook[18], bishop[19], and their pawns[20] repeatedly attacking the opponent according to a fixed plan. It is conceivable, furthermore, that the pattern of play might suggest to an observer a Model III assumption: a number of distinct players, with distinct objectives but shared power over the pieces, could be determining the moves as the resultant of collegial[21] bargaining. For example, the black rook's move might contribute to the loss of a black knight with no comparable gains for the black team, but with the black rook becoming the principal guardian of the palace on that side of the board.

Some Reservations

This bald[22] summary conveys none of my reservations about the persuasiveness of the argument in its present form. To make these points fully convincing would require greater length than seems reasonable here, and more success than I have had in coming to grips with[23] several hard problems. First, the argument that most analysts tend to rely on a single conceptual model sounds crudely reductionist. In spite of my recognition and description of several variants of Model I, my insistence on their logical similarity may, nonetheless, seem procrustean.[24] Second, because explanation and prediction of international events are not developed theoretical enterprises, few analysts proceed exclusively and single-mindedly within a pure conceptual model. Instead, they think predominantly in terms of one model, occasionally shifting from one variant of it to another and sometimes appropriating material that lies entirely outside the boundaries of the model. These first two problems give rise to a third. When examining uses of the Rational Actor Model, and especially when considering to what extent one has been relying upon some variant of this model, one can always find that it does not really capture all of his analytical activity. Fourth, the richness of variations on the classical theme makes a clearly specified account of the model seem little more than a caricature[25] or a strawman. Fifth, the alternative models are not fully developed. Finally, since the body of literature applying these alternative models to problems of foreign affairs is quite small, my applications of them are simply initial, tentative efforts.

In spite of my limited success in dealing with these difficult problems, many readers have found the general argument a suggestive contribution not only to discussion of the missile crisis but also to general thought about governmental behavior, especially in foreign and military affairs. Consequently, I have been persuaded to set these ideas down as the beginning, not the end, of an extended argument. In part, my compliance stems from the fact that defense of the stated propositions requires more than theoretical argument. The proof of the pudding is in the demonstration that the frameworks produce different explanations. The burden of the argument in this study is shared—some will insist carried—by three case studies that display the products of the conceptual models as each is applied in turn to the same problem: the central puzzles of the Cuban missile crisis. While differences among the conceptual models are examined systematically in the concluding chapter, these alternative explanations of the same happening are more revealing about the character of those differences—by showing the models at work.

A single case can do no more than suggest the kinds of differences among explanations produced by the three models. But the Cuban missile crisis is especially appropriate for the purposes of this study. In the context of ultimate danger to the nation, a small group of men, unhitched from the bureaucracy, weighed the options and decided. Such central, high-level, crisis decisions would seem to be the type of outcome for which Model I analysis is most suited. Model II and Model III are forced to compete on Model I's home ground. The dimensions and factors uncovered by Model II and Model III in this case will therefore be particularly suggestive.

【 Notes 】

This Selection is from Graham T. Allison, *Essence of Decision: Explaining the Cuban Missile Crisis*, Boston: Little, Brown and Company, 1971, pp. 1—9.

Graham T. Allison, a political scientist, was Professor of Government at Harvard University as a young man. Considered to be one of the most influential political science books of the 1970's, this book's aim is to take readers behind the scene of the Cuban Missile Crisis as it analyzed the international crisis. The author presents models for interpreting and studying America's foreign policy. Later Allison was the United States Assistant Secretary of Defense. In 1999 a new version of the book was published but this excerpt is from the first book.

【 New Words 】

①seminal /ˈseminl/ *adj.* 有重大影响的,产生巨大影响的
②precipice /ˈpresipis/ *n.* 悬崖
③awesome /ˈɔːsəm/ *adj.* 引起敬畏的, 可怕的
④pose /pəuz/ *v.* （使）摆好姿势

⑤entail /in'teil/ vt. 使必需，使蒙受，使承担
⑥retaliate /ri'tælieit/ v. 报复
⑦grist /'grist/ n. 有利的东西；谷物
⑧escalate /'eskəleit/ v. （使）逐步升高，（使）逐步增强
⑨conglomerate /kɔn'glɔmərit/ n. 集成物；聚集物；联合大企业；多种经营大公司
⑩inference /'infərəns/ n. 推论
⑪rational /'ræʃənl/ adj. 理性的，合理的，推理的
⑫supplant /sə'plɑ:nt/ vt. 排挤掉，代替
⑬Le. (abbr. Labor Exchange) 务实贸易
⑭monolith /'mɔnəuliθ/ n. 庞然大物；独块巨石
⑮intra- /'intrə/ prefix 表示"在内、内部"之义
⑯repertoire /'repətwɑ:/ n. （某个人的）全部技能
⑰resultant /ri'zʌltənt/ n. 结果；后果；合力，合成力
⑱rook /ruk/ n. （象棋）车，赌棍，骗子
⑲bishop /'biʃəp/ n. （国际象棋中的）相，象
⑳pawn /pɔ:n/ n. （象棋）兵、卒
㉑collegial /kə'li:dʒiəl/ adj. 分权的；平等分权的
㉒bald /bɔ:ld/ adj. 无掩饰的
㉓come to grips with (= get to grips with) 努力对付；认真谈论
㉔procrustean /prəu'krʌstiən/ adj. 残暴的，强求一致的
㉕caricature /'kærikətjuə/ n. 讽刺画，漫画，讽刺描述法，歪曲（或拙劣）的模仿

25. I Have a Dream
Martin Luther King

I am happy to join with you today in what will go down in history as the greatest demonstration for freedom in the history of our nation.

Fivescore[1] years ago, a great American, in whose symbolic shadow we stand today, signed the Emancipation Proclamation. This momentous decree came as a great beacon light of hope to millions of Negro slaves who had been seared[2] in the flames of withering injustice. It came as a joyous daybreak to end the long night of their captivity.

But one hundred years later, the Negro still is not free; one hundred years later, the life of the Negro is still sadly crippled by the manacles[3] of segregation and the chains of discrimination one hundred years later, the Negro lives on a lonely island of poverty in the midst of a vast ocean of material prosperity; one hundred years later, the Negro is still languished in the corners of American society and finds himself in exile in his own land.

So we've come here today to dramatize a shameful condition. In a sense we've come to our nation's capital to cash a check. When the architects of our republic wrote the magnificent words of the Constitution and the Declaration of independence, they were signing a promissory note to which every American was to fall heir. This note was the promise that all men, yes, black men as well as white men, would be guaranteed the unalienable[4] rights of life, liberty, and the pursuit of happiness.

It is obvious today that America has defaulted on this promissory note in so far as her citizens of color are concerned. Instead of honoring this sacred obligation, America has given the Negro people a bad check; a check which has come back marked "insufficient funds." We refuse to believe that there are insufficient funds in the great vaults of opportunity of this nation. And so we've come to cash this check, a check that will give us upon demand the riches of freedom and the security of justice.

We have also come to this hallowed spot to remind America of the fierce urgency of now. This is no time to engage in the luxury of cooling off or to take the tranquilizing drug of gradualism. Now is the time to make real the promises of democracy; now is the time to rise from the dark and desolate valley of segregation to the sunlit path of racial justice; now is the time to lift our nation from the quicksands[5] of racial injustice to the solid rock of brotherhood; now is the time to make justice a reality for all God's children. it would be fatal for the nation to overlook the urgency of the moment. This sweltering[6] summer of the Negro's legitimate discontent will not pass until there is an invigorating[7] autumn of freedom and equality.

Nineteen sixty-three is not an end, but a beginning. And those who hope that the Negro needed to blow off steam and will now be content, will have a rude awakening if the nation returns to business as usual.

There will be neither rest nor tranquility in America until the Negro is granted his citizenship rights. The whirlwinds of revolt will continue to shake the foundations of our nation until the bright day of justice emerges.

But there is something that I must say to my people who stand on the warm threshold which leads into the palace of justice. In the process of gaining our rightful place we must not be guilty of wrongful deeds.

Let us not seek to satisfy our thirst for freedom by drinking from the cup of bitterness and hatred. We must forever conduct our struggle on the high plane of dignity and discipline. We must not allow our creative protest to degenerate into physical violence. Again and again we must rise to the majestic heights of meeting physical force with soul force.

The marvelous new militancy which has engulfed[8] the Negro community must not lead us to a distrust of all white people, for many of our white brothers, as evidenced by their presence here today, have come to realize that their destiny is tied up with our destiny and they have come to realize that their freedom is inextricably bound to our freedom. This offense we share mounted to storm the battlements of injustice must be carried forth by a biracial army. We cannot walk alone.

And as we walk, we must make the pledge that we shall always march ahead. We cannot turn back. There are those who are asking the devotees of civil rights, 'When will you be satisfied? " We can never be satisfied as long as the Negro is the victim of the unspeakable horrors of police brutality.

We can never be satisfied as long as our bodies, heavy with fatigue of travel, cannot gain lodging in the motels of the highways and the hotels of the cities. We cannot be satisfied as long as the Negro's basic mobility is from a smaller ghetto[9] to a larger one.

We can never be satisfied as long as our children are stripped[10] of their selfhood and robbed of their dignity by signs stating "for whites only." We cannot be satisfied as long as a Negro in Mississippi cannot vote and a Negro in New York believes he has nothing for which to vote. No, we are not satisfied, and we will not be satisfied until justice rolls down like waters and righteousness like a mighty stream.

I am not unmindful that some of you come here out of excessive trials and tribulation. Some of you have come fresh from narrow jail cells. Some of you have come from areas where your quest for freedom left you battered by the storm-is of persecution and staggered by the winds of police brutality. You have been the veterans of creative suffering. Continue to work with the faith that unearned suffering is redemptive.[11]

Go back to Mississippi; go back to Alabama; go back to South Carolina; go back to Georgia; go back to Louisiana; go back to the slums and ghettos of the northern cities, knowing that somehow this situation can, and will be changed. Let us not wallow[12] in the valley of despair.

So I say to you, my friends, that even though we must face the difficulties of today and tomorrow, I still have a dream. It is a dream deeply rooted in the American dream that one day this nation will rise up and live out the true meaning of its creed—we hold these truths to be self-evident, that all men are created equal.

I have a dream that one day on the red hills of Georgia, sons of former slaves and sons of former slave-owners will be able to sit down together at the table of brotherhood.

I have a dream that one day, even the state of Mississippi, a state sweltering with the heat of injustice, sweltering with the heat of oppression, will be transformed into an oasis of freedom and justice.

I have a dream my four little children will one day live in a nation where they will not be judged by the color of their skin but by the content of their character. I have a dream today!

I have a dream that one day, down in Alabama, with its vicious racists, with its governor having his lips dripping with the words of interposition[13] and nullification,[14] that one day, right there in Alabama, little black boys and black girls will be able to join hands with little white boys and white girls as sisters and brothers. I have a dream today!

I have a dream that one day every valley shall be exalted,[15] every hill and mountain shall be made low, the rough places shall be made plain, and the crooked places shall be made straight and the glory of the Lord will be revealed and all flesh shall see it together.

This is our hope. This is the faith that I go back to the South with.

With this faith we will be able to hew out of the mountain of despair a stone of hope. With this faith we will be able to transform the jangling[16] discords of our nation into a beautiful symphony of brotherhood.

With this faith we will be able to work together, to pray together, to struggle together, to go to jail together, to stand up for freedom together, knowing that we will be free one day. This will be the day when all of God's children will be able to sing with new meaning, 'my country 'tis of thee; sweet land of liberty; of thee I sing; land where my fathers died, land of the pilgrim's pride; from every mountain side, let freedom ring—and if America is to be a great nation, this must become true.

So let freedom ring from the prodigious[17] hilltops of New Hampshire.

Let freedom ring from the mighty mountains of New York.

Let freedom ring from the heightening Alleghenies of Pennsylvania.

Let freedom ring from the snow-capped Rockies of Colorado. Let freedom ring from the curvaceous slopes of California. But not only that.

Let freedom ring from Stone Mountain of Georgia.

Let freedom ring from Lookout Mountain of Tennessee.

Let freedom ring from every hill and molehill of Mississippi, from every mountainside, let freedom ring.

And when we allow freedom to ring, when we let it ring from every village and hamlet, from every state and city, we will be able to speed up that day when all of God's children—black men and white men, Jews and Gentiles[18], Catholics and Protestants—will be able to join hands and to sing in the words of the old Negro spiritual, "Free at last, free at last; thank God Almighty, we are free at last."

【 Notes 】

This Selection is from Martin Luther King, "I Have a Dream," speech to the March on Washington for Civil Rights, August 28, 1963, in *I Have a Dream, Writings and Speeches That Changed the World*, Harper San Francisco, 1992, pp. 101—106.

Martin Luther King (1929—1967) gave this speech "I have a Dream" in 1963 in Washington, D. C. This is the complete speech, an example of an important primary document for historians. The year 1963 was the hundredth anniversary of the signing of the Emancipation Proclamation by President Lincoln freeing the slaves during the Civil War, a very significant year in American history and in the American Civil Rights Movement. During this 20th century movement which demanded equal treatment and equal civil rights for all Americans, the President of the United States, John F. Kennedy, authorized federal marshals to escort a few black students to register at the University of Mississippi and the University of Alabama, despite the opposition from the governors of the two states. However, the head of the Birmingham city police department, "Bull" Connor, ordered his officers to turn fire hoses and police dogs on the young demonstrators.

As television cameras captured this scene, the whole country watched. Riots occurred throughout the summer.

Martin Luther King, Jr. was the strongest leader of the American Civil Rights Movement and a black man. "I Have a Dream," is his most well-known and most often quoted speech. He spoke on the steps of the Lincoln Memorial in Washington, D.C., on August 28, 1963, at the March on Washington for Civil Rights attended by tens of thousands of black and white people from across the whole nation. Television cameras allowed the entire country to hear him plead for justice and freedom. King was assassinated by a sniper four years later.

【New Words】

①fivescore /ˈfaivˈskɔː(r)/ adj. 一百的
②sear /siə/ vt. 烤焦，使枯萎；vi. 凋谢，干枯
③manacle /ˈmænəkl/ n. 手铐，脚镣，束缚
④unalienable /ʌnˈeiliənəbl/ adj. 不可剥夺的；不可分割的
⑤quicksand /ˈkwiksænd/ n. 流沙；敏捷；危险而捉摸不定的事物
⑥sweltering /ˈsweltəriŋ/ adj. 闷热的，中暑的，酷热的
⑦invigorating /inˈvigəreitiŋ/ adj. 精力充沛的，爽快的
⑧engulf /inˈgʌlf/ vt. 卷入，吞没，狼吞虎咽
⑨ghetto /ˈgetəu/ n. 限制区，分离区；（美）城市中的黑人、波多黎各人等的集中居住区
⑩strip /strip/ vt., vi. （常与of连用）脱，剥，拆
⑪redemptive /riˈdemptiv/ adj. 赎回的，挽回的，用于补偿的
⑫wallow /ˈwæləu/ vi. （常与in连用）沉溺于
⑬interposition /inˌtəːpəˈziʃən/ n. 插入，妨害，干涉；调停；插入物
⑭nullification /ˌnʌlifiˈkeiʃən/ n. 无效，废弃，取消，使无价值，使变的无用
⑮exalt /igˈzɔːlt/ vt. 赞扬；歌颂；提升；晋升
⑯jangle /ˈdʒæɡl/ vt., vi. （使）发出刺耳声；乱响
⑰prodigious /prəuˈdidʒəs/ adj. 巨大的
⑱Gentile /ˈdʒentail/ n. 非犹太人，异教徒

Section 4 History of Popular Culture

26. The River of Rock
Adam Woog

... When rock and roll was new, the music industry ignored it. Record company executives, radio station managers, and concert promoters on the whole thought it was a silly fad[1] that would soon disappear.

They were wrong.

Rock and roll, which later became rock, is the dominant music of the twentieth century. Nearly a half century since the first rockers strutted[2] on stage, the music is still very much here. Around the world rock is... not only the theme music for the lives of millions, capable of carrying tremendous weight and influence, but it is also the background music of daily life, commonplace on radio and television, in supermarkets and malls.

......

Rock's ancestry winds through centuries of African and European music, and its immediate ancestors are idioms in American popular music that range from the blues to gospel,[3] commercial pop to bluegrass. More recently, rock has also been deeply influenced by "outsider" styles from around the world.

This history... is intense and complicated. Dividing rock history into eras is convenient but misleading since styles have a habit of never quite going away. Yesterday's sensations may be forgotten today, only to be "rediscovered" tomorrow. Others develop and grow, never fully losing their audiences.

Rock history can thus be thought of as a river; it continually carries material from upstream, mixes the old stuff with new material, and sends it all downstream. Rock also has a way of rediscovering its deepest roots every few years. [Someone has noted] that the music's history is "a matter of cycles within cycles ... a developing idiom that periodically refreshes itself by drinking from its own deepest wellsprings."

The Earthquakes

Despite this constant renewal, all popular music, rock included, periodically experiences the doldrums.[4] This happens, in large part, as the music industry tries to make it as palatable as possible to the widest audience, watering it down to make it commercially successful. Fans will turn away, however, if the music becomes so blandly commercial that it loses its spice. This has happened several times to rock, each time prompting predictions that the music is dead, that it has run its course. But rock has always experienced a jolt—an earthquake of sorts—that has brought it back to life.

The first jolt, the one that first gave life to rock and roll, came in the 1950s, when a small group of wildly gifted, gleefully[5] rebellious musicians began ripping up the stagnant[6] pop music scene. They came from musically rich cities like New Orleans and Memphis, and they recorded their music on shoestrings[7] in a succession of scrappy[8] little studios.

Inevitably, the power and creativity of this first wave of rock began to grow dull. Further earthquakes, notably the British invasion and psychedelia, were needed to stir things up. In the meantime, what had begun as music for dance and entertainment turned into a genuine art form; rock and roll became rock. Audiences also grew larger, as succeeding generations of fans came of age. By the seventies, rock was played in huge arenas, and a new class of entertainer—the millionaire rock star—had been born.

Then came another bracing jolt, as the punk[9] revolution of 1976 forced rock back to its raw, rebellious roots. Punk stripped the music to its bare essentials. Furthermore, punk's democratic spirit and do-it-yourself attitude (Anybody can be in a band! Who cares if you can't play an instrument?) were direct confrontations to the mainstream music industry.

There have been further developments since 1976—post-punk, MTV, thrash[10] metal, rap, grunge[11]—and there will be more in the future. Before exploring these rich possibilities, however, it is important to look at the roots of rock and roll: the music that first gave it life.

Growing from the Roots

In the early days of America, different strands of popular music arrived—as did Americans themselves—from many parts of the world. Black slaves brought African songs, Irish and English immigrants brought jigs[12] and reels,[13] and German and Polish settlers brought polkas.[14] For all of these people, music served as a powerful reminder of a homeland far away. Musical styles were generally divided by racial, social, and religious barriers. Religious people listened to religious music and condemned those who preferred "the devil's music." The upper classes preferred classical or light classical, and they disdained vulgar popular music. The racial barrier was probably the strongest, however: White audiences almost exclusively listened to music by white musicians in familiar European styles; black people, likewise, listened almost exclusively to black musicians playing in styles familiar to them.

Another barrier to the intermingling of styles was simply geographical. Pockets of distinctive regional music developed in culturally rich cities such as Nashville, Chicago, New York, Kansas City, New Orleans, and Memphis. Travel was difficult, however, and often musicians were not heard outside their immediate regions.

Beginning early in the century, radio and phonographs began breaking down these barriers. Thanks to these technological innovations, a fiddler[15] from Kentucky could hear a guitarist from Chicago; New Yorkers could hear the driving rhythms of Kansas City bands, and the Kansas City musicians could hear the sophisticated sounds of New York jazz bands.

Gradually, too, strictly divided styles began to blend and borrow from one another. One result of this blending of idioms, especially black and white styles, was a new music called rock and roll.

It was a slow process that took place over many years and in many places. In recorded music, black and white music had already begun mixing it up by the 1930s, as when, for example, black jazz trumpeter Louis Armstrong recorded with white bluegrass singer Jimmie Rodgers.

······

Out of Africa Perhaps the most important elements in rock's ancestry came from Africa, brought to the American South by slaves and developed further by their descendants. White traditions have been vital in rock's development, but most historians and fans agree that the primary influence has been black. Peter Gabriel, an English rocker who has been deeply influenced by music from around the world, states, "Part of what we consider our fundamental rock and roll heritage originated in Africa." Perhaps the most important of these influences is an emphasis on a steady beat—a rocking beat—adopted from the complex drumming styles that are common across Africa. Because drums were often forbidden to slaves on the theory that powerful instruments could incite[16] them to rebellion, slaves often created their rhythmic songs using only hand claps, foot stomps, and voices.

Vocal styles borrowed from Africa were also important predecessors to rock. One example was the technique called call and response, in which a chorus echoed a lead singer. Typically, the lead singer also used a high degree of improvisation[17] and an emotion-filled tone that seemed rough and coarse by European standards. Furthermore, musicians, singers, and audience members alike often entered a kind of ecstatic[18] trance[19] state that was called "getting happy." This became a cornerstone of both the black church tradition and, later, rock and roll.

Some of the earliest recorded examples of black music were made by a father-and-son team of musicologists, John and Alan Lomax. In the 1930s the Lomaxes recorded a significant collection of American folk music for the Library of Congress. This series includes "field shouts," songs used to maintain steady rhythms while picking cotton or otherwise working in fields, and songs sung by prison chain gangs.

One example, a 1934 recording of a church congregation singing a type of song called a ring shout, has words that seem like direct ancestors of rock and roll:

O my Lord

Well well well I've gotta[20] rock ... The Blues Perhaps the most important style of music that developed from African influences was the blues. It is not an exaggeration to say that the blues is the basic vocabulary of rock. The blues emerged in the early part of the century in the fertile Mississippi delta[21] as a style of acoustic (or "country") singing and playing that used commonly available instruments such as guitars, pianos, harmonicas,[22] basses made from washtubs, and bones or washboards for percussion.[23] The National steelbody guitar, often used with a slide to produce its characteristic haunting sound, was favored in those preamplification[24] days for its loud, bright tone.

The blues sound is created with "blue" or "bent" notes, formally the flattened third and seventh notes of a scale, which have a highly expressive and melancholy[25] feel. Also typical of the blues are a simple structure, usually twelve bars with a repeated three-chord progression, and lyrics[26] that express a bittersweet mixture of joy and pain.

The acknowledged king of early blues was Mississippi Robert Johnson, whose rough, hard-drinking life set the standard for the classic bluesman. Johnson gained his mastery of the slide guitar, according to legend, after making a pact with the devil at "the crossroads" in Clarksdale, Mississippi; he produced only a handful of recordings before his death at age twenty—he was apparently poisoned by a jealous girlfriend.

During and after World War 11, large numbers of African Americans moved from rural regions to cities in search of better jobs. Blues musicians were exposed to jazz and other sophisticated, big-city styles of popular music. At the same time, electrified instruments were more widely available.

Out of this combination of events emerged a type of amplified blues, harder edged and more aggressive. Memphis became a particular hotbed of this new urban style, nurturing such performers as singer-guitarist B. B. King and singer Bobby Bland. Chicago was the home of an important blues sound that was developed by artists such as singer-guitarist Muddy Waters and pianist Otis Spann.

. . . . . .

High Lonesome As black music was evolving into styles like electric blues and jump blues, white musicians were creating other idioms. Dominating white pop music of the time were crooners like Frank Sinatra, who interpreted songs by composers like George Gershwin, and swing musicians, who played a sophisticated, "sweetened" version of black jazz. More important to the history of rock and roll, however, was the development of country music and its close relative, bluegrass. Both drew heavily on traditional Irish-English music, typified by storytelling songs; stringed instruments such as the banjo, mandolin, and fiddle; and vocals characterized by "high lonesome" close harmonies.

Bluegrass was often the focus of dances in isolated mountain or prairie communities. Country music, the more commercial branch, was centered in the recording base of Nashville, Tennessee. It gave the music's traditional elements a glossy pop overlay with modern instruments, especially the trademark twang[27] of the pedal steel guitar.

A related hybrid[28] was Western swing, which combined elements of country with the powerful rhythms of horn-driven swing jazz and many other eccentric elements even the polkas of German and Polish immigrant groups. Western swing's best known proponent was Bob Wills and his Texas Playboys, whose many hits includes the now-classic "San Antonio Rose."

The most important of all, however, was Hank Williams, the father of modern country music ...

Growing up in Alabama, Williams played with blues artists and learned guitar from a black street musician. He later mixed black and white styles to create an extremely popular style that he dubbed honky-tonk.[29] The singer's magnetic stage presence, aching voice, and beautifully crafted songs set a high standard for future country music. They appealed to black audiences as well; many black musicians, including Ray Charles, have noted their affection for Williams's music.

Among the best of Williams's self-written songs are "jambalaya,"[30] "I'm So Lonesome I Could Cry," and "Your Cheatin' Heart." Though they may seem clichéd today, these intense, plain-spoken songs of lost love and hard drinking were bold departures from the bland[31] pop familiar to most white audiences of the day. Paul Friedlander writes that Williams "provided an alternative to the 'June, croon,[32] spoon' worldview of contemporary popular music."

"Good Rockin' Tonight" A final element in the genesis of rock and roll was a hybrid music called rhythm and blues, or R&B. R&B drew its main inspiration from a merger of jump blues and pop vocals, blending the characteristic emphasis on the backbeat and "gutty" tenor sax solos of jump blues with showy, gospel-influenced vocals. The term rhythm and blues was coined sometime in the 1940s—the exact date is uncertain—by Jerry Wexler, a writer for the music-industry magazine Billboard... The phrase was eventually used as a catchall[33] for all black pop music, replacing the archaic term race music.

A number of singers made R&B recordings in the late 1940s that skirt close to what can be considered rock and roll. These include Roy Brown's "Good Rockin, Tonight," Amos Milburn's "Chicken Shack Boogie," and Little Willie Littlefield's "K. C. Loving," later rewritten into a rock standard called "Kansas City."

For all intents and purposes, the pieces of rock and roll were ready. All the music needed now was a group of artists willing to bring the ingredients together—and to find an audience.

【 Notes 】

This Selection is from Adam Woog, *The History of Rock and Roll*, San Diego, CA: Lucent Books, 1999, pp. 8—17.

Adam Woog is an example of a historian of popular culture who concentrates on major figures and cultural modes that express the culture of the people. He has written biographies and on areas of popular culture in a simple direct style which appeals to general readers especially. His subjects have included the movie producer, Steve Spielberg; Bill Gates, founder of the Microsoft computer software company; and Fidel Castro. Here in this two volume work from which we have excerpts in two sections he traces the beginnings of Rock and Roll music from Africa and early Rhythm and Blues up to contemporary Pop music.

【New Words】

①fad /fæd/ n. 时尚，一时流行的狂热，一时的爱好
②strut /strʌt/ vi. 大摇大摆地走，肿胀；vt. 支撑，炫耀
③gospel /'gɔspəl/ n. 福音音乐
④doldrums /'dɔldrəmz/ n. [pl.] 消沉；经济无生气；赤道无风带
⑤gleefully /'gli:fuli/ adv. 愉快地
⑥stagnant /'stægnənt/ adj. 停滞的，迟钝的
⑦shoestring /'ʃu:striŋ/ n. 零星资金
⑧scrappy /'skræpi/ adj. （看似）零散的，片断的，杂乱无章的；斗志旺盛的
⑨punk /pʌŋk/ n.&adj. 庞克摇滚乐
⑩thrash /θræʃ/ v.&n. 打谷；击；颠簸，逆行
⑪grunge /grʌndʒ/ n. 肮脏，低下；令人讨厌或无聊的人
⑫jig /dʒig/ n. 快步舞，快步舞曲
⑬reel /ri:l/ n. 摇摆，蹒跚，眩晕，旋转
⑭polka /'pɔlkə/ n. 波尔卡舞
⑮fiddler /'fidlə/ n. 拉提琴的人，小提琴家；胡乱拨弄者
⑯incite /in'sait/ vt. 激动，煽动
⑰improvisation /imprərai'zeiʃən/ n. 即席创作
⑱ecstatic /eks'tætik/ adj. 狂喜的，心醉神迷的，入迷的
⑲trance /trɑ:ns/ n. 恍惚，出神，着迷；[医]迷睡
⑳gotta: got 的古英语形式
㉑delta /'deltə/ n. 三角洲，德耳塔（希腊字母的第四个字）
㉒harmonica /hɑ:'mɔnikə/ n. 口琴，玻璃或金属片的敲打乐器
㉓percussion /pə:'kʌʃən/ n. 打击乐器
㉔preamplification /priæmplifi'keiʃən/ 前置放
㉕melancholy /'melənkəli/ n. 忧郁
㉖lyric /'lirik/ n. 抒情诗；歌词
㉗twang /twæŋ/ n. 弦声；砰的一声；鼻音；意味
㉘hybrid /'haibrid/ n. 杂种，混血儿，混合物
㉙dub /dʌb/ vt. [电影]配音，轻点，授予称号，打击
honky-tonk /'hɔŋkitɔŋk/ n. 拉格泰姆钢琴曲，低级嘈杂的夜总会
㉚jambalaya /ˌdʒʌmbə'laiə/ n. 什锦菜肴
㉛bland /blænd/ adj. 温和的，柔和的；乏味的，冷漠的，刺激性少的

㉜croon /kruːn/ v. & n.　深情地、富有柔情地唱流行歌曲
㉝catchall /ˈkætʃɔːl/ n.　装零杂物品的容器

27. Rock and Roll
Adam Woog

A King Is Born

The roll call [of rockers in the 1950s] is long and distinguished, but one man more than any other, defined this golden age of classic rock and roll. Perhaps no other performer has had a greater impact on pop culture than Elvis Presley. More than twenty years after his death, his name, his face, and his music still evoke instant recognition even in distant corners of the world. For many people Elvis was—and is—rock and roll. In a saying frequently attributed to Bruce Springsteen, "There have been contenders[1], but there is only one King."

Elvis did not invent rock and roll. He was not the first to bring black and white musical styles together. It can be argued that he was not the music's most gifted singer. Nor did he write his own songs, relying instead on other (often mediocre[2]) writers. Nonetheless, Elvis remains the single most important person in the development of rock and roll.

This is because he was gifted not only as a performer and a synthesizer of styles but also as a popularizer. He was the first person to bring rock and roll to a truly widespread, mixed-race audience by successfully merging the intensity of black music with a mournful hillbilly[3] sound. In so doing, he introduced rock and roll to the world.

As a teenager fresh out of high school and working as a truck driver in Memphis, Presley made his first recording at a local studio. According to legend, it was a gift for his mother.

His voice caught the attention of the studio's owner. Sam Phillips, ... a fanatical[4] champion of black music, had often remarked that he could make a fortune if he found a singer with the passion of a black artist and a face that would appeal to white audiences. He thought that Elvis might just be that singer.

Phillips teamed the young singer with two professional musicians, guitarist Scotty Moore and bassist Bill Black. After months of practice they released their first single in 1954. Its two songs reflected Presley's ability to span white and black styles. One side was a blues song, "That's All Right (Mama)," and the other was a sped-up version of a country waltz, "Blue Moon of Kentucky."

The record was a regional hit, and Presley's fame slowly grew [and... the singer's career took off]. After his... contract was sold to a major record company, RCA, for the unheard-of sum of thirty-five thousand dollars, Presley's "Heartbreak Hotel" was his first national hit in 1956—and the first [step in his becoming] the most successful entertainment figure of all time.

......

Whaddya Got?[5]

Radio could get the message out, but rock and roll would not have flourished without the explosive development of teen culture in America after the war, and its acceptance of the music. Thanks to a strong postwar economy, American teens had far fewer responsibilities and far more leisure time and money than ever before. Translated into purchasing power, for the first time in history teens formed a pool of consumers control- ling billions of disposable[6] dollars.

Naturally, before long products specifically for teens appeared in quantity. As rock historian Paul Friedlander writes, "American business, recognizing the existence of a new consumer group, rushed to fill the void,[7] providing 'essential' items such as clothes, cosmetics, fast food, cars—and music."

Records (mostly singles with some long-play albums), radios (bulky table models or the thrilling new transistors), and hi-fi sets (stereo was still in the future) all absorbed the entertainment dollars teens were spending. However, the music industry often found it difficult to produce music that satisfied teens.

The pop music turned out by the major record labels was, almost without exception, bland and predictable. Teenagers preferred what they heard on small, scruffy,[8] independent labels—the far more exciting and dangerous sounds of R&B and rock and roll.

The new music struck a chord of rebellion against the conformist, complacent[9] society of the postwar years, an attitude summed up by Marlon Brando's famous line in The Wild One. In that movie a waitress asks Brando, who plays the leader of a motorcycle gang, what he's rebelling against. Brando coolly replies, "Whaddya got?"

An Evil Influence

Naturally, adults were disconcerted by such attitudes. How could kids be so rebellious when they had everything they wanted? Thus was laid one of the fundamental cornerstones of rock and roll: its long tradition of driving the old folks up the wall[10]. Parents and authorities, especially conservative lawmakers and clergy, increasingly railed against the influence of rock and roll on impressionable youth, juvenile delinquents, race mixing, violence, vandalism[11]—it was all clearly tied in with[12] the music.

......

The established music-industry response was to make rock tamer, more acceptable to a mainstream audience. It was the first attempt—but by no means the last—to tamp down[13] rock and roll's unruly[14] energy.

Pop Moves In: The Music Industry Discovers Rock and Roll

Until the breakthrough success of Elvis, rock and roll was known to a relatively small group of fans. It was thus outside the notice of the established music industry; the amount of money rockers generated was tiny compared to mainstream pop artists of the day like Perry Como, Frank Sinatra, and Patti Page.

However, as rock and roll began to gain nationwide popularity (and make serious money), the record industry took notice. Between 1958 and 1963 the music industry moved to embrace the new music and rock and roll became big business.

By 1963 record companies were selling $100 million in singles, making another $1.3 billion in television profits, and still another half-billion from five hundred thousand jukeboxes[15] spread across the country—and this was in America alone. An early 1960s press release from Decca Records boasted, "The recording industry, a fledgling[16] during the heyday of vaudeville,[17] has shown a steady, remarkable growth until today it stands as a major factor in the world's economy."

The tendency in all musical styles, as they move from fringe[18] phenomenon to mainstream entertainment, is to become watered down.[19] This decrease in intensity makes the "product," as the music industry calls its creations, acceptable to the widest audience possible. Rock and roll was no exception. John Tobler, a veteran music writer, writes that beginning in 1958 there was "a distinct trend towards the widespread softening and dilution[20] of rock 'n' roll into a more universally palatable product."

In some ways this thinning-down led to inferior music. In other ways, however, the music benefited from more diversity and polish, from access to better production values, and from a new emphasis on more sophisticated songwriting. The rawness of rock and roll was meeting the polish of pop, and the result was not always bad.

Several new styles emerged and flourished in this atmosphere, from emotionally lush[21] girl groups to silly dance crazes,[22] from elaborate mini-symphonies to wild-man instrumentals. Before, there had been essentially only one type of pop music in the mainstream; now there was something for everybody.

A Shortage

One reason for such diversity was that the first wave of rockers fell by the wayside, at least temporarily. By the early 1960s, for a variety of reasons, rock and roll had a distinct shortage of stars. ...

The music industry rushed to fill the void at the top left by the absence of these stars, especially Elvis. Loved or hated, the charismatic Elvis could not be ignored, and a frantic search was on for a replacement. As rock historian Charlie Gillett writes, "Presley's dark, heavy features, greasy black hair, and surly[23] expression became elements of an image that producers everywhere sought or attempted to re-create." [This was a time when] singing stars were picked by eager producers according to looks; musical ability was a secondary consideration.

. . . .

The British Invasion

On February 9, 1964, an estimated 70 million Americans tuned into the Ed Sullivan Show, the nation's most popular television show. It was the largest audience in history for a television entertainment show. In the live theater audience were 700 people chosen from over 50,000 applicants. Sullivan's show that night was the first American volley[24] of the amazing phenomenon called Beatlemania. Beatlemania[25] was a huge and unexpected tidal wave that touched off[26] an even larger upheaval in pop music. The bands of the British Invasion reintroduced audiences to the roots of rock, bringing a fresh perspective to the blues and R&B they had loved from afar.

Their freshness and energy was a needed antidote[27] to the faceless teen idols. Furthermore, the abundant gifts of the Beatles-especially the band's chief song writers and singers, John Lennon and Paul McCartney—set a new standard for future generations of rock music. They were the first major band, for instance, to write most of their own material and to play a significant role in producing their own records.

To some the advent of the Beatles signaled the change of the music from old- style rock and roll to something quite different. Critic Jon Landau writes, "The Beatles[28] shattered the dreariness[29] of the music business. And with them came rock ... a music quite different from rock 'n' roll."

The Beatles in England

Liverpool, a tough blue-collar town in northwestern England, was an unlikely but powerful breeding ground for the Beatles. Although isolated to a degree from mainstream British culture, as a major port city it had a direct pipeline to American pop culture; sailors eagerly brought in the latest American records, which were unavailable in most of England, and a lively underground of rockers thrived in the city.

Lennon, McCartney, guitarist George Harrison, and drummer Ringo Starr were part of this subculture: four scruffy lads linked by a shared love of American music. The rebel stance[30] of Elvis Presley, the weird passion of Little Richard, the clever wit of Chuck Berry, and the sweet harmonies of the Everly Brothers spoke straight to their hearts. As McCartney later recalled, "Every time I felt low I just put on an Elvis [record] and I'd feel great, beautiful... 'All Shook Up'! Oh, it was beautiful!"

The Beatles slowly forged a high-powered, crowd-pleasing stage act in the "beat clubs" of Liverpool and of Hamburg, Germany, another tough port city. A canny manager, Brian Epstein, then steered them toward a more polished stage act, trading in their greasy hair and leather jackets for the matching suits and "Beatle cuts"[31] that became their trademarks.

Hard work on Epstein's part also won the band a recording contract, and its first singles took England by storm. Soon the Beatles were headlining[32] a grueling[33] series of road shows, making appearances on the top television programs, and dodging[34] increasingly large crowds.

The audiences of screaming teenagers who swooned over[35] the Fab Four shocked and concerned the generally reserved British public. At the same time, Britons were charmed by the band's genuine wit and obvious talents. A comment by London's Daily Mirror newspaper was typical: "You have to be a real sour square[36] not to love the nutty,[37] noisy, happy, handsome Beatles. If they don't sweep your blues away, brother, you're a lost cause."

The Beatles in America

Success in England, however, did not guarantee success in the States. No British act had ever made a dent in the American pop charts, and early efforts to release Beatles records in America had met with dismal failure. Even after the group's British successes, the president of Capitol Records (the American subsidiary of their label) told their producer, George Martin, "We don't think the Beatles will do anything in this market." Through a fluke[38], however, an American disc jockey received a copy of a British single, "She Loves You." After he began playing it, its popularity spread from regional hit to nationwide smash. Capitol hastily arranged to release it in America and launched a fast publicity campaign (including large quantities of Beatle wigs) prior to their debut on the Ed Sullivan Show.

American critical reaction to the Beatles was mixed. The New York Herald-Tribune complained that they were "75% publicity, 20% haircut and 5% lilting lament[39]." The Washington Post called them "asexual and homely[40]." Religious leaders and other authorities, meanwhile, considered Beatlemania just another aspect of rock and roll's moral degeneracy.

But the public's response was what counted, and in this the band triumphed. The concerts were record-breaking sensations. Newsweek gave them a cover story, and sales of records and merchandise rocketed. There were even dozens of tribute records-songs with titles like "We Love You Beatles," "My Boyfriend Got a Beatle Haircut," and "Ringo for President." Rock critic David P. Szatmary summarizes: "From almost every standpoint, the Beatles' visit to America had been the nine most incredible and intense days in rock and roll history."

The publicity campaign, the sheer quality of the band's musicianship, and their personal charm were only some of the factors in the band's success in America. Another was their exotic nature: no American had ever heard a rock and roll band from overseas.

A final factor was a fluke of timing. In early 1964, America was a nation rocked by murder. The assassination of President John F. Kennedy in November 1963 had shaken the country to its core; all through the winter Americans had been wrapped in shock, grief, and disbelief. Finally ready for some light news, they found Beatlemania was the perfect answer. Noting how the nation's mood lifted in the wake of Beatlemania, critic Lester Bangs writes, "In retrospect,[41] it seems obvious that this elevation of our mood had to come from outside."

......

[In the late 1990s] Some musicians remain in the limelight[42] though they are no longer performing or even alive—Elvis Presley albums continue to sell in massive quantities. Likewise, after a 1996 retrospective, the Beatles essentially topped their own seemingly untoppable act. The London Observer notes that "the Beatles have achieved what every group since them has failed to do: become bigger than the Beatles."

【 Notes 】

This Selection is from Adam Woog, *The History of Rock and Roll*, San Diego, CA: Lucent Books, 1999, pp.23—42, 100.

【 New Words 】

①contender /kən'tendə/ *n.* 斗争者，竞争者
②mediocre /miːdi'əukə/ *adj.* 普普通通的
③hillbilly /'hilbili/ *n.* 山地内部的贫农，山地人
④fanatical /fə'nætikəl/ *adj.* 狂热的，盲信的
⑤Whaddya Got？：What do you have got?
⑥disposable /dis'pəusəbl/ *adj.* 可任意使用的
⑦void /vɔid/ *n.* 空间，空旷，空虚，怅惘
⑧scruffy /'skrʌfi/ *adj.* 肮脏的，不整洁的，破旧的
⑨conformist /kən'fɔːmist/ *adj.* 依照的(to; with)，遵从的(to) *n.* 遵奉者，墨守成规的人
 complacent /kəmp'leisnt/ *adj.* 自满的，得意的
⑩drive...up the wall：逼……至绝境，使……走投无路
⑪vandalism /'vændəliz(ə)m/ *n.* 故意破坏
⑫tie in (with) （使）连接起来；（使）协调；（与……）相一致
⑬tamp down 踏坏，踩碎；踏实
⑭unruly /ʌn'ruːli/ *adj.* 不受拘束的，不守规矩的，难驾驭的
⑮jukebox /'dʒuːkbɔks/ *n.* 自动唱片点唱机
⑯fledgling /'fledʒliŋŋ/ *n.* 刚学飞的幼鸟；无经验的人
⑰vaudeville /'vəudəvil/ *n.* 歌舞杂耍
⑱fringe /frindʒ/ *adj.* 边缘的，额外的
⑲water down 掺水，兑水 ；冲淡；打折扣
⑳dilution /dai'ljuːʃən/ *n.* 稀释，稀释法，冲淡物
㉑lush /lʌʃ/ *adj.* 茂盛的；青葱的；性感的
㉒craze /kreiz/ *n.* 狂热
㉓surly /'səːli/ 傲慢的；粗暴的
㉔volley /'vɔli/ *n.* （常与 of 连用）（质问等的）齐发，连发，连珠炮
㉕Beatlemania /biːtlmeinjə/ *n.* 披头士狂

㉖touch off： 引爆；放炮；引起；触发
㉗antidote /ˈætidəut/ n. 解毒剂，矫正方法
㉘Beatles /ˈbiːtlz/ n. 披头士（甲壳虫）乐队
㉙dreariness /ˈdriərinis/ n. 沉寂，可怕，凄凉
㉚stance /stæns/ n. 姿态
㉛"Beatle cuts" "甲壳虫款式"
㉜headline /ˈhedlain/ vt. 以明星身份推出或捧为明星
㉝grueling /ˈgruəliŋ/ adj. 筋疲力尽的
㉞dodge /ˈdɔdʒ/ vt., vi. （常与about, behind, round 连用）闪避；躲闪
㉟swoon /swuːn/ vi. 着迷；神魂颠倒
㊱sour square 苦恼忧郁、拘谨古板的人
㊲nutty /ˈnʌti/ 美味的；内容充实的
㊳fluke /fluːk/ n. 侥幸
㊴lilting lament 以明快的节奏演唱悲哀的歌
 lilt /lilt/ vt., vi. 以明快的节奏演唱
 lament /ləˈment/ n. 悲伤，哀悼，挽诗，悼词
㊵asexual and homely 无性的和不好看的
 asexual /ˌeiˈsekʃuəl/ adj. 无性的，非性的
㊶retrospect /ˈretrəspekt/ n. 回顾
㊷limelight /ˈlaimlait/ n. 引人注目的中心

Section 5　Women's History

28.　The Creation of Patriarchy
Gerda Lerner

Patriarchy[1] is a historic creation formed by men and women in a process which took nearly 2500 years to its completion. In its earliest form patriarchy appeared as the archaic state. The basic unit of its organization was the patriarchal family, which both expressed and constantly generated its rules and values. We have seen how integrally definitions of gender affected the formation of the state. Let us briefly review the way in which gender became created, defined, and established. The roles and behavior deemed appropriate to the sexes were expressed in values, customs, laws, and social roles. They also, and very importantly, were expressed in leading metaphors, which became part of the cultural construct and explanatory system. The sexuality of women, consisting of their sexual and their reproductive capacities and services, was commodified even prior to the creation of Western civilization. The development of agriculture in the Neolithic period fostered the inter-tribal "exchange of women," not only as a means of avoiding incessant[2] warfare by the cementing[3] of marriage alliances but also because societies with more women could produce more children. In contrast to the economic needs of hunting/gathering societies, agriculturists could use the labor of children to increase production and accumulate surpluses. Men-as-a-group had rights in women which women-as-a-group did not have in men. Women themselves became a resource, acquired by men much as the land was acquired by men. Women were exchanged or bought in marriages for the benefit of their families; later, they were conquered or bought in slavery, where their sexual services were part of their labor and where their children were the property of their masters. In every known society it was women of conquered tribes who were first enslaved, whereas men were killed. It was only after men had learned how to enslave the women of groups who could be defined as strangers, that they learned how to enslave men of those groups and, later, subordinates from within their own societies.

Thus, the enslavement of women, combining both racism and sexism, preceded the formation of classes and class oppression. Class differences were, at their very beginnings, expressed and constituted in terms of patriarchal relations. Class is not a separate construct from gender; rather, class is expressed in generic terms.

By the second millennium B. C. in Mesopotamian[4] societies, the daughters of the poor were sold into marriage or prostitution in order to advance the economic interests of their families. The daughters of men of property could command a bride price, paid by the family of the groom to the family of the bride, which frequently enabled the bride's family to secure more financially advantageous marriages for their sons, thus improving the family's economic position. If a husband or father could not pay his debt, his wife and children could be used as pawns,[5] becoming debt slaves to the creditor. These conditions were so firmly established by 1750 B. C. that Hammurabic[6] law made a decisive improvement in the lot of debt pawns by limiting their terms of service to three years, where earlier it had been for life.

The product of this commodification of women-bride price, sale price, and children-was appropriated by men. It may very well represent the first accumulation of private property. The enslavement of women of conquered tribes became not only a status symbol for nobles and warriors, but it actually enabled the conquerors to acquire tangible wealth through selling or trading the product of the slaves' labor and their reproductive product, slave children.

Claude Levi-Strauss, to whom we owe the concept of "the exchange of women," speaks of the reification[7] of women, which occurred as its consequence. But it is not women who are reified and commodified, it is women's sexuality and reproductive capacity which is so treated. The distinction is important. Women never became "things," nor were they so perceived. Women, no matter how exploited and abused, retained their power to act and to choose to the same, often very limited extent, as men of their group. But women always and to this day lived in a relatively greater state of unfreedom than did men. Since their sexuality, an aspect of their body, was controlled by others, women were not only actually disadvantaged but psychologically restrained in a very special way. For women, as for men of subordinate and oppressed groups, history consisted of their struggle for emancipation and freedom from necessity. But women struggled against different forms of oppression and dominance than did men, and their struggle, up to this time, has lagged behind that of men.

The first gender-defined social role for women was to be those who were exchanged in marriage transactions. The obverse[8] gender role for men was to be those who did the exchanging or who defined the terms of the exchanges.

Another gender-defined role for women was that of the "stand-in" wife, which became established and institutionalized for women of elite groups. This role gave such women considerable power and privileges, but it depended on their attachment to elite men and was based, minimally, on their satisfactory performance in rendering these men sexual and reproductive services. If a woman failed to meet these demands, she was quickly replaced and thereby lost all her privileges and standing.

The gender-defined role of warrior led men to acquire power over men and women of conquered tribes. Such war-induced[9] conquest usually occurred over people already differentiated from the victors by race, ethnicity, or simple tribal difference. In its ultimate origin, "difference" as a distinguishing mark between the conquered and the conquerors was based on the first clearly observable difference, that between the sexes. Men had learned how to assert and exercise power over people slightly different from themselves in the primary exchange of women. In so doing, men acquired the knowledge necessary to elevate[10] "difference" of whatever kind into a criterion for dominance.

From its inception[11] in slavery, class dominance took different forms for enslaved men and women: men were primarily exploited as workers; women were always exploited as workers, as providers of sexual services, and as reproducers. The historical record of every slave society offers evidence for this generalization. The sexual exploitation of lower-class women by upper-class men can be shown in antiquity, under feudalism, in the bourgeois households of nineteenth and twentieth-century Europe, in the complex sex/race relations between women of the colonized countries and their male colonizers-it is ubiquitous and pervasive.[12] For women, sexual exploitation is the very mark of class exploitation.

At any given moment in history, each "class" is constituted of two distinct classes—men and women.

The class position of women became consolidated and actualized through their sexual relationships. It always was expressed within degrees of unfreedom on a spectrum ranging from the slave woman, whose sexual and reproductive capacity was commodified as she herself was; to the slave-concubine,[13] whose sexual performance might elevate her own status or that of her children; then to the "free" wife, whose sexual and reproductive services to one man of the upper classes entitled her to property and legal rights. While each of these groups had vastly different obligations and privileges in regard to property, law, and economic resources, they shared the unfreedom of being sexually and reproductively controlled by men. We can best express the complexity of women's various levels of dependency and freedom by comparing each woman with her brother and considering how the sister's and brother's lives and opportunities would differ.

Class for men was and is based on their relationship to the means of production: those who owned the means of production could dominate those who did not. The owners of the means of production also acquired the commodity of female sexual services, both from women of their own class and from women of the subordinate classes. In Ancient Mesopotamia, in classical antiquity, and in slave societies, dominant males also acquired, as property, the product of the reproductive capacity of subordinate women—children, to be worked, traded, married off, or sold as slaves, as the case might be. For women, class is mediated[14] through their sexual ties to a man. It is through the man that women have access to or are denied access to the means of production and to resources. It is through their sexual behavior that they gain access to class. "Respectable women" gain access to class through their fathers and husbands, but breaking the sexual rules can at once declass them. The gender definition of sexual "deviance"[15] marks a woman as "not respectable," which in fact consigns[16] her to the lowest class status possible. Women who withhold heterosexual services (such as single women, nuns, lesbians[17]) are connected to the dominant man in their family of origin and through him gain access to resources. Or, alternatively, they are declassed. In some historical periods, convents and other enclaves[18] for single women created some sheltered space, in which such women could function and retain their respectability. But the vast majority of single women are, by definition, marginal[19] and dependent on the protection of male kin. This is true throughout historical time up to the middle of the twentieth century in the Western world and still is true in most of the underdeveloped countries today. The group of independent, self-supporting women which exists in every society is small and usually highly vulnerable to economic disaster.

Economic oppression and exploitation are based as much on the commodification of female sexuality and the appropriation by men of women's labor power and her reproductive power as on the direct economic acquisition of resources and persons.

The archaic state in the Ancient Near East emerged in the second millennium B. C. from the twin roots of men's sexual dominance over women and the exploitation by some men of others. From its inception, the archaic state was organized in such a way that the dependence of male family heads on the king or the state bureaucracy was compensated for by their dominance over their families. Male family heads allocated[20] the resources of society to their families the way the state allocated the resources of society to them. The control of male family heads over their female kin and minor sons was as important to the existence of the state as was the control of the king over his soldiers. This is reflected in the various compilations of Mesopotamian laws, especially in the large number of laws dealing with the regulation of female sexuality.

From the second millennium B. C. forward control over the sexual behavior of citizens has been a major means of social control in every state society. Conversely, class hierarchy is constantly reconstituted in the family through sexual dominance. Regardless of the political or economic system, the kind of personality which can function in a. hierarchical system is created and nurtured within the patriarchal family. The patriarchal family has been amazingly resilient and varied in different times and places. Oriental patriarchy encompassed polygamy[21] and female enclosure in harems. Patriarchy in classical antiquity and in its European development was based upon monogamy, but in all its forms a double sexual standard, which disadvantages women, was part of the system. In modern industrial states, such as in the United States, property relations within the family develop along more egalitarian[22] lines than those in which the father holds absolute power, yet the economic and sexual power relations within the family do not necessarily change. In some cases, sexual relations are more egalitarian, while economic relations remain patriarchal; in other cases the pattern is reversed. In all cases, however, such changes within the family do not alter the basic male dominance in the public realm, in institutions and in government.

The family not merely mirrors the order in the state and educates its children to follow it, it also creates and constantly reinforces that order.

It should be noted that when we speak of relative improvements in the status of women in a given society, this frequently means only that we are seeing improvements in the degree in which their situation affords them opportunities to exert some leverage[23] within the system of patriarchy.

Where women have relatively more economic power, they are able to have somewhat more control over their lives than in societies where they have no economic power. Similarly, the existence of women's groups, associations, or economic networks serves to increase the ability of women to counteract the dictates of their particular patriarchal system. Some anthropologists and historians have called this relative improvement women's "freedom." Such a designation is illusory and unwarranted. Reforms and legal changes, while ameliorating[24] the condition of women and an essential part of the process of emancipating them, will not basically change patriarchy. Such reforms need to be integrated within a vast cultural revolution in order to transform patriarchy and thus abolish it.

The system of patriarchy can function only with the cooperation of women. This cooperation is secured by a variety of means: gender indoctrination; educational deprivation; the denial to women of knowledge of their history; the dividing of women, one from the other, by defining "respectability" and "deviance" according to women's sexual activities; by restraints and outright: coercion[25]; by discrimination in access to economic resources and political power; and by awarding class privileges to conforming women.

For nearly four thousand years women have shaped their lives and acted under the umbrella of patriarchy, specifically a form of patriarchy best described as paternalistic dominance. The term describes the relationship of a dominant group, considered superior, to a subordinate group, considered inferior, in which the dominance is mitigated by mutual obligations and reciprocal[26] rights. The dominated exchange submission for protection, unpaid labor for maintenance. In the patriarchal family, responsibilities and obligations are not equally distributed among those to be protected. the male children's subordination to the father's dominance is temporary; it lasts until they themselves become heads of households. The subordination of female children and of wives is lifelong. Daughters can escape it only if they place themselves as wives under the dominance/protection of another man. The basis of paternalism is an unwritten contract for exchange: economic support and protection given by the male for subordination in all matters; sexual service, and unpaid domestic service given by the female. Yet the relationship frequently continues in fact and in law, even when the male partner has defaulted on his obligation.

It was a rational choice for women, under conditions of public powerlessness and economic dependency, to choose strong protectors for themselves and their children. Women always shared the class privileges of men of their class as long as they were under "the protection" of a man. For women, other than those of the lower classes, the "reciprocal agreement" went like this: in exchange for your sexual, economic, political, and intellectual subordination to men you may share the power of men of your class to exploit men and women of the lower class. In class society it is difficult for people "who themselves have some power, however limited and circumscribed"[27] to see themselves also as deprived and subordinated. Class and racial privileges serve to undercut the ability of women to see themselves as part of a coherent group, which, in fact, they are not, since women uniquely of all oppressed groups occur in all strata[28] of the society. The formation of a group consciousness of women must proceed along different lines. That is the reason why theoretical formulations, which have been appropriate to other oppressed groups, are so inadequate in explaining and conceptualizing the subordination of women.

【 Notes 】

This selection is from Gerda Lerner, *The Creation of Patriarchy*, New York: Oxford University Press, 1986, pp. 212—218.

Gerda Lerner (1920—) is a major feminist scholar and a pioneer in women's history. Born in Vienna, Austria, in the 1930's she fled with her family and eventually reached the United States and became an American citizen. During the 1940's she became a radical and joined the Communist Party but soon became critical of its approach to the woman question. Only in 1963 did she begin graduate studies in history. The Creation of Patriarchy, from which this excerpt is taken, is one of her major theoretical works, another being The Creation of Feminist Consciousness. In these two works she overturns Engels' theories about women's subordination and argues instead that the commodification of women by men predates even the formation of the concept of private property.

【 New Words 】

①patriarchy /ˈpeitriɑːki/ *n.* 家长统治，父权制
②incessant /inˈsesnt/ *adj.* 不断的，不停的
③cementing /siˈmentiŋ/ *n.* 胶接，黏合
④Mesopotamian /ˌmesəpəˈteimiən/ *adj.* 美索不达米亚的
⑤pawn /pɔːn/ *n.* 典当，抵押物；人质；（象棋）兵，卒；爪牙，被人利用的人
⑥Hammurabic /ˌhɑːmuˈrɑːbik/ law 汉穆拉比法典。巴比伦王国国王汉穆拉比在位期间（1790 BC—1750 BC），武力统一美索不达米亚地区，实行中央集权统治，所颁布的法典。
⑦reification /ˌriːifiˈkeiʃən/ *n.* 具体化；reify *vt.* 使具体化
⑧obverse /ˈɔbvəːs/ *adj.* 正面的
⑨induce /inˈdjuːs/ *vt.* 劝诱，促使，导致，引起，感应
⑩elevate /ˈeliveit/ *vt.* 举起；提拔；振奋；提升……的职位
⑪inception /inˈsepʃən/ *n.* 开端；开始
⑫ubiquitous /juːˈbikwitəs/ *adj.* 到处存在的，（同时）普遍存在的
　pervasive /pəːˈveisiv/ *adj.* 普遍深入的
⑬concubine /ˈkɔŋkjubai/ *n.* 妾，情妇，姘妇
⑭mediate /ˈmidieit, ˈmidiˌet/ *v.* 仲裁，调停，作为引起……的媒介，居中调停
⑮deviance /ˈdiviəns/ *n.* 偏常，不正常，异常，离经叛道；偏常性，变异性

⑯consign /kən'sain/ vt. （常与 to 连用）寄售,托卖；交付,托管
⑰lesbian /'lezbiən/ n 女性同性恋者
⑱convent /'kɔnvənt/ n. 女修道会，女修道院
　　enclave /'enkleiv/ n. 被包围中的领土，包体，包含物；残遗群落；小的孤立点
⑲marginal /'mɑːdʒinəl/ adj. 记在页边的；边缘的，边际的
⑳allocate /'æləkeit/ vt. 分派，分配
㉑polygamy /pɔ'ligəmi/ n. 一夫多妻，一妻多夫
　　harem /'hɛərem/ n. （伊斯兰教教徒之）闺房，闺房里的妻妾群
㉒egalitarian /iˌgæli'tɛəriən/ adj. 平等主义的
㉓leverage /'liːvəridʒ/ n. 杠杆作用
㉔ameliorate /ə'miːliəreit/ v. 改善，改进
㉕coercion /kəu'əːʃən/ n. 强迫，威压，高压政治
㉖reciprocal /ri'siprəkəl/ adj. 互惠的，相应的；倒数的，彼此相反的
㉗circumscribe /'səːkəmskraib/ vt. 在……周围画线，限制
㉘strata /'streitə/ n. stratum 的复数

Key to Exercises

1. The Meanings of the Term History

I.
(1) Through intermediary sources.
(2) Historical facts become known through such sources as: accounts from living witnesses; narrative records such as histories, memoirs, letters and literature; legal and financial records of courts, legislatures, religious institution and businesses; the unwritten information from physical remains of past civilizations such as architecture, art and crafts, burial grounds, cultivated land.
Additional sources might include those objects found in archeological investigations. Can you add more?
(3) Fact-finding is the foundation of historical research combined with: interpretation in every aspect. A subject must be chosen and a model or hypothesis formulated to guide the research project. The research proceeds with: a. selection, b. arrangement, c. explanation. The result will be the researcher's interpretation of the historical event.

III.
(1) is derived from　(2) connections　(3) memoirs　(4) testimony　(5) endeavored

IV.
(1) references　(2) committed　(3) address　(4) underwent　(5) assess

V.
(1) 写英格兰的历史不需要用其他的文字记载,因为各代皇帝和政治家都被称为历史的创造者。据说,有时历史学家只记载他们所创造的历史。
(2) 历史就其广义来说是指所发生的所有事情。它不仅包含人类生活的一切现象,而且也包括自然界的现象。
(3) 考证可能有偏见或错误,可能是支离破碎的,由于时间久远,文化和语言的变化使得这些考证几乎都模糊不清了。

2. An Overview of the Debates about Historical Writing

I.
(1) A. In the nineteenth century
B. World history and local history
C. Historical demography, labor history, urban history, rural history and others.
(2) "Rankean history," named after German historian, Leopold von Ranke. This history also called common sense view of history.
(3) A. False   B. 2
(4) C.

III.
(1) are opting for (2) transgression (3) converge (4) were emanating from
(5) consensus of opinion   (6) allocated to

IV.
(1) bidding   (2) on the grounds   (3) rather than   (4) related
(5) concentrates   (6) in terms of   (7) taking a brief account of
(8) independent   (9) competing

V.
(1) 例如,社会史,像某些新独立的国家一样,只是部分地独立于经济史而成为历史人口统计学、劳动史、城市史、农村史等。
(2) 费尔南·布罗代尔的《地中海史》是当代最著名的一部历史著作,他认为历史事件只不过是历史海洋无数波涛上的泡沫,不受青睐。
(3) 因此,很难对新史学下一个比较清楚的定义,想要将新史学描述成结构史那样就更不容易了。
(4) 过去曾经一直被认为一成不变的东西现在却被看作随着时空的流逝而容易千变万化的所谓文化结构。

3. History's Nature

I.
(1) What history is? What it is about? How it proceeds? What it is for?
(2) A. True   B. False   C. True
(3) D.

III.
(1) incidental   (2) fastened...on   (3) rid   (4) At best   (5) reflected on

  (6) entitles (7) finality (8) subject-matter

IV.

(1) With respect to/As to (2) with an eye (3) in particular (4) find out
(5) went through (6) put...together (7) gets into (8) the point

4. Culture and Society

I.

(1) Science, technology and politics.
(2) A. False.
  B. True.
  C. True.
  D. True.
(3) The French Revolution.
(4) B.
(5) The body of political and economic philosophy.

III.

(1) assiduity (2) middling (3) relations (4) stands for; stands for (5) Body
(6) with reference to (7) phase (8) bears witness

IV.

(1) in part (2) built on (3) build up (4) at least
(5) By means of (6) acknowledgement (7) substantially (8) mitigated
(9) rallied (10) characteristics (11) attributes (12) character

5. The Historian and His Day

I.

(1) False. (2) True. (3) True. (4) False.

III.

(1) called...off (2) obscured (3) at stake (4) have permeated
(5) go off half-cocked

IV.

(1) for better and worse (2) for a good while (3) with respect to (4) in controversy
(5) ruled out

V.

(1) There's no single panacea for the country's economic ills.

251

(2) Common preconceptions about life in this district are increasingly being challenged.//
(3) No trade union movement worth its salt could allow that to happen.
(4) Our discussions got bogged down in irrelevant detail.
(5) His salary vis-à-vis the national average is extremely high.

6. Introduction to World History

I.

(1) Herodotus, Christian and Buddhist travelers in Eurasia, Medieval Christianity, Ibn Khaldun in North Africa, Rashid al-din Fadl Allah of Persia, Max Weber, Oswald Spengler, Pitirim Sorokin, Arnold Toynbee, post world War II area studies programs and institutes.

(2) Stavrianos' theme: Stage theory of human development-hunting and gathering, agricultural, urban and industrial.
McNeill's theme: Increasing human interaction in world history-the expanding world of technological diffusion, migration, and cultural contact.

(3) A and C are the correct answers.
(4) True.
(5) C.
(6) True.

III.

(1) called on   (2) encompass   (3) betrayed   (4) posit
(5) elicited   (6) accounted for

IV.

(1) made ... contributions to   (2) hypothesis   (3) more than the sum of
(4) migration   (5) owns ... to   (6) at the expense of
(7) venture   (8) chronological   (9) draws on

V.

(1) 然后,沿着欧亚发达地区通商和朝圣的路线,基督教和伊斯兰教的商人以及思想家相对来说推进了,甚至可以说设想出了人类对世界的看法。

(2) 伊斯兰教庞大的宗教团体把神学的普遍特征和半球间的合作结合起来,然而,正是伊斯兰教处于包围之中(13到14世纪的蒙古和西班牙)时,世界史出现了。

(3) 哈德格森,他的支持者以及非洲、亚洲的历史学家们对历史时期所作的分期常常与以欧洲为中心的世界史相冲突。以欧洲为中心的世界史从文艺复兴时期到现代的世界画出了一条线,甚至提出世界处在静止不动的传统圈中,只有西方在不断地变化。

7. A Definition of Civilization

I.

(1) The achievement of most all of these: writing, cities, arts and sciences, formal political organization, social classes, taxation.

(2) 1) Minoa was on an island-Crete.
  2) It had the nature of a sea civilization.

(3) False.

(4) B.

(5) Equality.

III.

(1) on the move (2) for the moment (3) lived from hand to mouth (4) in place of
(5) in return (6) in the case of (7) serves as (8) derived from

IV.

(1) 这座金字塔如此巨大,甚至用它的石灰石砖块环绕着法国边界可以筑一道高3米 (10英尺),厚度为23厘米(9英寸)的墙。

(2) 满足生活必需品所余下的东西叫做过剩物。正是这些过剩物使得专门化和劳动分工成为可能。

(3) 正是这些进步终于使得现代人能够这样驾驭自然,并且通过科学和工业获得如此不可思议的生产力,使得多数人现在和少数人一起从中获益。

8. A Comparative Analysis of France, Russia, and China

I.

(1) state... class

(2) No recent colonial domination and all three ended in the consolidation of revolutionary state power.

(3) A, B, and C.

(4) False.

III.

(1) culminated in (2) had attended to (3) maxim (4) conjuncture
(5) played down

IV.

(1) justify (2) call for (3) gave rise to (4) premise
(5) lines (6) segregated (7) to take for granted

253

9. How the Greek World Grew

I.

(1) Knossos in Crete. Carbon 4 dating. End of 7th century—late 6000 BC.
(2) True.
(3) False.
(4) 5th and 4th centuries BC.
(5) 1) False, 2) True.
(6) A. About 7000 BC;
B. Early Bronze Age;
C. First Olympic Games;
D. Classical Greek civilization

III.

(1) liabilities   (2) elevation   (3) bulk   (4) scanty   (5) civic
(6) from stem to stem

IV.

(1) judge...from...   (2) attested to   (3) went off   (4) settled...into
(5) attached to

10. Chinese Economic History in Comparative Perspective

I.

(1) C.
(2) False.
(3) Sung agricultural technology and Social, political, and economic institutions perfected in the Sung period.
(4) 1) True, 2) False, 3) True, 4) True, 5) False.

III.

(1) elites   (2) unprecedented   (3) phased   (4) apart from
(5) swept over   (6) was awarded   (7) consequences

IV.

(1) The so-called division between the pure scientist and the applied scientist is more apparent than real.
(2) All things are interrelated and interact on each other and this event was almost simultaneous with that one.
(3) Three human beings have each lived by grace of another person's heart for seven years.

(4) Young students are advised to read edifying books to improve their mind.

(5) The new underground railway will facilitate the journey to all parts of the city.

11. Chinese Science Explorations of an Ancient Tradition

I.
(1) False.
(2) Change "making human relations understandable" to "making nature understandable."
(3) Medicine, alchemy, astrology, geomancy and physical studies.
(4) True.
(5) True.
(6) B.

III.
(1) embraces   (2) bore upon   (3) clout   (4) meditation   (5) telescoped

IV.
(1) have compounded   (2) extrinsic   (3) counterpart   (4) obscure
(5) arbitrary   (6) in turn   (7) shrugging off   (8) corresponded to

12. Ideology and Imperial Japan

I.
(1) False.
(2) B.
(3) D.
(4) False. In fact Gluck's idea is that Marxism influenced the later Japanese and Western writers to insist that ideology is "tied to the social groups that produce and are produced by them." (Paragraph 2, Section III.)

III.
(1) Articulate   (2) deplorable   (3) culminated in   (4) manifested
(5) ascendancy   (6) contour   (7) acute

IV.
(1) inculcate; by trial and error   (2) be imbued   (3) backdrop
(4) constellation   (5) Privation   (6) visceral
(7) equate   (8) blight   (9) conferred
(10) contended   (11) impelled   (12) deplore

13. On Some Aspects of the Historiography of Colonial India

I.
  (1) B.
  (2) A. Guha says it was not elitist caused but the result of the People themselves.
  (3) B.
  (4) D.
  (5) B.
  (6) True.

III.
  (1) endowed (2) protagonists (3) to enunciate (4) modicum (5) maze

IV.
  (1) has assimilated (2) to integrate (3) equate (4) intermediate
  (5) transactions (6) in the form of (7) geared to (8) relied on
  (9) derived from

14. Muhammad and the Appearance of Islam

I.
  (1) A, B, D, and E are all true.
  (2) True.
  (3) B.
  (4) B.
  (5) False, he is believed by Muslims to be the common ancestor of the Jews, Christians and Muslims.

III.
  (1) to mock (2) erased (3) vocation (4) breach (5) calamity

IV.
  (1) disputed (2) reveres (3) have levied (4) perverted (5) transmute
  (6) idol (7) accused of (8) extent (9) derives from

V.
  (1) A father has the custody of his children when they are young.
  (2) He commanded himself sufficiently to stammer out his regrets.
  (3) Her true nature was a revelation to me.
  (4) She avenged her mother's death upon the murderer.

(5) Dikes protected the lowland from incursions of the sea.

15. Africa after Independence

I.

(1) B.

(2) False. The sentence should read——"(including the Christian/Muslim god)".

(3) A, C, and D are weaknesses of the post-colonial African state.

(4) Matching:

Amin—c; Kenyatta—a; Nyerere—a; Mobuto—d; Nkrumah—a;

National Guard Council of Ghana—b.

III.

(1) call for   (2) interim   (3) having to do   (4) permeated   (5) attaches

(6) lurking   (7) sets out   (8) loath   (9) cut   (10) in the long run

IV.

(1) 但是,工业技术的手段只不过给文化的现实蒙上了一副面罩,再说,非洲的领导们也并不想将西方所提供的一切东西都照搬过来。

(2) 在诸如婚姻风俗、家庭事务、对待孩子以及教育孩子对待长辈的方式中,即使外观上看起来相当现代化,非洲的文化内涵依旧不变,这就是例证。

(3) 很少有人把国家理解成是每一个人都应该无限忠实于它的机构。

(4) 非洲人在两次世界大战中都浴血奋战,但是,公众几乎没有注意到军事被控制在刚刚取得独立的政府手中。

(5) 反之,这些政治状况在很大程度上又依赖于潜在的文化和殖民时期的历史。

16. From Balance of Power to World Politics

I.

(1) a) It marked a major shift from the age when Europe dominated the world to an age of world politics. b) After World War I was over the world was divided into two great power blocks in ideological struggle. These two blocks were guided by the ideologies of democracy and Bolshevism (Communism).

(2) Both rejected secret diplomacy, annexation, trade discrimination, the balance of power, and the control of the past over the present among states. They were both prophets of new ideas about the international order.

(3) True. He thinks the real turning point was WW I and immediately after that war. Lenin wanted universal revolution and rejected the system of self-balancing states. Wilson rejected the idea of the balance of power among the states, but the two men had very dif-

ferent aims in mind.

(4) B.

(5) C,D.

III.

(1) repudiated (2) modalities (3) cut loose (4) disrupted (5) concert
(6) precludes

IV.

(1) bids (2) monopoly (3) irrespective (4) belligerent (5) attributed
(6) On the contrary (7) sense (8) confronted

17. A Geographical Note

I.

(1) False.

(2) C.

(3) D.

(4) C and E.

(5) A.

(6) Four of the following: forests, oil, coal, gold, platinum.

(7) Finland.

III.

(1) rigid (2) mitigate (3) interlude (4) impact (5) in particular
(6) serves (7) may well (8) takes in (9) interminable

18. George Washington and the Enlightenment

I.

(1) a) His resignation as commander in chief.

　　b) His sponsoring the new constitution in 1787.

　　c) His farewell address as President of the United States.

(2) By resigning he actually gained more power.

(3) False—he accepted no pay.

(4) False—he argued for a strong central government.

(5) True.

(6) Washington emphasized to the soldiers that the call for them to mutiny was actually a real opportunity for each of them to show their public virtue—by refusing to mutiny and standing loyal to the army.

III.
    (1) elicited   (2) ardent   (3) tact   (4) disdained; irritable   (5) disposed
    (6) toil   (7) live up to   (8) clinging to

IV.
    (1) eludes   (2) baffled   (3) calls for   (4) grievances   (5) playing on
    (6) turned his back

19. Silent Spring

I.
    (1) B.
    (2) C.
    (3) 1) False 2) True
    (4) B.
    (5) Ultra-violet sunlight, cosmic rays, human disease spread by travelers.

III.
    (1) abode   (2) shattered   (3) tamper with   (4) futile   (5) brewed
    (6) vernacular

IV.
    (1) impetuous   (2) heredity   (3) advent   (4) mesmerized   (5) quarantined
    (6) keep... down (7) damped down

20. Chicago Manual of Style

I.

(1) The two kinds of sources are primary sources and secondary sources.

(2) The author-date system has two parts. The first part: at the point in the text where the source is being used, within parentheses, the author's last name is followed by the date of publication. The second part: a reference list at the end of the article or book contains a full bibliographic entry on this source.

    Part 1 example: (Collingwood, 1946)

    Part 2 example: Collingwood, R. G. The Idea of History. London: Oxford University Press, 1946.

(3) Endnotes are at the close of the chapter, article or book. They have the advantage over footnotes because the limited space at the bottom of the page limits the size of footnotes.

    With endnotes there is more space and more explanation can be included if necessary.

(4) This book uses endnotes following each of the reading selections.

(5) The bibliography is a list of books, documents and other sources used by the author in writing the work and preparing the notes and is usually at the end before the index. It is important to have a bibliography in a work so the readers can quickly see the sources that the author has used and also other works that the author thinks are related to the subject.

II.
  (1) relies on (2) identified (3) accommodate (4) have ruled out (5) particulars

III.
  (1) varied (2) In addition to (3) correspond (4) known as (5) concern

IV.
  (1) 第一手资料
  (2) 上标数字
  (3) 版权法
  (4) 学术论著
  (5) 社会科学和人文学科
  (6) 自然科学
  (7) 然而,当学者们跨越了自己学科的领域,而出版者为尚未出版的著作表现出了从未有过的关切而催促大家要意识到在学术上滥用引证的情况时,学科间引证规则原有的区别变得越来越模糊了。
  (8) 虽然有的著作在注释中用了不少引文,然而,除了注释以外,参考书目对于读者来说,是最有用的东西,对作者和出版人来说,也是最节省精力的办法。因为读者不仅很容易就能找到引文的出处,而且对作者所依靠和所挑选的与主题最密切相关的参考书目也一目了然。

Glossary

A

abandonment	/əˈbændənmənt/	n.	放弃	(U.7)
abdication	/ˌæbdiˈkeiʃən/	n.	弃权，让位，辞职	(U.11)
aberration	/ˌæbəˈreiʃən/	n.	脱离常轨；失常	(U.5)
abject	/ˈæbdʒekt/	adj.	卑鄙的；下贱的；不幸的；可怜的	(U.5)
abnegation	/ˌæbniˈgeiʃən/	n.	放弃；克制	(U.6)
abode	/əˈbəud/	n.	住所，住处	(U.12)
Abraham	/ˈeibrəhæm/	n.	(圣经)亚伯拉罕(相传为希伯来人的始祖)	(U.7)
abridgment	/əˈbridʒmənt/	n.	删节；缩短；节本；摘要；削减	(U.4)
abstraction	/æbˈstrækʃən/	n.	抽出；取出；分离出	(U.4)
accretion	/æˈkriːʃən/	n.	自然增加；增加之物；增值	(U.7)
acupuncture	/ˈækjupʌŋktʃə/	n.	针刺疗法	(U.4)
acute	/əˈkjuːt/	adj.	敏锐的；灵敏的	(U.5)
adept	/ˈædəpt/	n.	内行，熟手，名家	(U.4)
adjacent	/əˈdʒeisənt/	adj.	相邻的，邻近的	(U.10)
adjunct	/ˈædʒʌŋkt/	n.	附属物，附件，配件，添加剂	(U.13)
advent	/ˈædvənt/	n.	出现，到来	(U.2)
aesthete	/ˈiːsθiːt/	n.	审美家	(U.1)
aesthetics	/iːsˈθetiks/	n.	美学	(U.1)
afar	/əˈfɑː/	adv.	由远方；在远处；到远方	(U.4)
aggregation	/ægriˈgeiʃən/	n.	聚集；集合；总计；集合体	(U.6)
agitator	/ˈædʒiteitə/	n.	鼓动者；煽动者；搅拌器	(U.11)
agrarian	/əˈgreəriən/	adj.	土地的，农民的，农业的	(U.2)
aknowledgement	/əkˈnɔlidʒmənt/	n.	承认，致谢，感谢	(U.1)
alchemy	/ˈælkimi/	n.	炼金术，魔力	(U.4)
Allah	/ˈælə/	n.	(伊斯兰教的)阿拉，真主	(U.7)
allocate	/ˈæləukeit/	vt.	分配；把……纳入，把……划归	(U.1)
alloy	/ˈælɔi/	vt.	使成合金，减低成色	(U.3)
altruism	/ˈæltruizəm/	n.	利他主义	(U.6)
amalgam	/əˈmælgəm/	n.	混合物；汞合金	(U.5)
ameliorating	/əmiːliəˈreiʃən/	n.	改善，改进	(S.5)
anecdote	/ˈænikdəut/	n.	轶事，逸话，奇闻；(pl.) 秘史	(U.7)
anew	/əˈnjuː/	adv.	再，重新	(U.5)
Annapolis	/əˈnæpəlis/	n.	安纳波利斯(美国马里兰州首府)	(U.11)
annex	/æˈneks/	vt.	(常与to连用)附加；并吞	(U.3)

261

annexation	/ˌænek'seiʃən/	n.	(常与by或to连用)附加；合并，吞并	(U.9)
annotated	/'ænəuteitid/	adj.	有评注的，有注解的	(U.13)
anoint	/ə'nɔint/	v.	(with sth)涂油或膏于某人	(U.1)
anomalous	/ə'nɔmələs/	adj.	不规则的；异常的；反常的	(U.4)
antagonistic	/æntæg'nistik/	adj.	对抗性的；敌对的	(U.6)
antiabsolutist	/'ænti'æbsəlu:tist/	n.	专制主义者，专制政治论者	(U.2)
antidote	/'æntidəut/	n.	解毒剂，矫正方法	(S.4)
apace	/ə'peis/	adv.	快速地，急速地	(U.4)
apostle	/ə'pɔsl/	n.	(基督的)使徒；(早期的)基督教传教者	(U.7)
appreciably	/'æpri:ʃəb(ə)li/	adv.	略微，有一点；相当地(可观地)	(U.10)
arbiter	/'ɑ:bitə(r)/	n.	部落争端的仲裁人	(U.7)
arbitrary	/'ɑ:bitrəri/	adj.	任意的，武断的，独裁的，专断的	(U.4)
archaic	/ɑ'keiik/	adj.	古代的；过时的	(U.6)
ardent	/'ɑ:dənt/	adj.	热心的；热情的	(U.11)
arena	/ə'ri:nə/	n.	竞技场；活动场所；活动范围	(U.2)
Argentina	/ɑ:dʒən'ti:nə/	n.	阿根廷(南美洲南部国家)	(S.2)
arid	/'ærid/	adj.	干旱的；贫瘠的，荒芜的；枯燥无味的	(U.10)
aristocratic	/ˌəristə'krætik/	adj.	贵族的，贵族政治的	(S.1)
Aristotle	/æ'ristɔtl/	n.	亚里士多德	(U.4)
array	/ə'rei/	v.	部署(尤指兵力等)	
		n.	展示；显示；一系列	(U.1)
arsenic	/'ɑ:sənik/	n.	[化]砷，砒霜	(U.3)
articulate	/ɑ:'tikjuleit/	vt.vi	清楚明白地说	(U.1)
artisan	/'ɑ:tizn/	n.	(fml)技工，工匠	(U.1)
ascendancy	/ə'sendənsi/	n.	优势；权势；主权；支配地位	(U.5)
ascribe	/əs'kraib/	vt.	(常与to连用)归于，归因于	(U.11)
asexual	/æ'seksjuəl/	adj.	无性的，无性生殖的	(S.4)
aspiration	/ˌæspə'reiʃən/	n.	热望，渴望	(U.11)
assassinate	/'əsæsineit/	vt.	暗杀，行刺	(S.3)
assault	/ə'sɔ:lt/	vt.	突袭，突击	(U.1)
assault	/ə'sɔ:lt/	n.	攻击，袭击	
		v.	袭击	(U.12)
assiduity	/ˌæsi'dju:iti/	n.	(fml)专心致志，勤勉	(U.1)
assimilate	/ə'simileit/	vt.	吸收，消化；使同化	(U.6)
astrology	/ə'strɔlədʒi/	n.	占星术，占星学	(U.4)
Athenian	/ə'θinjən/	adj.	雅典的；雅典人的；雅典文化的	
		n.	雅典人	(U.3)
attest	/ə'test/	vt,vi.	证明；表明	(U.3)
attribute	/ə'tribju:t/	n.	属性，特点	(U.1)
austere	/ɔs'tiə/	adj.	束身自修的，苦行的；(指建筑物或地方)简朴的	(U.1)
authenticity	/ˌɔ:θen'tisiti/	n.	确实性，真实性；纯正性	(U.8)

autocracy	/ɔːˈtɔkrəsi/	n.	独裁政治,专制政治；独裁政府,专制国家	(U.2)
avenge	/əˈvendʒ/	vt.	为……复仇；向……报仇	(U.7)
awesome	/ˈɔːsəm/	adj.	引起敬畏的, 可怕的	(S.3)
awl	/ɔːl/	n.	锥子，尖钻	(U.3)

B

Babylonian	/bæbiˈləwnjən/	adj.	巴比伦城的；巴比伦人的	(U.2)
backdrop	/ˈbækdrɔp/	n.	背景幕,（事件的）背景	(U.5)
baffle	/ˈbæfl/	vt.	困惑, 阻碍, 为难	(U.11)
Baikal Lake			贝加尔湖	(U.10)
bald	/bɔːld/	adj.	无掩饰的	(S.3)
Balkhash Lake			巴尔喀什湖	(U.10)
baron	/ˈbærən/	n.	男爵（英国贵族的最低一级成员）	(U.1)
barrage	/ˈbærɑːʒ, bəˈrɑːʒ/	n.	掩护炮火；（指说话或写作）倾泻	(U.12)
bastard	/ˈbæstəːd/	n.	私生子；(作定语)假的；伪造的	
a bastard son			私生子；代用品；劣货	(U.3)
Beatle cuts			甲壳虫款式	(S.4)
Beatlemania	/biːtlmeinjə/	n.	披头士狂	(S.4)
Beatles	/ˈbiːtlz/	n.	披头士（甲壳虫）合唱队	(S.4)
behaviouristic	/beheivjəˈrisitik/	adj.	行动主义的	(U.6)
bibliography	/bibliˈɔgrəfi/	n.	节目，参考文献志书学，书籍学。	
belligerent	/biˈlidʒərənt/	adj.	好战的，交战国的，交战的	(U.9)
benevolence	/biˈnevələns/	n.	仁爱，善心；慈善；善行, 捐款	(U.7)
benevolent	/biˈnevələnt/	adj.	慈善的；善意的；行善的；仁爱的, 仁慈的	(U.5)
Benin	/beˈnin/		贝宁湾（几内亚湾一部分）	(U.8)
bid	/bid/		出价；投标；招标	(U.9)
bid	/bid/	v.	(过去时 bade 或 bid, 过去分词 bidden 或 bid) 企图；宣布	(U.1)
bipolarity	/baipəuˈlærəti/	n.	两极，双极	(U.9)
bishop	/ˈbiʃəp/	n.	（国际象棋中的）相, 象	(S.3)
bland	/blænd/	adj.	(-er,-est)文雅的；随和的；不动感情的；和蔼的	(U.1)
blight	/blait/	n.	枯萎病, 不良影响, 市容杂乱的地区	(U.5)
blur		v.	(-rr-)（使某事物）变得模糊不清	(U.1)
bog	/bɔg/	n.	[C, U]（地面为腐朽植物的）沼泽（地区）	(U.1)
Bolshevik	/ˈbɔlʃivik/	n.	布尔什维克	(U.9)
bolster	/ˈbəulstə/	v.	支持	
		n.	垫子	(S.2)
bombardment	/bɔmˈbɑːdmənt/	n.	炮击；轰击；碰撞；辐射	(U.12)
bourgeois	/ˈbuəʒwɑː/	adj.	中产阶级和资产阶级	
bourgeoisie	/ˌbuəʒwɑːˈziː/	n.	资产阶级	(S.1)

263

braiding	/ˈbreidiŋ/	n.	编织物；缠饰	(U.6)
Brazil	/brəzil/	n.	巴西	(S.2)
breach	/briːtʃ/	vt.	违背；不履行；破坏	(U.9)
		n.	破坏，违反，违背，不履行	(U.7)
brethren	/ˈbreðren/	n.	兄弟；教友；会友	(U.7)
brevity	/ˈbreviti/	n.	(时间)短暂，(讲话，文章等)简短	(U.13)
brew	/bruː/	vt, vi.	酿造(啤酒)；酝酿；孕育	(U.12)
brink	/briŋk/	n.	边，边沿；边缘	(S.3)
brood	/bruːd/	vt.	孵(卵)，孵出；沉思；筹划	(U.7)
Bukovina	/buːkəˈviːnə/	n.	布科维纳	(U.9)
bulk	/bʌlk/	n.	巨大的体积；大量，大部分	(U.3)
bureaucracy	/bjuəˈrɔkrəsi/	n.	官员；官僚政治；官僚机构	(U.2)
Burundi	/buˈrundi/	n.	布隆迪(非洲国家)	(U.8)
Byzantine	/biˈzəntizn/	n.	拜占庭	(U.7)

C

canonical	/kəˈnɔnikəl/	adj.	规范的；按照教规的；见于宗教经典的	(U.5)
caricature	/ˈkærikətjuə/	n.	讽刺画，漫画，讽刺描述法	(S.3)
catchall	/ˈkætʃɔːl/	n.	装零杂物品的容器	(S.4)
causal	/ˈkɔːzəl/	adj.	因果关系的，原因的	
celestial	/siˈlestiəl/	adj.	天的；天上的；天空的；天体的	(U.4)
cementing	/siˈmentiŋ/	n.	胶接，黏合	(S.5)
cereal	/ˈsiəriə/	n.	(常用复)禾谷类	(U.3)
ceremonial	/seriˈməuniəl/	n.	仪式	(U.4)
charioteer	/tʃæriəˈtiə/	n.	战车的御者，驾车者，御者	(U.2)
charisma	/kəˈrizmə/	n.	领袖人物的超凡魅力；神授的能力	(U.4)
Chile	/ˈtʃili/	n.	智利(南美洲西南部的一个国家)	(S.2)
chisel	/ˈtʃizl/	n.	凿子	(U.3)
choreograph	/ˈkɔ(ː)riəgrɑːf/	vt.	为(芭蕾舞)设计舞蹈动作；精心策划	(U.11)
Christianity	/kristiˈæniti/	n.	基督教	(U.7)
chronologically	/krɔnəˈlɔdʒikəli/	adv.	按年代顺序排列地	(U.2)
chronology	/krəˈnɔlədʒi/	n.	年代学，年表	(U.2)
circumscribe	/ˈsəːkəmskraib/	vt.	在……周围画线，限制	(S.5)
civic	/ˈsivik/	adj.	市的，市民的，公民的	(U.5)
clamity	/kəˈlæmiti/	n.	灾难，不幸事件	
cleavage	/kˈliːvidʒ/	n.	分裂；裂缝；分解；裂开	(U.9)
clergy	/ˈkləːdʒi/	n.	(集合称)圣职者，牧师，僧侣，神职人员	(S.1)
clout	/klaut/	n.	敲打，轻叩，破布；影响；引力	(U.4)
coercion	/kəuˈəːʃən/	n.	强迫，威压，高压政治	(S.5)
coercive	/kəuˈəːsiv/	adj.	强制的，胁迫的；高压的	(U.2)
coherent	/kəuˈhiərənt/	adj.	粘在一起的；连贯的；一致的	(U.2)

coincident	/kəu'insidənt/	adj.	一致的,符合的,巧合的	(U.6)
collegial	/kə'liːdʒiəl/		分权的;平等分权的	(S.3)
colonel	/'kɜːnl/	n.	上校	(U.11)
colossal	/kə'lɔsl/	adj.	巨像(似)的;巨大的	(U.2)
come to grips with			努力对付;认真谈论(= get to grips with)	(S.3)
comfortingly	/'kʌmfətiŋli/	adv.	安慰地;令人鼓舞地	(U.5)
commoner	/'kɔmənə/	n.	平民;(牛津大学等的)自费生	(U.1)
communal	/'kɔmjun(ə)l/	adj.	公社的;社区的;公有的;团体的	(U.7)
compete(against/with sb)			(in sth)(for sth)竞争;对抗;比赛	(U.1)
complacent	/kəm'pleisnt/	adj.	自满的,得意的	(S.4)
composite	/'kɔmpəzit/	adj.	合成的;混成的;拼凑成的(事物)	(U.2)
comprise	/kəm'praiz/	v.	包括,包含,构成,组成	(U.1)
Conakry	/'kɔnəkri/		科纳克里(几内亚首都)	(U.8)
concede	/kən'siːd/	vt.	勉强,承认,退让	
		vi.	让步	(S.1)
conceit	/kən'siːt/	n.	自负,自夸,骄傲自大,自高自大	(U.4)
concentric	/kɔn'sentrik/	adj.	同中心的,同轴的	(U.3)
concomitant	/kən'kɔmitənt/	adj.	相伴的,伴生的,附随的	(U.6)
concubine	/'kɔŋkjubai/	n.	妾,情妇,姘妇	(S.5)
concurrent	/kə'kʌrənt/	n.	直流,同向	(U.4)
condone	/kən'dəu/	vt.	原谅,宽容;宽恕;不咎(罪过)	(U.12)
confer	/kən'fəːn/	vt.	(conferred; conferring)授予,颁予(称号、学位等);赋予	(U.5)
configurations	/kənfigju'reiʃən/	n.	构造,结构,配置,外形	(U.2)
conformist	/kən'fɔːmist/	adj.	依照(to; with);遵从的(to)	(S.4)
Confucian	/kən'fjuːʃ(ə)n/	adj.	孔子学说的,儒学的	
		n.	儒家学者	(U.5)
conglomerate	/kɔŋ'lɔmərit/	n.	集成物;聚集物;联合大企业	(S.3)
coniferous	/kə'nifərəs/	adj.	松类的,结球果的	(U.10)
conjuncture	/kə'dʒʌŋktʃə/	n.	事态;局面;危机;时机	(U.2)
consecutively	/kən'sekjutivli/	adv.	连贯地,连续地	(U.13)
consensus	/kən'sensəs/	n.	(on sth/that...)意见一致,共同看法	(U.1)
consign	/kən'sain/	vt.	(常与 to 连用)寄售;托卖;交付;托管	(S.5)
constellation	/kɔnstə'leiʃən/	n.	[天]星群,星座,灿烂的一群;荟萃群集或会合	(U.5)
contamination	/kəntæmi'neiʃən/	n.	玷污,污染,污染物	(U.12)
contemplation	/kɔntem'pleiʃən/	n.	凝视;沉思,出神	(U.1)
contend	/kən'tend/	vi.	(常与 with 连用)竞争;争取	(U.5)
contender	/kən'tendə/	n.	斗争者,竞争者	(S.4)
contingent	/kən'tindʒənt/	adj.	(常与 on, upon 连用)偶然的;偶发性的;附带的	(U.5)
contours	/'kɔntuə/	n.	轮廓;外形;周线;海岸线;等高线	(U.5)

convent	/ˈkɔnvənt/	n.	女修道会，女修道院	(S.5)
convergence	/kənˈvəːdʒəns/	n.	趋于相同，相似	(U.1)
conversion	/kənˈvəːʃn/	n.	改变，转变；改变信仰	(U.2)
convoke	/kənˈvəuk/	vt.	召集	(S.1)
Corinthian	/kəˈrinθiən/	adj.	科林斯(人)的；古雅的；放荡的；奢侈的	(U.3)
corps	/kɔː/	n.	军团，团，技术兵种，特殊兵种	(S.2)
cosmic	/ˈkɔzmik/	adj.	宇宙的	
countenance	/ˈkauntinəns/	n.	面容；面部表情；赞同；支持；赞助	(U.11)
counterpart	/ˈkauntəpɑːt/	n.	副本，极相似的人或物，配对物	(U.4)
craze	/kreiz/	n.	狂热	(S.4)
credible	/ˈkredəbl/	adj.	可信的，可靠的	(U.4)
creed	/kriːd; krid/	n.	信条，教义(尤指宗教信仰)	(U.1)
croon	/ˈkruːn/	v., n.	深情地(的)唱，富有柔情地(的)唱流行歌曲	(S.4)
crossfire	/ˈkrɔsfaiə/	n.	交叉火力，困境	(U.12)
crumble	/ˈkrʌmbl/	vt., vi.	弄碎；把……弄成碎屑；崩毁；瓦解；灭亡	(U.2)
crusade	/kruːˈseid/	n.	十字军东侵，宗教战争，改革运动	(U.3)
crusader	/kruːˈseidə/	n.	十字军战士，改革者	(U.9)
culminate	/ˈkʌlmineit/	vi.	(与 in 连用) 达到……的顶点，完结	(U.2)
cult	/kʌlt/	n.	礼拜，祭仪，一群信徒，礼拜式	(U.3)
cumbersome	/ˈkʌmbəsəm/	adj.	讨厌的，麻烦的，笨重的	(U.13)
curb	/kəːb/	vt.	抑制；控制；勒住(马)	(U.12)
curtail	/kəːˈteil/	vt.	缩短；减缩；限制	(U.2)
custody	/ˈkʌstədi/	n.	监督；监视；保护；监护	(U.7)
Cyclades	/ˈsiklədiz/	n.	(希腊)基克拉迪群岛	
Cycladic	/siˈklædik/	adj.	基克拉迪群岛的	(U.3)
Cyprus	/ˈsaiprəs/	n.	塞浦路斯	(U.2)
Crimean	/kraiˈmiən/	adj.	克里米亚半岛的	(U.10)

D

dagger	/ˈdægə/	n.	短剑，匕首	(U.3)
dearth	/dəːθ/	n.	缺乏；饥荒	(U.10)
decipher	/diˈsaifə/	vt.	译解(密码等)；解释(古代文学)；辨认	(U.1)
deface	/diˈfeis/	vt.	损坏外观；损毁表面	(U.3)
definitive	/diˈfinitiv/	adj.	决定性的；最后的；明显的	(U.3)
delineate	/diˈlinieit/	vt.	(ated, -ating) 描画；画出；描述详情；详细记述	(U.2)
delta	/ˈdeltə/	n.	三角洲，德耳塔(希腊字母的第四个字)	(S.4)
demarcate	/diˈmɑːkeit/	vt.	定界线；划界；定范围	(U.6)
demark	/diˈmɑːk/	vt.	区别，区分	(U.4)
demise	/diˈmaiz/	n.	(不动产的)转让；遗赠；让位；逝世	(U.2)
demography	/diˈmɔgrəfi/	n.	人口统计学；人口学	(U.1)

denigration	/ˌdeniˈgreiʃən/	n.	抹黑，贬低，诋毁	(U.4)
denounce	/diˈnauns/	vt.	公开指责，公然抨击，谴责	(U.9)
depict	/diˈpikt/	vt.	画，刻画	(U.7)
depiction	/diˈpikʃən/	n.	描写，叙述	(U.5)
deplorable	/diˈplɔːrəbl/	adj.	可悲的，令人遗憾的；极糟糕的	(U.5)
deplore	/diˈplɔː/	vt.	悲悼，痛惜，悔恨；指责	(U.5)
depoliticize	/diːpəˈlitisaiz/	vt.	使非政治化，使不受政治影响	(U.5)
depose	/diˈpəuz/	vt.	免职，废(王位)，作证	(U.8)
despoiled	/disˈpɔil/	vt.	夺取，掠夺	(S.1)
despotism	/ˈdespətizəm/	n.	专制，暴政；专制统治	(U.10)
detestation	/ˌditesˈteiʃən/	n.	深恶，痛恨，讨厌；极讨厌的东西	(U.11)
detract	/diˈtrækt/	vi.	(与from连用)减损；去掉；诽谤；贬低	(U.9)
detrimental	/ˌdetriˈmentl/	adj.	有害的，伤害的	(U.12)
devastation	/ˌdevəsˈteiʃən/	n.	荒废；[pl.]劫后余迹	(U.10)
deviance	/ˈdiviəns/	n.	偏常，不正常，异常，离经叛道；变异性	(S.5)
dialectic	/ˌdaiəˈlektik/	n.	(与单数动词连用)辩证，辩证法；逻辑论证	(U.2)
dichotomy	/daiˈkɔtəmi/	n.	两分，二分法；分裂	(U.6)
didactic	/diˈdæktik/	adj.	教诲的，教训的；说教的	(U.4)
diffusion	/diˈfjuːʒən/	n.	传播，流传；扩散，弥漫	(U.2)
digging	/ˈdigiŋ/	n.	采(挖)掘，开凿；[pl.]开采物	(U.2)
dilution	/daiˈljuːʃən/	n.	稀释，稀释法，冲淡物	(S.4)
dipole	/ˈdaipəul/	n.	[物]偶极子；[化]偶极，偶极天线	(U.4)
disband	/disˈbænd/	v.	解散，裁减	(U.11)
discard	/disˈkɑːd/	vt.	扔掉，丢弃，不再使用	(U.1)
disclaimer	/disˈkleimə/	n.	否认某事物的声明	(U.1)
discourse	/ˈdiskɔːs/	n.	演说；讲演；谈话；论文	(U.6)
discredit	/disˈkredit/	vt.	损害，败坏名声，不可信，受怀疑	
discrepancy	/disˈkrepənsi/	n.	相差，差异，矛盾	(S.1)
discursive	/disˈkəːsiv/	adj.	散漫的，东拉西扯的，离题的；[哲]推论的	(U.13)
disdain	/disˈdein/	vt.	轻视；蔑视；不屑	(U.11)
disembodied	/ˌdisimˈbɔdid/	adj.	无实体的；空洞的；空虚的	(U.5)
dispatch	/disˈpætʃ/	n.	派遣；发送；急件；新闻电讯；迅速结束	(U.11)
disposable	/disˈpəusəbl/	adj.	可任意使用的	(S.4)
disposition	/ˌdispəˈziʃən/	n.	性情，性格	(U.1)
dispute	/disˈpjuːt/	n.	争论；辩论	(U.7)
disrupt	/disˈrʌpt/	vt.	使混乱；使瓦解	(U.9)
dissent	/diˈsent/	n.	异议；不同意；意见不一致	(U.5)
dissolution	/ˌdisəˈluːʃən/	n.	分解；分裂；腐朽；解体；解散	(U.9)
divergence	/daiˈvəːdʒəns/	n.	分歧，意见分歧	(U.9)
diverse	/daiˈvəːs/	adj.	不同的，变化多的	(S.2)
divine	/diˈvain/	adj.	神的；上帝的；天赐的；非常非常好的；极好的	(U.5)

docile	/'dəusail/	adj.	容易控制的,驯服的	(U.1)
documentation	/ˌdɔkjumen'teiʃən/	n.	证明文件,文献或参考资料	(U.13)
dodging	/'dɔdʒi/	vt.,vi.	(常与 about,behind,round 连用)闪避;躲闪	(S.4)
dogma	/'dɔgmə/	n.	教条;信条	(U.5)
dogmatic	/dɔg'mætik/	adj.	教条主义的,武断的	(U.1)
dogmatism	/'dɔgmətizm/	n.	(U)教条主义,武断	(U.1)
doldrums	/'dɔldrəmz/	n.	[pl.] 消沉;经济无生气;赤道无风带	(S.4)
Dominica	/ˌdɔmi'ni:kə/	n.	多米尼加(西印度群岛岛国)	(U.11)
dominion	/'dɔminjən/	n.	统治权;主权,领土;领地	(U.2)
dreariness	/'driərinis/	n.	沉寂,可怕,凄凉	(S.4)
drive...up the wall			将……逼至绝境,使……走投无路	(S.4)
dub	/dʌb/	vt.	[电影]配音,轻点,授予称号,打击	(S.4)
dubious	/'dju:bjəs/	adj.	半信半疑;可疑;不能确定的	(U.1)

E

eclectic	/ek'lektik/	adj.	折衷的,折衷学派的	(U.5)
eclipse	/ik'lips/	n.	蚀;失去,丧失(名声、威望等)	(U.3)
ecstatic	/eks'tætik/	adj.	狂喜的,心醉神迷的,入迷的	(S.4)
ecumene	/ekju'mi:n/	n.	有人居住的地区;定居区,核心区;发达区	(U.2)
edification	/ˌedifi'keiʃən/	n.	(尤指道德或精神方面的)教诲,启迪,熏陶	(U.5)
edify	/'edifai/	vt.	教育	(U.4)
efficacy	/'efikəsi/	n.	(= efficacity)效力(益,能)	(U.5)
egalitarian	/iˌgæli'teəriən/	adj.	平等主义的	(S.5)
elaborate	/i'læbəreit/	v.	详细制定,详尽解释,阐述	(U.1)
elevate	/'eliveit/	vt.	举起,提拔,振奋,提升...的职位	(S.5)
elevation	/ˌeli'veiʃn/	n.	提升;高尚;高雅;高地;海拔	(U.3)
elicit	/i'lisit/	vt.	引出,得出,探出	(U.2)
elite	/ei'li:t,i'li:t/	n.	精英,精华;中坚	(U.4)
elixir	/i'liksə/	n.	炼金药,长生不老药	(U.4)
elude	/i'lu:d/	vt.	逃避;逃脱;记不起;使人不解	(U.11)
elusive	/i'lu:siv/	adj.	逃避的;躲避的;难以捕捉的;难以理解的	(U.1)
emanate	/'eməneit/	v.	(from sth/sb)来自某物/某人	(U.1)
embark	/im'ba:k/	v.	(常与 on,in 连用)开始;从事	(U.9)
embryonic	/ˌembri'ɔnik/	adj.	萌发期的,未发达的	(S.1)
eminence	/'eminəns/	n.	卓越,显赫,著名	(U.9)
Empedocles	/em'pedəkli:z/	n.	恩培多克勒	(U.4)
enclave	/'enkleiv/	n.	被包围中的领土,包体,包含物;残遗群落	(S.5)
encompass	/in'kʌmpəs/	vt.	包括,包含;围绕;完工,促使	(U.2)
encroachments	/in'krəutʃmənt/	n.	侵蚀,侵犯	(S.1)
encyclopedic	/inˌsaikləu'pi:dik/	adj.	如百科辞典的,百科全书式的	(U.2)
endeavor	/in'devə/	n.	努力,尽力	

		v.	努力,尽力	(U.1)
endow	/in'dau/	vt.	捐赠;资助	(U.6)
enduring	/in'djnəriŋ/	adj.	持久的,耐久的	(U.1)
engraver	/in'greivə/	n.	雕刻师,雕工	(U.3)
engulf	/in'gʌlf/	vt.	卷入,吞没,狼吞虎咽	(S.3)
entail	/in'teil/	vt.	使必需,使蒙受,使承担	(S.3)
entangle	/in'tæŋgl/	vt.	使缠上,纠缠,卷入,使混乱	(U.6)
enunciate	/i'nʌncieit/	v.	阐明,清晰发言	(U.9)
enunciate	/i'nʌnsieit/	v.	阐明,清晰发言,宣布,发表(学说等)	(U.6)
eon	/'i:ən/	n.	(= aeon)世,纪,代,无限长的时代,永世	(U.12)
equate	/i'kweit/	vt.	(常与 to, with 连用)使相等	(U.5)
equilibrium	/ˌi:kwi'libriəm/	n.	平衡,平静,均衡	(U.9)
erase	/i'reiz/	vt.	擦掉,抹掉	(U.7)
erudition	/ˌeru:'diʃn/	n.	博学;学识;学问	(U.2)
escalate	/'eskəleit/	vi.	逐步升高,逐步增强;vt. 使逐步上升	(S.3)
escalation	/ˌeskə'leiʃn/	n.	自动调整;不断增加;逐步上升	(U.12)
eschew	/is'tʃu:/	v.	(文)避开;戒除;回避	(U.1)
escort	/is'kɔ:t/	v.	护卫,护送,陪同	(S.3)
esoteric	/ˌesəu'terik/	adj.	深奥的	(U.13)
ethos	/'i:θɒs/	n.	气质,道义,民族精神	(U.5)
evict	/i'vikt/	vt.	驱逐;赶出	(U.3)
exalt		vt.	赞扬;歌颂;提升;晋升	(S.3)
exalted	/ig'zɔ:ltid/	adj.	高的,崇高的	(U.1)
excrescence	/iks'kresns/	n.	多余物,长出物,赘疣,瘤	(U.5)
excruciating	/ikskru:ʃieitiŋ/	adj.	极痛苦的,折磨人的	(U.11)
exertion	/ig'zə:ʃn/	n.	努力,尽力;行使,运用	(U.11)
exhortation	/ˌegzɔ:'teiʃn/	n.	劝告,讲道词,训诫	(U.5)
exigency	/'eksidʒənsi/	n.	紧急的需要或要求;紧急情况;危急关头	(U.1)
exnihilo	/eks'naihiləu/		(拉)从无,出于无	(U.5)
expertise	/ekspə'ti:z/	n.	专门技能,知识;专家评价,鉴定	(U.2)
explicit	/iks'plisit/	adj.	详述的,明晰的;清楚的,直率的	(U.2)
explicitly	/iks'plisitli/	adv.	明白地,明确地	(U.7)
exploitation	/eksplɔl'teiʃn/	n.	开发,开采,剥削	(S.1)
explosive	/iks'pləusiv/	adj.	会爆炸的;激起感情的	(U.6)
extraterritoriality	/'ekstrəˌteriˌtɔ:ri'æliti/	n.	治外法权	(U.4)
extravagance	/ik'strævəgəns/	n.	奢侈,铺张,过度,放纵的言行	(U.5)
extrinsic	/eks'trinsk/	adj.	外界的	(U.4)

F

fabulously	/'fæbjuləsli/	adv.	难以置信地,惊人地	(U.10)
facilitate	/fə'siliteit/	vt.	使容易;使便利	(U.4)

facilitation	/fəˌsiliˈteiʃən/	n.	简易化，助长	(U.4)
fad	/fæd/	n.	时尚，一时流行的狂热，一时的爱好	(S.4)
fallow	/ˈfæləu/	adj.	休闲中的(田地)	(U.4)
fanatical	/fəˈnætikəl/	adj.	狂热的，盲信的	(S.4)
farthing	/ˈfɑːðiŋ/	n.	(英)1/4 旧便士，英国最小的钱币；极少量，一点儿	(U.11)
fathom	/ˈfæðəm/	n.	(长度单位)英寻(等于6英尺)	(U.1)
fertility	/fəˈtiliti/	n.	肥沃；丰饶；繁殖；生殖力	(U.4)
feudalism	/ˈfjuːdəlizəm/	n.	封建主义，封建制度	(S.1)
fiddler	/ˈfidlə/	n.	拉提琴的人，小提琴家，胡乱拨弄者	(S.4)
filial	/ˈfiliəl/	adj.	子女的；孝顺的	(U.5)
fivescore	/ˈfaivskɔː(r)/	adj.	一百的	(S.3)
flareback	/ˈfleəbæk/	n.	炮尾焰(火炮炮尾后曳的火焰)；激烈的反驳；回击	(U.12)
fledgling	/ˈfledʒliŋ/	n.	刚学飞的幼鸟；无经验的人	(S.4)
flicker	/fˈlikə/	vi.	闪现；忽隐忽现；摇晃	(U.2)
fluke	/fluːk/	n.	侥幸	(S.4)
foci	/ˈfəusai/	n.	focus的复数；焦距，配光	(U.8)
foreseeable	/fɔːˈsiːəbl/	adj.	可预知的，能预测的，能看透的	(U.9)
forge	/fɔːdʒ/	vi.	打(铁)，锻制；锻炼；编造(故事等)；伪造(文书等)	(U.11)
formative	/ˈfɔːmətiv/	adj.	格式化的；影响形成的；影响发展的	(U.5)
fringe	/frindʒ/	adj.	边缘的，额外的	(S.4)
full-fledged	/ˈfulfledʒd/	adj.	成熟的；完全有资格的	(U.6)
fundamentalist	/fʌndəˈmentəlist/	n.	原教旨主义者	(U.8)
futile	/ˈfuːtail/	adj.	琐细的,无用的,无效果的,(人)没有出息的	(U.12)

G

garrison	/ˈgærisn/	n.	卫戍部队，驻军，卫戍地，要塞	(U.11)
gauge	/gedʒ/	vt.	(用计量器)计量,度量；估量；评价；判断	(U.11)
generalist	/ˈdʒenərəlist/	n.	知识渊博者，有多方面才能的人，多面手	(U.2)
Gentiles	/ˈdʒentail/	n.	非犹太人，异教徒	(S.3)
geodetic	/dʒiːədetik/	adj.	大地测量学的；大地线的	(U.5)
geomancy	/ˈdʒiːəumænsi/	n.	泥土占卜；风水	(U.4)
germane	/dʒəˈmein/	adj.	~(to sth)(fml)有关	(U.1)
Ghana	/ˈgɑːnə/	n.	加纳	(U.8)
ghetto	/ˈgetəu/	n.	分离区；(美)城市中的黑人的集中居住区	(S.3)
gigantic	/dʒaiˈgæntik/	a.	巨大的,庞大的	(U.2)
gleefully	/ˈgliːfuli/	adv.	愉快地	(S.4)
globalization	/gləubəlaiˈzeiʃən/	n.	全球化,普及到世界范围	(U.2)
gospel	/ˈgɔspəl/	n.	福音音乐	(S.4)

gotta			got 的古英语形式	(S.4)
gracious	/'greɪʃəs/	adj.	亲切的，高尚的	(U.7)
granary	/'grænərɪ/	n.	谷仓；粮仓	(U.3)
grant	/grɑːnt/	n.	赠款；津贴，专用拨款	(S.2)
grievance	/'griːvəns/	n.	不满；不平；冤情；抱怨；牢骚	(U.11)
gripping	/'graɪpɪŋ/	adj.	引起人注意的；吸引人的	(U.5)
grist	/grɪst/	n.	有利的东西，谷物	(S.3)
grueling	/'gruəlɪŋ/	adj.	筋疲力尽的	(S.4)
grunge	/grʌndʒ/	n.	肮脏，低下，令人讨厌或无聊的人	(S.4)
Guinea	/'gɪnɪ/	n.	几内亚	(U.8)

H

habitat	/'hæbɪtæt/	n.	（动、植物的）产地,栖息地	(U.12)
hcclo	/heɪləʊ/	vt.	使有晕轮,围以光环	
Hammurabic	/hɑːmuˈrɑːpi/	n.	Law：汉穆拉比法典	(S.5)
hamstring	/'hæmstrɪŋ/	vt.	– strung 割断…的腿筋；使残废；破坏	(U.6)
haram	/'heərəm/	n.	(=harem)(伊斯兰教徒)女眷居住的内室,闺房	(U.7)
harbinger	/'hɑːbɪndʒə(r)/	n.	(修辞)预告者；先驱；前兆	(U.1)
harem	/'heərem/	n.	(伊斯兰教国家中的)闺房,后宫；女眷们	(U.2)
harmonicas	/hɑːˈmɒnɪkə/	n.	口琴，玻璃或金属片的敲打乐器	(S.4)
harmonics	/hɑːˈmɒnɪks/	n.	和声学	(U.4)
headline	/'hedlaɪn/	vt.	以明星身份推出或捧为明星	(S.4)
heedless	/'hiːdlɪs/	adj.	不注意的，不留心的；不谨慎的	(U.12)
hegemony	/hɪˈgemənɪ/	n.	霸权，霸权主义(尤指数国联盟中的)盟主权	(U.2)
heir	/eə/	n.	继承人；嗣子	(U.3)
Helladic	/heˈlædɪk/	adj.	铜器时代的；希腊文化的	(U.3)
hemispheric	/hemɪsˈferɪk/	adj.	半球的，半球状	(U.2)
hereditary	/hɪˈredɪtərɪ/	adj.	世袭的，遗传的	(S.1)
heredity	/hɪˈredɪtɪ/	n.	遗传；遗传性；遗传特征	(U.12)
heretic	/'herətɪk/	n.	异教徒,持异端者	(U.1)
hermetically	/həːˈmetɪklɪ/	adv.	密封地，炼金术地	(U.6)
Herodotus	/hɪˈrɒdətəs/	n.	希罗多德	(U.10)
hew	/hjuː; hju/	v.	(用斧、刀剑等)砍，劈(某物[某人])	(U.1)
hierarchical	/haɪəˈrɑːkɪkəl/	adj.	分等级的	(U.4)
hierarchy	/'haɪərɑːkɪ/	n.	统治集团，等级制度，特权阶级	(S.1)
hillbilly	/'hɪlbɪlɪ/	n.	山地内部的贫农，山地人	(S.4)
historiography	/ˌhɪstɔːrɪˈɒgrəfɪ/	n.	历史编纂学，编史工作；史评	(U.1)
homeostasis	/ˌhəʊmɪəʊˈsteɪsɪs/	n.	系统(动态)平衡；(似滞)	(U.4)
homogeneity	/ˌhɒməʊdʒɪˈniːɪtɪ/	n.	同种；同质；同性；(数)齐性,均匀性	(U.10)
homogeneous	/ˌhɒməʊˈdʒiːnɪəs/	adj.	同类的，相似的，均一的，均匀的	(U.2)
honky-tonk	/'hɒŋkɪtɒŋk/	n.	拉格泰姆钢琴曲，低级嘈杂的夜总会	(S.4)

hortatory	/ˈhɔːtətəri/	adj.	督促的；劝告的；激励的	(U.5)
horticultural	/ˌhɔːtiˈkʌltʃərəl/	adj.	园艺的	(U.4)
hubbub	/ˈhʌbʌb/	n.	吵闹声，呐喊声，叫嚷声	(U.11)
hybrid	/ˈhaibrid/	n.	杂种，混血儿，混合物	(S.4)
hygiene	/ˈhaidʒiːn/	n.	卫生学；保健法；卫生	(U.4)
hypothesize	/haiˈpɔθisaiz/	vi.,vt.	假设，假定	(U.2)

I

icon	/ˈaikən/	n.	图标，肖像，偶像	(U.11)
idiosyncratic	/ˌidiəsiŋˈkrætik/	adj.	具有个人气质、癖性、风格的	(U.1)
idol	/ˈaid(ə)l/	n.	神像；偶像；宠爱物；崇拜对象	(U.7)
illustrious	/iˈlʌstriəs/	adj.	杰出的；著名的；光荣的；辉煌的	(U.5)
imbue	/imˈbjuː/	vt.	（与with连用）（用感情）充满；灌输；影响	(U.5)
immortality	/iməːˈtæləti/	n.	不死（永生，永远性）	(U.4)
impel	/imˈpel/	vt.	-ll- 推进；驱使	(U.5)
impetuous	/imˈpetjuəs/	adj.	激烈的，猛烈的；激动的，冲动的	(U.12)
impetus	/ˈimpitəs/	n.	推动，刺激，促进	(U.1)
impinge	/imˈpindʒ/	v.	（upon sth）对某事物起作用或有影响	(U.1)
implicit	/imˈplisit/	adj.	暗含的；含蓄的	(U.10)
implicitly	/imˈplisitli/	adv.	含蓄地，暗中地	(U.4)
impoverish	/imˈpɔvəriʃ/	vt.	使贫困，使枯竭	(U.8)
impoverishment	/imˈpɔvəriʃmənt/	n.	贫穷，穷困	(U.3)
improvisation	/ˌimprəvaiˈzeiʃən/	n.	即席创作	(S.4)
imputable	/imˈpjuːtbl/	adj.	(to)可归罪的，可使负责的	(U.11)
incentive	/inˈsentiv/	n.	刺激；鼓励；动机	(U.4)
inception	/inˈsepʃən/	n.	开端；开始	(S.5)
incessant	/inˈsesnt/	adj.	不断的,不停的	
incidental	/insiˈdentl/	adj.	细小的，次要的	(U.1)
incite	/inˈsait/	vt.	激动，煽动	(S.4)
inclement	/inˈklemənt/	adj.	恶劣的，严寒的,狂风暴雨的(天气)	(U.10)
incorporate	/inˈkɔːpərent/	v.	包含；加上；吸收；把合并	(U.2)
inculcate	/inˈkʌlkeit/	vt.	谆谆教诲（劝导）	(U.5)
incursion	/inˈkəːʃən/	n.	侵入，侵略；袭击；（河水等）流入	(U.7)
indoctrination	/inˌdɔktriˈneiʃən/	n.	教导，教化	(U.5)
indubitably	/inˈduːbitəbli/	adv.	无疑地，确实地	(U.2)
induce	/inˈdjuːs/	vt.	劝诱，促使，导致，引起，感应	(S.5)
inference	/ˈinfərəns/	n.	推论	(S.3)
infrastructure	/infrəˈstrʌktʃə/	n.	基础；基础结构（设施）	(U.4)
ingenuity	/inˈdʒiːnjəs/	n.	机灵，独创性，精巧，灵活性	(U.3)
injunction	/inˈdʒʌŋkʃən/	n.	命令，责戒，训谕；(律)指令，禁令	(U.5)
insanity	/inˈsæniti/	n.	精神错乱，疯狂，愚顽	(U.12)

insipid	/in'sipid/	adj.	乏味的；枯燥的	(U.12)
insolent	/'insələnt/	adj.	粗野的；无礼的；侮慢的	(U.7)
integrate	/'intigreit/	vt.	使成整体，使一体化，结合	(U.6)
intelligible	/in'telidʒəbl/	adj.	可以理解的易领悟的	(U.1)
interact	/intər'ækt/	vi.	相互作用，相互影响；交相感应，反应	(U.4)
intermediate	/intə'mi:diət/	adj.	中间的；居中的	(U.6)
interminable	/in'tə:minəbl/	adj.	无终止的,没完没了的	(U.10)
intermingle	/intə(:)'miŋhl/	vt.	使混合；使搀和	
		vi.	（与……）混合	(U.12)
interposition	/intə'pə:siʃən/	n.	插入,妨害,干涉；调停,插入物	(S.3)
interim	/'inʃərim/	adj.	暂时的,临时的	
intra-	/'intrə/		prefix 表示"在内、内部"之义	(S.3)
intrinsic	/in'trinsik/	adj.	固有的；本身的；内在的	(U.4)
intrinsically	/in'trinsikli/	adv.	固有地,本质地,内在地	(U.4)
invigorating	/in'vigəreitiŋ/	adj.	精力充沛的，爽快的	(S.3)
irreconcilable	/i,rekən'sailəbl/	adj.	不能和解的人；不能调和的思想	(U.1)
irrecoverable	/iri'kʌvəbl/	adj.	不能恢复的；不能挽回的；不能治好的	(U.12)
irrefutable	/iri'fju:təbl/	adj.	（文）驳不倒的	(U.1)
irrespective	/iris'pektiv/	adj.	（与 of 连用）不顾……的;不考虑……的	(U.9)
irretrievably	/iri'tri:vəbli/	adv.	不能挽回地，不能补救地	(U.9)
irreversible	/iri'və:səbl/	adj.	不能撤回的，不能取消的	(U.12)
irrevocable	/i'revəkbəbl/	adj.	不能改变的；不能取消的	(U.9)
irritable	/'iritəbl/	adj.	易怒的；易激怒的	(U.11)
Islam	/'izlɑ:m, -læm, ləm/	n.	伊斯兰教；伊斯兰教徒；伊斯兰教国家	(U.7)
Ivory Coast	/'aivərikəust/		（非洲）象牙海岸	(U.8)

J

Jamaica	/dʒə'meikə/	n.	牙买加，牙买加甜酒	(U.11)
jambalaya	/dʒʌmbə'laiə/	n.	什锦菜肴	(S.4)
jangle	/'dʒæŋgl/	vt., vi.	（使）发出刺耳声；乱响	(S.3)
jig	/dʒig/	n.	快步舞；快步舞曲	(S.4)
Judaism	/'dʒu:deiizm/	n.	犹太教	(U.7)
juggle	/'dʒʌgl/	vt.	耍弄，歪曲，篡改；同时做使	(U.13)
jukebox	/'dʒu:kbɔks/	n.	自动唱片点唱机	(S.4)
jumble	/'dʒʌmbl/	n.	一堆；一团糟；混杂（混乱的）一团	(U.5)
juxtaposition	/ˌdʒʌkstəpə'ziʃən/	n.	并置，并列；接近；交叉重叠法	(U.2)

K

Khrushchev	/kruʃ'ʃɔ:f/	n.	赫鲁晓夫(前苏共第一书记)	(U.10)
Kievan	/'ki:jefən/	adj.	基辅的	(U.10)

kinship	/ˈkinʃip/	n.	亲属关系；相似	(U.4)

L

Ladoga Lake			拉多加湖	(U.10)
lament	/ləˈment/	n.	悲伤，哀悼，挽诗，悼词	(S.4)
latitudinally	/ˌlætiˈtjuːdinli/	adv.	纬度，向纬度方向	(U.10)
Le (Labor Exchange)			务实贸易	(S.3)
lesbians	/ˈlezbiən/	n.	女性同性恋者	(S.5)
lethal	/ˈliːθəl/	adj.	致命的	
		n.	致死因子	(U.12)
leverage	/ˈliːvəridʒ/	n.	杠杆作用	(S.5)
levy	/ˈlevi/	n.	征税；征募	(U.7)
liability	/ˌlaiəˈbiliti/	n.	责任；义务；负债	(U.3)
lilt	/lilt/	vt., vi.	以明快的节奏演唱	(S.4)
lilting lament			以明快的节奏演唱悲哀的歌	(S.4)
limelight	/ˈlaimlait/	n.	引人注目的中心	(S.4)
Linear B	/ˈliniəl/		B 类线形文字	(U.3)
linguistic	/ligˈwistik/	adj.	词的，语言学的，语言的	
Lifcurgy	/ˈlitə(ː)əʒi/	n.	圣餐仪式，礼拜仪式	
littoral	/ˈlitərəl/	n.	沿海地，沿海地区	(U.10)
loath	/ləuθ/	adj.	(to do/ that) 不情愿的，勉强的	(U.8)
longevity	/lɔnˈdʒeviti/	n.	长命，寿命，供职期限，资历	(U.4)
ludicrous	/ˈluːdikrəs/	adj.	可笑的；荒唐的；愚蠢的	(U.1)
lunatic	/ˈluːnətik/	adj., n.	精神失常(的)，疯(的)；极愚蠢(的)	(U.1)
lurk	/ləːk/	v.	埋伏；潜伏	(U.8)
lush	/lʌʃ/	adj.	茂盛的；青葱的；性感的	(S.4)
lyric	/ˈlirik/	n.	抒情诗，歌词	(S.4)
Levant	/liˈvænt/	n.	地中海东部沿岸诸国家和岛屿	(U.2)

M

Madagascar	/ˌmædəˈgæskə/	n.	马达加斯加岛（非洲岛国）	(U.8)
magnitude	/ˈmægnitjuːd/	n.	大小，数量，巨大，广大	(U.12)
magnum	/ˈmægnəm/	adj.	大的，发射能量大的	(U.2)
manacle	/ˈmænəkl/	n.	手铐，脚镣，束缚	(S.3)
Manichaean	/ˌmæniˈkiːən/	n.	摩尼教徒	(U.7)
manifest	/ˈmænifest/	vt.	显示，表明，指明；证明	(U.5)
manipulation	/məˌnipjuˈleiʃən/	n.	处理，操作，操纵，被操纵	(U.6)
manor	/ˈmænə/	n.	（封建领主的）领地，庄园	(S.1)
marginal	/ˈmɑːdʒinəl/	adj.	记在页边的，边缘的，边际的	(S.5)
marginalize	/ˈmɑːdʒinəlaiz/	v.	使处于社会边缘，忽视；排斥	(U.1)

mason	/ˈmeisn/	n.	泥瓦匠	(U.3)
maxim	/ˈmæksim/	n.	格言，箴言；谚语；座右铭；普遍真理	(U.2)
maze	/meiz/	n.	迷宫；错综复杂的曲径	(U.6)
Mecca	/ˈmeke/	n.	(＝Makkah, Mekka)麦加	(U.7)
meddle	/ˈmedl/	v.	干预；干涉	(U.11)
mediate	/ˈmidiːt, -djət/	v.	仲裁，调停，作为引起……的媒介，居中调停	(S.5)
mediocre	/miːdiˈəukə/	adj.	普普通通的	(S.4)
meditation	/mediˈteiʃən/	n.	熟虑	(U.4)
Mediterranean	/meditəˈreinjən/	n.	地中海	
		adj.	地中海的	(U.2)
melancholy	/ˈmelənkəli/	n.	忧郁	(S.4)
memoir	/ˈmemwaː/	n.	实录，传略；[pl.]自传，学术论文集	(U.1)
mercenary	/ˈməːsinəri/	adj.	为钱的，唯利是图的，贪财的；被雇佣的	(U.3)
mesmerize	/ˈmezməraiz/		给…施行催眠术，迷惑；吸引	(U.12)
Mesopotamian	/mesəpəˈteimiən/	adj., n.	美索不达米亚(的)	(U.2)
metallurgy	/meˈtælədʒi/	n.	冶金学；冶金术	(U.3)
middling	/ˈmidliŋ/	adj.	中等的，普通的	(U.1)
migration	/maiˈgreiʃn/	n.	移动；移居；迁徙的人；成群的候鸟	(U.2)
militia	/miˈliʃə/	n.	预备役部队	(U.11)
millennium	/miˈleniəm/	n.	(-nia)一千年；未来的太平盛世，幸福时代	(U.4)
Minerva	/miˈnəːvə/	n.	(罗神)密涅瓦	(U.2)
miniaturization	/ˌminiətʃəraiˈzeiʃən/	n.	小型化	(U.10)
Minoan	/miˈnəuən/	n.	弥诺斯	(U.3)
misinformation	/ˌmisinfəˈmeiʃən/	n.	误报，误传	(U.4)
mitigate	/ˈmitigeit/	vt.	减轻严重性；缓和，减低(坏处、伤害等)	(U.10)
mitigating	/ˈmitigeiti/	adj.	减轻的，和缓的，节制的	(U.1)
mock	/mɔk/	vt. vi.	(常与at连用)嘲笑；嘲弄	(U.7)
modality	/məuˈdæliti/	n.	形式，形态，特征	(U.6)
modicum	/ˈmɔdikəm/	n.	少量	(U.6)
monastic	/məˈnæstik/	n.	僧侣，修道士	(U.7)
monism	/ˈmɔnizəm/	n.	[哲]一元论	(U.6)
monk	/mʌŋk/	n.	修道士，僧侣	(U.7)
monograph	/ˈmɔnəugraf/	n.	专题文章；专著；专论	(U.2)
monolithic	/ˌmɔnəˈliθik/	adj.	巨石的；巨大而屹立的；单一的；统一的	(U.9)
monoliths	/ˈmɔnəuliθ/	n.	庞然大物；独块巨石	(S.3)
monopoly	/məˈnɔpəli/	n.	垄断，垄断者，专利权，专利事业	(U.9)
monotheistic	/ˌmɔnəuθiːˈstik/	adj.	一神论的	(U.7)
moribund	/ˈmɔ(ː)ribʌnd/	n.	垂死的人	
		adj.	垂死的	(S.1)
mortality	/mɔːˈtæliti/	n.	死亡人数；死亡率	(U.4)
mosque	/mɔsk/	n.	清真寺	(U.8)

Muhammad	/muˈhæməd/	adj.	(伊斯兰教创始人)穆罕默德	(U.7)
multilateral	/ˌmultiˈlætərəl/	adj.	多边的,多国的	(U.9)
multiplicity	/ˌmʌltiˈplisiti/	n.	大数目;多种多样;繁多	(U.5)
mummify	/ˈmʌmifai/	vt.	(-fied, -fying) 使为木乃伊;使干枯	(U.2)
Muslim	/ˈmuzlim; US mʌzlem/		伊斯兰教徒;穆斯林	(U.7)
mutation	/mjuːˈteiʃən/	n.	变化;[生]突变;变异;突变种;新种	(U.4)
mutiny	/ˈmjuːtini/	n.	兵变,叛变,造反。	
		v.	叛变,造反,兵变	(U.3)
Mycenaean	/ˌmaisiˈniːən/	adj.	迈锡尼的	
		n.	迈锡尼人;迈锡尼语	(U.3)

N

nauseam	/ˈnɔziːm/	n.	呕吐剂	(S.1)
nebulous	/ˈnebjuləs/	adj.	含糊的,模糊的;暧昧的	(U.10)
negritude	/ˈnegritjuːd/	n.	黑人文化传统的认同,黑人文化传统的自豪感	(U.8)
Neolithic	/ˌniːəuˈliθik/	adj.	新石器时代的	(U.3)
neurosis	/njuəˈrəusis/	n.	(-ses) 神经官能症;精神神经病	(U.5)
Nigeria	/naiˈdʒiəriə/	n.	尼日利亚(非洲中西部国家)	(U.8)
nomad	/ˈnəumæd/	n.	游牧部落的人,流浪者,游牧民	(U.10)
notable	/ˈnəutəbl/	adj.	值得注意的;显著的;显要的;优越的	(U.10)
notwithstanding	/ˌnɔtwiθˈstændiŋ/	prep.	虽然,尽管	
		adv.	尽管,还是	(U.5)
nullification	/ˌnʌlfiˈkeiʃən/	n.	无效,废弃,取消,使无价值	(S.3)
numerology	/ˌnjuːməˈrɔlədʒi/	n.	数字命理学	(U.4)
nutty	/ˈnʌti/	adj.	美味的;内容充实的	(S.4)

O

oared	/ˈɔːd/	adv.	有桨的	
oasis	/əuˈeisis/	n.	(pl. -ses)(沙漠中的)绿洲	(U.7)
obscure	/əbˈskjuə/	vt.	使 不分明;遮掩	(U.1)
observance	/əbˈzəːvəns/	n.	(法律、习俗等的)遵守,奉行	(U.7)
obsession	/əbˈseʃən/	n.	困扰;固定的想法;分心,分神;迷念	(U.2)
obsidian	/ɔbˈsidən/	n.	黑曜岩火山玻璃	(U.3)
obverse	/ˈɔbvəːs/	adj.	正面的	(S.5)
occidental	/ˌɔksiˈdəntəl/	n.	欧美人,西方人	(U.4)
offprint	/ˈɔfprint/	n.	选印本	(U.13)
offspring	/ˈɔːfspriŋ/	n.	(单复数同形)儿女,子孙,后代,产物	(U.3)
oligarch	/ˈɔligɑːk/	n.	寡头政治的执政者(支持者)	(U.5)
omen	/ˈəumen/	n.	预兆,征兆	(U.4)
Onega Lake			奥涅加湖	(U.10)

onset	/'ɔnset/	n.	攻击；开始	(U.4)
opt	/ɔpt/	v.	决定做某事物；选择	(U.1)
opus	/'əupəs/	n.	作品	(U.2)
ordinance	/'ɔːdinəns/	n.	法令；条例；布告；训令；传统的风俗习惯	(U.5)
orthodox	/'ɔːθədɔks/	adj.	正统的；正派的；传统的；习俗的	(U.7)
orthodoxy	/'ɔːθədɔksi/	n.	信奉正教；正教，正统派学说	(U.5)
ostentation	/ɔstenteiʃən/	n.	卖弄，夸耀，摆阔，风头主义	(U.11)
outlet	/'autlet, -lit/	n.	出口，出路	(S.2)
outmode	/aut'məud/	vt.	使不流行	
		vi.	变旧，变不流行	(U.6)
overture	/'əuvətʃuə(r)/	n.	序言，事件的开始	(U.1)

P

pagan	/'peigən/	n.	没有宗教信仰的人；异教徒	(U.7)
panacea	/ˌpænə'siə/	n.	治百病的药，万灵药	(U.1)
panhellenic	/ˌpænhe'liːnik/	adj.	泛希腊的，全大学校友会的	(U.3)
paradigm	/'pærədaim/	n.	范例，样式	(U.1)
parameter	/pə'ræmitə/	n.	参数，参量	(U.6)
parchment	/'pɑːtʃmənt/	n.	羊皮纸，羊皮纸文稿；仿羊皮纸	(U.1)
parochial	/pə'rəukiəl/	adj.	教区的；受限制的，狭隘的	(U.4)
pastoral	/'pɑːstərəl/	adj.	田园生活的；宁静的；乡村生活的	(U.7)
patriarchy	/'peitriɑːki/	n.	家长统治，父权制	(S.5)
patrician	/pə'triʃən/	n.	(古罗马的)贵族	(U.7)
pawn	/pɔːn/	n.	(象棋)兵，卒	(S.3)
pawn	/pɔːn/	n.	典当，抵押物，人质	(S.5)
pedagogic	/ˌpedə'gɔdʒik/	adj.	教师的，教学法的；教育学的	(U.1)
pedagogical	/ˌpedə'gɔdʒikəl/	adj.	教育学的，教学法的	(U.11)
per se	/pəː'sei/	adv.	本身；就其本身而论	(U.4)
percussion	/pəː'kʌʃən/	n.	打击乐器	(S.4)
perfunctory	/pə'fʌŋktəri/	adj.	马马虎虎的	(S.1)
periodization	/ˌpiəriədai'zeiʃən/	n.	(历史等的)时期划分，周期化	(U.2)
peripheral	/pə'rifərəl/	adj.	外围的，边缘的	(U.1)
periphery	/pə'rifəri/	n.	外围，界限；周边；外围设备，辅助设备	(U.2)
permeate	/'pəːmieit/	v.	(through sth)(fml) 弥漫；散布；充满	(U.1)
perpetuate	/pə(ː)'petjueit/	vt.	使永存，使不朽	(S.2)
pervasive	/pə'veisiv/	adj.	普遍深入的	(S.5)
pervert	/pə(ː)'vəːt/	vt.	使堕落；滥用；误解，曲解；使反常；颠倒	(U.7)
petrify	/'petrifai/	vt.	使石(质)化；使坚硬；使僵硬，使麻木；使僵化	(U.4)
pharaoh	/'fɛərəu/	n.	法老(古埃及王的尊称)；暴君	(U.2)
pharmacognosy	/ˌfɑːmə'kɔgnəsi/	n.	(研究天然药物的)生药学	(U.4)

word	pronunciation	pos	meaning	unit
phenomenal	/fiˈnɔminl/	adj.	异常的;非凡的；现象的;关于现象的	(U.2)
phony	/ˈfəuni/	adj.	假(冒)的, 伪造的, 不值钱的	(U.11)
piety	/ˈpaiəti/	n.	虔诚, 孝行	(U.5)
pious	/ˈpəiəs/	adj.	虔诚的	(U.1)
pilgrim	/ˈpilgrim/	n.	朝圣者；香客	(U.1)
pilgrimage	/ˈpilgrimidʒ/	n.	朝圣, 朝山进香, 参拜圣地	(U.2)
plague	/pleig/	vt.	使染瘟疫, 使得灾祸；折磨, 烦扰；使苦恼	(U.5)
platinum	/ˈplætinəm/	n.	白金, 铂	(U.10)
plausible	/ˈplɔːzəbl/	adj.	好像有道理的, 似乎可能的	(U.3)
plausibly	/ˈplɔːzəbli/	adv.	似真地	(U.3)
plebeian	/pliˈbiː(ː)ən/	n.	平民, 庶民；	
		adj.	平民的, 卑俗的	(S.1)
polity	/ˈpɔliti/	n.	政治组织, 国家组织, 政治, 政体	(U.4)
polka	/ˈpɔlkə/	n.	波尔卡舞	(S.4)
polar	/ˈpəulə/	adj.	极地的;正好相反的	(U.2)
polygamy	/pɔˈligəmi/	n.	一夫多妻, 一妻多夫	(S.5)
pompous	/ˈpɔmpəs/	adj.	(贬)自大的；自负的；浮夸的	(U.1)
portray	/pɔːˈtrei/	vt.	画(人物, 风景), 画(肖像)；描绘；描写	(U.7)
pose	/pəuz/	vt.,vi.	(使……)摆好姿势	(S.3)
posit	/ˈpɔzit/	vt.	假设,假定；提出以供考虑或研究	(U.2)
posterity	/pɔsˈterəti/	n.	后裔,后代,子孙	(U.1)
posthumously	/ˈpɔstʃuməsli/	adv.	身后地	(U.2)
praetorian	/priːˈtɔriən/	adj.	执政官的, 禁卫队的	(U.8)
preamplification	/priːˌæmplifiˈkeiʃən/	n.	前置放	(S.4)
precarious	/priˈkɛəriəs/	adj.	不安全的;危险的；臆断的	(U.10)
precedent	/priˈsidənt/	n.	先例	(U.4)
precipice	/ˈpresipis/	n.	悬崖	(S.3)
precipitate	/priˈsipiteit/	vt.	猛抛, 使陷入, 促成, 使沉淀	(S.1)
precipitation	/ˌprisipiˈteiʃən/	n.	急躁；仓促；降(雨)量；雨量；沉淀	(U.10)
preclude	/priˈkluːd/	vt.	(与 from 连用)避免；排除;阻止；妨碍	(U.9)
preconception	/ˌpriːkənˈsepʃə/	n.	事先形成的观点或思想,先入之见	(U.1)
predisposition	/ˌpriːdispəˈsiʃən/	n.	倾向, 素质；癖性	(U.5)
predominantly	/priˈdɔminəntli/	adv.	主要地,占主导地位地	(U.3)
preeminence	/priː(ː)ˈeminəns/	n.	卓越	(S.1)
preempt	/priː(ː)ˈempt/	vt.	以优先购买权取得;(为取得先买权)预先占据	(U.11)
prefectural	/priːˈfektjuərəl/	adj.	地方官	(U.5)
premise	/ˈpremis/	n.	前提	(U.2)
preponderance	/priˈpɔndərəns/	n.	优势, 占优势	(U.9)
presume	/priˈzjuːm/	vt,vi.	(常与 that 连用)假定;假设；认为	(U.2)
primacy	/ˈpraiməsi/	n.	首位;首要;首席	(U.9)
privation	/praiˈveiʃən/	n.	匮乏;穷困	(U.5)
procrustean	/prəuˈkrʌstiən/	adj.	残暴的, 强求一致的	(S.3)

prodigious	/prə'didʒəs/	adj.	巨大的	(S.3)
proliferation	/prə,lifə'reiʃn/	n.	再育，增生(现象)	(U.2)
promulgate	/'prɔməlgeit/	vt.	宣布，颁布，公布(法令等)；传播	(U.4)
prophets	/'prɔfit/	n.	[pl.]犹太诸圣徒，先知	(U.7)
propitiate	/prə'piʃieit/	v.	向(上帝)赎罪；劝解	(S.1)
proponent	/prə'pəunənt/	n.	提议者；建议者；支持者；辩护者	(U.4)
proposition	/,prɔpə'ziʃən/	n.	(to do/that)观点，定理，命题	(U.1)
propound	/prə'paund/	vt.	提请考虑,提出(某事物)以求解决	(U.1)
propriety	/prə'praiəti/	n.	礼节；规矩；行为规范	(U.5)
proselytize	/'prɔsilitaiz/	vt.	改变宗教；改变党籍	(U.5)
protagonist	/prə'tægənist/	n.	(故事的)主人公；领导者；拥护者	(U.1)
protogeometric	/,prəutəudʒiə'metrik/	adj.	原型几何的	(U.3)
prototype	/'prəutətaip/	n.	原型(体)，样机(品)，典型，模范，标准	(U.2)
protract	/prəu'træctid/	adj.	延长的，引长的，拖延的	(U.2)
providential	/,prɔvi'denʃəl/	n.	神助的；天意的，幸运的	(U.2)
provisional	/prə'viʒənl/	adj.	临时的,暂时的	(U.1)
pulse	/pʌls/	n.	豆，豆类；脉搏，脉冲	(U.3)
punch	/pʌntʃ/	n.	冲压机，冲床，打孔机	(U.3)
punk	/pʌŋk/	n.,adj.	庞克摇滚乐(的)	(S.4)
purge	/pə:dʒ/	vt.	清洗；洗涤	(U.5)

Q

qualitative	/'kwɔlitətiv/	adj.	性质的；定性的	(U.4)
quarantine	/'kwɔrənti:n/	n.	检疫,隔离,(政治或商业上的)封锁	(U.12)
quasi-family	/'kwɑ:zi(:)'fæmili/	n.	准家庭	(S.1)
quicksand	/'kwiksænd/	n.	流沙，敏捷，危险而捉摸不定的事物	(S.3)
Qur'an	/kɔ:'ræn/	n.	(=Koran)(伊斯兰教)可兰经	(U.7)

R

rabbi	/'ræbai/	n.	拉比(犹太教会众领袖)；大师,夫子	(U.7)
Raj	/rɑ:dʒ/	n.	统治；支配	(U.6)
rally	/'ræli/	v.	召集,集合,重新振作,恢复(健康)	(U.1)
rational	/'ræʃənl/	adj.	理性的，合理的，推理的	(S.3)
rationale	/ræʃə'nɑ:l/	n.	基本原理；基本理论，理论基础	(U.4)
rebuke	/ri'bju:k/	n.,vt.	指责；非难；谴责	(U.11)
recidivism	/ri'sidivizəm/	n.	累犯	(U.5)
reciprocal	/ri'siprəkəl/	adj.	互惠的，相应的，倒数的，彼此相反的	(S.5)
reciprocate	/ri'siprəkeit/	v.	互给，酬答，互换，报答	(U.8)
reckoning	/'rekəniŋ/	n.	计算；估计	(U.5)
reconciliation	/,rekənsili'eiʃən/	n.	和解，调和，顺从	(U.7)

recruit	/ri'kruːt/	vt., vi. 使恢复,补充,征募新兵	
		n. 新兵,新会员	(S.1)
rectitude	/'rektitjuid/	n. 正直,公正,清廉,笔直	(U.11)
redemptive	/ri'demptiv/	adj. 赎回的,挽回的,用于补偿的	(S.3)
reel	/riːl/	n. 摇摆,蹒跚,眩晕,旋转	(S.4)
regionalization	/ˌriːdʒənəlaiˈzeiʃən/	n. 地区化,区域化	(U.2)
reification	/ˌriːifiˈkeiʃən/	n. 具体化	(S.5)
reify		vt. 使具体化	(S.5)
reinstate	/'riːinsteit/	vt. 使恢复原状(原位);使恢复(权利等)	(U.5)
remuneration	/riˌmjuːnəˈreiʃən/	n. 报酬	(S.1)
Renaissance	/rəˈneisəns/	n. (前面与the连用)文艺复兴时期	(U.2)
rendering	/'rendəriŋ/	n. 翻译,表现,描写,透视图,复制图	(U.5)
renunciation	/riˌnʌnsiˈeiʃən/	n. 放(抛,废)弃;弃权;拒绝,否认	(U.7)
repertoire	/'repətwaː/	n. (某个人的)全部技能	(S.3)
repressive	/ri'presiv/	adj. 压抑的,压制的	(U.5)
repudiate	/ri'pjuːdieit/	vt., vi. 拒绝;断绝关系	(U.9)
residua	/ri'zidjuə/	n. 残余物;残基;残渣	(U.6)
resonance	/'rezənəns/	n. 共鸣,谐振,共振;回声;反响	(U.4)
resultant	/ri'zʌltənt/	n. 结果;后果;合力,合成力	(S.3)
resurgence	/ri'səːdʒəns/	n. 复兴;再起	(U.12)
retaliate	/ri'tælieit/	v. 报复	(S.3)
retardation	/ritaːˈdeiʃən/	n. 延迟,阻滞;延迟程度,妨碍量	(U.10)
retrospect	/'retrəuspekt/	n. 回顾	(S.4)
revelation	/ˌreviˈleiʃən/	n. 显示,揭露,被揭露的事,新发现,启示,揭示	(U.5)
revenue	/'revinjuː/	n. 收入,国家的收入,税收	(U.4)
revere	/ri'viə/	vt. 尊敬,崇敬	(U.7)
rigor	/'rigə/	n. 严峻;严肃;严厉;(法律等的)严格执行	(U.5)
rigorously	/'rigərəsli/	adv. 严格地;严肃地;严厉地,严密地	(U.12)
ripen	/'raipən/	vt., vi. (使)成熟	(U.9)
ritual	/'ritʃuəl/	n. 典礼,(宗教)仪式,礼节;	
		adj. 典礼的,(宗教)仪式的	(U.7)
Riviera	/riviˈeərə/	n. 里维埃拉	(U.10)
rodent	/'rəudənt/	n. 啮齿动物	(U.12)
rook	/ruk/	n. (象棋)车,赌棍,骗子	(S.3)
Rwanda	/ruˈændə/	n. 卢旺达(非洲国家)	(U.8)

S

sanctuary	/'sæŋktjuəri/	n. 圣所,圣殿;礼拜堂	(U.3)
sane	/sein; sen/	adj. (-r,-st)心智健全的;神志正常的,明智的	(U.1)
Sasanian	/sæˈseiniən/	n., adj. (=Sassanid)萨桑王朝(的);萨桑王朝特点(的)	(U.7)

scant	/skænt/	vt.	限制,节省,减少,藐视,忽略	(U.9)
scanty	/sˈkænti/	adj.	(数量)不是的,少量的	
schema	/skiːmə/	n.	图表;纲要;计划,方案	(U.1)
schemer	/skiːmə/	n.	设计者,计划者;阴谋家	(U.11)
scramble	/ˈskræmbl/	n.	攀登;爬；抢夺,争夺	(U.6)
scrappy	/skræpi/	adj.	(看似)零散的;片断的;杂乱无章的	(S.4)
scribe	/skraib/	n.	抄写员;书记；作者	(U.3)
scruffy	/skˈrafi/	adj.	肮脏的,不整洁的,破旧的	(S.4)
scrutiny	/ˈskrutini/	n.	认真,仔细审阅	(U.1)
sear	/siə/	vt.	烤焦,使枯萎	
		vi.	凋谢,干枯	(S.3)
sect	/sekt/	n.	派别,宗派,派系	(U.7)
secular	/ˈsekjulə/	adj.	不受宗教约束的,非宗教的,世俗的	(U.2)
segregate	/ˈsegrigeit/	vt.	分开,隔开;分离	(U.2)
self-conception	/selfkənˈsepʃən/	n.	自我概念	(U.2)
seminal	/ˈsiːminl/	adj.	有重大影响的,产生巨大影响的	(S.3)
Senegal	/ˌseniˈgɔːl/	n.	塞内加尔(西非国家)	(U.8)
sentiment	/ˈsentimənt/	n.	感情,情绪;情操	(U.5)
serf	/səːf/	n.	农奴,奴隶	(S.1)
serfdom	/ˈsəːfdəm/	n.	农奴身份,农奴境遇	(U.4)
serried	/ˈserid/	adj.	(旧或文)(指人或物的行列)排紧的,密集的	(U.1)
shack	/ʃæk/	n.	简陋木屋,棚屋	(U.2)
shackled	/ˈʃækl/	vt.	束缚;桎梏;上镣铐	(U.5)
shatter	/ˈʃætə(r)/	vt.,vi.	使粉碎,使破碎；损坏；摧毁	(U.12)
Shinto	/ˈʃintəu/	n.	日本之神道教	(U.5)
shoestring	/ˈʃuːstriŋ/	n.	零星资金	(S.4)
Siberia	/saiˈbiəriə/	n.	西伯利亚	(U.10)
siege	/siːdʒ/	n.	包围,围城	(U.2)
sifting	/ˈsiftiŋ/	n.	筛;过滤	(U.1)
simultaneous	/ˌsaimlˈteiniəs, siml-/	adj.	同时的;同步的	(U.4)
sinister	/ˈsinistə/	adj.	不吉的;不祥的;凶恶的	(U.12)
sizeable	/ˈsaizəbl/	adj.	相当大的;颇为可观的	(U.3)
skeptical	/ˈskeptikəl/	adj.	怀疑性的,好怀疑的,<口>无神论的	(S.2)
slacken	/ˈslækən/	v.	松弛,放慢,减弱,减少,减缓放慢	(S.1)
sluggish	/ˈslʌgiʃ/	adj.	行动迟缓的	(S.1)
smelt	/smelt/	vt.	[冶]熔炼;提炼;冶炼;熔解	(U.3)
sniper	/ˈsnaipə/	n.	狙击兵	(S.3)
solidify	/səˈlidifai/	vt.	使凝固;使硬,使结晶;使团结一致;充实,巩固	(U.5)
soothsayer	/ˈsuːθsei(r)/	n.	预言者;占卜者	(U.7)
sophistication	/səfistiˈkeiʃən/	n.	完善度,技巧;强词夺理,诡辩;混合	(U.4)
sour square			苦恼忧郁,拘谨古板的人	(S.4)
sovereignty	/ˈsɔvrinti/	n.	君权,统治权,主权；主权国家	(U.4)

spatiotemporal	/ˌspeʃiəu'tempərəl/	adj.	存在于时间和空间的；时空的	(U.2)
spew	/spjuː/	vt.,vi.	涌出；喷出；渗出	(U.10)
spine-chilling		adj.	令人毛骨悚然的	(U.5)
splinter	/'splintə/	vt.,vi.	(使)裂成碎片，(使)分裂	(U.5)
spurious	/'spjuəriəs/	adj.	伪造的，欺骗的；似是而非的；谬误的	(U.6)
staggering	/'stægəriŋ/	adj.	难以置信的；惊愕的	(U.10)
stagnant	/'stægnənt/	adj.	停滞的，迟钝的	(S.4)
stagnation	/stæg'neiʃən/	n.	停滞(性)；萧条；迟钝	(U.4)
stammer	/'stæmə/	vi.,vt.	口吃，结结巴巴地说	(U.7)
stance	/stæns/	n.	姿态	(S.4)
static	/'stætik/	adj.	静止的，静态的；呆板的；乏味的	(U.2)
statist	/'stætist/	n.	国家主义者	(U.2)
status quo	/ˌsteitəs'kwəu/	n.	(Lat.拉丁语)现状	(U.9)
steppe	/step/	n.	干草原；疏树大平原	(U.10)
stereotype	/'steriəutaip/	n.	陈规，老套，刻板模式	(U.1)
stern	/stəːn/	n.	船尾	(U.3)
straddle	/'strædl/	v.	跨坐或跨立在(某物)上	(U.1)
strand	/strænd/	n.	绳、线，海滨，河岸	(U.6)
strata	/'streitə/	n.	(stratum 的复数)层，地层	(U.6)
stratagem	/'strætədʒəm/	n.	(文)蒙蔽他人的计谋、策略或花招	(U.1)
strip	/strip/	vt.,vi.	(常与 of 连用)脱，剥，拆	(S.3)
Strontium	/'strɔntrəm/	n.	锶	(U.12)
strut	/strʌt/	vi.	大摇大摆地走；肿胀	
		vt.	支撑；炫耀	(S.4)
suasion	/'sweiʒən/	n.	劝告，说服	(U.5)
subaltern	/'sʌbəltən/	adj.	下的，副的，次的	(U.6)
subjugate	/'sʌbdʒugeit/	vt.	征服；压服；使屈服，使服从	(U.2)
subjugation	/ˌsʌbdju'geiʃən/	n.	镇压，平息，征服	(U.6)
sub-Saharan	/sʌbˌsə'hɑːrən/	adj.	(非洲)撒哈拉沙漠以南的	(U.8)
substantiality	/səbˌstænʃi'æliti/	n.	实在性，实质性，实体	(U.5)
substantially	/səb'stænʃəli/	adv.	可观地，大量地	(U.1)
subversive	/səb'vəːsiv/	adj.	削弱(某政治制度)的，颠覆的	(U.1)
succinct	/sək'siŋkt/	adj.	简洁的，紧身的，压缩在小范围内的	(U.13)
suffrage	/'sʌfridʒ/	n.	投票权；选举权	(U.9)
summon	/'sʌmən/	vt.	召集，召唤，号召；鼓起，振作	(U.9)
supplant	/sə'plɑːnt/	vt.	排挤掉，代替	(S.3)
supremacy	/sju'preməsi/	n.	地位最高的人，至高，无上，霸权	(U.11)
surly	/'səli/		傲慢的；粗暴的	(S.4)
Swahili	/'swɑːhili/	n.	斯瓦希里人(语)	(U.8)
sway	/swei/	v.	摇摆，摇动	(S.2)
swelter	/'sweltəriŋ/	adj.	闷热的，中暑的，酷热的	(S.3)
swoon	/swuːn/	vi.	着迷；神魂颠倒	(S.4)

synthetic	/sin'θetic/	adj.	合成的，人造的，综合的	(S.2)
Syria	/'siəriə/		叙利亚	(U.2)
Syrian	/'siriən/	adj.	叙利亚的；叙利亚人的；叙利亚语的	
		n.	叙利亚人；叙利亚语	(U.7)
Scythian	/'siðiən/	adj.	锡西厄的；锡西厄人的	
		n.	锡西厄人	(U.10)

T

tablet	/'tæblit/	n.	刻写板；简	(U.3)
tact	/tækt/	n.	机智；老练，圆滑	(U.11)
taiga	/'teigə/	n.	针叶树林地带	(U.10)
tamper	/'tæmpə/	vi.	(与 with 连用)擅改；篡改	(U.12)
Tanzania	/ˌtænzə'niə/	n.	坦桑尼亚(东非国家)	(U.8)
taper	/'teipə/	vt., vi.	(常与 off 连用)逐渐尖细，使逐渐尖细	(U.11)
taxation	/tæk'seiʃən/	n.	征税；税制；税，税款；估价征税	(U.2)
temporal	/'tempərəl/	adj.	时间的，时态的；世俗的；现世的	(U.4)
tenet	/'tenit/	n.	信念；信条；教义；主义	(U.9)
thalassocracy	/θælə'sɔkrəsi/	n.	制海权，海权	(U.2)
the Altai	/æl'teiai/		阿尔泰山	(U.10)
the Amu Daria			阿姆河	(U.10)
the Amur			黑龙江	(U.10)
the Aral sea			咸海	(U.10)
the Baltic	/'bɔːltik/		波罗的海	(U.10)
the Black Sea			黑海	(U.10)
the Bug			巴格河	(U.10)
the Carpathians	/'kɑːpeinθjənz/		喀尔巴阡山脉	(U.10)
the Caspian	/'kæspiən/		里海	(U.10)
the Caucasian chain			高加索山系	(U.10)
the Dnieper			第聂伯河	(U.10)
the Dniester	/'dnjestə/		德涅斯特河	(U.10)
the Don	/dɔn/		顿河	(U.10)
the Enisei river			叶尼塞河	(U.10)
the Indigirka			印迪吉尔卡河	(U.10)
the Kolyma			科累马河	(U.10)
the Lena			勒拿河	(U.10)
the Lovat			涅瓦河	(U.10)
the Northern Dvina			北德维纳河	(U.10)
the Ob	/əub/		鄂毕湾	(U.10)
the Pamir			帕米尔高原	(U.10)
the Pechora			北潮拉河	(U.10)
the Strait of Tartary			鞑靼海峡	(U.10)

the Syr Daria			锡尔河	(U.10)
the Ukraine	/ju(ː)ˈkrein/	n.	乌克兰	(U.10)
the Ural mountains			乌拉尔山脉	(U.10)
the Valdai hills			阿尔泰山	(U.10)
the Volga	/ˈvɔlgə/		伏尔加河	(U.10)
the Western Dvina			西德维纳河	(U.10)
theological	/θiəˈlɔdʒkəl/	adj.	神学的	(U.2)
therapeutic	/θerəˈpjuːtik/	adj.	治病的;治疗术的;治疗学的	(U.5)
therapeutics	/θerəˈpuːtiks/	n.	治疗学,疗法	(U.4)
thrash	/θræʃ/	v.,n.	打谷,击,颠簸,逆行	(S.4)
ticklish	/ˈtikliʃ/	adj.	难以处理的,棘手的,不好对付的(事);怕痒的	(U.11)
tie in (with)			(使)连接起来;(使)协调;(与……)相一致	(S.4)
tiller	/ˈtilə/	n.	(=farmer)耕作者,农夫;耕作机具	(U.10)
to tamp down			踏坏,踩碎;踏实	(S.4)
toil	/tɔil/	n.	苦工,难事;劳苦,辛苦	(U.11)
topography	/təˈpɔgrəfi/	n.	地形学;地形;地势	(U.5)
topological	/tɔpəˈlɔdʒikəl/	adj.	地质学的;拓扑学的	(U.4)
totalitarianism	/təutæliˈteəriənizm/	n.	极权主义	(U.5)
touch off			引爆;放炮;引起;触发	(S.4)
toxic	/ˈtɔksik/	adj.	毒的;中毒的;有毒的	(U.12)
trance	/trɑːns/	n.	恍惚,出神,着迷,[医]迷睡	(S.4)
tranquilize	/ˈtræŋkwilaiz/	v.	使……平静;使……变安静	(U.12)
transaction	/trænˈzekʃən/	n.	办理;处理;执行;事务,业务,交易	(U.6)
transcendent	/trænˈsendənt/	adj.	出类拔萃的,超群的;卓越的;超越宇宙的	(U.7)
transgression	/trænsˈgreʃən/	n.	违反,违法,罪过,过失,错误	(U.1)
transhumance	/trænsˈhjuːməns/	n.	季节性牲畜移动	(U.2)
transitory	/ˈtrænsitəri/	adj.	刹那间的,短暂的,暂时的	(U.2)
transmute	/trænzˈmjuːt/	vt.	使变形(质,化);使……转化	(U.7)
trappings	/ˈtræpiŋz/	n.	服饰,马饰	(U.8)
treatises	/ˈtriːtiz/	n.	论文,论述	(U.4)
tremor	/ˈtremə/	n.	震动;地震;震颤;颤抖;抖动	(U.5)
tribalism	/ˈtraibəlism/	n.	部落制,部落的特征,部落文化	(U.8)
trio	/ˈtriəu/	n.	三人一组	(U.2)
triumphant	/traiˈʌmfənt/	adj.	胜利的,成功的,凯旋的;得意洋洋的	(U.12)
tsarist	/ˈtsɑː/	adj.	沙皇的	(U.10)
tundra	/ˈtʌndrə/	n.	苔原,冻土地带	(U.10)
turnover	/ˈtəːnəuvə/	n.	翻覆;翻折;半圆卷饼;流通量;周转	(U.4)
twang	/twæŋ/	n.	弦声,砰的一声;鼻音;意味	(S.4)
tweezers	/ˈtwiːzəz/	n.	镊子,小钳	(U.3)

U

ubiquitous	/juːˈbikwitəs/	adj.	到处存在的,(同时)普遍存在的	(S.5)

Uganda	/juː(ː)ˈgændə/ /uːˈgændə/		(国名)乌干达(东非国家)	(U.8)
ultraviolet	/ˌʌltrəˈvaiəlit/	adj.	紫外线的	
unabated	/ˈʌnəˈbeitid/	adj.	不减弱的；不减轻的；猛烈如初的	(U.2)
unalienable	/ʌnˈeiljənəbl/	adj.	不可剥夺的；不可分割的	(S.3)
underscore	/ˌʌnderˈskɔː/	vt.	在…下划线；强调	(U.2)
underwrite	/ˈʌndərait/	vt.	签在……下，给……保险，签名，承保	(U.9)
uniqueness	/juːˈnːiknis/	n.	惟一性；单值性；独特性	(U.2)
universalism	/ˌjuːniˈvəːsəlizəm/	n.	宇宙神教，普遍性，普遍主义	(U.2)
unleash	/ʌnˈliːʃ/	vt.	解开……的皮带(链索)；(喻)释放；放纵；发动	(U.2)
unpalatable	/ʌnˈpælətəbl/	adj.	不合口味的，没味的；令人不快的	(U.12)
unprecedented	/ʌnˈpresidəntid/	adj.	空前的；没有前例的	(U.4)
unruly	/ʌnˈruːli/	adj.	不受拘束的，不守规矩的，难驾驭的	(S.4)
unseat	/ˌʌnˈsiːt/	vt.	使(从马背或自行车上)摔下来；罢免，免去……席位	(U.5)
Uruguay	/ˈurugwai/	n.	乌拉圭	(S.2)
usurpation	/ˌjuːzəːˈpeiʃən/	n.	篡夺	(S.1)

V

validate	/ˈvælideit/	vt.	证实；证明正确，使生效，使有法律效力	(U.2)
vandalism	/ˈvændəliz(ə)m/	n.	故意破坏	(S.4)
variable	/ˈvɛəriəbl/	n.	[数]变数，可变物，变量	(U.4)
vassalage	/ˈvæsəlidʒ/	n.	附庸地位，从属地位，隶属	(S.1)
vaudeville	/ˈvəudəvil/	n.	歌舞杂耍	(S.4)
verge	/vəːdʒ/		(与 on, upon 连用)将近，接近；向……倾斜	(U.11)
Verkhoiansk	/vjekəˈjænisk/		Range 维尔霍扬斯克山脉	(U.10)
vernacular	/vəˈnækjulə/	n.	本国语；方言；术语，行话；俗话	(U.12)
veterinary	/ˈveterinəri/	n.	兽医	(U.4)
veto	/ˈviːtəu/	vt.	否决，禁止	(U.8)
victor	/ˈviktə/		胜利者；征服者；战胜者	(U.11)
vindication	/ˌvidiˈkeiʃən/	n.	辩护，辩明，拥护，证明	(U.12)
virtuoso	/ˌvəːtjuˈəuzəu/	n.	(-sos 或 -si)艺术名家，艺术大师；音乐演奏名家	(U.11)
vis-a-vis	/viːzɑːˈviː/	prep.	关于(某事物)，同某事物相比	(U.1)
visceral	/ˈvisərəl/	n.	内脏的；出自内心的；内心深处的，深奥的	(U.5)
vitality	/vaiˈtæliti/	n.	生命力，活力；体力；生气	(U.2)
viticulture	/ˈvitikʌltʃə/	n.	葡萄栽培	(U.2)
vizier	/viˈziə/	n.	(伊斯兰教国家元老，高官)维齐尔，(伊斯兰国家的)大臣	(U.2)
vocation	/vəuˈkeiʃən/	n.	职业；行业；天职；使命	(U.7)
vogue	/vəug/	n.	时髦，时兴，流行，受欢迎	(U.3)

void	/vɔid/	n.	空间，空旷，空虚，怅惘	(S.4)
volley	/'vɔli/	n.	(常与 of 连用)(质问等的)齐发,连发, 连珠炮	(S.4)

W

wallow	/'wɔləu/	vi.	(常与 in 连用)沉溺于	(S.3)
water down			掺水，兑水；冲淡；打折扣	(S.4)
wearisome	/'wiərisʌm/	adj.	令人厌烦的；使人疲倦的，乏味的	(U.11)
welter	/'weltə/	n.	(与 of 连用)杂乱无章；混乱；翻腾；起伏	(U.5)
wicked	/'wikid/	adj.	邪恶的；不道德的；恶劣的；绝妙的	(U.7)
willy – nilly	/wili'nili/	adv.	无论想要不想要；不管愿意不愿意	(U.1)
wonted	/'wəuntid/	adj.	(仅作定语用)习惯的；平常的，照常的	(U.11)

Y

Yorktown	/'jɔːktaun/		约克镇(美国弗吉尼亚州东南部城镇)	(U.11)

Z

Zambia	/'zæmbiə/	n.	赞比亚	(U.8)
Zanzibar	/'zænzi'bɑː/	n.	桑给巴尔岛(坦桑尼亚东北部)；桑给巴尔	(U.8)